Moves Writers Make

James C. Raymond
The University of Alabama

Prentice Hall, Upper Saddle River, New Jersey 07458

Library of Congress Cataloging-in-Publication Data

Moves writers make / [compiled by] James C. Raymond.
    p. cm.
    Includes index.
    ISBN 0–13–440041–0
    1. College readers. 2. English language—Rhetoric—Problems,
exercises, etc. 3. Report writing—Problems, exercises, etc.
I. Raymond, James C.
PE1417.M655   1999
808' .0427—dc21   98–20021
                                          CIP

Editor in Chief: *Charlyce Jones-Owen*
Executive Editor: *Leah Jewell*
Editorial Assistant: *Patricia Castiglione*
Production Liaison: *Fran Russello*
Project Manager: *Marianne Hutchinson (Pine Tree Composition)*
AVP/Director of Manufacturing and Production: *Barbara Kittle*
Prepress and Manufacturing Buyer: *Mary Ann Gloriande*
Cover Director: *Jayne Conte*
Cover Designer: *Anthony Gemmellard*
Cover Art: *Two Figures Rising,* Nicholas Wilton/ Studio Zocolo

Credits appear on pages xxiv and 310, which constitute a continuation of the copyright page.

This book was set in 10/12 Times-Roman by Pine Tree Composition
and was printed and bound by Courier Companies, Inc.
The cover was printed by Phoenix Color Corp.

© 1999 by Prentice-Hall, Inc.
Upper Saddle River, New Jersey 07458

Printed in the United States of America

10 9 8 7 6 5 4 3

ISBN 0-13-440041-0

Prentice-Hall International (UK) Limited, *London*
Prentice-Hall of Australia Pty. Limited, *Sydney*
Prentice-Hall Canada Inc., *Toronto*
Prentice-Hall Hispanoamericana, S.A., *Mexico*
Prentice-Hall of India Private Limited, *New Delhi*
Prentice-Hall of Japan, Inc., *Tokyo*
Prentice-Hall Asia Pte. Ltd., *Singapore*
Editora Prentice-Hall do Brasil, Ltda., *Rio de Janeiro*

For Caroline
and all the "fam"
(Jeanne-Marie, Herschel,
Leslie & Susanna)

Rhetorical Contents

Thematic Contents

Just for Fun

Language

Science, Social Science, and Technology

A Preface for Teachers
Rhetoric in Four Dimensions

As director of a large composition program, the first thing I ask about rhetorical readers is "What's new? How is this book different from the rest?" Usually there are few differences. It is a very conservative genre. Now I have to imagine readers asking the same questions as they browse through this book. This is an adventurous textbook, despite its conventional form. It is postmodern in ways that may not be at all obvious at first, since it is free of the stylistic games that postmodern writers like to play. At the same time, it is rooted in rhetorical tradition, but with new understandings of terms that have been either mistranslated or glazed over with familiarity.

The rhetorical theory implicit in this textbook is four-dimensional. The first dimension includes stylistic options: figures, tropes, sentence patterns, tone, detail, and editorial conventions. Moves of this type are gathered in generic categories and captured in a scheme called "The Seven Common Moves"—that is, moves all essays have in common.

The second dimension includes the various framing devices to which information can be attached. These include the classical topoi and the traditional modes, methods of development—"conceptual moves," distinct ways of processing information.

The third dimension is a move that is generally neglected in traditional rhetorics: interpretation, the move that gives any essay its "so-what factor," the element that captures our interest even when we have no practical use for the information an essay contains. Interpretation is arguably one of the two defining characteristics of the essay as a genre—the other being the sense of an individual voice.

The fourth dimension is persuasion, which is the substance of any serious rhetoric. In this book, persuasion is treated not as the imposition of a point of view but as an anatomy of belief and the potential basis of a peaceable remedy for ideological differences.

THE FIRST DIMENSION: THE SEVEN COMMON MOVES

The history of rhetoric abounds in attention to figures and tropes and other stylistic moves that are more or less superficial. Sometimes the lists can become overwhelming, including hundreds of moves with Latin or Greek names that students are unlikely to master, or even find interesting.

And yet, there is something useful about naming the moves writers make, particularly if we want to make those moves ourselves. A skilled writer has lots of tricks and stratagems and tactics. Or to put it colloquially, a skilled writer has lots of good moves, in the sense in that an athlete or a dancer has good moves.

Normally, the moves writers make are invisible. Writers conceal them, following the old adage, "art hides its artifice" (*ars est celare artem*). Like magicians, they want us to react to the magic without noticing the skill that produces it. To make matters more difficult, good writers, even the best of them, perhaps especially the best of them, may not themselves know what their techniques are. "In truly good writing," Hemingway wrote to his friend Harvey Breit, "no matter how many times you read it you do not know how it is done." It's not easy to see how it's done because writing is most successful when its artifice is least apparent.

Normally when we read, we are not aware of writerly moves as moves; we simply respond to their effects. Or, to borrow a metaphor from Toni Morrison, texts are like fishbowls: our attention is drawn past the surface so that we see the fish (*Playing in the Dark,* p. 17). But to learn to write, we have to notice the bowl itself—the normally invisible surface that makes the whole thing possible. We have to become aware of subtle and normally invisible moves so we can make these moves ourselves.

Identifying the artifice—naming the moves—is the rhetorician's solution to this problem. Rhetorical names reveal the techniques and tactics that writers take pains to hide. In writing, as in sports, dance, and music, naming the moves may be unnecessary for those individuals who have a knack for imitating them; but naming them helps those without that knack to isolate what would otherwise be just a blur of expert performance.

There are literally hundreds of good moves writers make—so many, in fact, that any list that attempts to be complete will be tedious and pedagogically overwhelming. Perhaps the most practical innovation of this book is the checklist called "The Seven Common Moves," which reduces the limitless number to seven generic categories:

1. Beginning
2. Ending
3. Detail
4. Organization/Plot
5. Style
6. Voice/Attitude
7. Economy

These moves are explained more fully in chapter 1, and they are reexamined in each subsequent chapter. They are called Common Moves because they are, in fact, common to essays of every type. The Seven Common Moves serve multiple purposes in a writing class:

1. They serve as an iterable system for analyzing an essay whatsoever, replacing the *ad hoc* questions that are normally attached to individual essays.
2. They serve as a set of lenses that focus on techniques and tactics worth imitating, as opposed to debates about the subject matter of the essay.
3. They serve as a format for journal entries. Class discussion is much livelier and better focused if students have answered questions based on these common moves in advance.
4. They serve as a set of prompts to group workshops on task.
5. They serve as the basis of an analytic grading scale. A numerical value can be attached to each of the moves according to the instructor's priorities.

THE SECOND DIMENSION: MODES, METHODS, AND TOPES AS CONCEPTUAL MOVES

Everybody knows that traditional modes and methods of development (description, narration, exemplification, definition, and all the rest) are, at least from a theoretical perspective, defunct. Their knell was sounded by Robert Connors in "The Rise and Fall of the Modes of Discourse," College Composition and Communication 32 (December 1981): 444–55. And yet they survive, despite their inadequacies. They survive in part because they provide useful maps of a universe of discourse that would otherwise be undifferentiated and unteachable.

They survive for another reason: the modes and methods are heirs apparent to the "topics" of classical rhetoric. Aristotle's topoi ("topics" in English, close enough to "tropes" to cause confusion) may be defined as "moves the mind makes." It may seem odd to think of a "topic" as a move, since *topos* literally designates "place," not action. But when we examine the topoi, it becomes apparent that they are all conceptual moves, ways of framing or apprehending information. We can describe a subject, or tell a story about it, or compare it, or define it, or examine its causes or its effects, or in fact use any of the other modes or methods or classical topoi to come to grips with it.

Topics, modes, and methods are conceptual moves that we all learn when we learn language. They occur in any sort of discourse—written, oral, even purely interior, unspoken thought. They are common to all speakers in socioeconomic groups in all languages. They are universal moves; no normal speaker is without them. To appreciate their importance in writing, it may help to consider them in the context of literate versus oral societies. We do not need writing to describe, narrate, define, explain processes, categorize, divide, identify causes and effects, and argue. But without writing, we can do these things only in brief scope. Literacy, as an invention, as an artificial medium, makes possible an indefinite extension of each of these conceptual operations in ways that would be simply impossible in oral discourse.

The extension of these basic conceptual moves in writing is, for better or for worse, the foundation of what was once considered Western culture—though this particular aspect of Western culture no longer has any geographical limits. Without writing, systematic knowledge would be virtually impossible. The extended cause-and-effect analysis that we take for granted in scientific and other academic discourses is possible only in writing. History—extended factual narrative with an analytic and interpretive agenda—is possible only in writing; oral history is valuable, of course, but valuable in an entirely different way. In fact, the organizational framework of every academic discipline and of universities themselves—division and classification—would be impossible without writing. Without writing, our knowledge would be as chaotic as the Web before the advent of search engines (which are themselves cybernetic extensions of division and classification).

When we ask students to narrate or define or classify or argue or exemplify or explain a process in writing, we are not asking them to do anything they haven't done before; we are merely asking them to develop and extend conceptual operations that they have already acquired along with their spoken language. But in writing, these conceptual moves can be concentrated, cultivated, extended, organized, repeated in useful and interesting ways. Extending these moves is a skill that needs to be acquired through study and practice.

But the modes and methods are worse than useless if we expect the wrong things from them. As genres, they are patently artificial. Even when essays happen to resemble a particular mode or method, their authors are likely to have begun with a subject in mind (Grant and Lee, a dying moth, the meaning of "self-respect"), not with a genre, not with an impulse to write comparison and contrast, or exemplification, or definition. Furthermore, as a set of categories, the modes and methods are an embarrassment—like cats, dogs, corkscrews, and tinfoil in the same list—the sort of random collection that we would never tolerate in classification papers written by our students. In practice, they overlap with a dizzying redundancy.

Once we recognize and accept this artificiality and redundancy, however, we can turn them into a pedagogical and strategic advantage. Nothing is ever lost. The skills we teach in any one chapter turn out to be useful in all the others. Description can be attached to a narrative frame, exemplification can be part of a definition, process analysis can be part of an argument—in fact, every mode and method can turn up within each of the others. And if the modes and methods are artificial, well, yes of course; but so are scales and chords and pliés at the ballet bar and all the drills and exercises that athletes find effective in preparing for a game. Writing in the modes and methods are exercises for amplifying the power of conceptual muscles that can do only limited work without writing. They are practice for all kinds of writing—personal, vocational, and academic. But even when the modes and methods are mixed and combined within a composition, the result can be an uninteresting and formalistic exercise unless the writer adds what is the soul of any good essay: the act of interpretation that provides a so-what factor.

THE THIRD DIMENSION: INTERPRETATION, A HIGHER LITERACY, AND THE SO-WHAT FACTOR

As framing devices, the modes and methods are the rhetorical equivalent of tossing different tennis balls into the air. *Interpretation* is the equivalent of hitting them across a net. The first move is incomplete without the second. When description is just an inventory of sights and sounds, it is not yet an essay. It becomes an essay only when a writer provides an interpretation of the details that catches the reader by surprise. When narrative is just a record of events, it is not yet an essay. It becomes an essay when a writer interprets the events. Without interpretation, description and narration are just data, organized data, perhaps, but insignificant, unless perhaps a reader is disposed to discover meaning in them.

A process paper is not an essay if it merely reveals a process—how to bake a soufflé or trim a reed or assemble a bookshelf or install new software. Useful forms of writing, these—and worth teaching in vocational or technical courses—but they are not essays. A process essay interprets a process, shows us something significant about it that we may not have noticed on our own. This is why Jessica Mitford's "The American Way of Death" (p. 78) is an essay, while a textbook on embalming is, well, just a manual. Interpretation is the difference between a dictionary definition of a word, such as *self-respect* ("Due respect for oneself, one's character, and one's conduct"), and an essay, such as Joan Didion's tendentious musings about the "true" meaning of that term (p. 178). A definition of *essay* cannot merely rely on Webster—it cannot merely convey settled information. To write an essay, the writer has to take a stance, have an attitude: "You wanna know what 'self-respect' is, well I'll tell you what it is."

Interpretation also reveals the writer, indirectly, without the confessional revelations that were once thought necessary to persuade students that they had something worth saying within themselves. It reveals the writer by revealing a host of assumptions that guide the writer's choices—assumptions about what counts as good, what counts as evil, what counts as interesting, dull, funny, tasteless, worth knowing about, not worth explaining, and about innumerable other issues implicit in unstated judgments between the lines of every text. To recognize that the writer inhabits the text, either visibly in the form of a first person pronoun or simply by implication, is to return to Montaigne's recognition that the author is in fact the subject of every essay (*"Je suis moy-mesmes la matier de mon livre"*). It is also a recognition of what physicist and anthropologists have discovered in the twentieth century: that despite the ostensible absence of the author in scientific writing—ubiquitous passive voice and the banishment of the first person—it is simply impossible to separate the observer from the observed. Even if we concede the postmodern position—that the subject-observer is itself a fictional construct—the fictionally constructed subject-observer, the ineluctable mirage of personhood, is always and inevitably discernible in every essay.

Interpretation occurs precisely at that juncture where reading and writing are hard to distinguish from each other. It is the difference between primal literacy—the ability to encode spoken language in visual tokens—and literacy in a deeper sense, the ability to read the world and then to write it. Essayists usually make it seem as if they "find" the meaning in their material, as if it were already there, waiting to be recorded by any intelligent observer. But in fact interpretation involves the imposition of meaning, not the discovery of it. Interpretation is a creative act. A focus on interpretation—a requirement to view the data from a personal perspective—is what makes the essay an act of self-empowerment.

In this book, the Seven Common Moves are always preceded by a question about the "So-What Factor." The so-what factor is not just the thesis. It is not just the writer's interpretation. It is whatever is novel or interesting or surprising about the writer's interpretation. A thesis can be logical but predictable, indisputable (e.g., any statement of personal preference), or laden with unexamined assumptions—and therefore uninteresting. This is the risk we take when we focus on the forms of writing: students may produce the forms, but miss the element of surprise that makes an essay worth reading. The so-what factor, the surprise that makes an essay worth reading, is always the result of a departure from the norm: the writer sees the data in a way most readers would not have seen it on their own. By focusing on the so-what factor, we can teach students that the material in any essay is its subject only in secondary sense; the primary subject, the element that makes it worthy of a reader's attention, is always the writer's interpretation of the material.

THE FOURTH DIMENSION: THE EPISTEMOLOGY OF PERSUASION

Style, structure, and interpretation are all elements of rhetoric; but they are, as Aristotle called them, "ancillary" to rhetoric's main purpose, which is the study of the construction of belief.

I do not mean to suggest that Aristotle was a constructionist in the modern sense of that term, but only to exploit a rich ambiguity in a key term in the rhetoric, πιστισ (*pistis*). *Pistis* is generally translated as "persuasion," though in numerous other contexts it is translated as "belief." In recent years classical rhetoric's emphasis on persuasion has been characterized as agonistic and aggressive, a method for imposing beliefs on others, as opposed to a rhetoric of understanding and accommodation. Actually, both sorts of rhetoric are available in Aristotle.

According to Aristotle, there are different kinds of knowledge, each with its own rules, its own degree of certitude, and its own proper application. The ability to recognize these differences is the mark of an educated person. It might also be said, conversely, that a failure to recognize these differences is the root of dogmatism and intolerance, even among otherwise intelligent and well-intentioned people. In the *Nichomachean Ethics* Aristotle distinguishes only two kinds of knowledge, rhetorical and mathematical. In the modern university, however, there seem to be at least three.

One is geometry (or symbolic logic, or mathematics in general): absolute precision in a realm of absolute abstraction. There is no arguing with the logic of geometry; it is not just sometimes true, or approximately true. It is always and precisely true—at least for any community of readers that understands and accepts its implicit definitions.

The second is science—factual, reliable, less certain than mathematics because it always depends upon inductive leaps and problematic points of view and instruments that can never be absolutely precise; and it is always susceptible to the possibility that new data will compel us to revise what we thought were immutable laws.

The third kind of knowledge is rhetoric—reasoning that reaches probable conclusions based upon premises that are assumed rather than proven. Rhetoric goes out on an even more tenuous limb than science does. It derives categorical statements from assumptions that can never be proved (or disproved) and data that can never be entirely conclusive. In rhetoric, formal logic is replaced by enthymemes, and systemic data collection is replaced by reliance examples and paradigms that are necessarily inconclusive. The realm of rhetoric is the realm of the plausible and the merely probable.

Aristotle's rhetoric, at least as I read it, is remarkable in its recognition of the limits of logic, its recognition that some questions have no absolute answers and must be settled provisionally on the basis of evidence that is never entirely conclusive. In this fundamentally new/old (i.e., postmodern/Aristotelian) scheme, the analysis and dissemination of belief is the main business of rhetoric. Rhetoric can provide a basis for distinguishing ideological differences that we can live with from those that are truly incompatible. It can provide the epistemological framework not just for persuasion but for critical thinking, for negotiation, and for social and political accommodation. It may be too much to suggest that rhetoric could be a pharmakon for misunderstanding or a realistic alternative to violence. But it can be a system for understanding differences in a way that contributes to the peaceful resolution of conflict.

Sentence Exercises

The sentence exercises toward the back of this book (chapter 12) have been very popular with students and teachers at every level. Unlike many conventional sentence exercises, they are based on the commonsense notion that students need to be taught patterns that they don't already produce when they write. These sentence exercises do not include, for example, relative clauses or compound sentences. Students at every level already write relative clauses and compound sentences, because they speak them.

For this reason, the exercises focus on a series of structures that do not occur with great frequency in ordinary speech, including several varieties of what Francis Christensen used to call "free modifiers"—modifying phrases set off by parenthetical commas. The grammatical nomenclature in these exercises is not at all important; what is important is that students learn to notice, perhaps to "hear," these structures and then to imitate them in sentences of their own.

A Recipe (of Sorts) for Teaching Writing

Each chapter in this book implies a recipe for teaching writing. It's not a sure-fire recipe—writing is not the sort of process that can be reduced to an algorithm. But it is a sensible recipe, one that might be worth trying if you are a new teacher in search of a method, or even an experienced teacher looking for a different way to conduct your classes.

1. After choosing a model essay—an essay that makes the sort of moves you would like your students to acquire—construct an assignment that would have produced it. In other words, construct the assignment that you might have given Annie Dillard or Bruce Catton or Brent Staples if you wanted them to produce their essays that appear in this book.

2. Before showing students the model, give them the assignment and let them struggle with it for a while. This is the purpose of the "Journal Entry" in the headnotes to each essay.

3. After students have spent time working on the assignment, they will be ready to profit from analyzing the model, looking for techniques to imitate, using "So What and the Seven Common Moves" to reveal moves that would otherwise go unnoticed.

4. Have students prepare a draft.

5. Teach students to workshop the draft, providing "So What and the Seven Common Moves" as a checklist to keep their discussion focused.

6. Grade the final draft, using "So What and the Seven Common Moves" as an analytic grading system. If you are committed to process pedagogy, announce that all paper grades are "provisional": students who can provide you with a plan for substantial revision may be allowed to revise.

Because the modes and methods are interpenetrable, the chapters can be arranged on a syllabus in any sequence whatsoever. It may make sense to begin with description and narration, because invention and organization in these modes is relatively easy, so instruction can focus on style and other surface moves; then progress to modes that require more complex strategies for invention and organization, culminating with persuasion.

But a sequence beginning with persuasion is also possible, perhaps even preferable. Students could begin with the system for analyzing belief and persuasion explained in chapter 10 and then proceed through other chapters in almost any sequence, recognizing that each of the other modes and methods is transformed into a persuasive essay whenever the writer's interpretation of the subject is likely to encounter resistance from readers.

If you teach a research paper, sometimes it helps to have students write a personal paper first, drawing on what they have experienced or heard about a given issue, then to write a second paper, supplementing their personal knowledge with research. Two-stage research papers of this sort sometimes help students maintain a personal voice in their writing instead of submerging their own voices in those they have read.

The pedagogical approach implicit in this book is, compared to other rhetorics and readers, relatively simple. I have not attempted to reduce writing to an elaborate series of steps and strategies and cognitive processes, mainly because as a teacher I find myself overwhelmed by texts that attempt too much. After all, textbooks don't teach writing. Teachers do. The magic occurs at that critical moment when we respond to student papers. Textbooks are feeble substitutes for personal discussion and interaction, for making the right suggestion in the right manner at the right time. It's an art we can spend a lifetime learning.

Acknowledgments

This book could not have existed without the help of two very special people: Nancy Perry, who gave me the tough advice I needed at the outset; and Mark Gallaher, who selected most of the essays, wrote the biographical notes, and offered much generous and astute advice in the early going.

I have also benefited from the advice of numerous reviewers: Anita Pandey of University of Memphis; Meg Morgan of UNC-Charlotte; Cindy Brookey of Cisco Junior College; Patricia Harkin of Purdue; Miles S. McCrimmon of J. Sargeant Reynolds Community College; Cathryn Amdahl of Harrisburg Area Community College; Keith Coplin of Colby Community College; and Edward A. Kline of University of Notre Dame. They have saved me from numerous errors; those that remain are entirely my own doing.

Finally, I would like to thank the numerous graduate students and high school teachers and judges to whom I have presented much of this material in workshops over many years. Their encouragement and suggestions have been particularly valuable because they know better than anyone else when something doesn't work—and when it does.

J. C. R.

CREDITS

(*credits continued on page 310*)

1

Writing (and Reading) like a Writer:
So What and the Seven Common Moves

Something strange happens to ordinary speech when you write it down. It becomes boring. No matter how interesting it may be as speech—testimony from a celebrity trial, a President plotting politics with his closest advisors—write it down, and nobody wants to read it. Oh, people may read parts of it, searching for occasional moments of interest. But most of it will be skipped and forgotten. Speech rambles. It lacks the point and purpose and economy of good writing. It is inefficient—full of "uhs" and "you knows," of clichés and platitudes, of artless repetitions, of sentences that start and get sidetracked before they find a grammatical ending, of subjects that get changed before they are fully developed.

Writing, real writing, is different. As writers, we have a chance to inspect our thoughts, to correct them, to back them up with details and facts and references. When we write, time stands still. Sentences wait patiently for us to revise them, to rearrange them, to rid them of unnecessary words and substitute more precise ones for those that are merely generic, to add flourishes of style and wit and power, to cut out the trivial and replace it with news of some sort, surprises, things our readers would not have thought of on their own.

Writing is to speech what dance is to ordinary human movement. It selects moves that occur (or could occur) naturally and spontaneously, and then organizes these moves, cultivates, refines, and repeats them in pleasing ways. Almost all the moves writers make occur (or could occur) in speech; but in writing it is possible to develop, extend, and arrange these moves deliberately and with forethought. Speech happens too fast and disappears too quickly for this sort of planning and revision.

The moves writers make include not only stylistic devices (like simile, metaphor, and alliteration) but conceptual moves as well—moves we make to frame or organize information (narration, description, comparison and contrast, and all the rest that are treated as separate chapters in this book). In speech these conceptual moves occur, but they cannot be extended very far. We can describe a scene or tell a story or define a term in speech, but normally we have to do it in a few sentences. In writing, however, we can extend these conceptual moves indefinitely. We can describe or narrate or define for the length of an entire essay, even an entire book.

In fact, writing as a technology is important to civilization mainly for this reason. Other familiar tools are extensions of our bodies: shovels (and bulldozers) are extensions of our arms and hands; telescopes and microscopes are extensions of our eyes. Writing is an extension of our minds. It allows us to stretch basic conceptual moves far beyond what would be possible in normal conversation or private thought, and to preserve these moves beyond the life of any individual memory. Writing is the basis of all systematic knowledge. Without writing, there would be no science of any consequence (just folklore and practical wisdom handed down from each generation to the next); no history (just oral traditions and myths); and no humanities (there would be oral poetry, sculpture, and painting, but no extended prose narratives or systematic study of the arts). Without writing, we could not give our thoughts the depth and permanence and organization that provide the basic structure of all schools and colleges.

If writing could be arranged in a spectrum, you might put recipes, phone books, and airline schedules at one end and essays at the other. The first kinds of writing are designed to communicate information. They do not interpret their subjects; they do not reveal the personality of the writer. The second kind, essays, have just the opposite purpose: they interpret their subjects; and in the act of interpreting they imply a writer's personality, revealing not just peculiarities of style, but peculiarities of values and beliefs. This book concentrates on writing in the second category—essays—not just because essays tend to be more "literary" than other sorts of writing, and not just because essays include all the writing skills you'll need for writing of a more practical sort, but because writing essays requires you to do something that you will have to do to be truly successful in any profession or academic discipline. To write an essay, you cannot just convey information; you have to interpret it as well.

The most important question for an essay writer is not "What shall I write about?" but rather "What do I want my readers to believe, understand, or feel about my subject?" A good writer can make any subject interesting—a doorknob, a junkyard, statistical data, the making of a baseball, newly discovered forms of life on the ocean floor. Or to put it the other way around, all subjects are equally dull, like a pack of hound dogs snoozing in the sun. A writer's interpretation is a rabbit streaking past those hounds, making them yap and run as if they had discovered a purpose in life.

In this book you will find essays on subjects like "clog dancing" (p. 25) and "my experiences as a junior high cheerleader" (p. 29)—subjects that may not seem interesting in themselves. But good writers, like David Foster Wallace and Donna Tartt make them interesting because they find meaning in them that we might not have found for ourselves. These essays—and all successful essays—have one thing in common: a writer who has discovered something interesting about a particular subject and who wants to share this discovery with readers.

Interpretation is a skill you have already learned when you learned to speak, perhaps even earlier. You already interpret lots of persons, places, things and events in your life: you interpret weather conditions by looking at the sky; you interpret people's personalities or moods by observing their faces or the way they dress or move or talk. When you interpret, you are in fact "reading" the world around you.

But an interpretation that is obvious to everyone is not interesting enough to be the subject of an essay. You see black clouds and interpret them as signs of rain; you see a scowl on someone's face and interpret it as a sign of anger. No surprises here, no news. More important than any other move discussed in this book is the one we call the so-what factor—the original element, the news or surprise, in your interpretation. The so-what factor is the source of the essay's energy. It is attitude, a gentle aggression that says, "I've found something interesting in this subject, and I am going to make it interesting to you." You can spot the so-what factor by asking, "What is novel, interesting, surprising, or moving about the writer's thesis?"

Interpretation is always personal. When writers interpret the world around them, they are in fact revealing themselves—revealing their unique sense of good and evil or some analogous subset thereof (beauty/ugliness, fair/unfair, tragic/comic, interesting/dull, significant/trivial, question/answer, mystery/explanation, problem/solution . . .). Essays always show things in the context of an implied conflict between opposing forces that surge through inert information like opposing electrical charges. Essays reveal the author by revealing the assumptions, positive and negative, upon which the author builds an interpretive framework—the writer's personal and unique beliefs and values. That's why essays are always as much about the author as they are about the subject, no matter how objective they pretend to be.

Most of the assignments in this book suggest subjects that you have already interpreted: "Describe a place that has special meaning to you"; "Tell a story about something that happened to you as a child that you didn't fully understand until years later"; "Defend an opinion by citing lots of examples"; "Write an essay defining an abstract noun that has had special significance in your life." These assignments allow you to exploit, expand, and develop original interpretations you have already made. When you start writing, you may discover a new and interesting interpretation of things you thought you fully understood. Writing often works that way: it helps clarify your thoughts, helps you find out what you really think about a subject, once you put your mind to it. This book's contents can be viewed as a list of things to interpret—and in that sense, it is an aid to finding something to write about.

> Description is your interpretation of things you see, hear, feel, taste, or touch.
> Narration is your interpretation of a series of events.
> Process is your interpretation of how something is done.
> Comparison and contrast are your interpretation of similarities and differences.
> Classification and division are your interpretation of parts or categories.
> Cause and effect are your interpretation of the way things work.
> Definition is your interpretation of the meaning of a particular word.
> Exemplification is your interpretation of a series of instances or stories.
> Persuasion is your interpretation of any subject that other people interpret differently.

Essay writing is a way of making sense of the world around us. It freezes our thoughts and makes them visible so we can examine them, perhaps correct them or develop them. But essay writing is more than that. It is also a way of inventing ourselves on paper. It's not just that we reveal ourselves when we write; we actually invent a self to reveal, the self our readers will imagine as they read—our best self, if we take the time to do it well. All interpretive writing is self-revelation because it reveals the values and attitudes and insights that make us who we are. That's one reason we're so sensitive when people criticize our writing. It's much easier to accept criticism of the way we solve problems in math or work out formulas in chemistry. These things are separate from ourselves. But our writing—well, that's *us* on the page, and we tend to take criticism very personally.

For the most part, the assignments in this book will ask you to interpret a subject with willing and friendly readers in mind—readers who have no particular reason to argue with your interpretation. They have nothing at stake in your subject; they are willing to recognize you as an expert. Writing of this sort is called "exposition"—that is, writing that explains. All the conceptual moves—the modes and methods of development treated in the next nine chapters—are different ways of developing expository essays.

Writing of an entirely different sort occurs when your readers are not necessarily willing to accept your interpretation of things because they are aware of a competing interpretation. This kind of writing is called "persuasion," and it requires an entirely new set of techniques. All the tactics you learn in chapters 2 through 8 are still useful as part of persuasion; but persuasion has to come to grips with tactics of a different sort altogether, tactics based on an understanding of the difference between knowledge and belief, and an understanding of why human beings believe the things they believe. Rhetoric can be defined as the art of examining beliefs—our own as well as those of other people. As such, it can help resolve disagreements that arise when beliefs collide. This subject will be explored in the chapter on persuasive writing.

One way to learn to write well is to imitate writers you admire. But this is not always as easy as it might seem. We rarely see writers writing. We don't see the mistakes, the frustrations, the false starts, the seven or seventy pages that were sent to the wastebasket or to the dustbins of cyberspace for every one that was sent to the printer. All we see is the finished product, polished and self-assured as if the ideas had traveled effortlessly from brain to fingers to page. (It may surprise you to learn, for example, that the page you are reading right now was rewritten more than twenty times.) Writers don't necessarily tell us that they got one idea while showering, another in a dream, and yet another while shopping for groceries somewhere between the pickles and the pancakes. They don't always admit that sometimes they will do anything to avoid writing—bathe the dog, wash the dishes, straighten out the attic.

We don't even see the moves writers make right there on the page. We see straight through them, directly to the meaning. Good writers make their techniques invisible. They want us to react to what they write without our being aware of the moves that keep our interest alive: the figures of speech, the sentences carefully structured and rhythmically varied, the arrangement of information in a sequence that provides suspense or surprise at every point. Learning to write involves learning to notice the surfaces that we normally see straight through. If writers try to make the tricks of their trade invisible, then it's the job of a book about writing to do just the reverse: to isolate the writer's moves and give them names.

In addition to interpretation and the nine conceptual moves that are treated as separate chapters in this book, there are literally hundreds of other moves that good writers make, far too many to master completely. Because these moves are so numerous, we've gathered them under seven generic categories, which we call "The Seven Common Moves"—"common" because they occur in all kinds of essays and will be revisited in every chapter.

1. *Beginning.* Every essay has to have a beginning. A beginning is different from a "start." It is not just the first thing a writer happens to write. It's a move—a tactic with a purpose. A beginning has a job to do: it has to create interest in readers who are not obliged to continue reading.

As you read the essays in this book, notice the moves writers make in their opening paragraphs to grab the attention of their readers. There are lots of tactics to choose from: a quotation, an anecdote, a reference to something else in print, a conflict or problem, a striking metaphor, a provocative thesis or generalization, a partial event (like the ringing of a phone or the beginning of a journey), an opening scene, a pronoun without an antecedent ("She was new to her job," or "It all started at the game"). A beginning builds expectations, like a roller coaster clattering to the top of the first hill, gathering energy that will propel the reader into the rest of the essay.

2. *Ending.* A well-constructed essay doesn't just stop, as if the writer had run out of things to say. It ends. It has a sense of closure. If a beginning is like the first rise on a roller coaster, an effective ending provides the feeling of release you experience when the scream machine finally comes to a stop and allows you to climb out. As you read the essays in this book, notice the various techniques skilled writers use to create the sense of an ending: perhaps a climax in the form of a particularly powerful image or a startling revelation; perhaps a "coda"—a paragraph or two of reflection—either explaining what went before or coming to grips with the fact that it can never be explained; perhaps a return to the beginning, closing the loop. Look for closing moves you might like to use in essays of your own.

3. Detail. Details are the stuff of writing, the cargo, the goods, the beef in the burger. Details have to be interesting and plentiful, but never excessive. When you read a well-written essay, you tend to take the details for granted, as if the writer had no choice but to include them because, well, they were just there, waiting to turn up in an essay. But in fact, choosing details is a deliberate move, one that works hand in hand with interpretation. You have to select and present details in a way that will cause your readers to react the way you want them to. In descriptive and narrative writing, this requires what is called "the writer's eye"—the ability to pick out precisely the right image to convey a given interpretation of a scene or a series of events. Other sorts of writing call for an ability to choose just the right fact, the right examples. All writing requires a balance between "showing" (i.e., leading the readers to see and hear things for themselves) and "telling" (i.e., summarizing things you have seen or heard), between specific facts and generalizations.

4. Organization/Plot. Plot is a particular kind of organization. A dictionary is organized, but it doesn't have a plot. Neither does a phone book, a cookbook, or an encyclopedia. Reference books—like dictionaries, encyclopedias, and cookbooks— don't need plots; they just need to be organized in a way that enables readers to find the information they want as quickly as possible. Reference books are not intended to be read from beginning to end. But essays are like stories. They are intended to be read, not just consulted. That's why the organization of essays includes an element of "plot"—a continuous sense of unfinished business that keeps readers interested.

5. Style. Style has been given many definitions over the centuries. For purposes of this book, however, style can be defined as those surface moves that make careful writing more efficient, more pleasing, and often more powerful than ordinary speech. Many of these moves have traditional names, such as simile, metaphor, personification, allusion, alliteration, antithesis, and so on. Other moves do not have traditional names. You notice them when something leaps off the page and catches your attention. "That's a nice move," you think to yourself.

Toward the back of the book, you will find exercises to help you develop many of the stylistic moves that have been given names. They are analogous to musical exercises—basic patterns that turn up frequently in whatever you want to play (or write). Make a habit of looking for the writer's "best move" in every essay you read, and write a passage in which you imitate that move. You will soon become aware of an enormous range of stylistic tactics that you don't normally notice when you read, even though you react to them unconsciously.

6. Voice/Attitude. In speech we know how people sound: "I don't know who called, but it sounded like Charlie"; "Boy, did Mom sound angry this morning."

Voice and attitude can come across this way in writing, too—as a particular person in a particular mood. The voice—or more precisely, the "voicelessness"—of news stories might be considered a norm in American prose, the default option. Newspaper reporters try to be "objective," and so they try not to sound like particular individuals with particular styles and attitudes. Much scholarly writing strives for the same goal: to be objective, and in a sense, to be voiceless.

When academics and professionals write for other academics and professionals, they often suppress their individual voices, using instead what might be called their career voices. They sound like lawyers, or doctors, or social scientists, or English professors, using technical language and passive voice and avoiding the first person pronoun ("I"). Essayists, on the other hand, *like* to sound like individuals. They often have unique ways of writing and definite points of view—attitudes— that they do not mind revealing. They do not hesitate to use the first person pronoun ("I"), and to let us know how they feel about their subjects. This is why essays are always acts of self-revelation, even when they seem to be about something else.

7. Economy. Economy appears on the page as an absence. It's like fat on a racehorse: just not there. Good writers avoid details that have no purpose. They never give the same information twice, unless they put a new spin on it the second time. If you close your eyes and put your finger on a well-written page, whatever you touch will be relevant to the writer's purpose. Every word fits, tight as the pieces in a jigsaw puzzle. Pull one out and you miss it. (If you don't miss it, leave it out.) An extra piece—well, there just shouldn't be any extra pieces.

Good writers are stingy. They get the most said in the fewest words. They prefer active voice because it is always more economical than passive. They avoid the verb "to be" (*am, are, is, was, were, be, being, been*) if they can use a verb that expresses action instead. They use adjectives and adverbs only when they have to; they prefer nouns and verbs that include whatever meaning modifiers might have added. They don't use two words when one would do. They prune every "which" and "that" and restore only those that can't be done without. They know the best way to improve a draft is to cut until what's left is as smooth and efficient as the skin of a grape. In a well-written essay, it may be difficult to find words you could omit or details that serve no purpose. As writers, though, we have to continuously weed out irrelevant details and unnecessary words.

Each chapter in this book focuses on one of nine major conceptual moves— modes and methods for framing or developing information: description, narration, process analysis, comparison and contrast, division and classification, cause and effect, definition, exemplification, or persuasion. These are common ways of thinking and writing about the world. Although they are treated in separate chapters, they never occur in isolation. An essay that is predominantly in any one of these modes will always include passages in one or more of the other modes. Narration will generally include description. Cause and effect will often include definition. In fact, any of the modes and methods can occur within any of the others. Noticing moves within moves may help you find ideas for your own essays. How, for example, can you develop a classification and division essay? Well, you could describe things in detail, or tell stories about them, or explain their causes and effects, or give examples. Whatever you learn about any mode or method can be useful to you when you are writing in any of the other modes and methods. Nothing is wasted.

For analyzing your own writing, you need to add another move to the list: correctness. Correctness includes spelling, punctuation, grammar, and usage—what some people call "the basics." Like most basics, these things aren't very interesting, but they are extremely important. You never hear anyone recommending a book because its punctuation is terrific or its spelling flawless. Still, if you spot a misspelled word or grammatical error, it grabs your attention like a stain on the tablecloth or a bug in the soup. Breaking the rules—however trivial they might be—can make the difference between success and failure in a job application, a grant proposal, a research paper, an exam.

If you flip through the pages of this book, you will notice that it is full of essays—not poems or plays or stories, or lab reports, or business letters—but essays. You might ask, "Why should I learn to write essays? I'm majoring in business (or math or engineering or human resources or communications or nursing or music or political science)." One reason is that essays are, oddly enough, the most practical form of writing in the world. They require all the skills you'll need to write in any other form. Essays have to be clear and well organized. They have to be economical in content and style. They have to anticipate a reader's needs and interests. They have to observe conventions of spelling, punctuation, and grammar. And essays require a higher kind of literacy, the sort of literacy that enables you not merely to convey information, but to interpret it. Learn to write essays, and you will have no trouble applying a subset of these skills to business letters or job applications or lab reports or grant proposals.

Writing essays also has a value of its own, even if you never have to write a word to earn a living. Essays are a way of thinking. When you write an essay, you learn to interpret things for yourself—things you read as well as things you experience—you become freer, more independent, not just someone who sees the world as everybody around you sees it, but someone with a unique and examined point of view. That's why essay writing is traditionally associated with a "liberal" education—not "liberal" in the sense of a political preference, but "liberal" in the sense of "free and independent." Learning to interpret things for yourself is a liberating experience. It is the difference between job training and a true education.

Now you're ready to write—well, almost ready. First you have to find something to write about. Take a look at the Journal Entry that precedes whichever essay your instructor wants you to study first. After you've jotted down notes for an essay of your own, read the model that follows it. Use "So What and the Seven Common Moves" to find tactics you might imitate in your own essay. Once you finish your first draft, use the same checklist to see if you're making all the moves you can to make your subject come to life. If possible, swap drafts with classmates and have them use the same checklist to analyze your work while you analyze theirs. Good classmates can sometimes be your best teachers.

Don't expect instant success. You already know how to write; but learning to write well is another matter—a long process, like any art, full of trial and error, flashes of inspiration, and (at least for most people) lots of hard work. It's at least as hard as learning to dance or play tennis or improvise music. Improvement requires effort, dedication, and a willingness to accept constructive criticism. Be prepared to write several drafts of each essay, just as most professional writers do.

Above all, think of yourself as a person whose perspective on the world is unique and worth sharing.

Think of yourself as a Writer.

SUGGESTION FOR WRITING: THE PLURAL NOUN FORMULA

Write an essay about writing. For a thesis statement, compose a sentence with a plural noun in it, preferably one preceded by a number (e.g., "There are three ways to succeed in a composition course"; "All good writing has five qualities"). Make sure your thesis expresses an attitude, a judgment, but not just a personal preference that nobody can argue with (e.g., "My four favorite authors are . . . "; "There are seven things I'd like to learn in a composition course").

Once you compose a thesis sentence with a plural noun, organizing the paper is relatively easy: Write an introductory paragraph leading up to the thesis; write a paragraph or two about each of the "three ways," or "five qualities," or whatever you choose to write about; then add a concluding paragraph.

This method of writing is called, for obvious reasons, the "Plural Noun Formula." It is patently artificial: it is difficult to find a published essay that follows this pattern (though Deborah Tannen's essay, "But What Do You Mean?", p. 136, comes very close). But the Plural Noun Formula allows you to demonstrate some essential skills: the ability to extract a generalization (i.e., your thesis) from specific data; the ability to express this generalization as a thesis; and the ability to support it with evidence. The real challenge of this assignment is to make your writing interesting—which means that you have to come up with a new and persuasive interpretation of your subject, or else express an ordinary interpretation in an unusual way.

2

Things That Mean:
The Nature of Description

Description is about things: things you can see, taste, feel, smell, or hear; small things, large things, people, entire scenes. Descriptive writing makes things seem present by naming them with such specific detail that they produce something like virtual reality in the imagination of the reader.

But good description doesn't just name things. It interprets them. Description is about things that mean. It makes a judgment about the things described, gives things a so-what quality. Without this quality, description is just a list, and lists are boring. In fact, the lack of an original and surprising interpretation, the lack of a so-what factor, is a fatal flaw in descriptive writing. Uninterpreted things—things without meaning—are tedious:

> When you enter my bedroom, you will find a desk just to the left of the door. Beyond that desk, on the left side of the room, is my bed. On the far wall there is a window. To the right of the window is my stereo. Below the amplifier is a shelf with CDs. . . .

"So what?!" the reader wants to scream. "Why am I reading this? What's the point?" And in fact, the writer wants to scream almost the same thing: "So what?

Why am I writing this?" Because it is required, no doubt. Nobody writes this sort of stuff if they have a choice.

Anything—even a bedroom—can be an interesting subject for description, as long as the writer has an agenda. It may be a practical agenda or a speculative agenda or an entertaining agenda, just so long as it includes an original "take" on the subject, an interpretation that makes the subject worth paying attention to. A successful description of a bedroom, for example, would present unique details—its size, its shape, its furnishings, its history—in a way that conveys meaning or memories or associations to people who may never have seen them.

The things you describe can be unusual or exotic—but they don't have to be. There is nothing particularly unusual about a bunch of junior high cheerleaders, or clog dancers at a state fair, or the view from a filling station in Nowhere, Virginia. But as you will see later in this chapter, good writers make ordinary things seem unusual because they find meaning in them that we might have never discovered on our own. When we see cheerleaders and landscapes and country cloggers through the eyes of Donna Tartt or Annie Dillard or David Foster Wallace, we see them in ways that take us by surprise. When the subject is unusual—like debris left behind after a historic battle—it's not the debris that we find interesting. It's what that debris means to a writer like Ernie Pyle, and what he makes it mean to his readers.

When you choose a topic for a descriptive essay, choose something that is meaningful to you. What are the most meaningful things in your life, things you are most attached to? The most meaningful places? The most meaningful scenes? Let these be the subject of your essay.

Revealing meaning—interpreting things—may seem terribly difficult at first. But in fact, you wouldn't be reading this book if you hadn't already lived a life of successful interpretation. You've interpreted people's moods by reading the expression on their faces. You've interpreted neighborhoods by reading the looks of the houses. You've made judgments about people on the basis of the way they talk, and walk, and dress. Making sense of things, forming an impression, making judgments on the basis of appearances is interpretation. Writing a descriptive paper is just a matter of putting your interpretations on paper. Of course, to be interesting, you have to interpret things in a way that is both persuasive and yet not entirely obvious to everyone who has seen the same things.

Description is most powerful when it conveys a feeling or understanding without actually naming it. Good writers tend to avoid words like "tasty," "refreshing," "sad," "beautiful," or "terrifying"—label words, words that name a reaction instead of showing the things themselves in a way that makes readers perceive them as tasty, refreshing, beautiful, sad, or terrifying. The general rule is "Show, don't tell." Don't give your readers your interpretation of things directly; give them the things themselves in a way that gently compels them to react the way you want them to react.

In "Catch It If You Can" (p. 22), for example, instead of labeling a sunset with a reaction word like "beautiful," Annie Dillard gives us the sunset, showing instead of telling:

>Overhead, great strips and chunks of cloud dash to the north-west in a gold rush below.

If you let her words paint a picture in your imagination, you don't have to be told the sunset was beautiful. You see it for yourself.

Similarly, in "Clog Dancing at the Illinois State Fair" (p. 25), instead of telling us that the men he saw at the state fair were great dancers but quite ordinary in their appearance, David Foster Wallace shows the men dancing, letting us see them exactly as he wants us to see them:

>The men all have thinning hair and cheesy rural faces, and their skinny legs are rubberized blurs.

Wallace's words convey more than a scene; they convey an attitude as well. That's interpretation.

Writers like Dillard and Foster have what is called the "writer's eye," a knack for finding just the right details—the "strips and chunks of cloud," the "thinning hair and cheesy rural faces"—to convey the feeling or judgment they want their readers to share. Sometimes they heap detail after significant detail onto the page, like painters with quick and busy brushes. But they don't use just any details; they carefully select details that support a particular interpretation, ignoring countless other details that would be irrelevant to their purpose. Details for the sake of details are just clutter.

Description is not limited to images you can see. In fact, one of the best ways to discover details for a descriptive essay is to explore what you want to describe through each of the five senses. What do you see? What do you smell? Hear? Feel? Taste? Make a list much longer than you will need for your essay; then eliminate those details that have nothing to do with the feeling you want to convey.

Sometimes the point of description is expressed as a thesis, with descriptive details following a generalization. "The apartment was unfit for human beings to live in," a writer might say, and then provide a list of details to prove the point: a leaky roof, plaster peeling from the walls, exposed electrical wires, broken plumbing. Sometimes writers follow the opposite pattern: details first, generalization at the end. Often, however, the generalization—the agenda, the point—is not expressed explicitly, but quietly whispered between the lines as an unasked question: "Don't you think this is _____?" or "Don't you think this shows that _____?" When description is successful, the reader knows how to fill in the blanks.

Description can follow a spatial sequence in its organization—top to bottom, inside to outside, clockwise or counterclockwise. But it doesn't have to. Oddly enough, as long as the point is clearly stated or implied, details in a descriptive passage can be arranged in an apparently random order—as if the writer's eye were wandering from detail to detail in no particular order. You will notice, though, that in good description, what seems random usually isn't. Writers generally "plot" the sequence of details, saving the best for last. They seem to be reporting things in the sequence in which they were observed; but in fact, they have arranged their observations in the sequence that will have the most compelling effect on their readers.

Description is not just a literary art. Doctors and nurses describe symptoms. Scientists describe experiments and observations. Lawyers describe persons, places, and things involved in contracts or in alleged violations of the law. Almost every profession requires descriptive writing, the interpretation of things observed.

Normandy Beachhead

Ernie Pyle

In the preceding column we told about the D-Day wreckage among our machines of war that were expended in taking one of the Normandy beaches. 1

But there is another and more human litter. It extends in a thin little line, just like a high-water mark, for miles along the beach. This is the strewn personal gear, gear that will never be needed again, of those who fought and died to give us our entrance into Europe. 2

Here in a jumbled row for mile on mile are soldiers' packs. Here are socks and shoe polish, sewing kits, diaries, Bibles and hand grenades. Here are the latest letters from home, with the address on each one neatly razored out. One of the security precautions enforced before the boys embarked. 3

Here are toothbrushes and razors and snapshots of families back home staring up at you from the sand. Here are pocketbooks, metal mirrors, extra trousers, and bloody, abandoned shoes. Here are broken-handled shovels, and portable radios smashed almost beyond recognition, and mine detectors twisted and ruined. 4

Here are torn pistol belts and canvas water buckets, first-aid kits and jumbled heaps of lifebelts. I picked up a pocket Bible with a soldier's name in it, and put it in my jacket. I carried it half a mile or so and then put it back down on the beach. I don't know why I picked it up, or why I put it back down. 5

Soldiers carry strange things ashore with them. In every invasion you'll find at least one soldier hitting the beach at H-hour with a banjo slung over his shoulder. The most ironic piece of equipment marking our beach—this beach of first despair—is a tennis racket that some soldier had brought along. It lies lonesomely on the sand, clamped in its rack, not a string broken. 6

Two of the most dominant items in the beach refuse are cigarets and writing paper. Each soldier was issued a carton of cigarets just before he started. Today these cartons by the thousand, water-soaked and spilled out, mark the line of our first savage blow. 7

Writing paper and air-mail envelopes come second. The boys had intended to do a lot of writing in France. Letters that would have filled those blank, abandoned pages. 8

Always there are dogs in every invasion. There is a dog still on the beach today, still pitifully looking for his master. 9

He stays at the water's edge, near a boat that lies twisted and half sunk at the water line. He barks appealingly to every soldier who approaches, trots eagerly along with him for a few feet, and then, sensing himself unwanted in all this haste, runs back to wait in vain for his own people at his own empty boat. 10

Over and around this long thin line of personal anguish, fresh men today are rushing vast supplies to keep our armies pushing on into France. Other squads of men pick amidst the wreckage to salvage ammunition and equipment that are still usable. Men worked and slept on the beach for days before the last D-Day victim was taken away for burial. 11

I stepped over the form of one youngster whom I thought dead. But when I looked down I saw he was only sleeping. He was very young, and very tired. He lay on one elbow, his hand suspended in the air about six inches from the ground. And in the palm of his hand he held a large smooth rock. 12

I stood and looked at him a long time. He seemed in his sleep to hold that rock lovingly, as though it were his last link with a vanishing world. I have no idea at all why he went to sleep with the rock in his hand, or what kept him from dropping it once he was asleep. It was just one of those little things without explanation that a person remembers for a long time. 13

The strong, swirling tides of the Normandy coastline shift the contours of the sandy beach as they move in and out. They carry soldiers' bodies out to sea, and later they return them. They cover the corpses of heroes with sand, and then in their whims they uncover them. 14

As I plowed out over the wet sand of the beach on that first day ashore, I walked around what seemed to be a couple of pieces of driftwood sticking out of the sand. But they weren't driftwood. 15

They were a soldier's two feet. He was completely covered by the shifting sands except for his feet. The toes of his GI shoes pointed toward the land he had come so far to see, and which he saw so briefly. 16

The So-What Factor.   What is novel, interesting, surprising, or moving about Ernie Pyle's description of the Normandy beachhead? What does he want us to understand, feel, or believe after reading his report? There is no clear thesis statement. Instead, the interpretation is expressed in a question whispered between the lines: "Don't you think this is . . . ?" What? Because Pyle's purpose is rich, there are several ways to fill in the blank. Among them, the words "tragic," "heroic," "absurd," perhaps even "disgusting" flicker through our minds, though no single word is quite equal to what we feel. These would be "reaction" words, and Pyle avoids them, preferring instead to let us walk the beach with him, observing mementos of individual deaths, witnessing the details that made him feel the way he did, thinking, no doubt, that we will feel the same way.

What does Pyle consider good in what he finds on the Normandy beachhead? What does he consider evil? Do you think everybody would have been able to spot the same conflicting forces in the scene?

THE SEVEN COMMON MOVES

1. Beginning. Writers often create interest in their work by attaching it to other work in print, like spiders hanging webs from something already in place:

> In the preceding column we told about the D-Day wreckage among our machines of war that were expended in taking one of the Normandy beaches.

But Pyle's beginning is effective even for readers who may not have read his earlier column because in the second paragraph he adds a bit of mystery, announcing his topic in very general terms:

> But there is another and more human litter.

This is a generalization. You may have had teachers who wrote the word "generalization" on your papers, as if generalizations were errors. They can be, of course—but only if you fail to follow them with rich, cogent details. Generalizations arouse curiosity. In this case, Pyle satisfies our curiosity by providing the details that follow.

2. Ending. Description is complete when sufficient details have been provided to support the interpretation the writer wants to convey. But when writers reach this point, they don't just stop writing. They provide a sense of an ending. Often they do this by circling back to the beginning. Sometimes they end by stating the point, perhaps in the form of a thesis statement. Sometimes they provide a "zinger"—a final word or phrase or image that brings the passage to a fitting climax.

Pyle's essay ends with a zinger, a climatic image calculated to make the reader feel, "Ouch. I get the point." And in a sense, the ending circles back to the beginning, where "human litter" was mentioned: we didn't know, in the beginning, that this phrase referred not just to litter left by human beings, but to human beings as litter. The point, of course, is that the invasion of Normandy had tremendous human cost, and nothing could convey that cost more dramatically than the image of a young soldier buried on the beach, his feet poking up like sticks in the sand.

3. Detail. The two most fundamental rules for effective descriptive writing have to do with the quality of details:

1. Don't include just things, but *things that mean.*
2. Don't just tell, *show.*

The things Pyle shows us—letters, cigarettes, a banjo—are ordinary. They would be unexceptional if we found them around the house. But on a beach in Normandy, where they don't belong, left behind by people who may no longer be alive, they become more than inanimate objects. They become things that mean, emblems of lives cut off before they were well begun.

Notice that Pyle doesn't tell us how to react to these images. He doesn't use words like "sad," or "tragic," or "wasteful." Instead, he shows us the things themselves and lets us draw our own conclusions. Sometimes an individual item is examined in close detail, so that we see not a generic tennis racket, but a particular tennis racket, one that "lies lonesomely on the sand, clamped in its rack, not a string broken"; not just generic snapshots, but "snapshots of families back home staring up at you from the sand."

4. Organization/Plot. "Normandy Beach" has a narrative structure, with details floating along on the surface of time like leaves on a stream. We follow the writer as he walks along the beach, first past one item, then another, and another, reporting whatever comes into view along the way.

But Pyle does more than organize. He plots. He holds back information that he might well have given us at the outset, releasing it at the moment in which it could have its greatest impact. In fact, there is a steady heightening of images, each more moving than the one before: first the inanimate equipment of ordinary living; then the dog, still alive, but abandoned and pathetic; then the discovery of a soldier asleep on the sand; and finally the more startling discovery of a soldier who did not survive. Pyle may have encountered all these things in exactly the sequence in which he describes them. There is a good chance, though, that he wrote or revised his report after he had walked on the beach, ordering the details, not necessarily in the order in which he saw them, but in the order that would make the strongest impression on his readers, creating a sense of continually heightened interest, saving the strongest, the most startling image for last.

5. Style. Style *can* be conversational. In fact, essayists often try to write as if they were talking to a close friend or family member. But essayists also have a way of making stylistic moves that really would not be likely to occur in conversation, even though they seem perfectly natural on the page. To discover moves of this sort, read each sentence aloud and look for those that would seem odd as dialogue in a play. For instance, the following sentence seems natural enough on the page, but it is too finely constructed to be credible as dialogue:

> He barks appealingly to every soldier who approaches, trots eagerly along with him for a few feet, and then, sensing himself unwanted in all this haste, runs back to wait in vain for his own people at his own empty boat.

This sentence differs from ordinary speech in three ways: it has a neat series of parallel verbs ("barks," "trots," and "runs"); it includes a phrase embedded in a way that requires a bit of planning ("sensing himself unwanted in all this haste"); and it includes thick description (i.e., lots of details). It's not that we couldn't speak sentences like this; it's just that normally we don't. When we speak, we don't have time to arrange words and phrases this neatly. When we write, however, time runs in slow motion. We have time to plan and revise. Good writers take advantage of this extra time to develop stylistic moves that would be hard to achieve in the haste of ordinary conversation.

Another sentence that seems natural enough until you read it aloud is this one, in which the word order is a bit different from what you would expect in ordinary conversation:

> And in the palm of his hand he held a large smooth rock.

Normally we would say, "And he held a large smooth rock in the palm of his hand." Pyle inverts the normal order to put "rock" at the end because that's the word he wants to emphasize. This move illustrates an important principle of style: pay particular attention to endings. Sentences should end with something strong, not with a whimper or an afterthought. Notice this principle at work in the following example:

> Here are socks and shoe polish, sewing kits, diaries, Bibles and hand grenades.

Why does Pyle save hand grenades for last? How would the effect be altered if he had arranged these details in any other sequence? Notice, too, Pyle's attention to the tiniest details: Why does he put socks next to shoe polish? Diaries next to Bibles? Bibles next to hand grenades? All these choices Pyle made are elements of style. This is a very carefully crafted sentence, not one that anyone would be likely to speak.

Perhaps the most important sentence type to notice is what one scholar, Francis Christensen, called the "cumulative sentence":

> It lies lonesomely on the sand, clamped in its rack, not a string broken.

Cumulative sentences resemble freight trains: the main and essential clause comes first, like the engine, followed by a string of modifying phrases trailing behind like box cars:

> It lies lonesomely on the sand, (main clause)
>   clamped in its rack, (trailing phrase)
>   not a string broken. (trailing phrase)

Any or all of the trailing phrases could be detached, and the main clause would still chug along as if nothing had happened, a complete sentence in itself. Cumulative sentences are considered characteristic of modern American prose. You can find them in all sorts of good writing, but they are particularly abundant in narrative and descriptive passages. If you want to develop your ability to write sentences like this, practice the exercise on p. 287.

Pyle's style is characterized by very short sentences. This style was made famous by another war correspondent, Ernest Hemingway. In fact, it's not clear whether Hemingway influenced Pyle or vice versa.

6. *Voice/Attitude.* Voice and attitude reveal the writer implicit in the text. By tradition, front page newspaper stories are supposed to be "voiceless"—free of personal bias or interpretation, written in an "objective" voice, a voice in which the personality of the individual writer is concealed. Essayists, however, generally inhabit their work, revealing themselves by using the first person pronoun ("I") and giving lots of other signals to indicate just what sort of person this "I" might be. Voice and attitude are the result of any moves that would seem out of place in a story on the front page of a good newspaper, the moves that reveal mood, attitude, values, sometimes even social class or regional origin or professional status.

Because Ernie Pyle was a columnist, not just a reporter, he was entitled to a personal voice. He was allowed to reveal his moods and attitudes and values. He was allowed to "sound like" Ernie Pyle—a person readers would recognize even if his name had been omitted from the top of his columns. And, of course, because Ernie Pyle would have different moods on different occasions, he was allowed to adopt a voice in each column that revealed his mood and attitude in relation to the subject at hand.

Pyle injects himself into his essay by using the first person pronoun ("I picked up," "I carried," "I stepped," "I looked," "I saw"), making it clear that we are getting a personal point of view. He expresses his state of mind ("I don't know why," "I have no idea why"). He makes interpretive judgments, calling things "strange" or "ironic" or "savage." He even uses sentence fragments to establish a conversational tone ("One of the security precautions enforced before the boys embarked"). Each of these moves helps establish a "persona": they cause us to imagine the writer as a certain kind of person—not just a transparent observer.

Describing the personality implied in an essay is always subjective, always debatable, like interpreting a character in a play. One plausible description of the person we perceive in this essay, however, is that he is sensitive and sad. He has a certain toughness about him—not mean, but weary. Most of the sentences would seem natural enough in ordinary conversation, but they are clipped, as if the speaker had no words to waste:

> But there is another and more human litter.
> Soldiers carry strange things ashore with them.
> I stood and looked at him a long time.

The brevity creates a certain tone: laconic, matter-of-fact, no time for frills. The very plainness of these sentences—their tendency to understate what they describe, the sparseness of adjectives and adverbs—gives them a peculiar effect. They are like thin dams barely containing an overwhelming flood of sorrow.

7. Economy. Test for economy by putting your finger on any spot on the page and seeing if you can figure out a purpose for whatever word or phrase you happen to touch. If you touched "pocketbooks, metal mirrors, extra trousers, and bloody, abandoned shoes," for example, you would realize that these details indicate personal belongings that people would not normally leave behind. They are not just forgotten objects, but relics of young men killed in battle. Or if you touched the detail about "Letters that would have filled those blank, abandoned pages," you'd realize that the missing soldiers were not just isolated individuals; they had families and loved ones at home, hoping to hear from them.

There were lots of other things around that beach that Pyle could have described: the color of the water, perhaps a slate gray, rolling in whitecaps toward the beach, or, if the tide was out, gathered in glassy pools between sand bars; the seaside vegetation, grass waving like wheat in the wind, trees or fields off in the distance. But he chose not to describe these things, because although they might have been pleasant pictures on another occasion, they would not have helped us see the scene as Pyle wants us to see it.

Moves within Moves.   The dominant mode of this essay is description. It is a scene with meaning. But if you look closely, you will see that like all the other essays in this book, this one includes elements of other modes and methods of development that are treated as separate chapters. The structure, for example, is *narrative* (see chapter 3). It's as if we were walking along the beach with Pyle, observing the things he observed in chronological order.

Comparison (see chapter 5) occurs in its smallest form, a simile describing the litter:

> It extends in a thin little line, just like a high-water mark, for miles along the beach.

Comparison always implies contrast; if the litter was like a high-water mark, it is also unlike it in important ways.

Cause-and-effect analysis (see chapter 7) occurs briefly in paragraph 3, where Pyle explains why addresses had been "neatly razored out" of letters from home ("One of the security precautions enforced before the boys embarked"). *Exemplification* (see chapter 9) occurs in paragraph 6, which begins "Soldiers carry strange things ashore with them" and then provides examples of strange things.

Words, Phrases, and Allusions.   The following items were taken from "Normandy Beachhead" in the order of appearance. With the help of your classmates, locate these words in the essay and see if their context provides a clue to their meaning. If necessary, consult a dictionary, an encyclopedia, or other reference work to determine what each item means in its context. Pay particular attention to words and phrases that might be worth using in your own writing.

Normandy, D-Day, expended, high-water mark, embarked, mine detectors, H-hour, refuse (as a noun), contours

Suggestion for Writing

Return to the journal entry suggested at the beginning of this chapter. Using "Normandy Beachhead" as a model, write an essay describing things in a way that reveals something about the people associated with them or the nature of the activity that produced them. You may have thought of other topics as you read "Normandy Beachhead."

Journal Entry. Every once in a while you experience nature with an over-whelming freshness. Recall one such experience and make a list of all the details that made you feel the way you did. Explore the list through each of the five senses: what did you see, feel, taste, touch, hear? Be specific. Avoid reaction words (like "beautiful" or "awesome") and mushy personification (like trees dancing, the sun peeping, or birds chanting their morning prayers). Describe things honestly and accurately. The trick is to interpret a scene (i.e., to provide a "take" on it) and yet seem to be just reporting it as it is. After you've worked on this project for a while, read Annie Dillard's description of mountain scenery she suddenly noticed after she had been driving through it for hours. Look for tech-niques to imitate. Notice how she captures the shape and color and feel and smell of things in honest and direct language.

Catch It If You Can

Annie Dillard

It is early March. I am dazed from a long day of interstate driving homeward; I pull   1
in at a gas station in Nowhere, Virginia, north of Lexington. The young boy in charge ("Chick 'at oll?") is offering a free cup of coffee with every gas purchase. We talk in the glass-walled office while my coffee cools enough to drink. He tells me, among other things, that the rival gas station down the road whose FREE COF-FEE sign is visible from the interstate, charges you fifteen cents if you want your coffee in a Styrofoam cup, as opposed, I guess, to your bare hands.

All the time we talk, the boy's new beagle puppy is skidding around the office,   2
sniffing impartially at my shoes and at the wire rack of folded maps. The cheerful human conversation wakes me, recalls me, not to a normal consciousness, but to a kind of energetic readiness. I step outside, followed by the puppy.

I am absolutely alone. There are no customers. The road is vacant, the interstate   3
is out of sight and earshot. I have hazarded into a new corner of the world, an un-known spot, a *Brigadoon*. Before me extends a low hill trembling in yellow brome, and behind the hill, filling the sky, rises an enormous mountain ridge, forested, alive and awesome with brilliant blown lights. I have never seen anything so tremulous and live. Overhead, great strips and chunks of cloud dash to the northwest in a gold rush. At my back the sun is setting—how can I not have noticed before that the sun is setting? My mind has been a blank slab of black asphalt for hours, but that

doesn't stop the sun's wild wheel. I set my coffee beside me on the curb; I smell loam on the wind; I pat the puppy; I watch the mountain.

My hand works automatically over the puppy's fur, following the line of hair   4
under his ears, down his neck, inside his forelegs, along his hot-skinned belly.

Shadows lope along the mountain's rumpled flanks; they elongate like root   5
tips, like lobes of spilling water, faster and faster. A long purple pigment pools in each ruck and tuck of the rock; it deepens and spreads, boring crevasses, canyons. As the purple vaults and slides, it tricks out the unleafed forest and rumpled rock in gilt, in shape-shifting patches of glow. These gold lights veer and retract, shatter and glide in a series of dazzling splashes, shrinking, leaking, exploding. The ridge's bosses and hummocks sprout bulging from its side; the whole mountain looms miles closer; the light warms and reddens; the bare forest folds and pleats itself like living protoplasm before my eyes, like a running chart, a wildly scrawling oscillo-graph on the present moment. The air cools; the puppy's skin is hot. I am more alive than all the world.

This is it, I think, this is it, right now, the present, this empty gas station, here,   6
this western wind, this tang of coffee on the tongue, and I am patting the puppy, I am watching the mountain. And the second I verbalize this awareness in my brain, I cease to see the mountain or feel the puppy. I am opaque, so much black asphalt. But at the same second, the second I know I've lost it, I also realize that the puppy is still squirming on his back under my hand. Nothing has changed for him. He draws his legs down to stretch the skin taut so he feels every fingertip's stroke along his furred and arching side, his flank, his flung-back throat.

I sip my coffee. I look at the mountain, which is still doing its tricks, as you   7
look at a still-beautiful face belonging to a person who was once your lover in an-other country years ago: with fond nostalgia, and recognition, but no real feeling save a secret astonishment that you are now strangers. Thanks. For the memories. It is ironic that the one thing that all religions recognize as separating us from our cre-ator—our very self-consciousness—is also the one thing that divides us from our fellow creatures. It was a bitter birthday present from evolution, cutting us off at both ends. I get in the car and drive home.

UNDERSTANDING THE ESSAY

1. What does the title have to do with Dillard's subject matter? Is the essay re-ally about the scene itself, or about a way of seeing the scene?
2. What is the meaning of the next-to-last-sentence ("It was a bitter birthday present from evolution, cutting us off at both ends")?

3. What does Dillard consider good in the scene she describes? Of what do you think she is critical? Do you think you would react to the scene, the puppy, the attendant the same way Dillard does?

4. How do you feel about Annie Dillard as a person because of the beliefs and values that frame her description?

5. Dillard uses many unusual words. Can you find any that might have been replaced by more ordinary words? If so, would replacing them improve the essay?

So What and the Seven Common Moves.   Analyze this essay with the help of the questions about "So What and the Seven Common Moves" found on the back cover of this book.

Words, Phrases, and Allusions.   The following items were taken from "Catch It If You Can" in the order of appearance. With the help of your classmates, locate these words in the essay and see if their context provides a clue to their meaning. If necessary, consult a dictionary, an encyclopedia, or other reference work to determine what each item means in its context. Pay particular attention to words and phrases that might be worth using in your own writing.

impartially, *Brigadoon*, brome, tremulous, loam, lope, ruck, crevasses, bosses, hummocks, protoplasm, oscillograph, verbalize, opaque, taut, nostalgia

Suggestion for Writing

Using "Catch It If You Can" as a model, write an essay describing a scene in which you experienced nature with an unusual intensity. The journal entry suggested at the beginning of this selection may have given you an idea for a topic, or you may have thought of other topics as you read "Catch It If You Can."

Clog Dancing at the Illinois State Fair

David Foster Wallace

I'm on a teetery stool watching the Illinois Prairie Cloggers competition in a structure called the Twilight Ballroom that's packed with ag-folks and well over 100 degrees. I'd nipped in here only to get a bottle of soda pop on my way to the Truck and Tractor Pull. By now the pull's got to be nearly over, and in half an hour the big U.S.A.C. dirt-track auto race starts. But I cannot tear myself away from the scene in here. I'd imagined goony Jed Clampett types in tattered hats and hobnail boots, a-stompin' and a-whoopin', etc. I guess clogging, Scotch-Irish in origin and the dance of choice in Appalachia, did used to involve actual clogs and boots and slow stomps. But clogging has now miscegenated with square dancing and honky-tonk boogie to become a kind of intricately synchronized, absolutely kick-ass country tap dance. 1

There are teams from Pekin, Le Roy, Rantoul, Cairo, Morton. They each do three numbers. The music is up-tempo country or dance-pop. Each team has anywhere from four to ten dancers. Few of the women are under thirty-five, fewer still under 175 pounds. They're country mothers, red-cheeked gals with bad dye jobs and big pretty legs. They wear western-wear tops and midiskirts with multiple ruffled slips underneath; and every once in a while they grab handfuls of cloth and flip the skirts up like cancan dancers. When they do this they either yip or whoop, as the spirit moves them. The men all have thinning hair and cheesy rural faces, and their skinny legs are rubberized blurs. The men's western shirts have piping on the chest and shoulders. The teams are all color-coordinated—blue and white, black and red. The white shoes all the dancers wear look like golf shoes with metal taps clamped on. 2

Their numbers are everything from Waylon and Tammy to Aretha, Miami   3
Sound Machine, Neil Diamond's "America." The routines have some standard tap-
dance moves—sweep, flare, chorus-line kicking. But it is fast and sustained and
choreographed down to the last wristflick. And square dancing's genes can be seen
in the upright, square-shouldered postures on the floor, and there's a kind of florally
enfolding tendency to the choreography, some of which uses high-speed prome-
nades. But it is methedrine-paced and exhausting to watch because your own feet
move; and it is erotic in a way that makes MTV look lame. The cloggers' feet are
too fast to be seen, really, but they all tap out the exact same rhythm. A typical routine is something like: *ta*tatata*ta*tatata*ta*tata. The variations around the basic rhythm
are baroque. When they kick or spin, the two-beat absence of tap complexifies the
pattern.

The audience is packed in right to the edge of the portable hardwood flooring.   4
The teams are mostly married couples. The men are either rail-thin or have big
hanging guts. A couple of the men on a blue-and-white team are great fluid Astaire-
like dancers, but mostly it is the women who compel. The men have constant
smiles, but the women look orgasmic; they're the really serious ones, transported.
Their yips and whoops are involuntary, pure exclamation. They are arousing. The
audience claps savvily on the backbeat and whoops when the women do. It is almost all folks from the ag and livestock shows—the flannel shirts, khaki pants, seed
caps and freckles. The spectators are soaked in sweat and extremely happy. I think
this is the ag-community's special treat, a chance here to cut loose a little while
their animals sleep in the heat. The transactions between cloggers and crowd seem
synecdochic of the fair as a whole: a culture talking to itself, presenting credentials
for its own inspection, bean farmers and herbicide brokers and 4-H sponsors and
people who drive pickup trucks because they really need them. They eat non-fair
food from insulated hampers and drink beer and pop and stomp in perfect time and
put their hands on neighbors' shoulders to shout in their ears while the cloggers
whirl and fling sweat on the crowd.

There are no black people in the Twilight Ballroom, and the awakened looks on   5
the younger ag-kids' faces have this astonished aspect, like they didn't realize their
race could dance like this. Three married couples from Rantoul, wearing full western bodysuits the color of raw coal, weave an incredible filigree of high-speed tap
around Aretha's "R-E-S-P-E-C-T," and there's no hint of racial irony in the room;
the song has been made this people's own, emphatically. This Nineties version of
clogging does have something sort of pugnaciously white about it, a kind of perfor-
mative nose-thumbing at M. C. Hammer. There's an atmosphere in the room—not
racist, but aggressively white. It's hard to describe—the atmosphere is the same at a
lot of rural Midwest events. It is not like a black person who came in would be ill
treated; it's more like it would just never occur to a black person to come here.

I can barely hold the tablet still to scribble journalistic impressions, the floor is   6
rumbling under so many boots and sneakers. The record player is old-fashioned, the
loudspeakers are shitty, and it sounds fantastic. Two of the dancing Rantoul wives

are fat, but with great legs. Who could practice this kind of tapping as much as they must and stay fat? I think maybe rural Midwestern women are just congenitally big. But these people clogging get down. And they do it as a troupe, a collective, with none of the narcissistic look-at-me grandstanding of great dancers in rock clubs. They hold hands and whirl each other around and in and out, tapping like mad, their torsos upright and almost formal, as if only incidentally attached to the blur of legs below. It goes on and on. I'm rooted to my stool.

UNDERSTANDING THE ESSAY

1. What does Wallace find surprising and enjoyable about clog dancing and the clog dancers?
2. What attitude does Wallace express toward the clog dancers? Does he seem respectful or condescending, or is his attitude more complicated than either of these alone?
3. This essay was originally published in *Harper's*, a magazine of culture and criticism with a long history of appealing to an educated, discriminating audience. Do you think Wallace expected it to be read by cloggers? Do you think cloggers would be pleased or offended by the essay?
4. Wallace says that the fair represents "a culture talking to itself, presenting its own credentials for inspection" (paragraph 4). What does he mean?
5. Wallace remarks on the absence of black people (paragraph 5), and he describes clog dancing as "not racist, but aggressively white." Do you find that description offensive? Why or why not?

So What and the Seven Common Moves. Analyze this essay with the help of the questions about "So What and the Seven Common Moves" found on the back cover of this book.

Words, Phrases, and Allusions. The following items were taken from "Clog Dancing at the Illinois State Fair" in the order of appearance. With the help of your classmates, locate these words in the essay and see if their context provides a clue to their meaning. If necessary, consult a dictionary, an encyclopedia, or other reference work to determine what each item means in its context. Pay particular attention to words and phrases that might be worth using in your own writing.

Appalachia, Waylon, Tammy, Aretha, Miami Sound Machine, Neil Diamond's "America," methedrine-paced, Astaire-like, erotic, baroque, orgasmic, savvily, synecdochic, herbicide, filigree, pugnaciously, journalistic, narcissistic

Suggestion for Writing

Using "Clog Dancing at the Illinois State Fair" as a model, write an essay describing an activity or an event that you found yourself enjoying, even though you did not expect to. The journal entry suggested at the beginning of this selection may have given you an idea for a topic. Like Wallace, think of your readers as people who might need to be persuaded that the event or activity is really worth paying attention to. Use thick description, as Wallace does, to convey an honest but positive picture of your subject without the help of vague label words.

Team Spirit

Donna Tartt

The year I was a freshman cheerleader, I was reading *1984.* I was fourteen years old 1
then and failing algebra and the fact that I was failing it worried me as I would
worry now if the Mafia were after me, or if I had shot somebody and the police
were coming to get me. But I did not have an awful lot of time to brood about this.
It was basketball season then, and there was a game nearly every night. In Mississippi the schools are far apart, and sometimes we would have to drive two hundred
miles to get to Panola Academy, Sharkey-Issaquena, funny how those old names
come back to me; we'd leave sometime before school was out, not get home till
twelve or one in the morning. I was not an energetic teenager, and this was hard on
me. Too much exposure to the high-decibel world of teen sports—shrieking
buzzers, roaring stomping mob, thunderous feet of players charging up the
court—kept me in a kind of perpetual stunned condition; the tin-roof echo of rural
gymnasiums rang through all my silences, and frequently at night I woke in a panic
because I thought a player was crashing through my bedroom window or a basketball was flying at me, about to knock my teeth out.

I read *1984* in the backseats of Cadillacs, Buicks, Lincoln Town Cars, riding 2
through the flat wintry Delta with my saddle oxfords off and my schoolbooks piled
beneath my feet. Our fathers—professional men, mostly, lawyers and optometrists,

29

prosperous local plumbers—took turns driving us back and forth from the games. The other cheerleaders griped about not being allowed to ride with the players, but though I griped along with them, I was secretly appalled at the rowdy team bus, full of boys who shouted things when you walked by their table in the cafeteria. The cars, on the other hand, were wide, spacious, quiet. Somebody's mother usually would have made cookies; there were always potato chips and old issues of *Seventeen*. The girls punched listlessly at the radio, applied Bonne Bell lip gloss, did their homework or their hair.

Now that I think about it, I believe I read *Animal Farm* before *1984*. It upset me   3 a little, especially the end, but the statement ALL ANIMALS ARE EQUAL, BUT SOME ANIMALS ARE MORE EQUAL THAN OTHERS echoed sentiments that I recognized as prevalent in the upper echelons of the cheerleading squad. Our captain was a mean girl named Cindy Clark. She talked a lot about spirit and pep, and how important it was for us to work as a team, but she and her cronies ostracized the younger girls and were horrible to us off the court. Cindy was approximately my height and was forced to be my partner in some of the cheers, a circumstance that displeased her as much as it did me. I remember a song that was popular around that time; it had lyrics that went:

We are family
I've got all my sisters with me

This had for some reason been incorporated into one of the chants, and Cindy   4 and I were frequently forced to sing it together: arms around each other, leaning on each other like drunks, beaming with joy, and behaving in every way like the sisters that we, in fact, were most certainly not.

Though there was a sharp distinction between the older girls and the younger   5 ones, we were also divided, throughout our ranks and regardless of age, into two distinct categories: those of snob and slut. The snobs had flat chests, pretty clothes, and were skittish and shrill. Though they were always sugar-sweet to one's face, in reality they were a nasty, backbiting lot, always doing things like stealing one another's boyfriend and trying to rig the elections in the Beauty Revue. The sluts were from poorer families, and much better liked in general. They drank beer, made out with boys in the hallways, and had horrible black hickeys all over their necks. Our squad was divided pretty much half and half. Physically and economically, I fell into the category of snob, but I did poorly in school and was not gung ho or clubbish enough to fit in very well with the rest of them. (To be a proper snob, one had always to be making floats in some damn parade or other, or organizing potluck dinners for the Booster Club.) The sluts, I thought, took a more sensible view of such foolishness; they smoked and drank; I found them, as a rule, much nicer. Being big girls generally, they were the backbones of the stances, the foundations from which the pyramids rose and, occasionally, fell; I, being the smallest on the squad, had to work with them rather closely, in special sessions after the regular cheerleading practices, since they were the ones who lifted me into the air, who spotted me in gymnastics, upon whose shoulders I had to stand to form the obligatory pyramid. They all had pet names for me, and—though vigorously heterosexual—babied me in what I am sure none of them realized was a faintly lecherous way: tickles and pinches, slaps on the rump, pulling me into their laps in crowded cars and crooning stupid songs from the radio into my ear. At the games they completely ignored me, as every fiber of their attention was devoted to flirting with—and contriving to make out with—various boys. As I was both too young to be much interested in boys and lacking the fullness of bosom and broadness of beam that would have made them much interested in me, I was excluded from this activity. But still the sluts felt sorry for me and gave me tips on how to make myself attractive (pierced ears, longer hair, tissue paper in the bra)—and, when we were loitering around after practices, often regaled me with worldly tales of various sexual, obstetric, and gynecological horrors, some of which still make my eyes pop to think about. The gymnasiums were high-ceilinged, barn-like, drafty, usually in the middle of some desolate field. We were always freezing in our skimpy plaid skirts, our legs all goose pimples as we clapped and stamped on the yellowed wooden floor. At halftime there were the detested stances, out in the middle of the court, which involved perilous leaps, and complex timing, and—more likely than not—tears and remonstrations in the changing rooms.

As soon as they were over and the buzzer went off for the third quarter, the 6 younger girls rushed in a greedy flock to the snack bar for Cokes and french fries, Hershey bars, scattering to devour them in privacy while Cindy and her crew slunk out to the parking lot to rendezvous with their boyfriends. We were all of us, all the time, constantly sick—coughing, blowing our noses, faces flushed with fever: symptoms that were exacerbated by bad food, cramped conditions, exhaustion, and yelling ourselves hoarse every night. Hoarseness was, in fact, a matter of pride: we were accused of shirking if our voices weren't cracked by the end of the evening, the state to which we aspired being a rasping, laryngitic croak. I remember the only time the basketball coach—a gigantic, stone-faced, terrifying man who was also the principal of the school and who, to my way of thinking, held powers virtually of life or death (there were stories of his punching kids out, beating them till they had bruises, stories that perhaps were not apocryphal in a private school like my own, which prided itself on what it called "old-fashioned discipline" and where corporal punishment was a matter of routine); the only time this coach ever spoke to me was to compliment me on my burned-out voice, which he overheard in the hall the morning after a game. "Good job," he said. My companions and I were dumbfounded with terror. After he was gone they stared at me with awestruck apprehension and then, one by one, drifted gently away, not wishing to be seen in the company of anyone who had attracted the attention—even momentarily—of this dangerous lunatic.

There were pep squads, of a sort, in *1984.* I read about them with interest. Ban- 7 ners, processions, slogans, games were as popular in Airstrip One as they were at Kirk Academy. Realizing that there was a certain correspondence between this totalitarian nightmare and my own high school gave me at first a feeling of smug superiority, but after a time I began to have an acute sense of the meaninglessness of my words and gestures. Did I really care if we won or lost? No matter how enthusiastically I jumped and shouted, the answer to this was unquestionably No. This epiphany both confused and depressed me. And yet I continued—outwardly at least—to display as much pep as ever. "I always look cheerful and I never shirk anything," says Winston Smith's girlfriend, Julia. "Always yell with the crowd, that's what I say. It's the only way to be safe."

Our rival team was called the Patriots. I remember one rally, the night before a big game, when a dummy Patriot was hanged from the gymnasium rafters, then taken outside and burned amid the frenzied screams and stomps of the mob. I yelled as loud as anybody, even though I was suffused by an airy, perilous sense of unreality, a conviction—despite the apparently desperate nature of this occasion that none of it meant anything at all. In my diary that night—a document that was as secretive and, to my mind at least, as subversive as Winston's own—I noted tersely: "Hell's own Pep Rally. Freshmen won the spirit stick. Rah, rah."   8

It was on the rides home—especially on the nights we'd won—that the inequity of not being allowed on the team bus was most keenly felt by the cheerleaders. Moodily, they stared out the windows, dreaming of backseats, and letter jackets, and smooching with their repulsive boyfriends. The cars smelled like talcum powder and Tickle deodorant, and—if we were with one of the nicer dads, who had allowed us to stop at a drive-in—cheeseburgers and french fries. It was too dark to read. Everyone was tired, but for some reason we were all too paranoid to go to sleep in front of one another: afraid we might drool, perhaps, or inadvertently scratch an armpit.   9

Whispers, giggles, sighs. We rode four to a car and all four of us would be crammed in the backseat; bare arms touching, goosebumped knees pressed together, our silences punctuated by long ardent slurps of Tab. The console lights of the Cadillac dashboards were phosphorescent, eerie. The radio was mostly static that time of night, but sometimes you could get a late-night station coming out of Greenwood or Memphis: slow songs, that's what everyone wanted, sloppy stuff by Olivia Newton-John or Dan Fogelberg. (The cheerleaders had a virtual cult of Olivia Newton-John; they tried to do their hair like her, emulate her in every possible way, and were fond of speculating what Olivia would or would not do in certain situations. She was like the ninth, ghost member of the squad. I was secretly gratified when she plummeted—with alarming swiftness—from favor because someone heard a rumor that she was gay.)   10

Olivia or not, the favorite song that winter hands-down was "You Light Up My Life" by Debby Boone. It must have been number one for months; at least, it seemed to be played on the radio just about every other song, which was fine with everybody. When it came on the girls would all start singing it quietly to themselves, staring out the window, each in her own little world; touching the fogged window-glass gently with her fingertips and each thinking no one could hear her,   11 but all their voices combined in a kind of low, humming harmony that blended with the radio:

So many nights
I sit by my window
Waiting for someone
To sing me his song . . .

Full moon; hard frost on the stubbled cotton fields. They opened up on either   12
side of the car in long, gray spokes, like a fan.

UNDERSTANDING THE ESSAY

1. Does Tartt want you to think of team spirit as a good thing, a bad thing, or a mixed blessing? Explain by pointing out evidence in the text.
2. Is there any sense of team spirit among the cheerleaders on the ride home? If so, how would you compare it with the team spirit expressed at the games and at the pep rally?
3. How has Tartt's attitude toward the various kinds of girls in the cheerleading squad changed now that she is an adult?
4. What is significant about the details in paragraph 2—the title of the book, the make of cars, the kind of shoes, the jobs the fathers held?
5. What is the meaning of the image in the last paragraph, in which furrows "opened up on either side of the car in long, gray spokes, like a fan"?

So What and the Seven Common Moves.   Analyze this essay with the help of the questions about "So What and the Seven Common Moves" found on the back cover of this book.

Words, Phrases, and Allusions.   The following items were taken from "Team Spirit" in the order of appearance. With the help of your classmates, locate these words in the essay and see if their context provides a clue to their meaning. If necessary, consult a dictionary, an encyclopedia, or other reference work to determine what each item means in its context. Pay particular attention to words and phrases that might be worth using in your own writing.

decibel, saddle oxfords, listlessly, *Animal Farm, 1984,* lyrics, spotted, lecherous, loitering, obstetric, gynecological, perilous, remonstrations, exacerbated, laryngitic, apocryphal, corporal, dumbfounded, apprehension, totalitarian, smug, acute, epiphany, shirk, subversive, tersely, inequity, inadvertently, phosphorescent, emulate, stubbled

Suggestion for Writing

Using "Team Spirit" as a model, describe a scene or a series of scenes that reveals the groups, cliques, clubs, or extracurricular activities that were important to you as you were growing up. Write your essay in such a way that your readers will find your interpretation of the subject to be unusual and interesting. The journal entry suggested at the beginning of this selection may have given you an idea for a topic, or you may have thought of other topics as you read "Team Spirit."

RECIPES FOR WRITING DESCRIPTION

A. Writing from Personal Experience

The point of description is not just to describe, but to interpret: you have to have an angle, a point of view that makes your readers see things in a way they might not have seen them on their own. Instead of choosing a topic and then finding meaning in it, you might find it easier to choose a topic in which you have already found meaning. The energy in your essay will come from your ability to find meaning in those details that most other observers would have missed.

Here is a recipe for description:

1. Choose a person, place, thing, or scene that has special meaning for you, perhaps meaning that no one else has noticed.
2. Examine your topic from the perspective of each of the five senses. Make a list of the details that convey the meaning of your subject. It might help to write a topic sentence (e.g., "Toby's wharf is a great place to relax") and follow it with lots of supporting sentences. If you succeed in describing details in a way that makes their meaning clear, you may not need the topic sentence anymore.
3. One option for organizing a descriptive essay is spatial: top to bottom, bottom to top, inside to out, outside to in, left to right, right to left, clockwise, counterclockwise, and so on. But a descriptive essay can seem coherent even if the details occur in a random sequence, as long as each detail contributes to a point that is consistently implied throughout. Be sure to keep the reader's attention by saving the best details for last.
4. After you've selected and arranged your details, add an introduction and an ending.
5. Show a draft to fellow students in a formal or informal workshop, and see if your strategies are having the effects you want them to have. Use the checklist on the back cover to focus your discussion. Then look for errors in spelling, grammar, or punctuation that you will want to correct in your final draft.

B. Writing against the Text

An effective descriptive essay can seem as objective as a photograph, as if the writer had no choice but to record the scene exactly as it was. In fact, descriptive writing involves lots of personal choices, including choices about what to omit and what to include and how to interpret whatever details are selected. For example, Annie Dillard's description in "Catch It If You Can" may seem merely to represent what appeared before her eyes; but in fact, she selected the details that fit her purpose and ignored the rest. And while we appreciate her interpretation of nature as mystic and benign, we may also realize that nature can be indifferent, even cruel. Similarly, if you know anything about clog dancers or cheerleaders, they may seem quite different to you than they seemed to David Foster Wallace and Donna Tartt. Find room for disagreement or expansion in any essay in this chapter. Write a description of your own offering a different interpretation.

C. Writing from Research

Using the library and the Web, locate information about an interesting or exotic building (e.g., the Hagia Sophia or Taliesen West) or place (e.g., an ancient village in France, a remote outpost in Antarctica). After you have read as much as you can about that subject, write an essay describing it in a way that reveals its significance. It may help to choose two subjects instead of one—two Renaissance *palazzos*, for example, or two interesting villages—so you can compare their similarities and contrast their differences (see chapter 5). Put your sources aside as you write your first draft; then go back and add quoted material wherever you think it will make your paper more interesting or authoritative. Be sure to acknowledge the source of anything you quote or paraphrase.

3

Interpreting Events:
The Nature of Narrative

Storytelling is perhaps the most ancient and essential use of language. The oldest documents in history are generally stories: cave drawings portraying hunting expeditions; myths explaining the origin of the world or of a particular group of people; hieroglyphics recounting the exploits of queens and pharaohs, goddesses and gods. We crave stories for a reason deeply embedded in our souls. When we were children, the simple phrase "Once upon a time" was enough to keep us awake just a little longer. "There were three . . ." "Three what?" we wanted to know. "And what problem did they face? And how did they resolve it?"

We enjoy hearing or reading stories, and we love to tell them. We want people to know what happened to us, what problems we encountered, and how we resolved them—or, unhappily, failed to resolve them—because interpreting the things that happen to us is our way of defining, revealing, remembering, and making sense of ourselves. We care about stories other people tell, too, in part because we care about the people who tell them, and in part because other people's stories help us to create and understand our own.

A story is always more than a record of events. Herman Melville's novel *Moby-Dick* is a story, but a ship's log is just a record. John Grisham's novel *The Runaway*

Jury is a story, but the transcript of a trial is just a record. A story is a record of events to which an interpretive spin has been added. It makes no difference if the events are factual or fictional; a series of events cannot be interesting, cannot be a story, until someone puts them in a context that makes them meaningful.

Every storyteller brings a different set of values to any series of events, and therefore a different understanding of them, a different interpretive spin. If you were to narrate the events in your day from the time you woke up this morning to the time you read this sentence, your story would never be exactly the same as anyone else's, not even your roommate's, who may have had nearly identical experiences. If two political candidates were to review the events of the preceding four years, their stories would be different, even if the events were identical. Stories always reveal the personality, the values, the character of the storyteller. What some people find funny, others consider offensive; what some find serious, others consider trivial; some people see tragedy in events that others find ironic or even comic.

What actually happened—the actual series of events—is never fully, completely, and impartially represented. Every narrative is a "winning" story—a story the writer chooses over other stories that could have been told by selecting different events or by interpreting the same events from a different point of view. Perspective makes all the difference. That's why couples, friends, neighbors, and entire cultures can take it for granted that they will disagree from time to time. We are designed by nature to notice different events and to interpret them differently. The story of a battle or the story of a ballgame or of a political campaign will vary considerably, depending upon which side the teller happens to favor and which events the teller considers significant.

In every successful story, there is always something important at stake—usually a conflict between what is considered good (like happiness, knowledge, truth, safety, health, success, morality) and evil (like unhappiness, ignorance, falsehood, danger, sickness, failure, immorality). A conflict of opposing forces, often implied rather than explicitly stated, provides the context that makes each individual event meaningful. A story about how you spent your day would be dull unless you framed the events in the context of a pair of opposing forces—your own sense of fun and boredom, beauty and ugliness, fairness and injustice, importance and trivia, right and wrong. These opposites provide the interpretive ground that gives meaning to events. Events do not have any meaning in themselves.

Stories are descriptions in motion. A story doesn't just tell what happens; it shows it, projecting the experience itself onto the imagination of the reader. The skills discussed in chapter 2 (Description) are essential to successful storytellers. Details make the difference between a story and a mere summary of events. Details allow readers to see things—not just generic things, but unique things, as clear as props and scenery on a stage. Details allow readers to meet people—not just generic people, but individuals, like characters on stage, with one-of-a-kind warts and tics and smiles and habits and manners of speaking. Details also convey sounds and smells and tastes and textures whenever these other senses can help the writer make a point.

Narrative (storytelling) is not just a literary art. It is the way human beings create their identities both as individuals and as members of a group. It is no accident that the word "story" is hidden within the word "history." History is the story people tell in an attempt to make sense of their collective experiences. And because people rarely agree about the meaning of events (even when they can agree about the facts), it is important to understand that history is constructed: it is not just a record of facts, but an interpretation of facts from a particular perspective.

Stories are also the foundation of law. Every statute, contract, and treaty is an attempt to establish an interpretive framework (rules for distinguishing right from wrong) for future events. Every trial is an attempt to apply these interpretive rules to past events. Science is a story, too, a continual interpretation of physical events. Without stories, there could be no civilization, not even a primitive civilization. If aliens ever arrive from outer space, we can count on one thing in advance: they will be storytellers. Otherwise, they could have never have established the technology to get here.

Storytelling often occurs within all the other modes and methods treated as separate chapters in this book. Every essay in chapter 2 (Description) includes stories—about walking along a beach, or stopping at a rural filling station, or observing clog dancing, or bonding with fellow cheerleaders. And you will find stories embedded in the chapters to come: in exemplification essays, like "Just Walk on By" (p. 195) and "Virus Zero" (p. 203); in persuasive essays, like "Weedee Peepo" (p. 224); in cause-and-effect essays, like "The Origins of Anorexia Nervosa" (p. 148); in process essays, like "The Body Shop" (p. 73). Stories are especially useful as attention-getters at the beginning of an essay.

Because stories consist of events that occur sequentially, the most obvious way to organize a story is to put it in chronological order. And, in fact, chronological order is often the best way to organize legal, technical, and business writing—writing that needs to be as efficient as possible. Put the point up front and then relate the key events in the order in which they occurred.

But the purpose of a narrative essay is not just to enable readers to interpret events, but to experience them, to feel them in a way that makes the interpretation seem obvious and inevitable. When a story is well told, it may be unnecessary to announce the point in a thesis statement at the beginning or a moral tacked on to the end. In fact, putting the point up front might spoil the effect, like telling the punch line before the joke. Often, the point of a narrative essay is implied rather than stated, just as it is in descriptive essays—a question whispered between the lines: "Don't you think these events are _____?" or "Don't you think these events show that _____?" The blank is the interpretation that the writer wants readers to discover from the way the story is told.

Skilled writers do not necessarily tell stories in chronological order. Often they rearrange events, violating chronology to place events where they will have the maximum effect on the reader. This is called plotting—the difference between the actual chronology of events and the sequence in which the writer chooses to arrange them. It takes a great deal of skill to tell a story out of chronological order without making it seem jumbled and disorganized. But if you will read the essays in this chapter carefully, you will see how experienced writers make plotting—rearranging events for rhetorical purposes—seem easy and natural.

Journal Entry. Think of events in your childhood that you interpreted differently from the way the adults around you interpreted them. Maybe you turned out to be right in the long run, or maybe they did; in either case you did not really figure things out until years later. In your journal, start compiling the details you would need to tell that story on paper. Don't just summarize; dramatize. Let your readers see and hear for themselves. Don't just organize; plot. Keep your readers in suspense from the first line to the last. Try to make them get the point without your having to tell them.

After you've worked on this project for a while, read the following essay by Mike Royko as a tribute to baseball star Jackie Robinson just after he died. Notice how Royko interprets a particular baseball game, showing not just what happened, but what it meant.

Jackie's Debut: A Unique Day

Mike Royko

All that Saturday, the wise men of the neighborhood, who sat in chairs on the sidewalk outside the tavern, had talked about what it would do to baseball. 1

I hung around and listened because baseball was about the most important thing in the world, and if anything was going to ruin it, I was worried. 2

Most of the things they said, I didn't understand, although it all sounded terrible. But could one man bring such ruin? 3

They said he could and he would. And the next day he was going to be in Wrigley Field for the first time, on the same diamond as Hack, Nicholson, Cavarretta, Schmidt, Pafko, and all my other idols. 4

I had to see Jackie Robinson, the man who was going to somehow wreck everything. So the next day, another kid and I started walking to the ball park early. 5

We always walked to save the streetcar fare. It was five or six miles, but I felt about baseball the way Abe Lincoln felt about education. 6

Usually, we could get there just at noon, find a seat in the grandstands, and watch some batting practice. But not that Sunday, May 18, 1947. 7

By noon, Wrigley Field was almost filled. The crowd outside spilled off the sidewalk and into the streets. Scalpers were asking top dollar for box seats and getting it. 8

I had never seen anything like it. Not just the size, although it was a new record, more than 47,000. But this was 25 years ago, and in 1947 few blacks were seen in the Loop, much less up on the white North Side at a Cub game. 9

That day, they came by the thousands, pouring off the northbound Ls and out 　10 of their cars.

They didn't wear baseball-game clothes. They had on church clothes and fu- 　11 neral clothes—suits, white shirts, ties, gleaming shoes, and straw hats. I've never seen so many straw hats.

As big as it was, the crowd was orderly. Almost unnaturally so. People didn't 　12 jostle each other.

The whites tried to look as if nothing unusual was happening, while the blacks 　13 tried to look casual and dignified. So everybody looked slightly ill at ease.

For most, it was probably the first time they had been that close to each other in 　14 such great numbers.

We managed to get in, scramble up a ramp, and find a place to stand behind the 　15 last row of grandstand seats. Then they shut the gates. No place remained to stand.

Robinson came up in the first inning. 　16

When Robinson stepped into the batter's box, it was as if someone had flicked 　17 a switch. The place went silent.

He swung at the first pitch and they erupted as if he had knocked it over the 　18 wall. But it was only a high foul that dropped into the box seats. I remember think- ing it was strange that a foul could make that many people happy. When he struck out, the low moan was genuine.

I've forgotten most of the details of the game, other than that the Dodgers won 　19 and Robinson didn't get a hit or do anything special, although he was cheered on every swing and every routine play.

But two things happened I'll never forget. Robinson played first, and early in 　20 the game a Cub star hit a grounder and it was a close play.

Just before the Cub reached first, he swerved to his left. And as he got to the 　21 bag, he seemed to slam his foot down hard at Robinson's foot.

It was obvious to everyone that he was trying to run into him or spike him. 　22 Robinson took the throw and got clear at the last instant.

I was shocked. That Cub, a home-town boy, was my biggest hero. It was not 　23 only an unheroic stunt, but it seemed a rude thing to do in front of people who would cheer for a foul ball. I didn't understand why he had done it. It wasn't at all big league.

I didn't know that while the white fans were relatively polite, the Cubs and 　24 most of the other team kept up a steady stream of racial abuse from the dugouts. I thought that all they did down there was talk about how good Wheaties are.

Later in the game, Robinson was up again and he hit another foul ball. This 　25 time it came into the stands low and fast, in our direction. Somebody in the seats grabbed for it, but it caromed off his hand and kept coming. There was a flurry of arms as the ball kept bouncing, and suddenly it was between me and my pal. We both grabbed. I had a baseball.

The two of us stood there examining it and chortling. A genuine, major-league 　26 baseball that had actually been gripped and thrown by a Cub pitcher, hit by a Dodger batter. What a possession.

Then I heard the voice say: "Would you consider selling that?"   27

It was the black man who had applauded so fiercely.   28

I mumbled something. I didn't want to sell it.   29

"I'll give you $10 for it," he said.   30

Ten dollars. I couldn't believe it. I didn't know what $10 could buy because I'd   31
never had that much money. But I knew that a lot of men in the neighborhood considered $60 a week to be good pay.

I handed it to him, and he paid me with ten $1 bills.   32

When I left the ball park, with that much money in my pocket, I was sure that   33
Jackie Robinson wasn't bad for the game.

Since then, I've regretted a few times that I didn't keep the ball. Or that I hadn't   34
given it to him free. I didn't know, then, how hard he probably had to work for that
$10.

But last Tuesday I was glad I had sold it to him. And if that man is still around,   35
and has that baseball, I'm sure he thinks it was worth every cent.

The So-What Factor.   What is novel, interesting, surprising, or moving about
Mike Royko's account of Jackie Robinson's debut in Wrigley Field? What does he
want us to understand, feel, or believe after reading his story? There is no clear thesis statement. Instead, the so-what factor, the purpose, is expressed in a question
whispered between the lines: "Don't you think this shows . . . ?" What?

In "Jackie's Debut," we might hear the between-the-lines questions about individual events in the story: about the wise men at the tavern who thought integration
would ruin baseball ("Don't you think this was foolish?"), or about the runner who
tried to spike Robinson at first base ("Don't you think this was mean-spirited?"), or
about the man who would give a day's wages for a baseball ("Don't you think this
tells you how much Robinson meant to the African-American community?").

Perhaps the overall question underlying this story is "Don't you think a world
without racial prejudice is a lot nicer than one with it?" But to say that would be
"moralizing"—a move that always runs the risk of seeming trite. That's why Royko
never says it. He makes us feel it instead.

"Jackie's Debut" is a story about good and evil. It seems to be a boy's story,
but in fact it deals with issues that transcend age and gender and personal memories.
It is a story about prejudice, and a story about prejudice of one kind is a story about
prejudice of all kinds. Notice that Royko does not oversimplify: we are allowed to
see evil in the hearts of people who, in other circumstances, we would consider
quite good, even heroic—famous athletes, family men enjoying one another's company on a day off. It's not just good guys against bad guys; it's ugly attitudes and
behaviors in people who are otherwise not so bad. This is part of the surprise element in the so-what factor, part of the interpretive spin that would not have been obvious to everyone who witnessed the same events.

THE SEVEN COMMON MOVES

1. Beginning. Royko creates interest at the outset by setting out a mystery and a conflict. The first paragraph describes wise men who are worried about what "it" would do to baseball, and the second paragraph tells us that baseball seemed about to be ruined. Even people who don't follow the sport might be inclined to read just a little further. The use of a pronoun (in this case, "it") without an antecedent at the beginning of narrative is known as a "blind beginning." It is designed to create a mystery. Who or what are we talking about here? Our curiosity is piqued. And then a conflict is announced: something is about to ruin baseball. Royko hopes we will read on to find out what "it" is. Although this beginning seems natural and inevitable, it isn't. It is a strategic choice, an opening gambit, crafted by a writer who knows intuitively that the first thing to do is to grab the reader's attention.

2. Ending. "Jackie's Debut" ends with a "coda" (Italian for "tail"—a musical term describing something added at the end of a composition to bring it to a close). Royko's coda consists of a few lines of reflection many years after the game had ended. It has a contemplative air about it, a sense of respect for the subject, Jackie Robinson, who had died just days before the story was published, at a time when the United States was torn by deep racial hostility. It seemed to suggest in a gentle way that the conflict between meanness and generosity of spirit had not changed much since Jackie Robinson's first game.

3. Detail. Effective narrative is generally a mixture of telling events and showing. To tell is to summarize or give a reaction to things; to show is to dramatize, to let readers witness the scene, the actions, the words for themselves.

Telling (i.e., summarizing):

> I've forgotten most of the details of the game, other than that the Dodgers won and Robinson didn't get a hit or do anything special, although he was cheered on every swing and every routine play.

Showing (i.e., dramatizing):

> When Robinson stepped into the batter's box, it was as if someone had flicked a switch. The place went silent.
>
> He swung at the first pitch and they erupted as if he had knocked it over the wall. But it was only a high foul that dropped into the box seats.

When it comes to words spoken in a scene, the writer has two similar choices: paraphrase (which is analogous to telling) or dialogue (direct quotation, which is analogous to showing).

Paraphrase:

> [T]he wise men of the neighborhood . . . had talked about what it would do to baseball.

Dialogue:

> Then I heard the voice say: "Would you consider selling that?"
> "I'll give you $10 for it," he said.

Showing is always livelier than telling, and dialogue is always livelier than paraphrase. And yet, telling and paraphrase have their uses too. Writers really can't show everything and quote every word spoken. They would never finish their stories if they did. So although the usual advice teachers give—"Show, don't tell"—is generally sound, more precise advice would be to shout the rule and whisper the exception: "SHOW, DON'T TELL (except when showing seems irrelevant or inappropriate or when it slows the pace)." And a good rule for deciding when to quote and to paraphrase is this: Quote whenever the words are interesting in themselves or when they reveal something about the character who speaks them; otherwise, paraphrase.

4. Organization/Plot. For the most part, Royko follows ordinary chronological order. He tells us what happens before the game, during the game, and after the game. Although narrative can be organized in many other ways, chronological order is by far the easiest.

But Royko's story is not just organized; it is plotted. It is a series of mysteries and partial acts and unresolved conflicts from beginning to end. The mystery of the opening lines is solved in paragraph 5, when we discover what the men at the neighborhood tavern were worried about: Jackie Robinson's appearance in Wrigley Field. But as soon as Royko solves this mystery, he makes us curious again by describing a partial act:

> So the next day, another kid and I started walking to the ball park early.

A journey is begun, and we are inclined to stay with it until we arrive at the destination, Wrigley Field, where we are of course instantly made curious about the game itself. In short, the story is told in such a way that every time our curiosity is satisfied on one point, it is aroused again by another conflict or partial act.

That's what makes the difference between mere organization and a plot. If you want to feel the effect of plot—the continual sense of unfinished business—read "Jackie's Debut" to your friends, and see how they react if you stop reading at any point in the middle of the story.

5. Style. Some stylistic moves Royko makes have traditional names:

Allusion—a reference to well-known persons, places, stories, or objects, like the reference to "Wheaties," a cereal that was advertised for many years as the "Breakfast of Champions."

Irony—a statement that reveals more than its literal meaning, like the reference to Lincoln ("I felt about baseball the way Abe Lincoln felt about education"), which suggests that the young Royko's devotion to baseball may have been a bit excessive.

Simile—a comparison, using "like" or "as": "When Robinson stepped into the batter's box, it was as if someone had flicked a switch."

Thick Description—a cluster of descriptive details: "They had on church clothes and funeral clothes—suits, white shirts, ties, gleaming shoes, and straw hats."

Even though Royko's language seems natural and spontaneous, his sentences are all carefully crafted. Notice, for example, that Royko's sentences never end weakly; instead they focus our attention where Royko wants it focused:

> . . . what it would do to baseball.
> . . . I was worried.
> . . . it all sounded terrible.
> . . . bring such ruin?

His verbs, too, almost always indicate action: "hung," "listened," "said," "sounded," "wreck," "walked," "felt," "find," "watch," "spilled," "jostle," "shut," "flicked," "swung," "erupted," "hit," "swerved," "cheer," "grabbed," "caromed," "applauded," "mumbled," "regretted." Careful writers do not hesitate to use the verb "to be" when they need it (i.e., am, are, is, was, were, be, being, been), but they avoid it whenever they can use an action verb instead.

6. *Voice/Attitude.* Even though Royko's column appeared in a newspaper, it was an editorial column, where personal voice and attitude are appropriate. You can identify the moves that account for Royko's voice by circling all the words and phrases that would not be likely to occur in a front page story—every "I," for example, since reporters do not generally write in first person; and anything that indicates a personal attitude or judgment, like calling the neighborhood men "wise" (which turns out to be ironic), or saying that he was "worried." Voice and attitude are revealed by any word or expression that would vary from the level of formality normally expected on the front page of a newspaper, like "I hung around and listened," or "another kid and I started walking." Every deviation creates an individual voice. That voice implies a certain kind of person in a certain kind of mood.

For all its apparent simplicity, Royko's voice in "Jackie's Debut" is actually quite complex. The writer seems to be two persons at once—a naive adolescent who thinks baseball is the most important thing in the world, and a mature columnist who understands that Robinson's participation in the major leagues had an importance far greater than the sport itself.

7. *Economy.* Every detail in a well-written essay has a purpose. For example, the detail about people coming to a ballpark in "church clothes and funeral clothes" indicates, among other things, that for these people, the game they were about to witness had an historic importance far beyond what most baseball games have. What is the purpose of other details in the essay? Why does Royko bother telling us that the boys walked to the ballpark "to save the streetcar fare"? Why does he tell us that scalpers were getting top dollar for their tickets?

Economy doesn't just "happen," as if the writer had no choice. There were lots of other things that Royko could have described—the smell of popcorn, the voices of people hawking soft drinks in the stands, the condition of the field, the direction of the wind. But he didn't describe any of these things because they did not contribute to the interpretation of events that he wanted to convey to his readers.

Moves within Moves.   The dominant mode of this essay is narrative, a series of events. But if you look closely, you will see that this essay—like all the others in this book—includes some of the other modes and methods of development that are treated in separate chapters.

Cause and effect (see chapter 7):

> I hung around and listened because baseball was about the most important thing in the world, and if anything was going to ruin it, I was worried.

Comparison and contrast (see chapter 5):

> The whites tried to look as if nothing unusual was happening, while the blacks tried to look casual and dignified. So everybody looked slightly ill at ease.
> They didn't wear baseball-game clothes. They had on church clothes and funeral clothes—suits, white shirts, ties, gleaming shoes, and straw hats.

Exemplification (an incident intended to represent lots of similar instances; see chapter 9):

> Just before the Cub reached first, he swerved to his left. And as he got to the bag, he seemed to slam his foot down hard at Robinson's foot.

Words, Phrases, and Allusions.   One of the remarkable things about "Jackie's Debut" is that it has no extraordinary words—nothing that wouldn't be in the vocabulary of any ordinary fourteen-year-old. This is a good thing to notice, because although good writers often do use unusual words, it's a mistake to equate good writing with a fancy vocabulary. The trick is to put exactly the right word in exactly the right place, whether it's a fancy word or a simple one.

There are, however, a few allusions and local references that you might find unfamiliar:

> Wrigley Field, Jackie Robinson, "the way Abe Lincoln felt about education," scalpers, the Loop, Cub, northbound Ls, the Dodgers (Brooklyn), Wheaties, caromed, chortling.

With the help of your classmates, locate these words in the essay and see if their context provides a clue to their meaning. If necessary, consult a dictionary, an encyclopedia, or other reference work to determine what each item means in its context. Pay particular attention to words and phrases that might be worth using in your own writing.

Suggestion for Writing

Return to the journal entry suggested at the beginning of this chapter. Using "Jackie's Debut" as a model, tell a story about an experience you had as a child that you didn't fully understand until years later. You may have thought of other topics as you read "Jackie's Debut."

Journal Entry. Almost everyone remembers not being able to see or understand something that people around us expected us to see or understand. It can be a very uncomfortable feeling, particularly if we worry that expressing ourselves honestly will disappoint people we love or admire. Remember (or imagine) an incident of this sort and jot down all the details that would turn it into a story. It could be a story about yourself or about someone else—a real or fictitious person. After you've worked on this project for a while, read Langston Hughes's story about how he felt when people around him were expecting him to have a religious experience. Look for techniques to imitate. Notice how Hughes mixes description into the narrative, and how he allows us to hear the actual words people speak—words that reveal something about the nature of the people who speak them.

Salvation

Langston Hughes

I was saved from sin when I was going on thirteen. But not really saved. It happened like this. There was a big revival at my Auntie Reed's church. Every night for weeks there had been much preaching, singing, praying, and shouting, and some very hardened sinners had been brought to Christ, and the membership of the church had grown by leaps and bounds. Then just before the revival ended, they held a special meeting for children, "to bring the young lambs to the fold." My aunt spoke of it for days ahead. That night I was escorted to the front row and placed on the mourners' bench with all the other young sinners, who had not yet been brought to Jesus. 1

My aunt told me that when you were saved you saw a light, and something happened to you inside! And Jesus came into your life! And God was with you from then on! She said you could see and hear and feel Jesus in your soul. I believed her. I had heard a great many old people say the same thing and it seemed to me they ought to know. So I sat there calmly in the hot, crowded church, waiting for Jesus to come to me. 2

The preacher preached a wonderful rhythmical sermon, all moans and shouts and lonely cries and dire pictures of hell, and then he sang a song about the ninety and nine safe in the fold, but one little lamb was left out in the cold. Then he said: "Won't you come? Won't you come to Jesus? Young lambs, won't you come?" And he held out his arms to all us young sinners there on the mourners' bench. And the little girls cried. And some of them jumped up and went to Jesus right away. But most of us just sat there. 3

A great many older people came and knelt around us and prayed, old women with jet-black faces and braided hair, old men with work–gnarled hands. And the 4 church sang a song about the lower lights are burning, some poor sinners to be saved. And the whole building rocked with prayer and song.

Still I kept waiting to *see* Jesus. 5

Finally all the young people had gone to the altar and were saved, but one boy 6 and me. He was a rounder's son named Westley. Westley and I were surrounded by sisters and deacons praying. It was very hot in the church, and getting late now. Finally Westley said to me in a whisper: "God damn! I'm tired o' sitting here. Let's get up and be saved." So he got up and was saved.

Then I was left all alone on the mourners' bench. My aunt came and knelt at 7 my knees and cried, which prayers and songs swirled all around me in the little church. The whole congregation prayed for me alone, in a mighty wail of moans and voices. And I kept waiting serenely for Jesus, waiting, waiting—but he didn't come. I wanted to see him, but nothing happened to me. Nothing! I wanted something to happen to me, but nothing happened.

I heard the songs and the minister saying: "Why don't you come? My dear 8 child, why don't you come to Jesus? Jesus is waiting for you. He wants you. Why don't you come? Sister Reed, what is this child's name?"

"Langston," my aunt sobbed. 9

"Langston, why don't you come? Why don't you come and be saved? Oh, 10 Lamb of God! Why don't you come?"

Now it was really getting late. I began to be ashamed of myself, holding every- 11 thing up so long. I began to wonder what God thought about Westley, who certainly hadn't seen Jesus either, but who was now sitting proudly on the platform, swinging his knickerbockered legs and grinning down at me, surrounded by deacons and old women on their knees praying. God had not struck Westley dead for taking his name in vain or for lying in the temple. So I decided that maybe to save further trouble, I'd better lie, too, and say that Jesus had come, and get up and be saved.

So I got up. 12

Suddenly the whole room broke into a sea of shouting, as they saw me rise. 13 Waves of rejoicing swept the place. Women leaped in the air. My aunt threw her arms around me. The minister took me by the hand and led me to the platform.

When things quieted down, in a hushed silence, punctuated by a few ecstatic 14 "Amens," all the new young lambs were blessed in the name of God. Then joyous singing filled the room.

That night, for the last time in my life but one—for I was a big boy of twelve 15 years old—I cried. I cried, in bed alone, and couldn't stop. I buried my head under the quilts, but my aunt heard me. She woke up and told my uncle I was crying because the Holy Ghost had come into my life, and because I had seen Jesus. But I was really crying because I couldn't bear to tell her that I had lied, that I had deceived everybody in the church, and I hadn't seen Jesus, and that now I didn't believe there was a Jesus anymore, since he didn't come to help me.

UNDERSTANDING THE ESSAY

1. What does the title, "Salvation," lead you to expect the essay to be about? Does the essay itself change the way you think about the title?
2. Like Mike Royko as a boy (see "Jackie's Debut"), the young Langston Hughes did not see things the way older people expected him to. Who was right—Hughes, or the elders in his church? Would the adult Hughes side with the boy or with the elders? (Cite evidence in the text to support your answer.)
3. What do Westley's words (paragraph 6) reveal about Westley? Notice that dialogue generally works best when it reveals something about the character who speaks it.
4. What does Auntie Reed's explanation of Hughes's crying (final paragraph) reveal about Auntie Reed?
5. Why does Hughes tell us that the sermon was "all moans and shouts and lonely cries and dire pictures of hell"? Why does he tell us that his friend Westley was "knickerbockered"?

So What and the Seven Common Moves. Analyze this essay with the help of the questions about "So What and the Seven Common Moves" found on the back cover of this book.

Words, Phrases, and Allusions. The following items were taken from "Salvation" in the order of appearance. With the help of your classmates, locate these words in the essay and see if their context provides a clue to their meaning. If necessary, consult a dictionary, an encyclopedia, or other reference work to determine what each item means in its context. Pay particular attention to words and phrases that might be worth using in your own writing.

revival, mourners' bench, work–gnarled hands, rounder, deacons, serenely, knicker-bockered, ecstatic.

Suggestion for Writing

Using "Salvation" as a model, write a narrative essay about not being able to see or believe what people expect us to see or believe. The topic doesn't have to be religion: it could be art, or politics, or people, or things you are supposed to see through a microscope or a telescope. The journal entry suggested at the beginning of this selection may have given you an idea for a topic, or you may have thought of other topics as you read "Salvation."

Journal Entry.   Young people often harbor illusions about what it takes to impress members of the opposite sex. Some of us, in fact, never completely outgrow these illusions. Remember (or imagine) an incident in which someone goes to foolish lengths to make an impression. Jot down as many details as you can, using all your senses to make the people, the scenes, and the dialogue as vivid as possible. It could be a story about yourself or about someone else—a real or fictitious person. After you've worked on this project for a while, read Jaime O'Neill's account of his own youthful attempts to attract attention. Look for techniques to imitate. Notice how O'Neill mixes description into the narrative, and how he allows us to hear the actual words people speak—words that reveal something about the nature of the people who speak them.

Falling into Place

Jaime O'Neill

It is 1957 and I am up a tree. Though afraid of heights, I have taken to climbing the trees in the palmetto and mangrove swamp that spreads out from the little clearing where our house sits. 1

I cannot now remember what compelled me to climb trees when I was 13 years old, why I both liked and hated the twinge of fear as I scaled my way higher and higher, or what satisfactions might have settled over me when I found a niche between the branches where I could nest, more secure, and survey the swamp from that height. All that returns to me now is the way the breeze blew up there, stirring the leaves, not at all like the breeze on the ground. 2

The tree I am in towers over a hole, a gash in the sandy Florida soil, six or eight feet deep, packed hard, damp at the bottom. The swamp is slowly being cleared for development; the backhoes and the big Cats have been scraping away the tenacious vegetation, making way for homes. Soon we will have neighbors. 3

I am thinking about girls. If I thought of other things when I was 13, I can no longer imagine what those things might have been. It is, then, no wonder that I notice two girls who pass under my tree on that warm and humid afternoon, two girls from my class taking a shortcut home through the swamp. 4

I hear them before I see them; I see them before I know who they are. They are talking and keeping their eyes tight on the ground for fear of snakes, and they don't notice me. As they draw nearer, I know the pleasure of the spy, the Indian scout, the unseen watcher in hidden places. Perhaps I will overhear them saying wonderful things—"this cute boy in class, he just drives me wild"—and it will turn out to be me they are talking about. 5

No such luck. Still, it is good that they come by. Courage is much better when 6 it has a female audience, and it has taken some courage for me to have climbed so high.

Had I been another kind of boy, I might have let them pass, but the "look at 7 me" impulse is insistent, and one of the girls is exquisite, sporting breasts already, like cupcakes under her thin cotton blouse. Perhaps if she sees me up in this tree, a strange and solitary boy, friend of trees, neighbor of sky, mysterious creature of the swamps, she will love me at these heights—love me, and invite me to climb down.

"Hi," I call out. The two of them stop in their tracks, uncertain of where the 8 voice is coming from. I like it that they have to search the trees to find me.

"What are you," asks the one who is not cute, "some kind of monkey?" 9

"Tarzan, more like," I say, and I stand upright on my branch and beat my chest 10 with one hand while holding tight to a limb with my other.

"You're going to fall and hurt yourself," the cute girl says. I am further smitten 11 by her concern for me. Smitten, and imperiled. What is it in the male psyche that takes such words as encouragement toward further reckless self-endangerment?

"Nah," I say, and I step carelessly to another branch, "there's nothing to this." I 12 release my steadying grip on the limb and stand barehanded. "See."

What I hope they can't see is that my knees are going a little wobbly with fear. 13

The not-cute girl shades her eyes, peering up at me. "Well," she says, "why 14 don't you jump if you're so brave?"

I feign interest in her suggestion, survey the depression in the earth below, 15 gauge the distance.

"You think I'm crazy," I say. "It's probably 100 feet down from here." Though 16 this is surely a gross exaggeration, the actual distance is very great.

"Well, what are you, anyway," the girl calls back to me, "some kind of 17 chicken?"

Today, some 35 years later, I am an English teacher, one who routinely tries to 18 convince students of the power of words. There are few words more powerful to an adolescent boy than the word "chicken." For all practical purposes, brain function ceases, superseded by gonadal override.

Still, the chicken side of me, the side I wanted to keep secret, might have pro- 19 tected me from harm if the word had come from the not-cute girl alone. If she wanted to think me chicken, I could live with that.

What I could not live with was when the cute girl echoed the challenge. 20

"Yeah," she says, "what are you, chicken?" 21

And so I jump. I cover my eyes with one hand, step purposefully off the branch 22 and plummet like a spear to the hard-packed sand and dirt at the bottom of the Cat-scratched hole. I strike on my heels, fold up like an imploded building. It is as though every molecule of oxygen has been driven out my ears, out my nose, out the very pores of my scalp. In the pit, I cannot move. I gasp raspily, like an old man. The sound scares me; I have never made such a noise before.

Do the girls rush down into the pit, tend to me, beg me to forgive them for their 23 thoughtless challenge? In your dreams, they do. Mine, too.

What they do is laugh and leave. A life lesson. 24

I will live to know this experience again—the laughing and the leaving—be- 25
cause I am not, as I first suspect, killed.

What I am is unable to move. Faintly, from our house, I can hear the radio 26
playing. I try to call out, but the sound that escapes me is unintelligible and weak,
no match for the radio.

Around dusk, I hear my Mom calling me for supper. Then, a while later, I hear 27
movement in the brush and my brother's voice. I groan. He finds me, helps me up.

We hide it all from Mom, of course. My heels are bruised, and for a few days it 28
hurts to stand up straight.

Did I learn my life lesson, a lesson gained in pain and humiliation? 29

Hardly. 30

What man ever really does? 31

UNDERSTANDING THE ESSAY

1. Can you find two or three meanings in the title, "Falling into Place," after
   reading the essay?
2. Can you find more than one meaning in the first sentence ("It is 1957 and I
   am up a tree")?
3. What does the dialogue O'Neill imagines in paragraph 5 reveal about his
   state of mind?
4. What does the dialogue each person speaks in this essay reveal about the
   person who speaks it?
5. Why does O'Neill tell us that the girls were "keeping their eyes tight on the
   ground for fear of snakes"?

So What and the Seven Common Moves.   Analyze this essay with the help of the
questions about "So What and the Seven Common Moves" found on the back cover
of this book.

Words, Phrases, and Allusions.   The following items were taken from "Falling
into Place" in the order of appearance. With the help of your classmates, locate
these words in the essay and see if their context provides a clue to their meaning. If
necessary, consult a dictionary, an encyclopedia, or other reference work to determine what each item means in its context. Pay particular attention to words and
phrases that might be worth using in your own writing.

palmetto, mangrove, scaled, niche, survey, backhoes, the big Cats, tenacious, smitten,
imperiled, psyche, gauge, superseded, gonadal, imploded

Suggestion for Writing

Using "Falling into Place" as a model, write a narrative essay about someone's foolish attempt to make an impression. The topic doesn't have to be about gender relationships: it could be about an attempt to impress a teacher, or a coach, or a parent, or an admissions officer. The journal entry suggested at the beginning of this selection may have given you an idea for a topic, or you may have thought of other topics as you read "Falling into Place."

The Chase

Annie Dillard

Some boys taught me to play football. This was fine sport. You thought up a new strategy for every play and whispered it to the others. You went out for a pass, fooling everyone. Best, you got to throw yourself mightily at someone's running legs. Either you brought him down or you hit the ground flat out on your chin, with your arms empty before you. It was all or nothing. If you hesitated in fear, you would miss and get hurt: you would take a hard fall while the kid got away, or you would get kicked in the face while the kid got away. But if you flung yourself wholeheartedly at the back of his knees—if you gathered and joined body and soul and pointed them diving fearlessly—then you likely wouldn't get hurt, and you'd stop the ball. Your fate, and your team's score, depended on your concentration and courage. Nothing girls did could compare with it. 1

Boys welcomed me at baseball, too, for I had, through enthusiastic practice, what was weirdly known as a boy's arm. In winter, in the snow, there was neither baseball nor football, so the boys and I threw snowballs at passing cars. I got in trouble throwing snowballs, and have seldom been happier since. 2

On one weekday morning after Christmas, six inches of new snow had just fallen. We were standing up to our boot tops in snow on a front yard on trafficked Reynolds Street, waiting for cars. The cars traveled Reynolds Street slowly and 3 evenly; they were targets all but wrapped in red ribbons, cream puffs. We couldn't miss.

I was seven; the boys were eight, nine, and ten. The oldest two Fahey boys   4
were there—Mikey and Peter—polite blond boys who lived near me on Lloyd Street, and who already had four brothers and sisters. My parents approved Mikey and Peter Fahey. Chickie McBride was there, a tough kid, and Billy Paul and Mackie Kean too, from across Reynolds, where the boys grew up dark and furious, grew up skinny, knowing, and skilled. We had all drifted from our houses that morning looking for action, and had found it here on Reynolds Street.

It was cloudy but cold. The cars' tires laid behind them on the snowy street a   5
complex trail of beige chunks like crenellated castle walls. I had stepped on some earlier; they squeaked. We could have wished for more traffic. When a car came, we all popped it one. In the intervals between cars we reverted to the natural solitude of children.

I started making an iceball—a perfect iceball, from perfectly white snow, per-   6
fectly spherical, and squeezed perfectly translucent so no snow remained all the way through. (The Fahey boys and I considered it unfair actually to throw an iceball at somebody, but it had been known to happen.)

I had just embarked on the iceball project when we heard tire chains come   7
clanking from afar. A black Buick was moving toward us down the street. We all spread out, banged together some regular snowballs, took aim, and, when the Buick drew nigh, fired.

A soft snowball hit the driver's windshield right before the driver's face. It   8
made a smashed star with a hump in the middle.

Often, of course, we hit our target, but this time, the only time in all of life, the   9
car pulled over and stopped. Its wide black door opened; a man got out of it, running. He didn't even close the car door.

He ran after us, and we ran away from him, up the snowy Reynolds sidewalk.   10
At the corner, I looked back; incredibly, he was still after us. He was in city clothes: a suit and tie, street shoes. Any normal adult would have quit, having sprung us into flight and made his point. This man was gaining on us. He was a thin man, all action. All of a sudden, we were running for our lives.

Wordless, we split up. We were on our turf; we could lose ourselves in the   11
neighborhood backyards, everyone for himself. I paused and considered. Everyone had vanished except Mikey Fahey, who was just rounding the corner of a yellow brick house. Poor Mikey, I trailed him. The driver of the Buick sensibly picked the two of us to follow. The man apparently had all day.

He chased Mikey and me around the yellow house and up a backyard path we   12
knew by heart: under a low tree, up a bank, through a hedge, down some snowy steps, and across the grocery store's delivery driveway. We smashed through a gap in another hedge, entered a scruffy backyard and ran around its back porch and tight between houses to Edgerton Avenue; we ran across Edgerton to an alley and up our own sliding woodpile to the Halls' front yard; he kept coming. We ran up Lloyd Street and wound through mazy backyards toward the steep hilltop at Willard and Lang.

He chased us silently, block after block. He chased us silently over picket 13
fences, through thorny hedges, between houses, around garbage cans, and across
streets. Every time I glanced back, choking for breath, I expected he would have
quit. He must have been as breathless as we were. His jacket strained over his body.
It was an immense discovery, pounding into my hot head with every sliding, joyous
step, that this ordinary adult evidently knew what I thought only children who
trained at football knew: that you have to fling yourself at what you're doing, you
have to point yourself, forget yourself, aim, dive.

Mikey and I had nowhere to go, in our own neighborhood or out of it, but away 14
from this man who was chasing us. He impelled us forward; we compelled him to
follow our route. The air was cold; every breath tore my throat. We kept running,
block after block; we kept improvising, backyard after backyard, running a frantic
course and choosing it simultaneously, failing always to find small places or hard
places to slow him down, and discovering always, exhilarated, dismayed, that only
bare speed could save us—for he would never give up, this man—and we were losing speed.

He chased us through the backyard labyrinths of ten blocks before he caught us 15
by our jackets. He caught us and we all stopped.

We three stood staggering, half blinded, coughing, in an obscure hilltop back- 16
yard: a man in his twenties, a boy, a girl. He had released our jackets, our pursuer,
our captor, our hero: he knew we weren't going anywhere. We all played by the
rules. Mikey and I unzipped our jackets. I pulled off my sopping mittens. Our tracks
multiplied in the backyard's new snow. We had been breaking new snow all morning. We didn't look at each other. I was cherishing my excitement. The man's lower
pants legs were wet; his cuffs were full of snow, and there was a prow of snow beneath them on his shoes and socks. Some trees bordered the little flat backyard,
some messy winter trees. There was no one around: a clearing in a grove, and we
the only players.

It was a long time before he could speak. I had some difficulty at first recalling 17
why we were there. My lips felt swollen; I couldn't see out of the sides of my eyes;
I kept coughing.

"You stupid kids," he began perfunctorily. 18

We listened perfunctorily indeed, if we listened at all, for the chewing out was 19
redundant, a mere formality, and beside the point. The point was that he had chased
us passionately without giving up, and so he had caught us. Now he came down to
earth. I wanted the glory to last forever.

But how could the glory have lasted forever? We could have run through every 20
backyard in North America until we got to Panama. But when he trapped us at the
lip of the Panama Canal, what precisely could he have done to prolong the drama of
the chase and cap its glory? I brooded about this for the next few years. He could
only have fried Mikey Fahey and me in boiling oil, say, or dismembered us piece-
meal, or staked us to anthills. None of which I really wanted, and none of which any
adult was likely to do, even in the spirit of fun. He could only chew us out there in
the Panamanian jungle, after months or years of exalting pursuit. He could only

begin, "You stupid kids," and continue in his ordinary Pittsburgh accent with his normal righteous anger and the usual common sense.

If in that snowy backyard the driver of the black Buick had cut off our heads, 21 Mikey's and mine, I would have died happy, for nothing has required so much of me since as being chased all over Pittsburgh in the middle of winter—running terrified, exhausted—by this sainted, skinny, furious red-headed man who wished to have a word with us. I don't know how he found his way back to his car.

UNDERSTANDING THE ESSAY

1. Why does Dillard begin with references to football and baseball, when in fact the essay is going to be about neither sport? What connection does she find between these games and the chase?

2. What do you think motivated the man who chased the narrator? How can you tell? What is the narrator's attitude toward the man who chases her? How is it possibly different from his attitude toward her?

3. What is the effect of naming all the things the narrator ran through, around, and across in paragraph 12?

4. In paragraph 13, Dillard says, "you have to fling yourself at what you're doing, you have to point yourself, forget yourself, aim, dive"—echoing similar words in paragraph 1. How do these sentences connect playing football with chasing or being chased by a determined pursuer? Is the attitude expressed by these words applicable only to games, or do you think Dillard expects us to apply it to life itself?

5. Where does Dillard come closest to explicitly interpreting the events she related in her essay?

So What and the Seven Common Moves.   Analyze this essay with the help of the questions about "So What and the Seven Common Moves" found on the back cover of this book.

Words, Phrases, and Allusions.   The following items were taken from "The Chase" in the order of appearance. With the help of your classmates, locate these words in the essay and see if their context provides a clue to their meaning. If necessary, consult a dictionary, an encyclopedia, or other reference work to determine what each item means in its context. Pay particular attention to words and phrases that might be worth using in your own writing.

beige, crenellated, intervals, reverted, solitude, spherical, translucent, embarked, mazy, impelled, improving, labyrinths, captor, cherishing, perfunctorily, redundant, dismembered, exalting, righteous

Suggestion for Writing

Using "The Chase" as a model, write a narrative essay about someone breaking the rules. Make the events themselves as interesting as you can, but tell your story in a way that focuses on the interpretation of the events. Remember, it's your "take" on the topic that makes it an essay. The journal entry suggested at the beginning of this selection may have given you an idea for a topic, or you may have thought of other topics as you read "The Chase."

RECIPES FOR WRITING NARRATION

A. Writing from Personal Experience

When you narrate, think like a writer. Don't start out to prove a point. Start with a story that you consider memorable. Invent one if you have to, or combine several factual stories into a single narrative, embellishing with fictions as you go along. As you draft your story, try to discover what makes your story worth reading. That's the so-what factor. Once you've discovered it—which may not occur until your second or third draft—you have a basis for making a judgment about what to include and how to arrange it to create the effect that you want to create.

Here is a recipe for narration:

1. Choose a series of events about which you feel differently from the way most people feel. It does not have to be a true story.
2. Arrange the events in a series that will maintain the interest of your readers. The most obvious arrangement may be chronological order; but you may decide to weave back and forth in time, violating chronology for a specific purpose (e.g., to provide a surprise, or create a mystery, or build to a climax).
3. Look for opportunities to enrich your story with details that give the reader a sense of being on the scene, witnessing the events first hand.
4. Look for opportunities to use dialogue—the actual words spoken by the people in your story. Dialogue is most effective when it reveals something about the person who speaks it.
5. Create an ending. This is usually achieved by resolving all problems or answering all questions raised in the story. Normally, it is amateurish to end with a "moral."

6. Show a draft to fellow students in a formal or informal workshop, and see if your strategies are having the effects you want them to have. Use the checklist on the back cover to focus your discussion. Then look for errors in spelling, grammar, or punctuation that you will want to correct in your final draft.

B. Writing against the Text

Good narrative essays tend to seem "objective," as if the writer were merely recording what happened, not interpreting it. But in fact, every story reveals the values and beliefs of the person who tells it. Not everybody in the church Langston Hughes describes would have seen the events there the way he saw them. Not everybody who reads Jaime O'Neill's "Falling into Place" will agree with implicit assumptions about the gender relationships it implies. And while we may be extremely grateful for Mike Royko's interpretation of Jackie's debut, we have to admit that we are grateful precisely because it *is* an interpretation, one that not everyone who attended the game would have seen for themselves. Find room for disagreement or expansion in any essay in this chapter. Write a description of your own offering a different interpretation.

C. Writing from Research

Using the library and the Web, locate two or more conflicting narratives about the same series of events: an incident in Belfast, for example, told from both a Catholic and a Protestant point of view; a legal case, as told by the prosecution and the defense; a ballgame as reported by the home newspaper of each team. After you've studied your sources, put them aside and write, in your own words, what "really" happened. Then go back and add quoted material wherever it will make your paper more interesting or credible, and provide appropriate acknowledgments. If you come to a point in the narrative where you are really not sure which side to believe, tell both versions, and then indicate which, if any, you are inclined to believe.

4

Interpreting a Process:
How Things Are Done

If you've ever followed a recipe or directions for assembling a bookshelf or for installing a program on your computer, you've read a process paper. Process papers tell you how something is done. They turn up in owner's manuals and do-it-yourself books and instructions for filing income tax reports or filling out student aid applications. They turn up as chapters in textbooks, where processes like making alloys or altering DNA or writing an essay are explained. Process papers have been around for so long that we take them for granted; but without them, we could never have developed civilization as we know it. Process papers enable us to record and publish scientific and technical routines that would otherwise be available only to the people who happen to have invented them or learned them in personal apprenticeships.

There are several kinds of process writing, each valuable in its own way. One kind (a recipe, an instructional manual, technical directions) conveys information. It describes an "algorithmic" process—a sure-fire, step-by-step process that will produce a particular result, like a pecan pie, or a fusion reactor, or the square root of a number. Another kind of process writing does more than describe a process for readers who might want to try it; it interprets the process, making it interesting to readers who may never attempt it themselves. A third kind of process describes a process that really cannot be reduced to a sure-fire recipe—like how to paint a landscape, or how to have a happy marriage, or how to enjoy classical music, or how to write.

Some kinds of process writing presume the reader's need for the information they contain. Cookbooks, computer manuals, and technical instructions don't have to create interest at the outset. Ordinarily, people don't read about processes of this sort just for fun or enlightenment. They don't expect to be entertained. They don't expect a recipe to explain the cultural significance of meatloaf; they don't expect a computer manual to comment on the political or economic implications of hypertext. Process writing of this sort is useful, for sure, but it is not, strictly speaking, an essay.

The essence of a process essay is interpretation. We may not need the information, but the writer has earned our interest by interpreting the process in a way that makes it interesting, even if we may never want to perform it ourselves. Chances are you won't ever find yourself sprouting new tentacles, like a starfish, or embalming corpses for profit. But later in this chapter you will find essays on these processes. They are interesting because writers like Judith Herbst and Jessica Mitford have made them so. Even if the subject is algorithmic—a series of steps with a sure-fire result—a process paper can be an essay if it interprets the process. This is why Mitford's essay on embalming is an essay. It's not just a how-to-do-it manual for student morticians; it provides a commentary on the process, an interpretation.

Process writing always implies a writer who is an expert, explaining things to a reader who isn't. And that's just the problem. It's easy for experts to explain things in a way that will make sense to themselves and to other experts. But experts often find it tough to explain things to readers who don't already know the process. If a computer whiz tells us about "DOS command syntax," computer wonks will know exactly that means. But ordinary people may not. If a recipe begins with "First make a roux"—without further explanation—it will be perfectly clear to gourmet cooks like the ones who write cookbooks, but useless to readers who don't already know what a roux is and how one is made. You have probably read process papers of this sort. They make you want to shout, "But what *is* a roux (or a DOS command, or a widget, or whatever)?" The first task for a process writer, therefore, is to guess accurately what readers know and what they need to have defined or explained.

One nice thing about process papers is that they are easy to organize. If the subject is a linear process—like frying fish or installing a modem—you can just arrange the steps in chronological order, adding suitable comments, explanations, and definitions along the way. If the process is nonlinear—like listening to music or respecting the ecology—plotting becomes more important. There may be no natural, chronological order to processes of this sort, so you have to arrange the steps in the sequence that you think will best maintain the reader's interest.

Journal Entry. Think of a process you know better than most people in your class—like canning strawberries, or using a spreadsheet, or taking inventory, or building an architectural model, or resolving conflicts, or kayaking through whitewater. Or think of a zany process—like how to become famous by being really incompetent, or how to travel around the world without paying for it, or how to get someone else to wash your car. Make a list of steps, and then describe each step. To make an essay of a process paper, you have to interpret the process—make it interesting to people who have no intention of doing it them-selves.

After you've worked on this project for a while, read the following essay in which Merrill Markoe describes a process that you may not be inclined to try: showering with a dog. As you read the essay, look for moves that you can make in your own.

Showering with Your Dog

Merrill Markoe

Let's face it. Even the most beloved dog can be very stinky at times. And where pet   1
hygiene is concerned, the enlightened pet guardian (and, of course, by that I mean
me) has no choice but to share the indoor facilities with the animal.

Step 1: Choosing the Proper Wardrobe

When showering with your dog, it *is* advisable to wear swim wear. I don't know   2
whether the dog would know if you were naked, but *you* would know.

Step 2: Getting the Dog into the Shower

Nothing can really proceed until this is accomplished. Often the dog will exhibit a   3
little initial reluctance . . . perhaps because he has watched too many horror movies
on TV in which showers are presented in an unfortunate light. Many dogs have
never given any thought to the concept of "fiction" and so do not know that most
showers are not just another death trap. Rather than confront the animal with a lot of
mind-blowing philosophical concepts, I recommend one of the two less complicated strategies that work for me. The first is what I call the old "ball in the shower"
approach, in which you, the parent or guardian, relocate to the inside of the shower
with some favorite sports equipment, making it appear that you have selected the

location *not* because of its showering capabilities but simply because it is the best damn place for miles around to hit fungoes. If, after fifteen or twenty minutes of enthusiastic solo sports maneuvers, you have not managed to interest the animal in joining you, I suggest you switch to the immediately effective "chicken skin around the drain" approach. It's a well-documented fact that only a minute amount of chicken skin can accumulate in the lower third of any area of the world before it will be joined by a dog.

Once this has happened, simply close the shower door behind him, or pull the 4 curtain. (For the more squeamish among you, who worry about the mess in the shower, you can count on the dog to clean it all up. If he should happen to miss a little, and some chicken skin remains, don't worry. It will simply be taken by any future showerers as a remarkable indication of how seriously you scrub yourself when you wash.)

Step 3: Moistening and Soaping the Animal

This may be trickier than it appears, because the animal tends to move to the parts 5 of the shower where there is no water. And so it becomes your perpetual task to keep moving to the parts of the shower where there is a dog. During this phase, apply shampoo and try not to take personally the animal's expression, which indicates a hatred and loathing so extreme that he is trying to figure out how he can reconnect with his long-buried primitive instincts to kill and eat a human being. It may be useful to let the dog know that showering is not a punishment but something *you* actually find pleasurable and relaxing. If this does not help, now is an excellent time to explain to the animal that the legal system is built primarily around the rights of humans, and if you want to, you can take him back to the pound where you got him and then his life won't be worth a plug nickel.

Step 4: Rinsing

You are now dealing with increasing desperation on the part of the dog, 6 who may be getting ready to make a break for it. This is why nature gave the dog a tail, to help you as you try to restrain him before he runs through the house all matted and soapy and gets big hair-encrusted stains all over your cherished possessions.

Step 5: Toweling the Dog

This process is designed to help you avoid the splattered, soaking mess that results 7 when the dog shakes himself off. No matter how diligently you perform toweling, it is futile. When you're through, the dog will disperse the same astonishing amounts of water and hair as if he had never been toweled at all.

Now you may release the animal, perhaps deluding yourself that he is thrilled 8 at his cleaner condition. You should return immediately to the shower and shovel out the three to five pounds of hair you will find lodged in your drain. This brings me to the final but most important step.

Step 6: Remove Any Bottles of Flea and Tick Shampoo

Take it from someone who has lived through every unfortunate scenario that can result from simply leaving the bottle around. . . . I know I have helped you. 9

The So-What Factor. What is novel, interesting, surprising, or moving about Merrill Markoe's instructions for showering with a dog? When an essay does not have an explicit thesis, the point can usually be discovered by completing the question implied between the lines: "Don't you think this is . . . ?" What? In the case of "Showering with Your Dog," the words "funny" or "ridiculous" leap to mind. The purpose of the essay is not really to tell us how to shower with a dog (though there are some otherwise normal readers who will take it seriously). The purpose is to entertain, to make us smile. The measure of Markoe's success is whether you were amused when you read the essay. Not everyone is, of course; many readers do not share Markoe's sense of humor. Still, the intent of the essay is clear. The so-what factor is simple. So what? So relax, so lighten up a bit.

THE SEVEN COMMON MOVES

1. Beginning. Markoe knows we are not likely to be seriously interested in showering with dogs, so she has to capture our interest quickly. She begins, as many essayists do, by presenting an unsettling or unsettled situation. In this case, it's a stinky dog, combined with a proposition that Markoe hopes we will find interesting precisely because we can't take it very seriously: that sometimes we have "no choice" but to shower with an animal. We don't believe this for a second, but the assertion is so preposterous that we may be inclined to continue reading, just to see if she can keep us entertained.

2. Ending. A process paper usually has a natural ending. It ends when the process ends—when the cake is baked, the program installed, or in this case, when the dog emerges from the shower, no longer stinky. But Markoe takes us one step further, in effect going beyond the process to its possible effects. She adds a coda in the form of a joke, having us imagine what would happen if we left flea and tick shampoo in the shower, where someone might use it to wash their own hair. To this, Markoe adds yet another joke: "I know I have helped you," she says, with mock seriousness, knowing full well she hasn't helped us at all. We have no intention of showering with a . . . oh, well, there we go, taking things too seriously.

3. *Detail.* To keep her readers interested in an inane process, Markoe invents details that surprise and amuse us, using the writer's eye to create striking and humorous images. Even without looking back at the essay, you probably find it easy to remember some of the images—perhaps the chicken skin on the drain, or the author wearing a bathing suit in the shower. Return to those images you find easiest to remember and see if you can determine what Markoe did to make them effective.

4. *Organization/Plot.* "Showering with Your Dog" pretends to be a classic process paper ("pretends" because it is really a spoof, a parody, not intended to be taken seriously). But just like a serious process paper—a recipe or an instruction manual—it describes a linear process, following steps in chronological order. The outline is clearly indicated in bold headings—Step 1 . . . Step 2, and so forth. Once you describe the first step in a process, there will be a continuous sense of unfinished business until you describe the last. Once the author decides to shower with a pup, our curiosity will remain unsatisfied until task is done.

5. *Style*. Even though Markoe's style is deliberately conversational, she makes some moves that have traditional rhetorical names. One example occurs in the first sentence of Step 3:

> . . . the animal tends to move to the parts of the shower where there is no water. And so it becomes your perpetual task to keep moving to the parts of the shower where there is a dog.

The two elements (animal/shower) in the first sentence return in the second, but in the reverse order (shower/dog). This is a neat move, a criss-cross arrangement called "chiasmus" (after *chi*, the Greek *X*). Perhaps the most famous example in modern times is John F. Kennedy's "ask not what your country can do for you . . . ask what you can do for your country."

Another traditional stylistic move is personification—treating an animal or an inanimate object as if it were human. Personification can be a serious poetic device. But it can also be funny, as it is when we imagine a dog watching horror movies, or engaging in mind-blowing philosophical conversations, or listening to an explanation of the legal system.

Another move with a traditional name is "hyperbole" or "exaggeration." It is hyperbole to imagine that a shower would be a great place for hitting fungoes—when you realize that fungoes are the sort of fly balls a baseball coach hits to fielders for practice. A shower stall would have to be large indeed to accommodate a fungo drill. It is also hyperbole to imagine, as Markoe has us do in Step 3, that dogs resent showers so much that they have difficulty suppressing an urge to attack and devour their owners. And hyperbole to imagine that a pet owner would return a dog to the pound because of its unhappy expression in the shower.

6. *Voice/Attitude.* "Showering with Your Dog" is full of moves that suggest an individual writer, moves that would seem out of place in an unsigned news article. Markoe wants to seem conversational. "Let's face it," she says at the outset, as if she and her readers were pals having a chat, "Even the most beloved dog can be very stinky at times." Not fetid, foul, musty, putrid, or malodorous. Not rancid or rank. Just stinky. This is not the formal language of a scholar or the anonymous diction of a news reporter. Markoe uses italics to emphasize words that she might have emphasized in speech: "it *is* advisable to wear swim wear"; "but *you* would know"; "you have selected the location *not* because of its showering capabilities." All these moves contribute to the intimacy and informality of her attitude and voice.

Or at least one of her voices—she uses several in this piece. Sometimes she mimics someone seriously giving instructions: "During this phase, apply shampoo. . . ." Sometimes she uses learned words (like "hygiene" for bathing a dog, and "indoor facilities" for showers, and "parent or guardian" for a pet's owner) or affects the theoretical loftiness of a scholar or scientist: "It's a well-documented fact that only a minute amount of chicken skin can accumulate in the lower third of any area of the world before it will be joined by a dog." But Markoe uses these voices satirically, connecting lofty language with a silly subject. And her attitude is personal, playful, and friendly. You don't imagine a scholar or a judge behind the words on the page; you imagine the deliberately ditzy comedienne that Markoe actually is.

7. Economy. Test for economy by looking for words, phrases, or details that could be omitted without being missed. What does chicken skin have to do with the essay? What purpose is served by mentioning hair in the drain? Would the essay be improved or worsened without these details? Can you find any details that don't serve a purpose and therefore wouldn't be missed if omitted?

Moves within Moves.   The dominant mode of this essay is process analysis. But if you look closely, you will see some of the other patterns of development within individual sentences or passages.

Contrast (See chapter 5)

> I don't know whether the dog would know if you were naked, but *you* would know.

> Rather than confront the animal with a lot of mind-blowing philosophical concepts, I recommend one of the two less complicated strategies that work for me.

> . . . making it appear that you have selected the location *not* because of its showering capabilities but simply because it is the best damn place for miles around to hit fungoes.

> . . . showering is not a punishment but something *you* actually find pleasurable and relaxing.

Cause and effect (See chapter 7)

> Often the dog will exhibit a little initial reluctance . . . perhaps because he has watched too many horror movies on TV in which showers are presented in an unfortunate light.

Definition (See chapter 8)

> The first is what I call the old "ball in the shower" approach, in which you, the parent or guardian, relocate to the inside of the shower with some favorite sports equipment . . .

Description (See chapter 2)

> . . . the animal's expression, which indicates a hatred and loathing so extreme that he is trying to figure out how he can reconnect with his long-buried primitive instincts to kill and eat a human being.

> . . . he runs through the house all matted and soapy and gets big hair-encrusted stains all over your cherished possessions.

> . . . the three to five pounds of hair you will find lodged in your drain.

And of course the essay as a whole is framed as *narrative* (See chapter 3)—a chronological sequence of events.

Words, Phrases, and Allusions.   Except for "fungoes" (which may be familiar to you if you've ever played baseball) there are no unusual words in "Showering with Your Dog." And yet the essay is successful. There's a lesson in this. Good writing doesn't necessarily require fancy words. Just the right words, in the right place—words with the level of formality or informality that best suits the writer's purpose.

The few words this essay does have are often mixed with colloquialisms for comic effect, as in "mind-blowing philosophical concepts." The following items were taken from "Showering with Your Dog" in order of appearance. With the help of your classmates, locate these words in the essay and see if their context provides a clue to their meaning. If necessary, consult a dictionary, an encyclopedia, or other reference work to determine what each item means in its context. You probably know most of these words from conversation and reading, but you may not yet feel comfortable using them in your own writing.

hygiene, fungoes, minute, loathing, desperation, futile, disperse, deluding, scenario

Suggestion for Writing

Using "Showering with Your Dog" as a model, write a whimsical process paper. The journal entry suggested in the introduction to the essay might provide you with a process worth writing about, but you may have thought of other topics as you read "Showering with Your Dog." Reread the model for specific techniques you might imitate in your own essay.

Journal Entry.   You have already done a lot of reading and a lot of writing in your life. Pick some aspect of your experience with the printed word and write a "How To" paper, or if you prefer, a "How Not To" paper. Topics could include "How to find a good book," "How to find what you need in the library," "How to find ideas for writing a paper," "How to organize a bibliography," "How to find a publisher for your writing," "How to write about sports (or music, or art, or social events)," "How to find things on the Internet." Think of your classmates as readers: make sure you explain terms that they might otherwise not understand, and try to make the process interesting even to those who may never attempt it themselves. After you've worked on this project for a while, read the following advice about "How to Write with Style," by Kurt Vonnegut, one our most successful novelists. Look for techniques to imitate.

How to Write with Style

Kurt Vonnegut

Newspaper reporters and technical writers are trained to reveal almost nothing about themselves in their writings. This makes them freaks in the world of writers, since almost all of the other ink-stained wretches in that world reveal a lot about themselves to readers. We call these revelations, accidental and intentional, elements of style. 1

These revelations tell us as readers what sort of person it is with whom we are spending time. Does the writer sound ignorant or informed, stupid or bright, crooked or honest, humorless or playful—? And on and on. 2

Why should you examine your writing style with the idea of improving it? Do so as a mark of respect for your readers, whatever you're writing. If you scribble your thoughts any which way, your readers will surely feel that you care nothing about them. They will mark you down as an egomaniac or a chowderhead—or, worse, they will stop reading you. 3

The most damning revelation you can make about yourself is that you do not know what is interesting and what is not. Don't you yourself like or dislike writers mainly for what they choose to show you or make you think about? Did you ever admire an empty-headed writer for his or her mastery of the language? No. 4

So your own winning style must begin with the ideas in your head. 5

6

1. Find a subject you care about. Find a subject you care about and which you in your heart feel others should care about. It is this genuine caring, and not your games with language, which will be the most compelling and seductive element in your style.

I am not urging you to write a novel, by the way—although I would not be sorry   7
if you wrote one, provided you genuinely cared about something. A petition to the mayor about a pothole in front of your house or a love letter to the girl next door will do.

2. *Do not ramble, though.* I won't ramble on about that.   8

3. *Keep it simple.* As for your use of language: Remember that two great mas-   9
ters of language, William Shakespeare and James Joyce, wrote sentences which were almost childlike when their subjects were most profound. "To be or not to be?" asks Shakespeare's Hamlet. The longest word is three letters long. Joyce, when he was frisky, could put together a sentence as intricate and as glittering as a necklace for Cleopatra, but my favorite sentence in his short story "Eveline" is this one: "She was tired." At that point in the story, no other words could break the heart of a reader as those three words do.

Simplicity of language is not only reputable, but perhaps even sacred. The   10
Bible opens with a sentence well within the writing skills of a lively fourteen-year-old: "In the beginning God created the heaven and the earth."

4. *Have the guts to cut.* It may be that you, too, are capable of making neck-   11
laces for Cleopatra, so to speak. But your eloquence should be the servant of the ideas in your head. Your rule might be this: If a sentence, no matter how excellent, does not illuminate your subject in some new and useful way, scratch it out.

5. *Sound like yourself.* The writing style which is most natural for you is bound   12
to echo the speech you heard when a child. English was the novelist Joseph Conrad's third language, and much that seems piquant in his use of English was no doubt colored by his first language, which was Polish. And lucky indeed is the writer who has grown up in Ireland, for the English spoken there is so amusing and musical. I myself grew up in Indianapolis, where common speech sounds like a band saw cutting galvanized tin, and employs a vocabulary as unornamental as a monkey wrench.

In some of the more remote hollows of Appalachia, children still grow up hear-   13
ing songs and locutions of Elizabethan times. Yes, and many Americans grow up hearing a language other than English, or an English dialect a majority of Americans cannot understand.

All these varieties of speech are beautiful, just as the varieties of butterflies are   14
beautiful. No matter what your first language, you should treasure it all your life. If it happens not to be standard English, and if it shows itself when you write standard English, the result is usually delightful, like a very pretty girl with one eye that is green and one that is blue.

I myself find that I trust my own writing most, and others seem to trust it most,   15
too, when I sound most like a person from Indianapolis, which is what I am. What alternatives do I have? The one most vehemently recommended by teachers has no doubt been pressed on you, as well: to write like cultivated Englishmen of a century or more ago.

6. *Say what you mean to say.* I used to be exasperated by such teachers, but   16
am no more. I understand now that all those antique essays and stories with which I

was to compare my own work were not magnificent for their datedness or foreignness, but for saying precisely what their authors meant them to say. My teachers wished me to write accurately, always selecting the most effective words, and relating the words to one another unambiguously, rigidly, like parts of a machine. The teachers did not want to turn me into an Englishman after all. They hoped that I would become understandable—and therefore understood. And there went my dream of doing with words what Pablo Picasso did with paint or what any number of jazz idols did with music. If I broke all the rules of punctuation, had words mean whatever I wanted them to mean, and strung them together higgledy-piggledy, I would simply not be understood. So you, too, had better avoid Picasso-style or jazz-style writing, if you have something worth saying and wish to be understood.

Readers want our pages to look very much like pages they have seen before. Why? This is because they themselves have a tough job to do, and they need all the help they can get from us. 17

7. *Pity the readers.* They have to identify thousands of little marks on paper, and make sense of them immediately. They have to read, an art so difficult that most people don't really master it even after having studied it all through grade school and high school—twelve long years. 18

So this discussion must finally acknowledge that our stylistic options as writers are neither numerous nor glamorous, since our readers are bound to be such imperfect artists. Our audience requires us to be sympathetic and patient teachers, ever willing to simplify and clarify—whereas we would rather soar high above the crowd, singing like nightingales. 19

That is the bad news. The good news is that we Americans are governed under a unique Constitution, which allows us to write whatever we please without fear of punishment. So the most meaningful aspect of our styles, which is what we choose to write about, is utterly unlimited. 20

8. *For really detailed advice.* For a discussion of literary style in a narrower sense, in a more technical sense, I commend to your attention *The Elements of Style*, by William Strunk, Jr., and E. B. White. E. B. White is, of course, one of the most admirable literary stylists this country has so far produced. 21

You should realize, too, that no one would care how well or badly Mr. White expressed himself, if he did not have perfectly enchanting things to say. 22

UNDERSTANDING THE ESSAY

1. Kurt Vonnegut claims that newspaper reporters and technical writers do not reveal their individuality in what they write. Is this true?
2. Does Vonnegut seem to think that newspaper reporters and technical writers *should* reveal their individuality in what they write? Do you agree with him?

3. Vonnegut claims that varieties of English are like varieties of butterflies: all beautiful. Do you agree? Do you agree that elements of nonstandard English can be "delightful" when they show up in otherwise formal prose? (As you think about these questions, you might consult Amy Tan's essays on the varieties of English spoken, on various occasions, by a Chinese-American.)

4. Why is (or isn't) Vonnegut's advice about writing with style an essay? Does he interpret a process, or merely describe one? Does he presume the interest of his readers, or does he make efforts to create and maintain it? Are the steps arranged in chronological order? Should they be?

5. Is writing with style the sort of thing that can truly be reduced to a recipe, or is Vonnegut, like other writers on this subject, doomed to give personal advice that may or may not be effective?

So What and the Seven Common Moves.   Analyze this essay with the help of the questions about "So What and the Seven Common Moves" found on the back cover of this book.

Words, Phrases, and Allusions.   There are few allusions or unusual words in "How to Write with Style," proving once again that good writing requires right words in the right places, not necessarily fancy or formal words. The following items were taken from "How to Write with Style" in order of appearance. With the help of your classmates, locate these words in the essay and see if their context provides a clue to their meaning. If necessary, consult a dictionary, an encyclopedia, or other reference work to determine what each item means in its context. You probably know most of these words from conversation and reading, but you may not yet feel comfortable using them in your own writing.

egomaniac, chowderhead, James Joyce, intricate, Cleopatra, reputable, eloquence, illuminate, Joseph Conrad, piquant, galvanized, hollows, Appalachia, dialect, standard English, vehemently, exasperated, unambiguously, Pablo Picasso, higgledy-piggledy

Suggestion for Writing

Using "How to Write with Style" as a model, write an essay explaining a process that you care about. The journal entry suggested at the beginning of this selection may have given you an idea for a topic, or you may have thought of other topics as you read Vonnegut's essay.

Journal Entry. Think of a fixing process that you understand better than most people: how to repair interior walls or broken hard drives; how to repair a relationship, or a musical instrument, or a torn sail. Jot down everything you know about how these things occur. But before you start your first draft, read Judith Herbst's essay about how certain animals regenerate missing body parts. Keep your own repair process in mind as you study the way Herbst explains one of nature's most fascinating tricks.

The Body Shop

Judith Herbst

It often comes as something of a shock to be told by your biology teacher to "gently   1
make three horizontal slices" in the living, breathing animal waiting patiently on your
lab tray. Even the toughest shrink back. For several minutes, the air in the classroom
is heavy with 1) loathing for the teacher, 2) self-disgust at the murderous act you are
about to commit, and 3) cowardice in technicolor. Scalpels hang poised. Throats gulp.
And then almost in unison, the entire class gently makes three horizontal slices.

The recipient of such treatment is a small, cross-eyed flatworm called a planarian,   2
a staple of school biology labs. Despite the drastic surgery, however, it never appears
to be the least bit bothered and, most significantly, goes right on living just as it did before you and your band of mercenaries showed up. Curious, indeed.

If you have a conscience, you think about your little planarian all through the   3
week, wondering how it is faring and if its severed head misses its body, its body
misses its tail, and its tail misses everything that once grew above it. The planarian,
though, is busy with far more important matters than musing over some stranger.
Like a handful of others in its animal-amazing fraternity, it is working on a recon-
struction project the likes of which the greatest scientific minds in the world cannot
duplicate. In a few days, you will see the dramatic results.

At the appointed time, the students retrieve their respective planarian trays, but   4
even before they have returned to their lab tables, they can see that an apparent mir-
acle of zoology has occurred. On each tray, there are now three fully formed pla-
naria, all of which bear a striking family resemblance to the original model. What
has happened in the course of a couple of weeks?

With remarkable exactitude, the individual pieces of planarian have regener-   5
ated themselves: The head has regrown a body and tail, the body has fashioned itself a head and tail, and the tail has supplied its missing head and body. If students
are not allowed to peek at the intermediate stages of the process, the planarian's re-

generation feat is shocking, but it becomes positively fascinating when you watch this simple animal slowly but surely making itself whole again—or rather, making its three selves whole again. Even better than that, however, is the fact that this regenerative power is the planarian's secret, a mysterious gift from nature that science has yet to understand.

Regeneration is an ability given in varying degrees to few members of the animal world. Salamanders, for example, can grow a new tail, but their tail cannot grow a new body. Lobsters can manage claws, but claws cannot make new lobsters. The starfish, though, runs a complete body shop and can grow a whole new self from just an arm, a feat that Maine oystermen (and women) are not too crazy about. 6

Starfish love oysters and can devastate an oyster bed in a very short period of time. Now, since oysters are decidedly quite delicious to eat and starfish are not, the oystermen are out gunning for starfish. 7

One of the rangers at Acadia National Park in Maine tells the story of an irate (and not too clever) oysterman who, fed up and disgusted with the whole starfish business, hauled in a big bunch of the spiny little things and proceeded to chop them into tiny pieces. "That'll teach ya!" he screamed, and hurled the pieces back into the sea. But each piece did what came naturally, and in very short order the starfish were back in greater numbers than ever before. The oysterman, one can only hope, has figured out the error of his ways. 8

Limb regeneration always has fascinated us, and we have watched in awe as salamanders slowly but surely grow their tails back and planarians replace their heads. Even more astonishing are the reports of a human baby's ability to regrow the tips of its fingers! This was seen, not once, but several times at the Children's Hospital in Sheffield, England. According to Dr. Cynthia Ellingsworth, the severed finger, dressed but otherwise untreated, regenerates in about three months on the average. And all the details are there—fingernail, sensation, even the loops and whorls of the original fingerprint! 9

But it is really in the lower animals—the newts and salamanders, the lizards and starfish, and of course, the planarian—that we see regeneration at its most impressive. These are creatures that can repair themselves after severe physical trauma. How do they do it? And why are there so few regeneration magicians in the animal world? And why, perhaps most of all, can't we do it? After age ten even fingertip regeneration is lost to us, and about all we can manage is limited bone and skin regrowth. What does the salamander have that a human being doesn't have? 10

You might at first think that the salamander can regenerate its limbs because it has *less* than we do. It's a simple animal, not nearly as complicated, and the blueprint for a new limb is probably equivalent to, say, a crayon drawing. Easy stuff. But scientists have found that the so-called "lower" animals are just as complex as we are. A leg is a leg. Period. It doesn't seem to matter to nature that some legs are smaller than others, covered with scaly green skin, or end in funny-looking toes. The basic structure, the thing that becomes *leg*, has the same basic design whether you are a frog, a zebra, or even Bigfoot. So, okay. All legs are created equal, but surely there must be *some* difference between salamanders and human beings. 11

Interestingly enough, scientists already had part of the answer as far back as the eighteenth century; they just didn't know it. They had discovered that when an animal suffers an injury, the wound immediately begins to generate a positive electrical charge. Furthermore, the greater the injury, the higher the voltage. But this was only a piece of the puzzle, so it didn't look like much to the scientists, and they filed it away for use later on—much later on as it turned out.

It wasn't until the mid 1950s that an anatomy professor studying regeneration in animals hit on this little gem: When an animal that cannot regenerate loses a limb, the electrical charge emitted by the stump grows slowly weaker and weaker as scar tissue is formed. When the stump scars over completely, the electrical charge shuts down for good. But if the animal can regrow its lost limb, then scar tissue *doesn't* form. The stump doesn't seal itself off but instead begins to regenerate new bone, muscle, tissue, and nerves—and that is the difference between salamanders and people. Our body forms scar tissue.

Furthermore, in a stump that is regenerating, not only does the electrical voltage remain as strong as ever, the charge flips from positive to negative. Like a fabulous craftsman, the animal fashions a new leg with painstaking accuracy. Every detail is there, right down to the tiniest, most seemingly insignificant skin fold, a precise duplicate of the original. When the regeneration process is at last complete, the electrical charge fades to nothing, presumably because there is no longer any wound.

Well, now. What have we here? Electricity as the great healer? It seems extraordinary. But in the 1800s, charlatans peddled all kinds of doodads and gizmos that plugged in and supposedly cured people of everything short of bubonic plague—and maybe even that, too. There were electricity chairs to sit in, hats and bizarre-looking electrical tiaras. There was even a washtublike device touted by its manufacturer to cure gout and rheumatism.

As you might expect, the scientific community thought all this electricity business was a pack of laughs, but that was then and this is now, and nobody's laughing anymore. In the 1970s, Dr. Steven Smith, working out of the University of Kentucky, performed a dramatic experiment that dethroned Godzilla as the most famous amphibian. Smith amputated the right foreleg of a frog—an animal that doesn't handle regeneration any better than we do—and implanted a tiny battery and an electrode leading to the end of the stump. The battery gave off a continuous negative charge similar, Smith hoped, to the negative electrical current that is present in regenerating limbs. While the results were truly eye-popping, they did not occur overnight. The entire process took about a year, but yes, indeed, the frog actually regrew its entire leg—toes and all!

How did the frog's stump know what to make? How did it know that it had to refashion so much bone, so much muscle, nerves of such and such a length, green skin, and four skinny toes?

To find the answer we have to go back to the womb. All of us, as you probably know, begin life as a single fertilized cell. Almost at once, the cell begins dividing—two, four, eight, sixteen, thirty-two—in a geometric progression that quickly becomes a little ball of cells called a blastula. The word *blastula* is from the Greek *blastos* meaning a "bud," and indeed, that's exactly what it is. Like a tiny bud on a branch, the blastula soon will bloom into all the details that make a living organism: heart, lungs, muscles, bone, arms, legs, fingernails, even individual hair shafts. The instructions for each organ, each feature, is contained in the long, twisted strands of DNA in the cells that make up the blastula. The blastula is then the original body shop where all the parts are made.

But the body shop does not remain in operation for very long. Nearly every an- 19
imal quickly loses the mysterious ability to make limbs and organs as the cells of the blastula did in the earliest days of life. Yes, we can manage skin. We can re-grow some bone and a little bit of muscle, but once severed, the body part is gone forever.

Only in the cells of the blastula lies the secret of regeneration. Except . . . 20

Newts and salamanders, starfish and planarians can create a sort of makeshift 21
blastula at the site of the amputation. It is a bundle of cells that scientists call a blastema. The blastema *somehow* knows just what is missing and how to make it. A salamander that loses its toes produces a blastema that makes toes—not a leg or an-other foot, only toes, only what has been lost. Truly, it is a remarkable process.

Over the years, scientists have learned a great deal about regeneration, but the 22
closer we look, the more blurred the picture seems to get. For example, animals that regenerate do not get cancer. The lizard can regenerate its tail but nothing else. If cancer cells are implanted into the lizard's body, the cancer flourishes; if they are implanted into its tail, the cancer vanishes.

Hormones appear to play some role in regeneration. When a lizard's adrenal 23
gland is removed, the animal loses its ability to regenerate its tail. However, if a hormone called prolactin is injected into the lizard, the ability returns. Even more fascinating, prolactin is found in the pituitary gland, and one of the jobs of the pitu-itary gland is to regulate growth!

The plot does indeed thicken. 24

There will come, no doubt, a brave new world in which we are able to regener- 25
ate bits and pieces of ourselves as easily as the starfish and the planarian. The artifi-cial limbs and hearts, the hearing aids and implants will no longer have to be shipped in from the body shop.

The body shop will be us. 26

UNDERSTANDING THE ESSAY

1. What is the main difference between the healing process of animals that re-generate body parts and those that don't?

2. Has the identification of this difference explained how body parts are regenerated?

3. Although Herbst is writing primarily about the regeneration of body parts in relatively simple animals, what hopes does she seem to raise that makes her topic of particular interest to humans?

4. Why is (or isn't) Herbst's description about the regeneration of body parts an essay? Does she interpret a process, or merely describe one? Does she presume the interest of her readers, or does she make efforts to create and maintain it?

5. Does Herbst reveal an attitude, or is she merely a neutral observer, a pure scientist, like a video camera that observes and records without commentary? Do you think other observers would have exactly the same "take" on this subject that Herbst has? Cite the passages in the text to support your answers to these questions.

So What and the Seven Common Moves.   Analyze this essay with the help of the questions about "So What and the Seven Common Moves" found on the back cover of this book.

Words, Phrases, and Allusions.   The following items were taken from "The Body Shop" in order of appearance. With the help of your classmates, locate these words in the essay and see if their context provides a clue to their meaning. If necessary, consult a dictionary, an encyclopedia, or other reference work to determine what each item means in its context. You probably know most of these words from conversation and reading, but you may not yet feel comfortable using them in your own writing.

technicolor, scalpels, unison, recipient, planarian, mercenaries, respective, zoology, salamanders, irate, whorls, newts, trauma, anatomy, emitted, charlatans, bubonic, bizarre, tiaras, gout, rheumatism, Godzilla, blastula, blastema, adrenal gland, pituitary gland

Suggestion for Writing

Using "The Body Shop" as a model, write an essay explaining a repair process that you happen to know and understand. The journal entry suggested at the beginning of this selection may have given you an idea for a topic, or you may have thought of other topics as you read Herbst's essay. You may decide to do some research for this topic—using the library, the Web, and if possible consulting experts who might give you some clues about the process you have chosen to write about.

The American Way of Death

Jessica Mitford

The drama begins to unfold with the arrival of the corpse at the mortuary. 1

Alas, poor Yorick! How surprised he would be to see how his counterpart of 2 today is whisked off to a funeral parlor and is in short order sprayed, sliced, pierced, pickled, trussed, trimmed, creamed, waxed, painted, rouged and neatly dressed—transformed from a common corpse into a Beautiful Memory Picture. This process is known in the trade as embalming and restorative art, and is so universally employed in the United States and Canada that the funeral director does it routinely, without consulting corpse or kin. He regards as eccentric those few who are hardy enough to suggest that it might be dispensed with. Yet no law requires embalming, no religious doctrine commends it, nor is it dictated by considerations of health, sanitation, or even of personal daintiness. In no part of the world but in Northern America is it widely used. The purpose of embalming is to make the corpse presentable for viewing in a suitably costly container; and here too the funeral director routinely, without first consulting the family, prepares the body for public display.

Is all this legal? The processes to which a dead body may be subjected are after 3 all to some extent circumscribed by law. In most states, for instance, the signature of next of kin must be obtained before an autopsy may be performed, before the deceased may be cremated, before the body may be turned over to a medical school for research purposes; or such provision must be made in the decedent's will. In the case of embalming, no such permission is required nor is it ever sought. A textbook, *The Principles and Practices of Embalming*, comments on this: "There is some question regarding the legality of much that is done within the preparation room." The author points out that it would be most unusual for a responsible member of a bereaved family to instruct the mortician, in so many words, to "embalm" the body of a deceased relative. The very term "embalming" is so seldom used that the mortician must rely upon custom in the matter. The author concludes that unless the family specifies otherwise, the act of entrusting the body to the care of a funeral establishment carries with it an implied permission to go ahead and embalm.

Embalming is indeed a most extraordinary procedure, and one must wonder at   4
the docility of Americans who each year pay hundreds of millions of dollars for its perpetuation, blissfully ignorant of what it is all about, what is done, how it is done. Not one in ten thousand has any idea of what actually takes place. Books on the subject are extremely hard to come by. They are not to be found in most libraries or bookshops.

In an era when huge television audiences watch surgical operations in the com-   5
fort of their living rooms, when, thanks to the animated cartoon, the geography of the digestive system has become familiar territory even to the nursery school set, in a land where the satisfaction of curiosity about almost all matters is a national pastime, the secrecy surrounding embalming can, surely, hardly be attributed to the inherent gruesomeness of the subject. Custom in this regard has within this century suffered a complete reversal. In the early days of American embalming, when it was performed in the home of the deceased, it was almost mandatory for some relative to stay by the embalmer's side and witness the procedure. Today, family members who might wish to be in attendance would certainly be dissuaded by the funeral director. All others, except apprentices, are excluded by law from the preparation room.

A close look at what does actually take place may explain in large measure the   6
undertaker's intractable reticence concerning a procedure that has become his major *raison d'être*. Is it possible he fears that public information about embalming might lead patrons to wonder if they really want this service? If the funeral men are loath to discuss the subject outside the trade, the reader may, understandably, be equally loath to go on reading at this point. For those who have the stomach for it, let us part the formaldehyde curtain. . . .

The body is first laid out in the undertaker's morgue—or rather, Mr. Jones is   7
reposing in the preparation room—to be readied to bid the world farewell.

The preparation room in any of the better funeral establishments has the tiled   8
and sterile look of a surgery, and indeed the embalmer–restorative artist who does his chores there is beginning to adopt the term "dermasurgeon" (appropriately corrupted by some mortician-writers as "demi-surgeon") to describe his calling. His equipment, consisting of scalpels, scissors, augers, forceps, clamps, needles, pumps, tubes, bowls and basins, is crudely imitative of the surgeon's, as is his technique, acquired in a nine- or twelve-month post-highschool course in an embalming school. He is supplied by an advanced chemical industry with a bewildering array of fluids, sprays, pastes, oils, powders, creams, to fix or soften tissue, shrink or distend it as needed, dry it here, restore the moisture there. There are cosmetics, waxes and paints to fill and cover features, even plaster of Paris to replace entire limbs. There are ingenious aids to prop and stabilize the cadaver: a Vari-Pose Head Rest,

the Edwards Arm and Hand Positioner, the Repose Block (to support the shoulders during the embalming), and the Throop Foot Positioner, which resembles an old-fashioned stocks.

Mr. John H. Eckels, president of the Eckels College of Mortuary Science, thus   9
describes the first part of the embalming procedure: "In the hands of a skilled practitioner, this work may be done in a comparatively short time and without mutilating the body other than by slight incision—so slight that it scarcely would cause serious inconvenience if made upon a living person. It is necessary to remove the blood, and doing this not only helps in the disinfecting, but removes the principal cause of disfigurements due to discoloration."

Another textbook discusses the all-important time element: "The earlier this is   10
done, the better, for every hour that elapses between death and embalming will add to the problems and complications encountered. . . ." Just how soon should one get going on the embalming? The author tells us, "On the basis of such scanty information made available to this profession through its rudimentary and haphazard system of technical research, we must conclude that the best results are to be obtained if the subject is embalmed before life is completely extinct—that is, before cellular death has occurred. In the average case, this would mean within an hour after somatic death." For those who feel that there is something a little rudimentary, not to say haphazard, about this advice, a comforting thought is offered by another writer. Speaking of fears entertained in early days of premature burial, he points out, "One of the effects of embalming by chemical injection, however, has been to dispel fears of live burial." How true; once the blood is removed, chances of live burial are indeed remote.

To return to Mr. Jones, the blood is drained out through the veins and replaced   11
by embalming fluid pumped in through the arteries. As noted in *The Principles and Practices of Embalming*, "every operator has a favorite injection and drainage point—a fact which becomes a handicap only if he fails or refuses to forsake his favorites when conditions demand it." Typical favorites are the carotid artery, femoral artery, jugular vein, subclavian vein. There are various choices of embalming fluid. If Flextone is used, it will produce a "mild, flexible rigidity. The skin retains a velvety softness, the tissues are rubbery and pliable. Ideal for women and children." It may be blended with B. and G. Products Company's Lyf-Lyk tint, which is guaranteed to reproduce "nature's own skin texture . . . the velvety appearance of living tissue." Suntone comes in three separate tints: Suntan; Special Cosmetic Tint, a pink shade "especially indicated for young female subjects"; and Regular Cosmetic Tint, moderately pink.

About three to six gallons of a dyed and perfumed solution of formaldehyde,   12
glycerin, borax, phenol, alcohol and water is soon circulating through Mr. Jones, whose mouth has been sewn together with a "needle directed upward between the upper lip and gum and brought out through the left nostril" with the corners raised slightly "for a more pleasant expression." If he should be bucktoothed, his teeth are cleaned with Bon Ami and coated with colorless nail polish. His eyes, meanwhile, are closed with flesh-tinted eye caps and eye cement.

The next step is to have at Mr. Jones with a thing called a trocar. This is a long, 13
hollow needle attached to a tube. It is jabbed into the abdomen, poked around the
entrails and chest cavity, the contents of which are pumped out and replaced with
"cavity fluid." This done, and the hole in the abdomen sewn up, Mr. Jones's face is
heavily creamed (to protect the skin from burns which may be caused by leakage of
the chemicals), and he is covered with a sheet and left unmolested for a while. But
not for long—there is more, much more, in store for him. He has been embalmed,
but not yet restored, and the best time to start the restorative work is eight to ten
hours after embalming, when the tissues have become firm and dry.

The object of all this attention to the corpse, it must be remembered, is to make 14
it presentable for viewing in an attitude of healthy repose. "Our customs require the
presentation of our dead in the semblance of normality . . . unmarred by the ravages
of illness, disease or mutilation," says Mr. J. Sheridan Mayer in his *Restorative Art*.
This is rather a large order since few people die in the full bloom of health, unrav-
aged by illness and unmarked by some disfigurement. The funeral industry is equal
to the challenge: "In some cases the gruesome appearance of a mutilated or disease-
ridden subject may be quite discouraging. The task of restoration may seem impossible and shake the confidence of the embalmer. This is the time for intestinal fortitude and determination. Once the formative work is begun and affected tissues are
cleaned or removed, all doubts of success vanish. It is surprising and gratifying to
discover the results which may be obtained."

The embalmer, having allowed an appropriate interval to elapse, returns to the at- 15
tack, but now he brings into play the skill and equipment of sculptor and cosmetician.
Is a hand missing? Casting one in plaster of Paris is a simple matter. "For replacement
purposes, only a cast of the back of the hand is necessary; this is within the ability of
the average operator and is quite adequate." If a lip or two, a nose or an ear should be
missing, the embalmer has at hand a variety of restorative waxes with which to model
replacements. Pores and skin texture are simulated by stippling with a little brush, and
over this cosmetics are laid on. Head off? Decapitation cases are rather routinely handled. Ragged edges are trimmed, and head joined to torso with a series of splints, wires
and sutures. It is a good idea to have a little something at the neck—a scarf or a high
collar—when time for viewing comes. Swollen mouth? Cut out tissue as needed from
inside the lips. If too much is removed, the surface contour can easily be restored by
padding with cotton. Swollen necks and cheeks are reduced by removing tissue
through vertical incisions made down each side of the neck. "When the deceased is
casketed, the pillow will hide the suture incisions . . . as an extra precaution against
leakage, the suture may be painted with liquid sealer."

The opposite condition is more likely to present itself—that of emaciation. His 16
hypodermic syringe now loaded with massage cream, the embalmer seeks out and
fills the hollowed and sunken areas by injection. In this procedure the backs of the
hands and fingers and the under-chin area should not be neglected.

Positioning the lips is a problem that recurrently challenges the ingenuity of the 17
embalmer. Closed too tightly, they tend to give a stern, even disapproving expression. Ideally, embalmers feel, the lips should give the impression of being ever so

slightly parted, the upper lip protruding slightly for a more youthful appearance. This takes some engineering, however, as the lips tend to drift apart. Lip drift can sometimes be remedied by pushing one or two straight pins through the inner margin of the lower lip and then inserting them between the two front upper teeth. If Mr. Jones happens to have no teeth, the pins can just as easily be anchored in his Armstrong Face Former and Denture Replacer. Another method to maintain lip closure is to dislocate the lower jaw, which is then held in its new position by a wire run through holes which have been drilled through the upper and lower jaws at the midline. As the French are fond of saying, *il faut souffrir pour être belle.*

If Mr. Jones has died of jaundice, the embalming fluid will very likely turn him   18 green. Does this deter the embalmer? Not if he has intestinal fortitude. Masking pastes and cosmetics are heavily laid on, burial garments and casket interiors are color-correlated with particular care, and Jones is displayed beneath rose-colored lights. Friends will say "How well he looks." Death by carbon monoxide, on the other hand, can be rather a good thing from the embalmer's viewpoint: "One advantage is the fact that this type of discoloration is an exaggerated form of a natural pink coloration." This is nice because the healthy glow is already present and needs but little attention.

The patching and filling completed, Mr. Jones is now shaved, washed and   19 dressed. Cream-based cosmetic, available in pink, flesh, suntan, brunette and blond, is applied to his hands and face, his hair is shampooed and combed (and, in the case of Mrs. Jones, set), his hands manicured. For the horny-handed son of toil special care must be taken; cream should be applied to remove ingrained grime, and the nails cleaned. "If he were not in the habit of having them manicured in life, trimming and shaping is advised for better appearance—never questioned by kin."

Jones is now ready for casketing (this is the present participle of the verb "to   20 casket"). In this operation his right shoulder should be depressed slightly "to turn the body a bit to the right and soften the appearance of lying flat on the back." Positioning the hands is a matter of importance, and special rubber positioning blocks may be used. The hands should be cupped slightly for a more lifelike, relaxed appearance. Proper placement of the body requires a delicate sense of balance. It should lie as high as possible in the casket, yet not so high that the lid, when lowered, will hit the nose. On the other hand, we are cautioned, placing the body too low "creates the impression that the body is in a box."

Jones is next wheeled into the appointed slumber room where a few last touches   21 may be added—his favorite pipe placed in his hand or, if he was a great reader, a book propped into position. (In the case of little Master Jones, a Teddy bear may be clutched.) Here he will hold open house for a few days, visiting hours 10 A.M. to 9 P.M.

All now being in readiness, the funeral director calls a staff conference to make   22 sure that each assistant knows his precise duties. Mr. Wilber Kriege writes: "This makes your staff feel that they are a part of the team, with a definite assignment that must be properly carried out if the whole plan is to succeed. You never heard of a football coach who failed to talk to his entire team before they go on the field. They have drilled on the plays they are to execute for hours and days, and yet the successful coach knows the importance of making even the bench-warming third-string substitute feel that he is important if the game is to be won." The winning of *this* game is predicated upon glass-smooth handling of the logistics. The funeral director has notified the pallbearers whose names were furnished by the family, has arranged for the presence of clergyman, organist, and soloist, has provided transportation for everybody, has organized and listed the flowers sent by friends. In *Psychology of Funeral Service* Mr. Edward A. Martin points out: "He may not always do as much as the family thinks he is doing, but it is his helpful guidance that they appreciate in knowing they are proceeding as they should. . . . The important thing is how well his services can be used to make the family believe they are giving unlimited expression to their own sentiment."

The religious service may be held in a church or in the chapel of the funeral   23 home; the funeral director vastly prefers the latter arrangement, for not only is it more convenient for him but it affords him the opportunity to show off his beautiful facilities to the gathered mourners. After the clergyman has had his say, the mourners queue up to file past the casket for a last look at the deceased. The family is *never* asked whether they want an open-casket ceremony; in the absence of their instruction to the contrary, this is taken for granted. Consequently well over 90 per cent of all American funerals feature the open casket—a custom unknown in other parts of the world. Foreigners are astonished by it. An English woman living in San Francisco described her reaction in a letter to the writer:

> I myself have attended only one funeral here—that of an elderly fellow worker of mine. After the service I could not understand why everyone was walking towards the coffin (sorry, I mean casket), but thought I had better follow the crowd. It shook me rigid to get there and find the casket open and poor old Oscar lying there in his brown tweed suit, wearing a suntan makeup and just the wrong shade of lipstick. If I had not been extremely fond of the old boy, I have a horrible feeling that I might have giggled. Then and there I decided that I could never face another American funeral—even dead.

The casket (which has been resting throughout the service on a Classic Beauty   24 Ultra Metal Casket Bier) is now transferred by a hydraulically operated device called Porto-Lift to a balloon-tied, Glide Easy casket carriage which will wheel it to yet another conveyance, the Cadillac Funeral Coach. This may be lavender, cream, light green—anything but black. Interiors, of course, are color-correlated, "for the man who cannot stop short of perfection."

At graveside, the casket is lowered into the earth. This office, once the preroga-   25 tive of friends of the deceased, is now performed by a patented mechanical lowering device. A "Lifetime Green" artificial grass mat is at the ready to conceal the sere earth, and overhead, to conceal the sky, is a portable Steril Chapel Tent ("resists the intense heat and humidity of summer and the terrific storms of winter . . . available in Silver Grey, Rose or Evergreen"). Now is the time for the ritual scattering of earth over the coffin, as the solemn words "earth to earth, ashes to ashes, dust to dust" are pronounced by the officiating cleric. This can today be accomplished "with a mere flick of the wrist with the Gordon Leak-Proof Earth Dispenser. No grasping of a handful of dirt, no soiled fingers. Simple, dignified, beautiful, reverent! The modern way!" The Gordon Earth Dispenser (at $5) is of nickel-plated brass construction. It is not only "attractive to the eye and long wearing"; it is also "one of the 'tools' for building better public relations" if presented as "an appropriate noncommercial gift" to the clergyman. It is shaped something like a salt-shaker.

Untouched by human hand, the coffin and the earth are now united.   26

It is in the function of directing the participants through this maze of gadgetry   27
that the funeral director has assigned to himself his relatively new role of "grief therapist." He has relieved the family of every detail, he has revamped the corpse to look like a living doll, he has arranged for it to nap for a few days in a slumber room, he has put on a well-oiled performance in which the concept of *death* has played no part whatsoever—unless it was inconsiderately mentioned by the clergyman who conducted the religious service. He has done everything in his power to make the funeral a real pleasure for everybody concerned. He and his team have given their all to score an upset victory over death.

UNDERSTANDING THE ESSAY

1. Although Mitford is writing primarily about the funeral business, in what sense is she also writing about the culture in which the funeral business thrives?

2. Mitford quotes several people who represent the funeral business. Compare or contrast her attitude toward what they do with theirs.

3. What processes take place in funeral parlors without consultation with the people who are expected to pay for them? What is Mitford's opinion about the practice of presuming that people want these services and are willing to pay for them? Do you agree with her?

4. Why is (or isn't) Mitford's description about the embalming an essay? Does she interpret a process, or merely describe one? Does she presume the interest of her readers, or does she make efforts to create and maintain it?

5. Does Mitford reveal an attitude, or is she merely a neutral observer, a social scientist reporting facts without taking a position? Do you think other observers would have exactly the same "take" on this subject that Mitford has? Cite the passages in the text to support your answers to these questions.

So What and the Seven Common Moves.   Analyze this essay with the help of the questions about "So What and the Seven Common Moves" found on the back cover of this book.

Words, Phrases, and Allusions. The following items were taken from "The American Way of Death" in order of appearance. With the help of your classmates, locate these words in the essay and see if their context provides a clue to their meaning. If necessary, consult a dictionary, an encyclopedia, or other reference work to determine what each item means in its context. You probably know most of these words from conversation and reading, but you may not yet feel comfortable using them in your own writing.

> Yorick, trussed, eccentric, dispensed, cremated, decedent's, bereaved, mortician, docility, perpetuation, mandatory, dissuaded, intractable, reticence, raison d'être, patrons, loath, the formaldehyde curtain, reposing, scalpels, augers, forceps, array, distend, cadaver, disfigurements, elapses, rudimentary, somatic, dispel, carotid artery, femoral artery, jugular vein, subclavian vein, pliable, glycerin, borax, phenol, trocar, entrails, semblance, unmarred, ravages, elapse, stippling, casketed, suture, emaciation, syringe, ingenuity, *il faut souffrir pour être belle,* jaundice, casket, discoloration, queue, hydraulically, prerogative, sere, cleric, revamped

Suggestion for Writing

Using "The American Way of Death" as a model, write an essay explaining an institutional process that you happen to know and understand. The journal entry suggested at the beginning of this selection may have given you an idea for a topic, or you may have thought of other topics as you read Mitford's essay.

RECIPES FOR PROCESS WRITING

A. Writing from Personal Experience

A process *paper* has a very practical objective: it explains how something is done. A process *essay* has a different purpose: it *interprets* the process, gives the writer's "take" on it, reveals an attitude.

Here is a recipe for process writing:

1. Choose a process that you understand better than most of your readers do.
2. If the process occurs in a set sequence of steps (e.g., baking a cake, changing a tire), create an outline by naming the steps and arranging them in the right sequence.
3. If the process is one that does not necessarily occur in a set sequence of steps (e.g., winning at chess, succeeding in college), create an outline by naming the necessary activities and arranging them in a sequence that will best maintain the interest of your readers.

4. If your purpose is just to explain the process, expand each step into a sentence, a paragraph, or a few paragraphs—depending on how complex the step is. Be sure to define any terms that may not be clear to your readers.

5. If your purpose is to *interpret* the process, describe each step in a way that makes your readers feel, understand, or believe what you want them to feel, understand, or believe about it.

6. After you've selected and arranged parts of the process, add an introduction and an ending.

7. Show a draft to fellow students in a formal or informal workshop, and see if your strategies are having the effects you want them to have. Use the checklist on the back cover to focus your discussion. Then look for errors in spelling, grammar, or punctuation that you will want to correct in your final draft.

B. Writing against the Text

A process *paper* is usually hard to disagree with—unless, of course, the writer doesn't really know how to go about showering with a dog or about how certain animals can generate new organs. A process *essay*, however, always leaves room for disagreement. For example, while many people would find useful advice in Kurt Vonnegut's essay on how to write, some might take issue with his assumption that newspaper reporters and technical writers should reveal their individuality in their prose. Similarly, not everyone sees the funeral industry with quite the same critical eye through which Jessica Mitford sees it. Choose a process essay with room for disagreement, summarize the essay, and then show how and why you disagree.

C. Writing from Research

Using the library and the Web, locate information about a process that interests you. It could be a natural process (e.g., how mountains or canyons are formed, or how the sun produces energy), or a sociological process (e.g., how various churches or political parties evolved or how the Internet is managed). Choose a process that has some mystery to it, or at least some practical application, so that both you and your readers will be interested in your explanation of it. After you've completed your research, write a draft in your own words without consulting your sources; this will help you avoid being overwhelmed by what you read and perhaps unintentionally plagiarizing material. Then go back and add material from your research wherever you think it will make your paper more interesting or authoritative. Be sure to acknowledge the source of anything you quote or paraphrase.

5

Significant Differences:
Comparison and Contrast

A famous basketball coach once revealed the secret of his success. It was a method of teaching based on an incredibly simple pattern. "Do this," he would tell his players, demonstrating the move he wanted them to make, "not this," demonstrating the move he wanted them to stop making. In teaching this way, he was recognizing one of the most basic of all human thought processes: learning what something is by recognizing what it isn't. In fact, it is the act that marks the beginning of our individual self-consciousness—when as infants we begin to notice that there is a difference between what's us and what's not-us.

Comparing and contrasting are ways of seeing things. Like all the other modes and methods of development, they are universal ways of framing our experience. In conversation, they generally occur in short units; but in writing, they can frame a phrase, a sentence, or even, paragraph, or even an entire essay. You may have already noticed compact comparison in similes and metaphors, like the one Ernie Pyle used (p. 14) to describe the litter on the beach at Normandy ("It extends in a thin little line, just like a high-water mark, for miles along the beach"), or the one Annie Dillard used (p. 23) to describe the shadows on a mountainside ("they elongate like root tips, like lobes of spilling water"). You may have noticed contrast in the essay on clog dancing (p. 27), where David Foster Wallace says that clog dancers dance as a team, not like some other dancers: "they do it as a troupe, a collective, with none of the narcissistic look-at-me grandstanding of great dancers in rock clubs." Or you may have noticed it in the essay on Jackie Robinson, where Mike Royko mentions that some people were wearing, not one kind of clothes, but another kind: "They didn't wear baseball-game clothes. They had on church clothes and funeral clothes—suits, white shirts, ties, gleaming shoes, and straw hats" (p. 41).

In this chapter, you will see how comparison and contrast can frame an entire essay. But comparing and contrast are never sufficient in themselves to make an essay interesting. OK, so grass is green and the sky is blue. So what? And New York is big and your home town is small. Who cares? Differences and similarities become interesting only when we discover meaning in them, something that makes them worth noticing and knowing about—a so-what factor.

Once you find two things with differences or similarities that you care about, your next task is to arrange them in a pattern that makes sense. The most obvious pattern—though not necessarily the most effective—is AAA/BBB. Some people call this a "block pattern." First you say everything you have to say about one term (apples, for example), and then everything you have to say about the second term (say, bananas). This can be an effective structure, but it has one inherent weakness: it separates the points of comparison and contrast, possibly making them less striking.

Normally it is more effective to switch back and forth from one term to the other—first saying something about the taste of apples, then something about the taste of bananas; then something about the cost of apples, then something about the cost of bananas. This would be the A/B A/B A/B pattern (an "alternating" pattern), the pattern that Bruce Catton follows in one of the most famous of all comparison and contrast essays, his portrait of two Civil War generals, Grant and Lee (see pp. 111–113). One advantage of this pattern is that it puts similarities and differences right next to each other, making the points of contrast or comparison more vivid.

There is no single "right" way to organize a comparison/contrast paper. The important thing is to arrange the As and Bs in whatever sequence you think will best maintain your reader's interest. Sometimes it can be effective to follow a mixed pattern: a few paragraphs of A/B A/B followed by a passage of AAA/BBB. Sometimes it makes sense to compare one thing (an apple, for example), not with just one contrasting thing, but with a lot of contrasting things—with bananas, cherries, strawberries, peaches, pears and any other fruit that is significantly different from apples. And sometimes you can develop characteristics of just one of the terms, assuming that your readers know the other term so well that they do not need to be told how different it is. "On the moon," you might say, "the average person could leap over a seven-foot wall." You don't have to tell us that this is impossible on earth. It goes without saying.

Journal Entry. Think of a pair of things you happen to know better than most people in your class: two jobs, two colleges, two people, two places, two kinds of anything at all. The trick is to choose similarities or differences that will be interesting to your readers—perhaps even surprising. Street gangs and college fraternities, for example, are obviously different; so pointing out their similarities— that they both have initiation rituals, they both have secret symbols, they both serve as surrogate families—may make for an interesting paper.

On the other hand, lots of things have so many similarities that people tend to lump them together—like the two Carolinas, or two baseball teams, or a pair of identical twins. Pointing out the differences might be an interesting tactic. Or you could write a "things-just-aren't-what-they-used-to-be" essay—an essay comparing any aspect of today's world (your former high school, for example) with the way it used to be, the point being that things have gotten much better or much worse, much tougher or much easier.

After you've picked out some significant similarities or differences, read the following essay in which Marie Winn contrasts childhood in the past with childhood as she sees it now. It is not just a list of differences; it's a list of surprising and alarming differences, differences that mean, described in such a way that you are not likely to forget them. You may not agree entirely with Winn's perspective, but that's beside the point. The point is to see if you can use some of her technique as a writer to develop a compelling comparison and contrast essay of your own.

Something Has Happened

Marie Winn

Once upon a time, a fictional twelve-year-old from New England named Lolita Haze slept with a middle-aged European intellectual named Humbert Humbert and profoundly shocked American sensibilities. It was not so much the idea of an adult having sexual designs on a child that was appalling. It was Lolita herself, unvirginal long before Humbert came upon the scene. Lolita, so knowing, so jaded, so unchildlike, who seemed to violate something America held sacred. The book was banned in Boston. Even a sophisticated book reviewer of the New York Times called Nabokov's novel "repulsive" and "disgusting."

No more than a single generation after *Lolita*'s publication, Nabokov's vision of American childhood seems prophetic. There is little doubt that schoolchildren of the 1980s are more akin to Nabokov's nymphet than to those guileless and innocent creatures with their shiny Mary Janes and pigtails, their scraped knees and trusting ways, that were called children not so long ago.

Something has happened to the joys of childhood. The child of a generation   3
ago, observes the satirical magazine *National Lampoon*, spent his typical Saturday afternoon "climbing around a construction site, jumping off a garage roof and onto an old sofa, having a crabapple war, mowing the lawn." The agenda for today's child, however, reads: "Sleep late, watch TV, tennis lesson, go to shopping mall and buy albums and new screen for bong, play electronic WW II, watch TV, get high." The bulging pockets of the child of the past are itemized: "knife, compass, 36¢, marble, rabbit's foot." The contemporary tot's pocket, on the other hand, contains "hash pipe, PopRocks, condom, $20.00, 'ludes, Merits."

Something has happened to the limits of childhood. An advertisement for a   4
new line of books called "Young Adult Books" defines a young adult as a person facing the problems of adulthood. The books, however, which deal with subjects such as prostitution, divorce, and rape, are aimed at readers between the ages of ten and thirteen, "persons" who were formerly known as children.

Something has happened to the image of childhood. A full-page advertisement in   5
a theatrical newspaper showing a sultry female wearing dark lipstick, excessive eye-shadow, a mink coat, and possibly nothing else bears the legend: "Would you believe I'm only ten?" We believe it. For beyond the extravagances of show business lies the evidence of a population of normal, regular children, once clearly distinguishable as little boys and little girls, who now look and act like little grown-ups.

Something has happened to blur the formerly distinct boundaries between   6
childhood and adulthood, to weaken the protective membrane that once served to shelter children from precocious experience and sorrowful knowledge of the adult world. All over the country newly single mothers are sitting down with their children and making what has come to be known as The Speech: "Look, things are going to have to be different. We're all in this together and we're going to have to be partners." Things truly are different for great numbers of children today as the traditional, hierarchical structure of the family in which children are children and parents are adults is eroded and new partnerships are forged.

What's going on with children today? Is everything happening too soon? There   7
is nothing wrong with sex, the modern adult has come to understand, but what about sex at age twelve? Marijuana and alcohol are common social accessories in today's society, but is sixth grade the right time to be introduced to their gratification? Should nine-year-olds have to worry about homosexuality? Their parents hardly knew the word until their teens. Lassitude, indifference, cynicism, are understand-able defenses against the hardships of modern adult life, but aren't these states anti-thetical to childhood? Shouldn't these kids be out at the old fishing hole or playing with their dolls or stamp albums instead of reading *Screw* and *Hustler*, or flicking the TV dial to see what's playing, just like weary adults after a hard day's work? Should childhood be special and different?

We are at the beginning of a new era, and like every time of transition from one ⁸ way of thinking to another, ours is characterized by resistance, anxiety, and no small amount of nostalgia for those familiar landmarks that most contemporary adults still recall from their own "old-era" childhoods. And yet the change has occurred so swiftly that most adults are hardly aware that a true conceptual and behavioral revolution is underway, one that has yet to be clearly defined and understood. At the heart of the matter lies a profound alteration in society's attitude towards children. Once parents struggled to preserve children's innocence, to keep childhood a carefree gold age, and to shelter children from life's vicissitudes. The new era operates on the belief that children must be exposed early to adult experience in order to survive in an increasingly complex and uncontrollable world. The Age of Protection has ended. An Age of Preparation has set in.

Every aspect of contemporary children's lives is affected by this change in the ⁹ way adults think about children. Indeed, it is a change as consequential as the transformation in thinking and behaving that occurred at the end of the Middle Ages. Not until then was childhood recognized as a distinct entity and children perceived as special creatures with special needs, not miniature versions of adults. Today's integration of children into adult life marks a curious return to that old, undifferentiated state of affairs in which childhood and adulthood were merged into one.

To be sure, today's changed approach to children did not result from some de- ¹⁰ liberate adult decision to treat kids in a new way; it developed out of necessity. For children's lives are always a mirror of adult life. The great social upheavals of the late 1960s and 1970s—the so-called sexual revolution, the women's movement, the proliferation of television in American homes and its larger role in child rearing and family life, the rampant increase in divorce and single parenthood, political disillusionment in the Vietnam and post-Vietnam era, a deteriorating economic situation that propels more mothers into the work force—all these brought about changes in adult life that necessitated new ways of dealing with children.

No single societal change, however important, can account for the end of a ¹¹ centuries-old conviction about childhood and the emergence of a brave new relationship between adults and children. It was the confluence of all these changes at one time, acting upon each other and upon society as a whole, that helped to alter long-established patterns within the course of a single decade. Only with the rise in two-career families and only with the mounting divorce rate, two factors to come up again and again in the course of this discussion, did parents have cause to withdraw their close, protective attention from children. Only with the fascinating presence of television in every home, mesmerizing and sedating normally unpredictable and demanding children, was the actual decrease in adult attention and supervision made possible. The conjunction occurred in the 1960s. Suddenly the idea of childhood as a special and protected condition came to seem inadvisable if not actually dangerous, and in any event, quite impossible to maintain.

Which came first, the unchildlike child or the unprotecting adult? There is an in- ¹² tricate interconnection to be found between society's underlying concepts of childhood and children's perceivable behavior. A circular pattern always comes into view. For instance, as today's children impress adults with their sophisticated ways, adults begin to change their ideas about children and their needs; that is, they form new conceptions of childhood. Why, these tough little customers don't require protection and careful nurture! No longer need adults withhold information about the harsh realities of life from children. No longer need they hide the truth about their own weaknesses. Rather, they begin to feel it is their duty to prepare children for the exigencies of modern life. However, as adults act less protectively (not entirely as a reaction to the seeming worldliness of their children, of course, but also because of their own adult concerns, their work, their marital problems) and as they expose children to the formerly secret underside of their lives—adult sexuality, violence, injustice, suffering, fear of death—these former innocents grow tougher, perforce, less playful and trusting, more skeptical—in short, more like adults. We have come full circle. . . .

The So-What Factor.   What is novel, interesting, surprising, or moving about Marie Winn's interpretation of childhood behavior? What does she want us to understand, feel, or believe? Assuming that Winn thinks of her readers as having basically the same values as she does, you can guess what sort of reaction she hopes you will have. She hopes you will be alarmed by the unwholesome things children seem to be involved in, dismayed by the loss of the long seasons of fantasy and play and innocence that we once considered a normal part of growing up. And she hopes you share her belief that changes she disapproves of in the adult world have resulted in change in the world of children. Whether you agree with Winn or not, the so-what factor of her essay is easy enough to grasp: Unless we do something to prevent children from rushing headlong into troubled adulthood, the fictional Lolita of the first paragraph will be an ordinary factual norm, not an exception.

What opposing forces of good and evil provide the basis for Winn's interpretation? Do you share Winn's alarm about the differences between what childhood once was and what it seems to have become? Why or why not? What sort of people benefit from the advertising attached to the TV shows Winn laments?

Are Winn's generalizations about children universally valid in all segments of American society today? Are there any groups in America for whom childhood is still a protected state? Are there any groups for whom early adulthood has been a historical fact, long before the cultural changes Winn describes? Are there any advantages to early adulthood for society or for individual children? In paragraph 10 Winn lists the "sexual revolution, the women's movement, the proliferation of television, . . . the rampant increase in divorce and single parenthood, political disillusionment in the Vietnam and post-Vietnam era, [and] a deteriorating economic situation that propels more mothers into the work force" as primary culprits. Do you agree? Are these all bad things? Can you think of any other causes for the exploitation of children and their premature adulthood (poverty, for example, or the willingness of commercial interests to target children as consumers or to exploit them as advertising icons)? Using evidence from personal experience or common knowledge, write an essay in which you offer a different interpretation of the differences between the way childhood once was and the way it is now.

Do you accept all of Winn's historical generalizations? What evidence does she offer for the assertion that "Not until then [the end of the Middle Ages] was childhood recognized as a distinct entity and children perceived as special creatures with special needs, not miniature versions of adults"? Were there other times and other cultures in which children were regarded as children before the end of the Middle Ages in Europe? Were there other times and other cultures in which children became adults early on? In frontier America, for example, or during the Great Depression? Find as many sources as you can in your library and write a documented paper that either supports or contests Winn's sense of the history of childhood.

THE SEVEN COMMON MOVES

1. Beginning. Winn's first paragraph is a combination of several moves writers often make to create interest at the beginning of an essay:

It tells a story that embodies the problem of the essay as a whole.
It is an allusion—in this case, it alludes to a once-famous novel.
It relies on shock value, announcing the sexual exploits of a twelve-year-old
    girl—a move not unlike the sort of headlines you see on tabloids as you
    check out of a supermarket.

This last quality—the shock value of the story—could be considered sleazy if, as normally happens in the tabloids, it merely titillates or actually misleads the reader. In this case, however, Winn seems to think the story is entirely appropriate: what was once a scandalous fiction, she argues, has become a commonplace reality.

2. Ending. In the final paragraph, Winn makes two moves that writers often make to bring an essay to a close: she summarizes what she has said before; and she ends with a sentence that, in context, is a zinger ("We have come full circle."). The "circle" reminds us of the circular process Winn describes—adults expecting children to be more like adults, and then treating them more like adults because they act that way, until finally there is very little left of childhood. We have come full circle in another sense, a historical sense, returning to the Middle Ages' concept of children as miniature adults. And by saying we have come full circle, Winn suggests that we have gone back to the beginning of her essay, where in fact we find the disturbing story of Nabokov's Lolita.

3. Detail. The meat of this essay is the imagery—words that appeal to the imagination, showing rather than merely telling the differences between then and now. Mary Janes (shoes with a single strap across an open top, once popular among little girls), pigtails, scraped knees, fishing holes, dolls, stamp collections, crabapple wars and a rabbit's foot are among the images Winn uses to evoke a vanishing past;

TV, electronic games, drug paraphernalia, and pornographic magazines are among the images she uses to evoke an alarming present. Try to conjure up concrete, specific images of this sort to convey what you consider to be the significant similarities or differences that are the subject of your next paper.

   4. Organization/Plot. "Something Has Happened" is unusual in that it includes lots of traditional paragraphs—paragraphs with topic sentences followed by examples. Topic sentences are effective as organizing devices, but they are also effective as plotting devices—techniques for creating suspense. They announce generalizations—sometimes even vague ones, as in "Something has happened"—and these generalizations make readers curious, make them want to read on for substantiating details. Paragraph 3 is a good example. Notice that Winn uses what we described as the A/B, A/B structure—in which the differences are placed right next to each other for emphasis. She weaves from old-style childhood to new-style childhood and back again:

   Topic Sentence: Something has happened to the joys of childhood.

A. Old-Style Childhood	B. New-Style Childhood
The child of a generation ago, observes the satirical magazine *National Lampoon*, spent his typical Saturday afternoon "climbing around a construction site, jumping off a garage roof and onto an old sofa, having a crabapple war, mowing the lawn."	The agenda for today's child, however, reads: "Sleep late, watch TV, tennis lesson, go to shopping mall and buy albums and new screen for bong, play electronic WW II, watch TV, get high."
The bulging pockets of the child of the past are itemized: "knife, compass, 36¢, marble, rabbit's foot."	The contemporary tot's pocket, on the other hand, contains "hash pipe, PopRocks, condom, $20.00, 'ludes, Merits."

   The As and Bs are distributed fairly evenly in this passage; but if you were to continue this analysis, you would discover that they are distributed unevenly throughout the essay. This is normal in mature writing. The writer assumes that the reader is more familiar with one term than with the other, and so the unfamiliar term gets more attention. Winn gives us a few reminders of what childhood used to be—pigtails and pocket knives and crabapple wars; but then she focuses our attention on what she sees as the concerns of modern childhood—prostitution, divorce, rape, pornography, drugs—assuming that we'd know without being told that children did not have to worry about these things in the past as she remembers it.

   On a larger scale, the paragraphs are arranged in a way that gains and sustains the reader's attention. Winn gains her reader's attention with the Lolita story in the first two paragraphs. Then she elaborates on the problem in vivid detail in paragraphs 3 through 6. Paragraph 7 provides a transition from problem to analysis. Paragraphs 8 through 11 provide the analysis. Paragraph 11 reviews the analysis and drives home the significance of Winn's argument. Notice how Winn uses extra white space between several paragraphs to divide her essay into four sections (between paragraphs 2 and 3, 6 and 7, 11 and 12).

5. *Style.* The longest sentence in "Something Has Happened" is a classic "periodic sentence"—a long sentence in which the possibility of a period is delayed until the very end. Here it is, broken up to help you see its structure:

> The great social upheavals of the late 1960s and 1970s
> —the so-called sexual revolution,
> the women's movement,
> the proliferation of television in American homes and its larger role in child rearing and family life,
> the rampant increase in divorce and single parenthood,
> political disillusionment in the Vietnam and post-Vietnam era,
> a deteriorating economic situation that propels more mothers into the work force—
> all these brought about changes in adult life that necessitated new ways of dealing with children.

Even though this sentence is very long, it is not particularly difficult to read because it is structured in neat, parallel phrases. Periodic sentences can sound "rhetorical"—they sound like someone really getting worked up about a topic. For more information about this stylistic move, see Sentence Exercises, p. 288.

But short sentences can have lots of power, too. The shortest sentence in this essay has only three words: "We believe it." Locate that sentence (in paragraph 5) and see how context can transform a seemingly ordinary sentence into a zinger. Look for other short sentences in the essay, and notice how they acquire force from their contexts.

Several other stylistic moves Winn makes have traditional names. One of the most powerful moves she makes is called anaphora: a series of phrases beginning with the same word. It is a highly charged rhetorical figure—the verbal equivalent of pointing a finger in someone's face to punctuate a series of parallel points. One example of anaphora occurs in the first sentences of paragraphs three through six:

> Something has happened . . .
> Something has happened . . .
> Something has happened . . .
> Something has happened . . .

Other examples include the repetition of "Only with the . . ." in paragraph 11 and "No longer need . . ." in paragraph 12.

6. *Voice/Attitude.* Winn uses a number of voices, some of them fairly dripping with attitude. One voice might be described as "intimate," the sort of voice Winn imitates when she has us imagine an imaginary conversation between a mother and her child:

"Look, things are going to have to be different. We're all in this together and we're going to have to be partners."

In another place, she sounds sarcastic:

"Why, these tough little customers don't require protection and careful nurture!"

The sarcasm actually starts in the opening lines: "Once upon a time," Winn begins, as if she were telling a fairy tale, inviting us just for a second to read on with the innocent eyes of children; only the tale turns out to be the shocking behavior of a twelve-year-old girl, whom she describes in the next paragraph as a "nymphet." A nymph is, literally, a minor goddess of woods and streams in classical mythology; but in modern English, "nymphet" suggests a young woman of loose morals, a nymphomaniac. Winn employs the word "nymphet"—a little nymph—to show her disdain for Lolita and her kind.

At times Winn's voice would be appropriate in a formal speech or sermon, and her passion for her subject is also apparent in her word choice. It would be hard to find even a single sentence with the sort of detached neutrality you would find on the front page of a serious newspaper. Instead, a judgmental attitude is packed in everywhere: approval expressed in words like "sacred," "guileless," and "innocent," and disapproval expressed in words like "appalling," "unvirginal," "jaded," "repulsive," and "disgusting."

Words that convey attitude, either positive or negative, are considered "charged." They are traditionally avoided in writing that pretends to be scholarly or objective, but we do expect to find them in essays—writing about beliefs we want others to share.

7. Economy. What do Mary Janes, and crabapple wars, and a rabbit's foot have to do with the purpose of the essay? Why does Winn mention magazines like *Screw* and *Hustler*? Would the essay be improved or worsened without these details? Pick other details at random and see if you can discover their purpose.

Moves within Moves. The dominant mode of Winn's essay is comparison and contrast—mainly pointing out significant differences. But if you look closely, you will see that this essay—like all the others in this book—includes some of the other modes and methods of development that are treated as separate chapters. The essay as a whole is a series of examples. As you will see in chapter 9, examples—or "likely stories"—can be very persuasive forms of evidence. In this case, the persuasiveness of Winn's essay depends to some extent on whether you, the reader, consider her examples "likely" or sufficiently typical of contemporary childhood.

Another method of development in this essay is cause-and-effect analysis (see chapter 7). Winn argues that alarming changes in the nature of childhood are caused by changes in adult behavior—particularly by changes in the ways adults think about children, by the sexual revolution, the women's movement, television, and a number of other causes listed in paragraphs 9 through 12.

Winn also uses narration (see chapter 3) in paragraph 1 and description (see chapter 2) in paragraph five. The essay could also be considered both definition (see chapter 8) and persuasion (see chapter 10)—an attempt to argue what childhood is or ought to be.

Words, Phrases, and Allusions. The following items were taken from "Something Has Happened" in order of appearance. With the help of your classmates, locate these words in the essay and see if their context provides a clue to their meaning. If necessary, consult a dictionary, an encyclopedia, or other reference work to determine what each item means in its context. You probably know most of these words from conversation and reading, but you may not yet feel comfortable using them in your own writing.

sensibilities, designs, appalling, jaded, sophisticated, nymphet, guileless, satirical, contemporary, sultry, hierarchical, eroded, forged, gratification, lassitude, indifference, antithetical, nostalgia, vicissitudes, consequential, undifferentiated, proliferation, disillusionment, mesmerizing, exigencies

Suggestion for Writing

Using "Something Has Happened" as a model, describe and interpret the differences between two things you know well. The journal entry suggested in the introduction to the essay might provide you with a subject worth developing, but you may have thought of other topics as you read "Something Has Happened."

"Help Me, God. I'm a Girl."

Myra Sadker and David Sadker

"Suppose you woke up tomorrow and found you were a member of the other sex. How would your life be different?" During the past decade we have posed that question to hundreds of students across the country. The question fascinates them; their answers reveal the value they place on each gender as well as on themselves.

Girls' reactions run the gamut when it comes to changing their gender. Many would rather stay girls. As an eleven-year-old said, "Being female is what I'm all about. It would be confusing to be a boy." Still, girls are intrigued at the thought of becoming boys, at least for a little while. "I don't think being a boy would be that bad," said twelve-year-old Hannah. "I would not want to be a boy permanently, but I would like to try it for a week to see how it feels. If I liked it, I would stay longer."

Other girls embrace their new roles enthusiastically; they see many advantages. "When I grow up, I will be able to be almost anything I want, including governor and president of the United States," wrote twelve-year-old Dana. "People will listen to what I have to say and will take me seriously. I will have a secretary to do things for me. I will make more money now that I am a boy." Anita said, "I would feel sort of more on top. I guess that's what a lot of boys feel."

For boys the thought of being female is appalling, disgusting, and humiliating; it is completely unacceptable. "If I were a girl, my friends would treat me like dirt," said a sixth-grade boy from a rural school. "My teachers would treat me like a little hairy pig-headed girl," said Michael from an urban classroom. The essays of desperate horror continue:

"If I was a girl, I would scream. I would duck behind corners so no one would   5
see me."

"I would hide and never go out until after dark."   6

Many choose the final exit: "If I were turned into a girl today, I would kill my-   7
self."

Between 1988 and 1990, almost eleven hundred children in Michigan wrote   8
essays about what life would be like if they experienced a gender change. Forty-
two percent of the girls found many good things to say about being male: They
would feel more secure and less worried about what other people thought, they
would be treated with more respect, they looked forward to earning more money at
better jobs. Ninety-five percent of the 565 boys saw no advantage at all to being female. Only 28 boys saw any benefits. Some of the reasons offered by this 5 percent were sincere. They talked about not being punished as much, getting better
grades, not needing to pay for dates, and not getting hurt in fights. But the advantages were often phrased as stereotypic putdowns: "crying to get out of paying traffic tickets" and getting out of trouble by "turning on the charm and flirting my way
out of it."

Sixteen percent of the Michigan boys wrote about fantasy escapes from their   9
female bodies, with suicide the most frequent getaway selection:

"I would *kill* myself *right away* by setting myself on fire so no one knew."   10

"I'd wet the bed, then I'd throw up. I'd probably go crazy and kill myself."   11

"And I would never wake up again and would be heading over to the cemetery   12
right now and start digging."

"If I woke up tomorrow as a girl, I would stab myself in the heart fifty times   13
with a dull butter knife. If I were still alive, I would run in front of a huge semi in
eighteenth gear and have my brains mashed to Jell-O. *That would do it.*"

"No cat liked me. No dog. No animal in the world. I did not like myself."   14

When we analyzed the hundreds of essays students wrote in response to our   15
question, we found similar themes. Boys took imaginative, desperate measures to
get out of being girls. A twelve-year-old wrote: "To have my boy body I would
walk off a cliff. I would bungee jump without a bungee cord off the tallest mountain." Stephen, also twelve, said he would "walk around the world on hot coals,"
and Jesse offered to "jump out of a plane into a glass of milk to get my boy body
back."

As girls move into adolescence, being popular with boys becomes overwhelm-   16
ingly important, the key to social success. They look to males for esteem, hoping to
see approval and affirmation in their eyes. But if the attitudes expressed in the male
stories of gender changing are any measure, girls are seeking comfort in a carnival
mirror, one sending back an image so grotesque and misshapen that its distortion is
startling. Although we have read hundreds of boys' stories about waking up as a
girl, we remain shocked at the degree of contempt expressed by so many. If the students were asked to consider waking up as a member of a different religious, racial,
or ethnic group, would rejection be phrased with such horror and loathing?

When we talked with students about these essays, we tried to understand why   17
the boys made such disparaging comments about girls, why their stories were
marked by such jolting themes of revulsion. Part of the reason appeared to lie in
boys' perception of the female body as fragile, limited, and incompetent, especially
in athletics and sports. More than one in four elementary school boys regard athletics as the best thing about being male, and almost three-quarters dream about being
sports stars when they grow up. Twenty-eight percent say their first career choice is
to become an athlete or a sports star. One regret that repeatedly emerged in fifth-
and sixth-grade boys' essays of gender change was loss of the ability to play sports.
Boys said: "Being a girl sucks. Now instead of basketball I have to play boring
jump rope." "Now that I'm a girl, they won't let me play football. But I'll play it
anyway. I'll play in a dress if I have to." Eleven-year-old Keith told how becoming
female meant losing the most important fantasy of his life: "So many times I wish I
was still a boy because of all my dreams to become a baseball player. But now
they've perished into the night, and I'm just a little old bag lady sitting in a card-
board box. And whenever I go to a baseball game I cry my eyes out because my
dreams have been lost forever."

While a female body represents loss of sports, a male body means access. Fifth-   18
and sixth-grade girls who imagined they had turned into boys said: "People would
call me slugger instead of sweetie." "When the boys play ball, they never pass to
the girls, but if I was a boy, I would probably get the ball thrown to me all the time."
"At school the boys would say 'Nice shot' if I scored a goal and not 'Ewwwww,
busted by a girl.'" "I would get to play with a *real* basketball instead of a *beach* ball
like girls in our class use now."

With boy bodies some of the girls allowed themselves a new dream, that of be-   19
coming a professional sports star. In her essay, "Cool, I'm a Boy!" sixth grader
Maddy said, "I've always wanted to be a boy so I could play Professional hockey."
And twelve-year-old Melissa wrote: "I feel that being a girl is fun and I love it, but
if I were a boy, I could fulfill my dream to become a star in the NBA."

As middle school students grow older, the focus on sports ability broadens to a   20
more general admiration for boys' physical advantages. Twenty-one percent of
boys and 34 percent of girls chose physical advantage as the reason boys were
lucky. In contrast, both boys (21 percent) and girls (41 percent) considered physical
characteristics to be disadvantageous.

Even the sense of being attractive, fundamental to female self-esteem, is dimin-   21
ished during middle school. In elementary school 31 percent of white girls said they
always liked the way they looked. This feeling of being pretty took a 20-point dive
to 11 percent in middle school; in high school it remained level as only 12 percent
said they were satisfied with their appearance. Between elementary and middle
school, pride in appearance took a 26-point plunge for Hispanic girls, from 47 percent to 21 percent. Another 10-point drop occurred between middle school and high
school when only 11 percent of Hispanic girls always liked the way they looked.

While African-American girls took more pride in their appearance, they also expressed more concern about pregnancy.

For girls, adolescence means pregnability. For some, menstruation is a moment   22
of triumph, a signal of maturity. For others, it is humiliating, even scary. Now girls
are restricted in where they are allowed to go. According to the AAUW survey, 13
percent of boys and 22 percent of girls cited personal freedom as the reason boys
were lucky. Hispanic girls were especially aware of restraint and confinement.
Twenty-eight percent said sexism or the greater freedom boys had was "a bad thing
about being a girl."

Awareness of physical changes girls go through—and the vulnerability that ac-   23
companies these developments—became the topic of discussion when we talked
about the gender-switching essays with a radically diverse and unusually forthright
eighth-grade class.

The students have just finished writing their essays. Three black males have   24
written a group rap poem instead and ask if they can say it out loud. Nelson, one of
the best-liked students in the class, ambles to the front of the room and reads what it
would be like to wake up as a girl:

> Wake up in the morning
> I'm the opposite sex.
> Look at your private parts and check,
> Sit up and cry.
> I'll do anything but die.
> Would my friends tease me?
> I have to sit down and pee.
> Oh no, I lost my hairy chest,
> And I'm stuck with a big breast.
> I'll hide my hair in my hat
> Push in my breasts so they are flat,
> I'd have to wear pink underwear
> And spend forever with gook in my hair.
> Would I like it, no or yes?
> What if I get PMS?
> Would my name be Sue or Chrissy?
> On the 28th day would I act all pissy?
> I hate playing with girls' dolls.
> Turn me back so I can have balls.

Soft-spoken and smiling, Nelson has given a humorous rather than a hostile   25
rendition, and by the end of the poem the class is laughing and clapping. The students sneak furtive glances at the teacher to catch her reaction to some of the vocabulary, but even she is smiling—although a little uneasily.

"Is this really what you think it would be like to be a girl?" we ask.   26

"Yes!" several of the boys shout, putting their thumbs skyward in a victory   27
sign.

"Being a girl can't be all bad. What are some of the advantages?" We start a list 28
on the board. Several girls shout from different parts of the room:

"Going shopping." 29

"Going to the mall." 30

"Talking on the phone." 31

"Looking gorgeous." 32

"You get to wear better clothes—boy clothes and girl clothes." 33

The initial burst of enthusiasm is over, and the room grows quiet. Then a His- 34
panic girl raises her hand and says softly, "You get to bring new life into the world.
I would never want to give that up."

No boy has yet offered an advantage, so we call on a group sitting together to- 35
ward the back of the room to name one good thing about being female. "Nothin',"
they say. "There's nothin' good at all."

"Not a single thing?" we probe. 36

"Well, you don't get into as much trouble," one boy finally volunteers. "The 37
girls just bat their eyelashes, and we get blamed for everything."

We ask for the disadvantages. This list grows more quickly, and it is much 38
longer. Both males and females contribute:

"Going through labor." 39

"Getting pregnant." 40

"Getting periods." 41

"PMS." 42

"Cooking and cleaning." 43

"Sexual harassment." 44

"Getting raped." 45

"Not getting respect." 46

"People don't pay as much attention to you." 47

"Weaker." 48

"Smaller." 49

"Not as good in sports." 50

"Can't be a professional football star." 51

"Can't be president of the United States." 52

"Sex discrimination." 53

"Don't have as much freedom." 54

"Don't have as much fun." 55

"Have to worry about your hair." 56

"Have to wear bras." 57

"High heels." 58

"Have to put on makeup." 59

"Diet all the time." 60

"Don't get as many jobs or make as much money." 61

"Have to spend all your money to look pretty." 62

"Have to go through too many changes." 63

"Did any of you write your essays about these?" we ask. An Asian boy raises 64
his hand and reads his paragraph about the work it takes to maintain the female
body: "I'd have to douche, wear tampons, shave my legs, and wear heels. I'd buy a
Thighmaster, but every day I would grow more cellulite."

Other boys laugh, but Nelson, coauthor of the rap poem, is now serious. "I 65
think the worst thing is that you're vulnerable," he volunteers. "In this school boys
are always touching girls. They bump into them in the halls and touch their behinds.
If you're a girl, you've got to worry about being sexually harassed or raped. I
couldn't stand it if people messed with me like they do with girls."

"Do you feel that way?" we asked the girls. Almost all of them nodded. "What 66
do boys do that frightens or embarrasses you?"

"They say things like 'Look at that juicy behind.'" 67

"They snap our bras in gym." 68

"Sometimes they squeeze breasts." 69

"They say mean things, like if you're not developed, they say, 'You're about as 70
curvy as that blackboard up there.'"

"They say, 'You're so fat and ugly. Get outta my face.'" 71

"They say, 'Your bra is showing.'" The blonde who volunteers this comment 72
turns beet red. "I never wore that bra again."

"Like Nelson said, they bump into us in the hallway, and they pinch us and 73
touch us."

"Did any of you write your essays about these things?" 74

The girls nod. 75

"Would you read them?" 76

Thirteen-year-old Latoya volunteers: "I think my life and relationships would 77
be totally different. People would respect me more. As it is now, I think people look
at me and see a target. I also bet my mother would let me do more on my
own—walk to my friends' houses, ride my bike where I want. She is very worried
that when older men see a young girl like me, they see an easy target."

"Let me read mine," says Charlene. She saunters to the front of the room, 78
smiles, and reads: "I wouldn't mind being a boy. I'd order *Playboy*. Knock the
shower down. Buy beer. Get a car. Have parties. Have a body-building workout.
Talk dirty. Pig out. Walk like an ape. Nobody would dare fool with me. I wouldn't
have to deal with date rape. I wouldn't mind it for a change."

Several girls laugh and cheer. Others raise their hands to read, but the bell 79
rings. As we leave, a slight girl, an immigrant from Vietnam, runs to catch up with
us. "I'm the only child in my family, and my father wishes I was a boy. I worry, but
I never have anybody to talk to. It helps to speak about these things in class. I'm
glad we did it."

UNDERSTANDING THE ESSAY

1. In most of the selections in this book, you can detect a personal voice—an individual author with an attitude. "Help Me, God. I'm a Girl" was written by two people, rather than one. Do you think this results in a lack of personal voice? Would you consider this selection an essay, or would you consider it some other kind of writing?

2. Although there may not be an individual voice expressed in this selection, is there an attitude? Do the Sadkers merely report their findings, or do they subtly suggest that they are not particularly happy about what they found?

3. In what ways does the style of this essay differ from what you normally consider scholarly writing? (You might browse through a few journals of psychology or sociology to provide a basis for comparison and contrast.) If you think these styles are different, which do you prefer?

4. Is this selection about similarities and differences, or is it about the way a particular group of people react to similarities and differences?

5. What effect do the Sadkers achieve by allowing us to hear the students describe their reactions in their own words?

So What and the Seven Common Moves.   Analyze this essay with the help of the questions about "So What and the Seven Common Moves" found on the back cover of this book.

Words, Phrases, and Allusions.   "Help Me, God. I'm a Girl." is like "Jackie's Debut" (p. 40) in that it has no extraordinary words—nothing that wouldn't be in the vocabulary of any ordinary eighth grader. This is a good thing to notice, because although good writers often do use unusual words, it's a mistake to equate good writing with a fancy vocabulary. The trick is to put exactly the right word in exactly the right place, whether it's a fancy word or a simple one.

Suggestion for Writing

Using "Help Me, God. I'm a Girl." as a model, write an essay explaining significant similarities and differences between two roles in life, two ways of experiencing the world. The journal entry suggested at the beginning of this selection may have given you an idea for a topic, or you may have thought of other topics as you read the Sadkers' essay.

Journal Entry. Pick two languages or two varieties of a single language that you know well. Make a long list of examples of things these languages have in common—or things that they do not have in common. Make a judgment about these similarities and differences. Do they mean that the two languages are equal, but different, as Kurt Vonnegut suggests in his essay on style (p. 69)? Do the differences represent that one language has the ability to grasp realities in ways that the other doesn't? Is one language more suited for literary work than the other? Would one be more effective than the other in certain specific contexts?

After you've made your judgment, assemble your lists of similarities and differences in a sequence that will maintain the interest of your readers as you express your opinion about them. When you have worked on this project for a while, read the following essay, in which Amy Tan explains the different varieties of English she finds herself using in different situations.

Mother Tongue

Amy Tan

I am not a scholar of English or literature. I cannot give you much more than per- 1
sonal opinions on the English language and its variations in this country or others.

I am a writer. And by that definition, I am someone who has always loved lan- 2
guage. I am fascinated by language in daily life. I spend a great deal of my time
thinking about the power of language—the way it can evoke an emotion, a visual
image, a complex idea, or a simple truth. Language is the tool of my trade. And I
use them all—all the Englishes I grew up with.

Recently, I was made keenly aware of the different Englishes I do use. I was 3
giving a talk to a large group of people, the same talk I had already given to half a
dozen other groups. The nature of the talk was about my writing, my life, and my
book, *The Joy Luck Club.* The talk was going along well enough, until I remembered one major difference that made the whole talk sound wrong. My mother was
in the room. And it was perhaps the first time she had heard me give a lengthy
speech, using the kind of English I have never used with her. I was saying things
like, "The intersection of memory upon imagination" and "There is an aspect of my
fiction that relates to thus-and-thus"—a speech filled with carefully wrought grammatical phrases, burdened, it suddenly seemed to me, with nominalized forms, past
perfect tenses, conditional phrases, all the forms of standard English that I had
learned in school and through books, the forms of English I did not use at home
with my mother.

Just last week, I was walking down the street with my mother, and I again 4
found myself conscious of the English I was using, and the English I do use with
her. We were talking about the price of new and used furniture and I heard myself
saying this: "Not waste money that way." My husband was with us as well, and he
didn't notice any switch in my English. And then I realized why. It's because over
the twenty years we've been together I've often used that same kind of English with
him, and sometimes he even uses it with me. It has become our language of intimacy, a different sort of English that relates to family talk, the language I grew up
with.

So you'll have some idea of what this family talk I heard sounds like, I'll quote 5
what my mother said during a recent conversation which I videotaped and then tran-
scribed. During this conversation, my mother was talking about a political gangster
in Shanghai who had the same last name as her family's, Du, and how the gangster
in his early years wanted to be adopted by her family, which was rich by comparison. Later, the gangster became more powerful, far richer than my mother's family,
and one day showed up at my mother's wedding to pay his respects. Here's what
she said in part:

"Du Yusong having business like fruit stand. Like off the street kind. He is Du 6
like Du Zong—but not Tsung-ming Island people. The local people call putong, the
river east side, he belong to that side local people. That man want to ask Du Zong
father take him in like become own family. Du Zong father wasn't look down on
him, but didn't take seriously, until that man big like become a mafia. Now important person, very hard to inviting him. Chinese way, came only to show respect,
don't stay for dinner. Respect for making big celebration, he shows up. Mean gives
lots of respect. Chinese custom. Chinese social life that way. If too important won't
have to stay too long. He come to my wedding. I didn't see, I heard it. I gone to
boy's side, they have YMCA dinner. Chinese age I was nineteen."

You should know that my mother's expressive command of English belies how 7
much she actually understands. She reads the *Forbes* report, listens to *Wall Street
Week*, converses daily with her stockbroker, reads all of Shirley MacLaine's books
with ease—all kinds of things I can't begin to understand. Yet some of my friends
tell me they understand 50 percent of what my mother says. Some say they understand 80 to 90 percent. Some say they understand none of it, as if she were speaking
pure Chinese. But to me, my mother's English is perfectly clear, perfectly natural.
It's my mother tongue. Her language, as I hear it, is vivid, direct, full of observation
and imagery. That was the language that helped shape the way I saw things, expressed things, made sense of the world.

Lately, I've been giving more thought to the kind of English my mother speaks. 8
Like others, I have described it to people as "broken" or "fractured" English. But I
wince when I say that. It has always bothered me that I can think of no way to describe it other than "broken," as if it were damaged and needed to be fixed, as if it
lacked a certain wholeness and soundness. I've heard other terms used, "limited
English," for example. But they seem just as bad, as if everything is limited, including people's perceptions of the limited English speaker.

I know this for a fact, because when I was growing up, my mother's "limited"   9
English limited *my* perception of her. I was ashamed of her English. I believed that
her English reflected the quality of what she had to say. That is, because she expressed them imperfectly her thoughts were imperfect. And I had plenty of empirical evidence to support me: the fact that people in department stores, at banks, and
at restaurants did not take her seriously, did not give her good service, pretended not
to understand her, or even acted as if they did not hear her.

My mother has long realized the limitations of her English as well. When I was   10
fifteen, she used to have me call people on the phone to pretend I was she. In this
guise, I was forced to ask for information or even to complain and yell at people
who had been rude to her. One time it was a call to her stockbroker in New York.
She had cashed out her small portfolio and it just so happened we were going to go
to New York the next week, our very first trip outside California. I had to get on the
phone and say in an adolescent voice that was not very convincing, "This is Mrs.
Tan."

And my mother was standing in the back whispering loudly, "Why he don't   11
send me check, already two weeks late. So mad he lie to me, losing me money."

And then I said in perfect English, "Yes, I'm getting rather concerned. You had   12
agreed to send the check two weeks ago, but it hasn't arrived."

Then she began to talk more loudly. "What he want, I come to New York tell   13
him front of his boss, you cheating me?" And I was trying to calm her down, make
her be quiet, while telling the stockbroker, "I can't tolerate any more excuses. If I
don't receive the check immediately, I am going to have to speak to your manager
when I'm in New York next week." And sure enough, the following week there we
were in front of this astonished stockbroker, and I was sitting there red-faced and
quiet, and my mother, the real Mrs. Tan, was shouting at his boss in her impeccable
broken English.

We used a similar routine just five days ago, for a situation that was far less hu-   14
morous. My mother had gone to the hospital for an appointment, to find out about a
benign brain tumor a CAT scan had revealed a month ago. She said she had spoken
very good English, her best English, no mistakes. Still, she said, the hospital did not
apologize when they said they had lost the CAT scan and she had come for nothing.
She said they did not seem to have any sympathy when she told them she was anx-
ious to know the exact diagnosis, since her husband and son had both died of brain
tumors. She said they would not give her any more information until the next time
and she would have to make another appointment for that. So she said she would
not leave until the doctor called her daughter. She wouldn't budge. And when the
doctor finally called her daughter, me, who spoke in perfect English—lo and be-
hold—we had assurances the CAT scan would be found, promises that a conference
call on Monday would be held, and apologies for any suffering my mother had gone
through for a most regrettable mistake.

I think my mother's English almost had an effect on limiting my possibilities in   15
life as well. Sociologists and linguists probably will tell you that a person's developing language skills are more influenced by peers. But I do think that the language

spoken in the family, especially in immigrant families which are more insular, plays a large role in shaping the language of the child. And I believe that it affected my results on achievement tests, IQ tests, and the SAT. While my English skills were never judged as poor, compared to math, English could not be considered my strong suit. In grade school I did moderately well, getting perhaps B's, sometimes B-pluses, in English and scoring perhaps in the sixtieth or seventieth percentile on achievement tests. But those scores were not good enough to override the opinion that my true abilities lay in math and science, because in those areas I achieved A's and scored in the ninetieth percentile or higher.

This was understandable. Math is precise; there is only one correct answer. Whereas, for me at least, the answers on English tests were always a judgment call, a matter of opinion and personal experience. Those tests were constructed around items like fill-in-the-blank sentence completion, such as, "Even though Tom was _____, Mary thought he was _____. And the correct answer always seemed to be the most bland combinations of thoughts, for example, "Even though Tom was shy, Mary thought he was charming," with the grammatical structure "even though" limiting the correct answer to some sort of semantic opposites, so you wouldn't get answers like, "Even though Tom was foolish, Mary thought he was ridiculous." Well, according to my mother, there were very few limitations as to what Tom could have been and what Mary might have thought of him. So I never did well on tests like that. 16

The same was true with word analogies, pairs of words in which you were supposed to find some sort of logical, semantic relationship—for example, "*Sunset* is to *nightfall* as _____ is to _____." And here you would be presented with a list of four possible pairs, one of which showed the same kind of relationship: *red* is to *stoplight, bus* is to *arrival, chills* is to *fever, yawn* is to *boring.* Well, I could never think that way. I knew what the tests were asking, but I could not block out of my mind the images already created by the first pair, "*sunset* is to *nightfall*"—and I would see a burst of colors against a darkening sky, the moon rising, the lowering of a curtain of stars. And all the other pairs of words—red, bus, stoplight, boring—just threw up a mass of confusing images, making it impossible for me to sort out something as logical as saying: "A sunset precedes nightfall" is the same as "a chill precedes a fever." The only way I would have gotten that answer right would have been to imagine an associative situation, for example, my being disobedient and staying out past sunset, catching a chill at night, which turns into feverish pneumonia as punishment, which indeed did happen to me. 17

I have been thinking about all this lately, about my mother's English, about achievement tests. Because lately I've been asked, as a writer, why there are not more Asian Americans represented in American literature. Why are there few Asian Americans enrolled in creative writing programs? Why do so many Chinese students go into engineering? Well, these are broad sociological questions I can't begin to answer. But I have noticed in surveys—in fact, just last week—that Asian students, as a whole, always do significantly better on math achievement tests than in 18

English. And this makes me think that there are other Asian-American students whose English spoken in the home might also be described as "broken" or "limited." And perhaps they also have teachers who are steering them away from writing and into math and science, which is what happened to me.

Fortunately, I happen to be rebellious in nature and enjoy the challenge of disproving assumptions made about me. I became an English major my first year in college, after being enrolled as premed. I started writing nonfiction as a freelancer the week after I was told by my former boss that writing was my worst skill and I should hone my talents toward account management.   19

But it wasn't until 1985 that I finally began to write fiction. And at first I wrote   20 using what I thought to be wittily crafted sentences, sentences that would finally prove I had mastery over the English language. Here's an example from the first draft of a story that later made its way into *The Joy Luck Club*, but without this line: "That was my mental quandary in its nascent state." A terrible line, which I can barely pronounce.

Fortunately, for reasons I won't get into today, I later decided I should envision   21 a reader for the stories I would write. And the reader I decided upon was my mother, because these were stories about mothers. So with this reader in mind—and in fact she did read my early drafts—I began to write stories using all the Englishes I grew up with: the English I spoke to my mother, which for lack of a better term might be described as "simple"; the English she used with me, which for lack of a better term might be described as "broken"; my translation of her Chinese, which could certainly be described as "watered down"; and what I imagined to be her translation of her Chinese if she could speak in perfect English, her internal language, and for that I sought to preserve the essence, but neither an English nor a Chinese structure. I wanted to capture what language ability tests can never reveal: her intent, her passion, her imagery, the rhythms of her speech and the nature of her thoughts.

Apart from what any critic had to say about my writing, I knew I had succeeded   22 where it counted when my mother finished reading my book and gave me her verdict: "So easy to read."

UNDERSTANDING THE ESSAY

1. Why does Tan seem not to want to describe her mother's English as "broken" (see paragraph 8)?
2. Why does she now seem to regret feeling "ashamed" of her mother's English (paragraph 9)?
3. Why do you suppose the hospital decided it was able to find the missing CAT scan after talking to the patient's daughter (paragraph 14)?

4. Why did Tan choose to imagine her mother as the audience for her writing (paragraph 21), and what effect did this choice have on her style?
5. Does Tan consider one variety of language inferior, or just different? If she doesn't consider one variety inferior, what other reason might she have for avoiding it in certain circumstances?

So What and the Seven Common Moves.   Analyze this essay with the help of the questions about "So What and the Seven Common Moves" found on the back cover of this book.

Words, Phrases, and Allusions.   The following items were taken from "Mother Tongue" in order of appearance. With the help of your classmates, locate these words in the essay and see if their context provides a clue to their meaning. If necessary, consult a dictionary, an encyclopedia, or other reference work to determine what each item means in its context. You probably know most of these words from conversation and reading, but you may not yet feel comfortable using them in your own writing.

> carefully wrought, nominalized forms, past perfect tenses, conditional phrases, transcribed, Shanghai, belies, *Forbes*, *Wall Street Journal*, Shirley MacLaine's books, portfolio, impeccable, CAT scan, sociologists, linguists, insular, semantic opposites, mental quandary, nascent state

Suggestion for Writing

Using "Mother Tongue" as a model, write an essay explaining significant similarities and differences between two languages or two varieties of the same language. The journal entry suggested at the beginning of this selection may have given you an idea for a topic, or you may have thought of other topics as you read Tan's essay.

Grant and Lee: A Study in Contrasts

Bruce Catton

When Ulysses S. Grant and Robert E. Lee met in the parlor of a modest house at Appomattox Court House, Virginia, on April 9, 1865, to work out the terms for the surrender of Lee's Army of Northern Virginia, a great chapter in American life came to a close, and a great new chapter began. 1

These men were bringing the Civil War to its virtual finish. To be sure, other armies had yet to surrender, and for a few days the fugitive confederate government would struggle desperately and vainly, trying to find some way to go on living now that its chief support was gone. But in effect it was all over when Grant and Lee signed the papers. And the little room where they wrote out the terms was the scene of one of the poignant, dramatic contrasts in American history. 2

They were two strong men, these oddly different generals, and they represented the strengths of two conflicting currents that, through them, had come into final collision. 3

Back of Robert E. Lee was the notion that the old aristocratic concept might somehow survive and be dominant in American life. 4

Lee was tidewater Virginia, and in his background were family culture, and tradition . . . the age of chivalry transplanted to a New World which was making its own legends and its own myths. He embodied a way of life that had come down through the age of knighthood and the English country squire. America was a land that was beginning all over again, dedicated to nothing much more complicated than the rather hazy belief that all men had equal rights, and should have an equal chance in the world. In such a land Lee stood for the feeling that it was somehow of advantage to human so- 5 ciety to have a pronounced inequality in the social structure. There should be a leisure class, backed by ownership of land; in turn, society itself should be keyed to the land as the source of wealth and influence. It would bring forth (according to this ideal) a class of men with a strong sense of obligation to the community; men who lived not to gain advantage for themselves, but to meet the solemn obligation which had been laid on them by the very fact that they were privileged. From them the country would get its leadership; to them it could look for the higher values—of thought, of conduct, of personal deportment—to give it strength and virtue.

Lee embodied the noblest elements of this aristocratic ideal. Through him, the   6
landed nobility justified itself. For four years, the Southern states had fought a desperate war to uphold the ideals for which Lee stood. In the end, it almost seemed as if the Confederacy fought for Lee; as if Lee himself was the Confederacy . . . the best thing that the way of life for which the Confederacy stood could ever have to offer. He had passed into legend before Appomattox. Thousands of tired, underfed, poorly clothed Confederate soldiers, long-since past the simple enthusiasm of the early days of the struggle, somehow considered Lee the symbol of everything for which they had been willing to die. But they could not quite put this feeling into words. If the Lost Cause, sanctified by so much heroism and so many deaths, had a living justification, its justification was General Lee.

Grant, the son of a tanner on the Western frontier, was everything Lee was not.   7
He had come up the hard way, and embodied nothing in particular except the external toughness and sinewy fiber of the men who grew up beyond the mountains. He was one of a body of men who owed reverence and obeisance to no one, who were self-reliant to a fault, who cared hardly anything for the past but who had a sharp eye for the future.

These frontier men were the precise opposites of the tidewater aristocrats. Back   8
of them, in the great surge that had taken people over the Alleghenies and into the opening Western country, there was a deep, implicit dissatisfaction with a past that had settled into grooves. They stood for democracy, not from any reasoned conclusion about the proper ordering of human society, but simply because they had grown up in the middle of democracy and knew how it worked. Their society might have privileges, but they would be privileges each man had won for himself. Forms and patterns meant nothing. No man was born to anything, except perhaps to a chance to show how far he could rise. Life was competition.

Yet along with this feeling had come a deep sense of belonging to a national   9
community. The Westerner who developed a farm, opened a shop, or set up in business as a trader could hope to prosper only as his own community prospered—and his community ran from the Atlantic to the Pacific and from Canada down to Mexico. If the land was settled, with towns and highways and accessible markets, he could better himself. He saw his fate in terms of the nation's own destiny. As its horizons expanded, so did his. He had, in other words, an acute dollars-and-cents stake in the continued growth and development of his country.

And that, perhaps, is where the contrast between Grant and Lee becomes most   10
striking. The Virginia aristocrat, inevitably, saw himself in relation to his own re-

gion. He lived in a static society which could endure almost anything except change. Instinctively, his first loyalty would go to the locality in which that society existed. He would fight to the limit of endurance to defend it, because in defending it he was defending everything that gave his own life its deepest meaning.

The Westerner, on the other hand, would fight with an equal tenacity for the 11 broader concept of society. He fought so because everything he lived by was tied to growth, expansion, and a constantly widening horizon. What he lived by would survive or fall with the nation itself. He could not possibly stand by unmoved in the face of an attempt to destroy the Union. He would combat it with everything he had, because he could only see it as an effort to cut the ground out from under his feet.

So Grant and Lee were in complete contrast, representing two diametrically op- 12 posed elements in American life. Grant was the modern man emerging; beyond him, ready to come on the stage, was the great age of steel and machinery, of crowded cities and a restless, burgeoning vitality. Lee might have ridden down from the old age of chivalry, lance in hand, silken banner fluttering over his head. Each man was the perfect champion of his cause, drawing both his strengths and his weaknesses from the people he led.

Yet it was not all contrast, after all. Different as they were—in background, in 13 personality, in underlying aspiration—these two great soldiers had much in common. Under everything else, they were marvelous fighters. Furthermore, their fighting qualities were really very much alike.

Each man had, to begin with, the great virtue of utter tenacity and fidelity. Grant 14 fought his way down the Mississippi Valley in spite of acute personal discouragement and profound military handicaps. Lee hung on in the trenches at Petersburg after hope itself had died. In each man there was an indomitable quality . . . the born fighter's refusal to give up as long as he can still remain on his feet and lift his two fists.

Daring and resourcefulness they had, too; the ability to think faster and move 15 faster than the enemy. These were the qualities which gave Lee the dazzling campaigns of Second Manassas and Chancellorsville and won Vicksburg for Grant.

Lastly, and perhaps greatest of all, there was the ability, at the end, to turn 16 quickly from war to peace once the fighting was over. Out of the way these two men behaved at Appomattox came the possibility of a peace of reconciliation. It was a possibility not wholly realized, in the years to come, but which did, in the end, help the two sections to become one nation again . . . after a war whose bitterness might have seemed to make such a reunion wholly impossible. No part of either man's life became him more than the part he played in their brief meeting in the McLean house at Appomattox. Their behavior there put all succeeding generations of Americans in their debt. Two great Americans, Grant and Lee—very different, yet under everything very much alike. Their encounter at Appomattox was one of the great moments of American history.

UNDERSTANDING THE ESSAY

1. What does Bruce Catton mean when he describes Lee as a tidewater aristocrat?
2. How were Grant's personality and politics shaped by the region in which he grew up?
3. What, according to Catton, did Grant and Lee have in common?
4. How does any knowledge you bring to this essay affect your ability to share Catton's description of each general? Do you know anything about either of them that you disapprove of?
5. Grant is described as the more modern General, Lee as the more traditional. What are the limitations of Grant's modernity? What are the limitations of Lee's traditionalism?

So What and the Seven Common Moves. Analyze this essay with the help of the questions about "So What and the Seven Common Moves" found on the back cover of this book.

Words, Phrases, and Allusions. The following items were taken from "Grant and Lee" in order of appearance. With the help of your classmates, locate these words in the essay and see if their context provides a clue to their meaning. If necessary, consult a dictionary, an encyclopedia, or other reference work to determine what each item means in its context. You probably know most of these words from conversation and reading, but you may not yet feel comfortable using them in your own writing.

> virtual, poignant, aristocratic, tidewater Virginia, age of chivalry, leisure class, personal deportment, tanner, sinewy fiber, obeisance, Alleghenies, static society, tenacity, diametrically opposed, acute, indomitable

Suggestion for Writing

Using "Grant and Lee" as a model, write an essay explaining significant similarities and differences between two people with similar roles in life. The journal entry suggested at the beginning of this selection may have given you an idea for a topic, or you may have thought of other topics as you read Catton's essay.

RECIPES FOR WRITING COMPARISON/CONTRAST

A. Writing from Personal Experience

When you write a comparison and contrast essay, it's not enough just to point out similarities or differences. The Yankees play baseball and the Jets play football. So what? They are both professional teams, both located in New York. So what? Your paper will be interesting only if you find differences or similarities that strike you as odd or paradoxical, or that help you understand the subject of your essay

Here is a recipe for writing a comparison and contrast essay:

1. Choose a pair of things that you know more about than most of your readers do.
2. If the similarities between the two things are obvious, look for interesting differences; if the differences are obvious, look for interesting similarities. The key word here is *interesting*. If your paper points out only what is already obvious to your readers, it will lack a so-what factor.
3. Write the similarities and differences on note cards or separate slips of paper.
4. Arrange the cards or slips in the sequence that will best maintain the interest of your readers. Usually it is more effective to weave back and forth between the things you are comparing or contrasting rather than treating one first and then the other.
5. After you've selected and arranged your details, add an introduction and an ending.
6. Show a draft to fellow students in a formal or informal workshop, and see if your strategies are having the effects you want them to have. Use the checklist on the back cover to focus your discussion. Then look for errors in spelling, grammar, or punctuation that you will want to correct in your final draft.

B. Writing against the Text

Do not be intimidated by the appearance of objectivity in the essays in this chapter: Marie Winn's interpretation of modern childhood, for example, is arguably a bit skewed, colored by what she sees in a particular part of the country, and by what she *wants* to see. Even a great historian, like Bruce Catton, may be tempted to romanticize his famous pair of generals, to let us see them as he wants us to see them. Find room for disagreement in any essay in this chapter. Write a comparison/contrast essay of your own offering a different interpretation.

C. Writing from Research

Using the library and the Web, locate information about two people or things that have something important in common: for example, two battles (e.g., the attack on Pearl Harbor and the bombing of Hiroshima), two famous people (e.g., Washington and Jefferson), two cities (e.g., New York and Paris). Or consider one person or thing before and after a significant event: for example, London before and after the Great Fire, or American welfare policy before and after the Great Depression, or

Muhammad Ali before and after his debilitating illness. Look for similarities and differences that you find interesting. After you've completed your research, write a draft in your own words without consulting your sources; this will help you avoid being overwhelmed by what you read and perhaps unintentionally plagiarizing material. Then go back and add material from your research wherever you think it will make your paper more interesting or authoritative. Be sure to acknowledge the source of anything you quote or paraphrase.

6

Division and Classification:
A Pair of Two-Steps

"All Gaul is divided into three parts," wrote Julius Caesar in his famous memoirs about how he conquered what is now France and made it part of the Roman Empire. "Divide and conquer" was one Caesar's favorite strategies. And in fact, dividing things into parts is one of the most effective ways of conquering them intellectually, making manageable knowledge of them.

Division is often mentioned in the same breath with classification. Both are ways of framing a subject so we can study it better. Division begins with one thing (a country, a computer, a book, a company, an airplane) and mentally takes it apart. Normally, division is exhaustive; that is, it covers its subject entirely. When Caesar divided Gaul into the three parts, he didn't leave any of it out. "Classification," on the other hand, begins with many things—individual Gallic people, for example, or a random collection of books, or an assortment of fish. If Caesar had been classifying rather than dividing, he might have said something like "Every Gallic person belongs to one of three major tribes." He would have been putting individuals into categories instead of separating one thing into its parts. In general, "classifying" is putting individuals or things into conceptual pigeonholes so we can organize our knowledge about them. And in general, dividing is a form of analysis—mentally taking something apart to understand it better.

Of course, we divide and classify things in our ordinary conversation. But writing enables us to develop and expand these moves beyond what would be possible in speech. Writing, which is an invented technology every bit as artificial as a computer or a steam engine, makes it possible to divide and classify huge subjects—like all living things, or all kinds of speeches, or every known disease and cure—and store the results, so they become part of an evolving body of knowledge that can be passed on from one generation to the next.

It would be hard to exaggerate the importance of division and classification as ways of organizing knowledge. On a small scale, think how you would feel if your composition instructor returned your paper with, say, twenty or thirty individual errors marked on it. Then think how you would feel if your instructor wrote you a note explaining that those twenty or thirty errors actually fell into three categories—so that, essentially, you have only three lessons to learn, not twenty or thirty. Dividing and classifying would give you some control over information that would otherwise be unwieldy.

On a large scale, how would you manage all the knowledge in the world? A typical university is designed to do just that. A university is divided into colleges according to the different kinds of knowledge they impart. And colleges are often divided into departments—traditionally based on divisions of subject matter. And then each department divides and classifies the things it studies. Chemistry divides and classifies the numberless physical things in the universe into a fairly limited number of atomic elements. Zoology divides and classifies living things with charts that show how they are all related to one another. English divides and classifies texts. The purpose is always the same: dividing and classifying helps us conquer things mentally, helps us discover and remember relationships that would otherwise elude us. A university may not actually contain all knowledge, but it is structured according to categories in which virtually any sort of knowledge could find a place. And libraries, of course, are also designed to divide and categorize knowledge so that every sort of knowledge imaginable can be assigned to a place.

Sometimes it is hard to distinguish division from classification. For example, if we study literature as three genres (poetry, fiction, and drama), have we divided one thing, literature, into three parts, or have we classified individual works under those three headings? Something about the nature of language makes this problem impossible to solve. Normally, it really doesn't matter. And once in a while we encounter something that is interesting precisely because it refuses to be classified (a platypus, for example, or a play that is both tragic and comic) or refuses to be neatly divided (e.g., light, or a literary movement). The important thing is that taking things apart or putting them into categories generally helps us understand them better—even though every once in a while, things will refuse to be treated in this way.

Organization is a relatively easy task in division and classification papers. Once you have determined the parts or categories, start your rough draft with a "plural-noun" sentence: "There are three kinds of X"; or "Y can be divided into five parts." Then you have a choice about arranging the order of the parts or categories: sometimes, it will make more sense to arrange them in a logical or spatial order—like top to bottom, or left to right, or inside to outside, or largest to smallest, or vice versa. Sometimes, however, you may decide that the arrangement of parts or categories is not dictated by a logical or spatial sequence, and so you find the sequence you think will best maintain the interest of your readers. By the time you get to your final draft, your original plural-noun sentence may be absorbed into or replaced by a more interesting opening paragraph; but still, it is a handy device for getting your first draft underway.

After you have established the categories or named the parts, you need to say something interesting about each part or category—usually by describing each one, or by telling a story about it, or by explaining how it works, or by comparing it, or by contrasting it, or by discussing its causes or its effects, or by defining it, or by giving examples, or by proving something about them. In other words, classification and division always work in conjunction with at least one of the other conceptual moves treated as separate chapters in this book. That's why we call them a pair of two-steps: one step, dividing or classifying, is never enough to make an essay worth reading.

What Are Friends For?

Marion Winik

I was thinking about how everybody can't be everything to each other, but some people can be something to each other, thank God, from the ones whose shoulder you cry on to the ones whose half-slips you borrow to the nameless ones you chat with in the grocery line.

Buddies, for example, are the workhorses of the friendship world, the people out there on the front lines, defending you from loneliness and boredom. They call you up, they listen to your complaints, they celebrate your successes and curse your misfortunes, and you do the same for them in return. They hold out through innumerable crises before concluding that the person you're dating is no good, and even then understand if you ignore their good counsel. They accompany you to a movie with subtitles or to see the diving pig at Aquarena Springs. They feed your cat when you are out of town and pick you up from the airport when you get back. They come over to help you decide what to wear on a date. Even if it is with that creep.

What about family members? Most of them are people you just got stuck with, and though you love them, you may not have very much in common. But there is that rare exception, the Relative Friend. It is your cousin, your brother, maybe even your aunt. The two of you share the same views of the other family members. Meg never should have divorced Martin. He was the best thing that ever happened to her. You can confirm each other's memories of things that happened a long time ago. Don't you remember when Uncle Hank and Daddy had that awful fight in the middle of Thanksgiving dinner? Grandma always hated Grandpa's stamp collection; she probably left the window open during the hurricane on purpose.

While so many family relationships are tinged with guilt and obligation, a relationship with a Relative Friend is relatively worry-free. You don't even have to hide your vices from this delightful person. When you slip out Aunt Joan's back door for a cigarette, she is already there.   4

Then there is that special guy at work. Like all the other people at the job site, at first he's just part of the scenery. But gradually he starts to stand out from the crowd. Your friendship is cemented by jokes about co-workers and thoughtful favors around the office. Did you see Ryan's hair? Want half my bagel? Soon you know the names of his turtles, what he did last Friday night, exactly which model CD player he wants for his birthday. His handwriting is as familiar to you as your own.   5

Though you invite each other to parties, you somehow don't quite fit into each other's outside lives. For this reason, the friendship may not survive a job change. Company gossip, once an infallible source of entertainment, soon awkwardly accentuates the distance between you. But wait. Like School Friends, Work Friends share certain memories which acquire a nostalgic glow after about a decade.   6

A Faraway Friend is someone you grew up with or went to school with or lived in the same town as until one of you moved away. Without a Faraway Friend, you would never get any mail addressed in handwriting. A Faraway Friend calls late at night, invites you to her wedding, always says she is coming to visit but rarely shows up. An actual visit from a Faraway Friend is a cause for celebration and binges of all kinds. Cigarettes, Chips Ahoy, bottles of tequila.   7

Faraway Friends go through phases of intense communication, then may be out of touch for many months. Either way, the connection is always there. A conversation with your Faraway Friend always helps to put your life in perspective: when you feel you've hit a dead end, come to a confusing fork in the road, or gotten lost in some crackerbox subdivision of your life, the advice of the Faraway Friend— who has the big picture, who is so well acquainted with the route that brought you to this place—is indispensable.   8

Another useful function of the Faraway Friend is to help you remember things from a long time ago, like the name of your seventh-grade history teacher, what was in that really good stir-fry, or exactly what happened that night on the boat with the guys from Florida.   9

Ah, the Former Friend. A sad thing. At best a wistful memory, at worst a dangerous enemy who is in possession of many of your deepest secrets. But what was it that drove you apart? A misunderstanding, a betrayed confidence, an unrepaid loan, an ill-conceived flirtation. A poor choice of spouse can do in a friendship just like that. Going into business together can be a serious mistake. Time, money, distance, cult religions: all noted friendship killers. You quit doing drugs, you're not such good friends with your dealer anymore.   10

And lest we forget, there are the Friends You Love to Hate. They call at inop- 11
portune times. They say stupid things. They butt in, they boss you around, they em-
barrass you in public. They invite themselves over. They take advantage. You've
done the best you can, but they need professional help. On top of all this, they love
you to death and are convinced they're your best friend on the planet.

So why do you continue to be involved with these people? Why do you tolerate 12
them? On the contrary, the real question is, What would you do without them?
Without Friends You Love to Hate, there would be nothing to talk about with your
other friends. Their problems and their irritating stunts provide a reliable source of
conversation for everyone they know. What's more, Friends You Love to Hate
make you feel good about yourself, since you are obviously in so much better shape
than they are. No matter what these people do, you will never get rid of them. As
much as they need you, you need them too.

At the other end of the spectrum are Hero Friends. These people are better than 13
the rest of us, that's all there is to it. Their career is something you wanted to be
when you grew up—painter, forest ranger, tireless doer of good. They have beautiful homes filled with special handmade things presented to them by villagers in the
remote areas they have visited in their extensive travels. Yet they are modest. They
never gossip. They are always helping others, especially those who have suffered a
death in the family or an illness. You would think people like this would just make
you sick, but somehow they don't.

A New Friend is a tonic unlike any other. Say you meet her at a party. In your 14
bowling league. At a Japanese conversation class, perhaps. Wherever, whenever,
there's that spark of recognition. The first time you talk, you can't believe how
much you have in common. Suddenly, your life story is interesting again, your insights fresh, your opinion valued. Your various short-comings are as yet completely
invisible.

It's almost like falling in love. 15

The So-What Factor.   What is novel, interesting, surprising, or moving about
Marion Winik's classification of friends? Do you recognize some of your own
friends in her categories? What does she want us to understand, feel, or believe after
reading her essay?

Although the essay is lighthearted, it employs the same sort of categorization
that a psychologist or a physicist or a historian or a rhetorician might use to bring
order and intelligibility to any group of things. Usually the purpose is to produce an
"aha!" reaction—a feeling that you suddenly see something clearly that had been
fuzzy at first. In this case, you may have found yourself saying, "Yes, that's right! I
have friends just like these." The so-what factor in this essay, then, is the pleasure
of seeing familiar things more clearly.

What does Winik count as a good kind of friendship as opposed to a less satisfactory kind? Do you share Winik's assumptions about the value of various kinds of friendship? Why or why not?

Are Winik's categories of friends universally valid, or do they apply merely to her friends? Would your friends fall into the same categories? Would you need to add some categories to account for some of your friends, or invent new categories that better express the nature of certain kinds of friendships?

THE SEVEN COMMON MOVES

1. Beginning. Read Winik's opening sentence aloud. Its structure rambles like a train derailed. It sounds as if Winik tried to pack in more material than a single sentence could contain, so her ideas come sputtering out like a mouthful of cookie crumbs. The inelegance of this sentence has a curious effect. "How's that again?" you might think after reading it. It doesn't really tell a story, or jump into the middle of some action, or pose a problem. It just generalizes about people in a confusing way, making you curious enough to look ahead to the next paragraph to see if you can figure out what in the world Winik is talking about.

2. Ending. Unlike many essays, this one does not end with a conclusion, a final paragraph that wraps things up. Instead, the ending is just one more item in a list of items—one more category of friends. But Winik achieves a sense of finality (and actually, a sense of new possibilities) by saving the best, the most interesting category for last. In a sense, this last category brings her discussion full circle; the ending is also a beginning. The last line—"It's almost like falling in love"—is a zinger in itself, but it is even more fun if you recognize it as an allusion to a famous love song, "Almost Like Being in Love" (from the musical *Brigadoon*).

3. Detail. In division and classification the interest is in the details. Winik makes her definitions of each category fun by illustrating them with details we might find surprising—like half-slips, and diving pigs, grandpa's stamp collection, half a bagel, Chips Ahoy, bottles of tequila. Without looking back at the text, what other details stick in your mind? Find those details and see if you can determine how Winik made it so memorable.

One of Winik's strengths as a writer is to suggest things between the lines rather than spelling them out. For example, she makes an ironic commentary on the sort of mail we receive every day when she writes, "Without a Faraway Friend, you would never get any mail addressed in handwriting." And instead of telling stories in full, Winik just hints at them in a line or two, choosing the sort of details that create huge blanks for her readers to fill in (e.g., "Meg never should have divorced Martin"; "exactly what happened that night on the boat with the guys from

Florida"). Locate other instances of suggestive details in the essay and see if you can explain why they work the way they do.

4. Organization/Plot. The structure of this essay is fairly straightforward: after an introductory paragraph, Winik lists eight kinds of friends and defines and describes each of them in either one or two or three paragraphs. Actually, nine kinds of friends, if you count "School Friends," who are mentioned once in paragraph 6. There is no concluding paragraph.

The arrangement of the categories is not dictated by any strict logic; the categories could have been treated in almost any order whatsoever. Winik does, however, arrange her categories in a sequence of increasing interest. Buddy Friends are ordinary, so she starts with these. Hero Friends and New Friends are both, in some way, extraordinary, so Winik ends with these. Friends You Love to Hate are the opposite of Hero Friends, so she places these two categories next to each other. And the remaining categories seem to reflect decreasing degrees of personal involvement: relatives, work friends, faraway friends, and former friends. In general, the plot moves from the commonplace to the extraordinary in an attempt to maintain the reader's interest.

5. Style. Winik's sentences seem conversational, but they include a number of moves that have been given learned names in classical rhetoric—names like anaphora, asyndeton, and chiasmus. Don't let the Greek words bother you. Winik's style just goes to show that virtually all those dusty old classical moves are alive and well in modern prose, even when the writer is in a lighthearted mood.

Anaphora is a series of sentences or phrases beginning with the same word. Winik gives us two excellent examples, one in paragraph 2—

> They call . . . they listen . . . they celebrate . . . They hold out . . . They accompany . . . They feed . . . They come over . . .

—and another in paragraph 11—

> They call . . . They say . . . They butt in . . . they embarrass you in public. . . . They invite . . . They take . . . they need . . . they love . . .

It's easy to imagine an excited person using anaphora in speech; most of the moves that have fancy Greek names can occur in speech, particularly in emotional speech. It is also easy to imagine a politician or a preacher or a lawyer using premeditated anaphora to provide an emotional lift to a point on a very formal occasion.

Asyndeton—the omission of "and" between the last two elements in a series— is another move that occurs in emotionally charged speech and can be used in emotionally charged writing. A good example occurs in paragraph 14:

> Suddenly, your life story is interesting again, your insights fresh, your opinion valued.

Grammatically, it would make sense to put an "and" before the last "your." But try it that way, and you will see why the sentence is better without it. Whether you learn the name of this move is not nearly as important as learning the move itself— learning to consider omitting the conjunction at the end of every series you write. Often you will find that asyndeton improves a sentence, makes it punchier.

Finally, there is a tiny chiasmus at the end of paragraph 12—the criss-cross arrangement named for the Greek letter *X* (*chi*):

As much as they need you, you need them too.

You may have seen this move before in Merrill Markoe's essay on showering with a dog (p. 63).

6. Voice/Attitude. Winik sounds friendly and informal right from the first word, "I," and the conversational structure of her first sentence, rambling as if she were actually speaking it. She uses colloquial words and expressions like "creep" and "just got stuck with" and "some crackerbox subdivision of your life," and "just make you sick"—expressions that would not show up in a formal newspaper story because they reveal more personality and individuality than a reporter is allowed to display. She also uses deliberate sentence fragments (see if you can find them in paragraphs 2, 7, 10, and 14) to make her voice casual and intimate. She uses contractions in abundance (you can find them in every paragraph except 7 and 9). And the phrase "just like that" (paragraph 10) is particularly effective in establishing a conversational tone, since it makes sense only in real conversation, when the word "that" is punctuated with a snap of the fingers.

Sentence fragments, contractions, first-person pronouns—aren't these things writers are supposed to avoid? Not necessarily. The smart thing is to know that they give your writing a casual, informal tone. Use them when you want to achieve that tone. But if you use them in more formal situations, like research papers and other scholarly writing, they are likely to seem like errors—not because they are errors in themselves, but because in those contexts they would be out of place.

7. Economy. What purpose is served by details like "Cigarettes, Chips Ahoy, bottles of tequila" in paragraph 7? What is the purpose of the question asked in paragraph 12, "So why do you continue to be involved with these people?" Can you find any details that seem irrelevant to the point Winik is trying to make, or to the tone she wants to creates?

Moves within Moves.   In addition to dividing and classifying her subject—friends—Winik makes the list interesting by defining each category. She does this, usually, by exemplification, in the form of likely stories, often hinted at in a phrase or two. One category, School Friends, is defined very quickly, by an implied comparison/contrast. School Friends, we must infer, are like Work Friends. As you read other essays in this chapter, notice that division and classification are always accompanied by at least one of the other modes or methods of development treated elsewhere in this book as devices for framing entire essays.

Words, Phrases, and Allusions.   "What Are Friends For?" is an example of good writing that doesn't depend upon fancy or unusual words; just the right words in the right places. Still there are some words that you may not yet feel comfortable writing, even though you may know their meaning when you see them in print. The following items were taken from the essay in the order of appearance:

> counsel, Aquarena Springs, infallible, accentuates, nostalgic, perspective, inopportune, spectrum, extensive

With the help of your classmates, locate these words in the essay and see if their context provides a clue to their meaning. If necessary, consult a dictionary, an encyclopedia, or other reference work to determine what each item means in its context.

Suggestion for Writing

Using "What Are Friends For?" as a model, write an essay in which you help your readers understand several types of things better by collecting them into categories and giving an example or two of each (if you have just a single instance in each category, the paper will be "exemplification," which we will discuss in chapter 9). The journal entry suggested at the beginning of this selection may have given you an idea for a topic, or you may have thought of other topics as you read Winik's essay.

The Sphere of Air

Jerry Dennis

Taken all in all, the sky is a miraculous achievement.
                                        —Lewis Thomas, *The Lives of a Cell*

If we could look at the earth in cross section, the thin membrane of gas and clouds 1
enveloping it would have the relative thickness of an apple's skin. Contained within
that skin are almost all the ingredients essential to life on our planet. It is where we
live. Without it we could have no hope of surviving.

The atmosphere is often described in terms that make it seem like an assembly 2
of well-lubricated parts working together to produce rain, snow, sleet, and hurri-
canes—a machine for the production of meteorological phenomena. Yet the atmosphere itself might be the greatest meteorological phenomenon of all. It is such a
complex structure that mechanical models of how it works are always in danger of
collapsing. The meteorologists who try to make sense and order of it are correct
barely half the time when they try to predict weather more than two or three days in
advance. Meteorology is an imprecise science not because of faulty computers or
lack of data, but because the atmosphere is subject to so many variables that it de-
fies easy understanding.

A century and a half ago, the amateur meteorologist Luke Howard, an English- 3
man who would earn world fame for devising the system of cloud classification still
used today, wrote, "The ocean of air in which we live and move, in which the bolt
of heaven is forged, and the fructifying rain condensed, can never be to the zealous
Naturalist a subject of tame and unfeeling contemplation." Zealous naturalists like
Luke Howard look at the sky and can not help wondering what keeps it from seep-
ing away into deep space, how it cleanses itself of smoke and dust and poison, why

127

it appears blue in daylight and transparent at night. Like countless people before and after him, Luke Howard must have wondered what, exactly, this thing was that the Greeks called the "sphere of air."

In text-book definitions, atmosphere is simply a gaseous envelope contained by   4
gravity around a planet. It can be a poisonous mixture of carbon dioxide and sulfur dioxide, as on Venus, or a seemingly bottomless cloud of methane and ammonia, as on Jupiter. Earth's atmosphere extends hundreds of miles above the ground, yet 90 percent of the air it contains is compressed within the lowest ten miles. At ground level air is composed of approximately 78 percent nitrogen, 21 percent oxygen, and 1 percent such gases as argon, carbon dioxide, helium, krypton, neon, and xenon. The amount of water vapor it contains fluctuates greatly, but on average is equal to about 2 percent of the volume of other gases. The atmosphere contains as well a rich and varying brew of dust, smoke, volcanic debris, oceanic salt particles, pollen, seeds, bacteria, and insects.

Such analysis gives little hint of the complex nature of earth's atmosphere, or   5
of its role in the daily weather, the annual seasons, and the long-term climate of the planet. It is active in three dimensions, affected by (and affecting) both vertical and horizontal winds, influenced by the uneven heating of the sun on the earth's surface, by the motion of the earth's orbit, and by such cataclysms as volcanoes and nuclear explosions.

Significant progress in the study of the atmosphere did not begin until about the   6
turn of the twentieth century, when the French meteorologist Léon-Philippe Teisserenc de Bort began sending up unmanned balloons carrying barometers, thermometers, and other scientific instruments. Until then the only explorations of the atmosphere had been in manned balloon flights that had reached only to about six miles, the height at which cold and insufficient oxygen made further exploration dangerous. For centuries it had been assumed that temperatures decreased steadily with altitude until the atmosphere blended with the unimaginable cold of space. Teisserenc de Bort discovered that temperatures in the atmosphere declined steadily from the ground up to about seven miles, then remained constant as high above that level as his balloons could reach. Based on those observations, he suggested in 1902 that the atmosphere be divided into layered segments. He called the lowest layer, from the ground to about seven miles up, the *troposphere*, from Greek roots meaning "sphere of change," because it is the level where temperatures vary and produce winds and clouds. The level above the troposphere, where temperatures were constant, he called the *stratosphere*, from Greek for "sphere of layers," because it was his theory that in the steady temperatures at those altitudes there would be no winds, thus gases would settle into layers, with the heavier gases arranged below the lighter ones.

In the years since, Teisserenc de Bort's observations have been refined and ad-   7
justed, and additional levels of atmosphere have been identified and studied using high-altitude balloons, aircraft, and satellites, yet his ideas about the lower reaches of the atmosphere have proven to be mostly correct. We now know the troposphere varies from about ten miles high at the equator, to about seven miles high in temper-

ate regions, to about five miles high at the poles, and that it contains all the warm air, most of the clouds and water vapor, most of the wind, most of the oxygen and other gases, and most of the living organisms contained in the atmosphere.

When parcels of heated air from the surface rise by convection, they expand 8 and cool as they rise through the troposphere, and are almost always stopped at its top, a ceiling known as the *tropopause*. The tropopause causes the distinctive anvil-shape at the top of enormous, towering thunderheads. Temperatures in the troposphere vary from 100 degrees Fahrenheit or more at ground level, to a low of about −70 degrees Fahrenheit at the tropopause, declining at a rate of about 3.6 degrees for every 1,000 feet of altitude.

Above the tropopause, reaching to a height of about thirty miles, is the strato- 9 sphere. Temperatures throughout most of the stratosphere range from −40 degrees to −100 degrees Fahrenheit, and it is windless except for the undulating jet streams, which sometimes extend into its lower reaches.

The *mesosphere* extends from about thirty miles to about fifty miles above sea 10 level. So few gases are found at this level that there is little to absorb solar heat. Temperatures once again plummet with altitude, reaching as low as −225 degrees Fahrenheit at the top of the mesosphere. Paradoxically, the lower temperatures in the mesosphere occur in summer, the warmest in winter, perhaps the result of a not-yet-understood global exchange of cold and warm air. Most meteors burn up at this level.

The next layer of atmosphere, the *thermosphere*, extends from 50 to 180 miles 11 above the ground, and contains less than 1/100,000 of the air in the entire atmosphere. Yet even this extremely rarified layer of atmosphere absorbs a great deal of the sun's radiation, enough that temperatures fluctuate from daytime highs of 3,600 degrees Fahrenheit to nighttime lows more than 1,000 degrees cooler. Because there is no wind or convection, the thermosphere satisfies Teisserenc de Bort's original theory about the nature of the stratosphere; its gases settle into distinctive layers, with heavy nitrogen and oxygen at the bottom, and lighter helium and hydrogen at the top.

At the top of the atmosphere is the final layer, the *exosphere*, a bleak, stark re- 12 gion 180 to 300 or more miles high where solitary atoms of helium, hydrogen, and oxygen are likely to drift for six miles on average before colliding with other atoms or molecules. At sea level, in comparison, molecules of gas can travel only 3/1,000,000 inch before colliding. A few of those scattered atoms of air in the upper exosphere, heated by solar radiation to temperatures of 3,600 degrees Fahrenheit, speed away from the earth at 25,000 miles an hour and escape into space.

There is no clearly defined boundary between the atmosphere and space. Some- 13 where in the region located 300 to 900 miles above the surface of the earth, molecules are so scarce that you can safely say there are none at all.

UNDERSTANDING THE ESSAY

1. Explain the analogy of the apple's skin (paragraph 1). What surprising fact does it tell you about the earth's atmosphere?
2. What common misunderstandings about the earth's air does Dennis's essay clear up?
3. Dennis draws no conclusion from his division of the atmosphere, but can you?
4. In what way might understanding the structure of the air alter your appreciation of space travel or your concern for the environment?
5. Find out who among your classmates find this essay interesting and who find it boring. See if you can discover what each reader brings to the text that determines the way he or she reacts to it.

So What and the Seven Common Moves.   Analyze this essay with the help of the questions about "So What and the Seven Common Moves" found on the back cover of this book.

Words, Phrases, and Allusions.   The following items were taken from "The Sphere of Air" in order of appearance. With the help of your classmates, locate these words in the essay and see if their context provides a clue to their meaning. If necessary, consult a dictionary, an encyclopedia, or other reference work to determine what each item means in its context. You probably know most of these words from conversation and reading, but you may not yet feel comfortable using them in your own writing.

cross section, meteorological phenomena, forged, fructifying, zealous Naturalists, volcanic debris, cataclysms, barometers, troposphere, stratosphere, convection, tropopause, thunderheads, undulating, mesosphere, plummet, thermosphere, exosphere

Suggestion for Writing

Using "The Sphere of Air" as a model, write an essay in which you help your readers understand something better by breaking it down into its constituent parts. The journal entry suggested at the beginning of this selection may have given you an idea for a topic, or you may have thought of other topics as you read Dennis's essay.

The Men We Carry in Our Minds

Scott Russell Sanders

The first men, besides my father, I remember seeing were black convicts and white   1
guards, in the cotton field across the road from our farm on the outskirts of Memphis. I must have been three or four. The prisoners wore dingy gray-and-black zebra suits, heavy as canvas, sodden with sweat. Hatless, stooped, they chopped weeds in the fierce heat, row after row, breathing the acrid dust of boll-weevil poison. The overseers wore dazzling white shirts and broad shadowy hats. The oiled barrels of their shotguns flashed in the sunlight. Their faces in memory are utterly blank. Of course those men, white and black, have become for me an emblem of racial hatred. But they have also come to stand for the twin poles of my early vision of manhood—the brute toiling animal and the boss.

When I was a boy, the men I knew labored with their bodies. They were   2
marginal farmers, just scraping by, or welders, steelworkers, carpenters; they swept floors, dug ditches, mined coal, or drove trucks, their forearms ropy with muscle; they trained horses, stoked furnaces, built fires, stood on assembly lines wrestling parts onto cars and refrigerators. They got up before light, worked all day long whatever the weather, and when they came home at night they looked as though somebody had been whipping them. In the evenings and on weekends they worked on their own places, tilling gardens that were lumpy with clay, fixing broken-down cars, hammering on houses that were always too drafty, too leaky, too small.

The bodies of the men I knew were twisted and maimed in ways visible and in-   3
visible. The nails of their hands were black and split, the hands tatooed with scars.

Some had lost fingers. Heavy lifting had given many of them finicky backs and guts weak from hernias. Racing against conveyor belts had given them ulcers. Their ankles and knees ached from years of standing on concrete. Anyone who had worked for long around machines was hard of hearing. They squinted, and the skin of their faces was creased like the leather of old work gloves. There were times, studying them, when I dreaded growing up. Most of them coughed, from dust or cigarettes, and most of them drank cheap wine or whisky, so their eyes looked bloodshot and bruised. The fathers of my friends always seemed older than the mothers. Men wore out sooner. Only women lived into old age.

As a boy I also knew another sort of men, who did not sweat and break down 4 like mules. They were soldiers, and so far as I could tell they scarcely worked at all. During my early school years we lived on a military base, an arsenal in Ohio, and every day I saw GIs in the guard shacks, on the stoops of the barracks, at the wheels of olive drab Chevrolets. The chief fact of their lives was boredom. Long after I left the Arsenal I came to recognize the sour smell the soldiers gave off as that of souls in limbo. They were all waiting—for wars, for transfers, for leaves, for promotions, for the end of their hitch—like so many braves waiting for the hunt to begin. Unlike the warriors of older tribes, however, they would have no say about when the battle would start or how it would be waged. Their waiting was broken only when they practiced for war. They fired guns at targets, drove tanks across the churned-up fields of the military reservation, set off bombs in the wrecks of old fighter planes. I knew all this was play. But I also felt certain that when the hour for killing arrived, they would kill. When the real shooting started, many of them would die. This was what soldiers were for, just as a hammer was for driving nails.

Warriors and toilers: those seemed, in my boyhood vision, to be the chief des- 5 tinies for men. They weren't the only destinies, as I learned from having a few male teachers, from reading books, and from watching television. But the men on television—the politicians, the astronauts, the generals, the savvy lawyers, the philosophical doctors, the bosses who gave orders to both soldiers and laborers—seemed as removed and unreal to me as the figures in tapestries. I could no more imagine growing up to become one of these cool, potent creatures than I could imagine becoming a prince.

A nearer and more hopeful example was that of my father, who had escaped 6 from a red-dirt farm to a tire factory, and from the assembly line to the front office. Eventually he dressed in a white shirt and tie. He carried himself as if he had been born to work with his mind. But his body, remembering the years of slogging work, began to give out on him in his fifties, and it quit on him entirely before he turned sixty-five. Even such a partial escape from man's fate as he had accomplished did not seem possible for most of the boys I knew. They joined the Army, stood in line for jobs in the smoky plants, helped build highways. They were bound to work as their fathers had worked, killing themselves or preparing to kill others.

A scholarship enabled me not only to attend college, a rare enough feat in my 7 circle, but even to study in a university meant for the children of the rich. Here I met for the first time young men who had assumed from birth that they would lead lives of comfort and power. And for the first time I met women who told me that men were guilty of having kept all the joys and privileges of the earth for themselves. I was baffled. What privileges? What joys? I thought about the maimed, dismal lives of most of the men back home. What had they stolen from their wives and daughters? The right to go five days a week, twelve months a year, for thirty or forty years to a steel mill or a coal mine? The right to drop bombs and die in war? The right to feel every leak in the roof, every gap in the fence, every cough in the engine, as a wound they must mend? The right to feel, when the lay-off comes or the plant shuts down, not only afraid but ashamed?

I was slow to understand the deep grievances of women. This was because, as   8
a boy, I had envied them. Before college, the only people I had ever known who were interested in art or music or literature, the only ones who read books, the only ones who ever seemed to enjoy a sense of ease and grace were the mothers and daughters. Like the menfolk, they fretted about money, they scrimped and made-do. But, when the pay stopped coming in, they were not the ones who had failed. Nor did they have to go to war, and that seemed to me a blessed fact. By the comparison with the narrow, ironclad days of their fathers, there was an expansiveness, I thought, in the days of the mothers. They went to see neighbors, to shop in town, to run errands at school, at the library, at church. No doubt, had I looked harder at their lives, I would have envied them less. It was not my fate to become a woman, so it was easier for me to see the graces. Few of them held jobs outside the home, and those who did filled thankless roles as clerks and waitresses. I didn't see, then, what a prison a house could be, since houses seemed to me brighter, handsomer places than any factory. I did not realize—because such things were never spoken of—how often women suffered from men's bullying. I did learn about the wretchedness of abandoned wives, single mothers, widows; but I also learned about the wretchedness of lone men. Even though I could see how exhausting it was for a mother to cater all day to the needs of young children. But if I had been asked, as a boy, to choose between tending a baby and tending a machine, I think I would have chosen the baby. (Having now tended both, I know I would choose the baby.)

So I was baffled when the women at college accused me and my sex of having   9
cornered the world's pleasures. I think something like my bafflement has been felt by other boys (and girls as well) who grew up in dirt-poor farm country, in mining country, in black ghettos, in Hispanic barrios, in the shadows of factories, in Third World nations—any place where the fate of men is as grim and bleak as the fate of women. Toilers and warriors, I realize now how ancient these identities are, how deep the tug they exert on men, the undertow of a thousand generations. The miseries I saw, as a boy, in the lives of nearly all men I continue to see in the lives of many—the body-breaking toil, the tedium, the call to be tough, the humiliating powerlessness, the battle for a living and for territory.

When the women I met at college thought about the joys and privileges of men,   10
they did not carry in their minds the sort of men I had known in my childhood. They

thought of their fathers, who were bankers, physicians, architects, stockbrokers, the big wheels of the big cities. These fathers rode the train to work or drove cars that cost more than any of my childhood houses. They were attended from morning to night by female helpers, wives and nurses and secretaries. They were never laid off, never short of cash at month's end, never lined up for welfare. These fathers made decisions that mattered. They ran the world.

The daughters of such men wanted to share in this power, this glory. So did I.   11
They yearned for a say over their future, for jobs worthy of their abilities, for the right to live at peace, unmolested, whole. Yes, I thought, yes yes. The difference between me and these daughters was that they saw me, because of my sex, as destined from birth to become like their fathers, and therefore as an enemy to their desires. I was an ally. If I had known, then, how to tell them so, would they have believed me? Would they now?

UNDERSTANDING THE ESSAY

1. At first Sanders divides men into two categories: "the brute toiling animal and the boss" (paragraph 1). How many other categories of men does he describe in this essay?
2. How does Sanders feel about the quality of the lives lived by the men he knew as a child?
3. How does Sanders feel about the quality of the lives lived by the women he knew as a child?
4. Sanders seems to be writing his essay in opposition to a different notion of what men are and what sorts of lives they lead. What is this different notion, and where does Sanders first encounter it?
5. Where does Sanders make concession to the opposing point of view? What effect do these concessions have on his credibility?

So What and the Seven Common Moves.   Analyze this essay with the help of the questions about "So What and the Seven Common Moves" found on the back cover of this book.

Words, Phrases, and Allusions.   "The Men We Carry in Our Minds" is like "Help Me, God. I'm a Girl" (p. 98) and "Jackie's Debut" (p. 40) in that it has no extraordinary words—nothing that wouldn't be in the vocabulary of any ordinary eighth grader, confirming again the notion that good writing does not necessarily involve unusual words. In what sense, though, is the very plainness of Sander's vocabulary particularly appropriate to his topic and to the way he interprets it?

Suggestion for Writing

Using "The Men We Carry in Our Minds" as a model, write an essay in which you help your readers understand how categories we learn as children affect the way we see the world when we grow up. The journal entry suggested at the beginning of this selection may have given you an idea for a topic, or you may have thought of other topics as you read Sanders's essay.

Journal Entry. Life is full of misunderstandings: a group of people read the same newspaper, and each person takes entirely different meaning from it; a couple look at the same household budget and reach entirely different conclusions about necessary and optional expenses; co-workers in a business review production and sales data and arrive at entirely different judgments about the company's problems and possibilities. Think of a context in which you have witnessed misunderstandings. It could be at home, at work, or in some extracurricular activity. See if you can devise categories of misunderstanding. If you succeed, you will have gone a long way toward resolving or even preventing them. After you've worked on this project for a while, read the following essay in which Deborah Tannen helps us understand several kinds of misunderstanding between men and women in the workplace. Notice that Tannen doesn't merely place the types of misunderstanding into categories; she has something interesting to say about each category. As you read the essay, look for moves you can imitate in your own essay.

But What Do You Mean?

Deborah Tannen

Conversation is a ritual. We say things that seem obviously the thing to say, without thinking of the literal meaning of our words, any more than we expect the question "How are you?" to call forth a detailed account of aches and pains. 1

Unfortunately, women and men often have different ideas about what's appropriate, different ways of speaking. Many of the conversational rituals common among women are designed to take the other person's feelings into account, while many of the conversational rituals common among men are designed to maintain the one-up position, or at least avoid appearing one-down. As a result, when men and women interact—especially at work—it's often women who are at the disadvantage. Because women are not trying to avoid the one-down position, that is unfortunately where they may end up. 2

Here, the biggest areas of miscommunication. 3

1. Apologies

Women are often told they apologize too much. The reason they're told to stop doing it is that, to many men, apologizing seems synonymous with putting oneself down. But there are many times when "I'm sorry" isn't self-deprecating, or even an 4 apology; it's an automatic way of keeping both speakers on an equal footing. For example, a well-known columnist once interviewed me and gave me her phone number in case I needed to call her back. I misplaced the number and had to go through the newspaper's main switchboard. When our conversation was winding down and we'd both made ending-type remarks, I added, "Oh, I almost forgot—I lost your direct number, can I get it again?" "Oh, I'm sorry," she came back instantly, even though she had done nothing wrong and *I* was the one who'd lost the number. But I understood she wasn't really apologizing; she was just automatically reassuring me she had no intention of denying me her number.

Even when "I'm sorry" *is* an apology, women often assume it will be the first step in a two-step ritual: I say "I'm sorry" and take half the blame, then you take the other half. At work, it might go something like this: 5

A: When you typed this letter, you missed this phrase I inserted.
B: Oh, I'm sorry. I'll fix it.
A: Well, I wrote it so small it was easy to miss.

When both parties share blame, it's a mutual face-saving device. But if one person, usually the woman, utters frequent apologies and the other doesn't, she ends up looking as if she's taking the blame for mishaps that aren't her fault. When she's only partially to blame, she looks entirely in the wrong. 6

I recently sat in on a meeting at an insurance company where the sole woman, Helen, said "I'm sorry" or "I apologize" repeatedly. At one point she said, "I'm thinking out loud. I apologize." Yet the meeting was intended to be an informal brainstorming session, and *everyone* was thinking out loud. 7

The reason Helen's apologies stood out was that she was the only person in the room making so many. And the reason I was concerned was that Helen felt the annual bonus she had received was unfair. When I interviewed her colleagues, they said that Helen was one of the best and most productive workers—yet she got one of the smallest bonuses. Although the problem might have been outright sexism, I suspect her speech style, which differs from that of her male colleagues, masks her competence. 8

Unfortunately, not apologizing can have its price too. Since so many women use ritual apologies, those who don't may be seen as hard-edged. What's important is to be aware of how often you say you're sorry (and why), and to monitor your speech based on the reaction you get. 9

2. Criticism

A woman who cowrote a report with a male colleague was hurt when she read a rough draft to him and he leapt into a critical response—"Oh, that's too dry! You have to make it snappier!" She herself would have been more likely to say, "That's a really good start. Of course, you'll want to make it a little snappier when you revise." 10

Whether criticism is given straight or softened is often a matter of convention. 11
In general, women use more softeners. I noticed this difference when talking to an
editor about an essay I'd written. While going over changes she wanted to make,
she said, "There's one more thing. I know you may not agree with me. The reason I
noticed the problem is that your other points are so lucid and elegant." She went on
hedging for several more sentences until I put her out of her misery: "Do you want
to cut that part?" I asked—and of course she did. But I appreciated her tentative-
ness. In contrast, another editor (a man) I once called summarily rejected my idea
for an article by barking, "Call me when you have something new to say."

Those who are used to ways of talking that soften the impact of criticism may 12
find it hard to deal with the right-between-the-eyes style. It has its own logic, however, and neither style is intrinsically better. People who prefer criticism given
straight are operating on an assumption that feelings aren't involved: "Here's the
dope. I know you're good; you can take it."

3. Thank-Yous

A woman manager I know starts meetings by thanking everyone for coming, even 13
though it's clearly their job to do so. Her "thank-you" is simply a ritual.

A novelist received a fax from an assistant in her publisher's office; it con- 14
tained suggested catalog copy for her book. She immediately faxed him her suggested changes and said, "Thanks for running this by me," even though her contract
gave her the right to approve all copy. When she thanked the assistant, she fully expected him to reciprocate: "Thanks for giving me such a quick response." Instead,
he said, "You're welcome." Suddenly, rather than an equal exchange of pleas-
antries, she found herself positioned as the recipient of a favor. This made her feel
like responding,"Thanks for nothing!"

Many women use "thanks" as an automatic conversation starter and closer; 15
there's nothing literally to say thank you for. Like many rituals typical of women's
conversation, it depends on the goodwill of the other to restore the balance. When
the other speaker doesn't reciprocate, a woman may feel like someone on a seesaw
whose partner abandoned his end. Instead of balancing in the air, she has plopped to
the ground, wondering how she got there.

4. Fighting

Many men expect the discussion of ideas to be a ritual fight—explored through ver- 16
bal opposition. They state their ideas in the strongest possible terms, thinking that if
there are weaknesses someone will point them out, and by trying to argue against
those objections, they will see how well their ideas hold up.

Those who expect their own ideas to be challenged will respond to another's 17
ideas by trying to poke holes and find weak links—as a way of *helping*. The logic is
that when you are challenged you will rise to the occasion: Adrenaline makes your
mind sharper; you get ideas and insights you would not have thought of without the
spur of battle.

But many women take this approach as a personal attack. Worse, they find it 18 impossible to do their best work in such a contentious environment. If you're not used to ritual fighting, you begin to hear criticism of your ideas as soon as they are formed. Rather than making you think more clearly, it makes you doubt what you know. When you state your ideas, you hedge in order to fend off potential attacks. Ironically, this is more likely to *invite* attack because it makes you look weak.

Although you may never enjoy verbal sparring, some women find it helpful to 19 learn how to do it. An engineer who was the only woman among four men in a small company found that as soon as she learned to argue she was accepted and taken seriously. A doctor attending a hospital staff meeting made a similar discovery. She was becoming more and more angry with a male colleague who'd loudly disagreed with a point she'd made. Her better judgment told her to hold her tongue, to avoid making an enemy of this powerful senior colleague. But finally she couldn't hold it in any longer, and she rose to her feet and delivered an impassioned attack on his position. She sat down in a panic, certain she had permanently damaged her relationship with him. To her amazement, he came up to her afterward and said, "That was a great rebuttal. I'm really impressed. Let's go out for a beer after work and hash out our approaches to this problem."

5. Praise

A manager I'll call Lester had been on his new job six months when he heard that 20 the women reporting to him were deeply dissatisfied. When he talked to them about it, their feelings erupted; two said they were on the verge of quitting because he didn't appreciate their work, and they didn't want to wait to be fired. Lester was dumbfounded: He believed they were doing a fine job. Surely, he thought, he had said nothing to give them the impression he didn't like their work. And indeed he hadn't. That was the problem. He had said *nothing*—and the women assumed he was following the adage "If you can't say something nice, don't say anything." He thought he was showing confidence in them by leaving them alone.

Men and women have different habits in regard to giving praise. For example, 21 Deirdre and her colleague William both gave presentations at a conference. Afterward, Deirdre told William, "That was a great talk!" He thanked her. Then she asked, "What did you think of mine?" and he gave her a lengthy and detailed critique. She found it uncomfortable to listen to his comments. But she assured herself that he meant well, and that his honesty was a signal that she, too, should be honest when he asked for a critique of his performance. As a matter of fact, she had noticed quite a few ways in which be could have improved his presentation. But she never got a chance to tell him because he never asked—and she felt put down. The worst part was that it seemed she had only herself to blame, since she *had* asked what he thought of her talk.

But had she really asked for his critique? The truth is, when she asked for his 22 opinion, she was expecting a compliment, which she felt was more or less required following anyone's talk. When he responded with criticism, she figured, "Oh, he's playing 'Let's critique each other'"—not a game she'd initiated, but one which she was willing to play. Had she realized he was going to criticize her and not ask her to reciprocate, she would never have asked in the first place.

It would be easy to assume that Deirdre was insecure, whether she was fishing 23 for a compliment or soliciting a critique. But she was simply talking automatically, performing one of the many conversational rituals that allow us to get through the day. William may have sincerely misunderstood Deirdre's intention—or may have been unable to pass up a chance to one-up her when given the opportunity.

6. Complaints

"Troubles talk" can be a way to establish rapport with a colleague. You complain 24 about a problem (which shows that you are just folks) and the other person responds with a similar problem (which puts you on equal footing). But while such commiserating is common among women, men are likely to hear it as a request to *solve* the problem.

One woman told me she would frequently initiate what she thought would be 25 pleasant complaint-airing sessions at work. She'd talk about situations that bothered her just to talk about them, maybe to understand them better. But her male office mate would quickly tell her how she could improve the situation. This left her feeling condescended to and frustrated. She was delighted to see this very impasse in a section in my book *You Just Don't Understand*, and showed it to him. "Oh," he said, "I see the problem. How can we solve it?" Then they both laughed, because it had happened again: He short-circuited the detailed discussion she'd hoped for and cut to the chase of finding a solution.

Sometimes the consequences of complaining are more serious: A man might 26 take a woman's lighthearted griping literally, and she can get a reputation as a chronic malcontent. Furthermore, she may be seen as not up to solving the problems that arise on the job.

7. Jokes

I heard a man call in to a talk show and say, "I've worked for two women and nei- 27 ther one had a sense of humor. You know, when you work with men, there's a lot of joking and teasing." The show's host and the guest (both women) took his comment at face value and assumed the women this man worked for were humorless. The guest said, "Isn't it sad that women don't feel comfortable enough with authority to see the humor?" The host said, "Maybe when more women are in authority roles, they'll be more comfortable with power." But although the women this man worked for *may* have taken themselves too seriously, it's just as likely that they each had a terrific sense of humor, but maybe the humor wasn't the type he was used to. They may have been like the woman who wrote to me: "When I'm with men, my wit or cleverness seems inappropriate (or lost!) so I don't bother. When I'm with my women friends, however, there's no hold on puns or cracks and my humor is fully appreciated."

The types of humor women and men tend to prefer differ. Research has shown 28 that the most common form of humor among men is razzing, teasing, and mock-hostile attacks, while among women it's self-mocking. Women often mistake men's teasing as genuinely hostile. Men often mistake women's mock self-deprecation as truly putting themselves down.

Women have told me they were taken more seriously when they learned to joke 29 the way the guys did. For example, a teacher who went to a national conference with seven other teachers (mostly women) and a group of administrators (mostly men) was annoyed that the administrators always found reasons to leave boring seminars, while the teachers felt they had to stay and take notes. One evening, when the group met at a bar in the hotel, the principal asked her how one such seminar had turned out. She retorted, "As soon as you left, it got much better." He laughed out loud at her response. The playful insult appealed to the men—but there was a trade-off. The women seemed to back off from her after this. (Perhaps they were put off by her using joking to align herself with the bosses.)

There is no "right" way to talk. When problems arise, the culprit may be style dif- 30 ferences—and all styles will at times fail with others who don't share or understand them, just as English won't do you much good if you try to speak to someone who knows only French. If you want to get your message across, it's not a question of being "right"; it's a question of using language that's shared—or at least understood.

UNDERSTANDING THE ESSAY

1. Deborah Tannen claims that conversation is a ritual. In what sense is it a ritual?
2. What does Tannen say is the essential difference in the goals among men and among women in conversation (see paragraph two)?
3. Tannen uses lots of examples. Do they strike you as typical? Do they support her arguments about the differences between the way men and women conduct conversations?
4. How many of her examples seem factual, and how many fictitious? Are the fictitious examples any less persuasive than the real ones? Why does Tannen give the people in her examples first names only, or pseudonyms, or sometimes no names at all?
5. How could a person's competence on the job be masked by her speech habits (see paragraph eight)?

So What and the Seven Common Moves.   Analyze this essay with the help of the questions about "So What and the Seven Common Moves" found on the back cover of this book.

Words, Phrases, and Allusions.   The following items were taken from "But What Do You Mean" in order of appearance. With the help of your classmates, locate these words in the essay and see if their context provides a clue to their meaning. If necessary, consult a dictionary, an encyclopedia, or other reference work to determine what each item means in its context. You probably know most of these words from conversation and reading, but you may not yet feel comfortable using them in your own writing.

> synonymous, self-deprecating, utters, monitor (as a verb), lucid, hedging, tentativeness, summarily, intrinsically, reciprocate, recipient, adrenaline, contentious, potential attacks, verbal sparring, adage, critique, soliciting, rapport, commiserating, condescended to, impasse, chronic malcontent, razzing, mock-hostile attacks, retorted, align

Suggestion for Writing

Using "But What Do You Mean" as a model, write an essay in which you help your readers understand misunderstandings by putting them into categories. The journal entry suggested at the beginning of this selection may have given you an idea for a topic, or you may have thought of other topics as you read Tannen's essay.

RECIPES FOR WRITING DIVISION OR CLASSIFICATION

A. Writing from Personal Experience

Two things are essential to making a division or classification essay interesting: First, you have to find a division or classification that you care about—one that reveals something interesting about your subject matter. The second is to do something with each division or classification—for example, to define it, or describe it, or tell a story about it.

Here is a recipe for writing a division and classification essay:

1. If your subject is one that can be best understood by examining its parts (e.g., the parts of a flower or the parts of an engine), you are writing a "division" paper. If your subject is best understood by placing it in the context of other, related subjects (e.g., twelve kinds of roses or seven kinds of optical illusions), you are writing a classification paper.
2. Once you choose a topic, see if you can say something general about it in a sentence that includes a plural noun, preferably one with a number in front

of it—for example, "There are nine kinds of friends," or "Nuclear reactors have three major components."

3. Write the parts or categories on separate slips of paper and arrange the slips in the sequence that will work best for this topic: either a logical sequence, a spatial sequence, or perhaps a sequence in which you group similar observations together, saving the best for last to maintain the interest of your readers.

4. Develop each part or category by describing, narrating, exemplifying, or using any of the other conceptual moves treated as separate chapters in this book.

5. After you've selected and arranged your details, add an introduction and an ending.

6. Show a draft to fellow students in a formal or informal workshop, and see if your strategies are having the effects you want them to have. Use the checklist on the back cover to focus your discussion. Then look for errors in spelling, grammar, or punctuation that you will want to correct in your final draft.

B. Writing against the Text

It is hard to argue with a paper that divides something into its parts if that thing has a definite number of parts. But it is almost always possible to divide those parts into parts. And it is almost always possible to add new categories to a classification paper—examples that do not quite fit anywhere in whatever scheme the writer proposes. Can you, for example, think of friends that do not quite match any of the types that Marion Winik describes? Or can you think of female speech habits in addition to those Deborah Tannen describes, or female speech patterns that actually give women the upper hand over their less skillful male colleagues? Find a division or classification essay to which you can add more parts or more categories, and write a new essay of your own.

C. Writing from Research

Using the library and the Web, locate information about anything that interests you. You might look for ways to classify a group of things (e.g., trees, birds, colleges, computer programs, accounting techniques, rock bands) or ways to understand a single thing by dividing it into its parts (e.g., a computer, a frog, a university, a double helix). After you've completed your research, write a draft in your own words without consulting your sources; this will help you avoid being overwhelmed by what you read and perhaps unintentionally plagiarizing material. Then go back and add material from your research wherever you think it will make your paper more interesting or authoritative. Be sure to acknowledge the source of anything you quote or paraphrase.

7

Probable Causes
(and Likely Effects)

Children generally go through what their parents call a questioning stage. "Why is the sky blue?" they'll ask, and "Why do cats have whiskers?" and "How do bats see in the dark?" and "What makes the wind blow?" Asking cause-and-effect questions is one of the universal conceptual moves that everybody can make in conversation—even children.

But writing provides a system for asking these questions and recording the answers in ways that were simply unthinkable before writing was invented. In fact, the foundation of every academic discipline is precisely this: answering, in writing, the sort of how and why questions that all normal children ask. It is the main business of scientists and social scientists. It is a fundamental activity in economics, political science, sociology, history, philosophy, education, engineering, marketing, management, nursing, English, even the fine and performing arts. That's why learning to write a cause-and-effect essay in a composition course is not an artificial exercise. It is an opportunity to develop a way of thinking that you will need in your major, no matter what that might be.

There are two kinds of cause-and-effect analysis. One kind attempts to explain physical phenomena; the other attempts to explain human behavior. The first kind is scientific. It seeks answers to questions like "What causes lightning?" or "What effect will smoking have on a patient's blood pressure?" The second kind explores questions that science cannot answer, like "What caused the Soviet Union to collapse?" or "What effect would merging two supermarket chains have on the price of squash?" or "What causes intelligent students to fail?" or "What will happen if we pass a balanced budget amendment?"

According to Aristotle, the sign of a true education is the ability to tell the difference between these two sorts of questions. Educated people do not settle for "probable" and "likely" answers when the questions could be answered with solid data. Neither do they look for scientific answers to questions that have none. If the question is whether alcohol causes birth defects or whether fish floating in a river were killed by industrial waste, we should demand scientific certitude in the answers. For those other kinds of questions, however—questions about morality, art, politics, personal decisions, and economics—the best we can find are "probable" causes and "likely" effects. We can only make educated guesses about the causes of artistic genius or happy marriages or the madness that compels people to storm department stores in search of toys that mysteriously and unpredictably become crazes.

Scientific questions are often extremely important and urgent. But many of our most interesting and important questions belong to that second category, the kind involving human factors that cannot be directly measured or observed: beliefs, values, and our ability to make choices that other people find unmotivated, unpredictable, surprising, brilliant, or foolish.

The first step in writing a cause-and-effect essay is to choose a topic. Personal experience is perhaps the handiest source. You could find something to write about by filling in the blank in either of these questions:

Why did I _____?
What happened because I _____?

Look for some puzzling or important behaviors or surprising effects to explore. The advantage of writing about personal experience is that it requires no research: you are (or at least you could be) the world's greatest expert on your own behavior.

Other topics for cause-and-effect essays require collecting and analyzing data. You could, for example, write about the behavior of other people: "Why do women tend to vote for Democratic candidates?" "How have rating schemes for television shows affected the viewing habits of children?" "Why did Bonnie and Clyde become criminals?" "What would happen if the United States eased economic sanctions against Cuba?" Or you could write about sequences of physical events: "What are the causes and the effects of acid rain—or migraine headaches, or holes in the ozone layer, or global warming?" Notice, however, that these topics require research. You will have to collect and analyze data—or else find someone else who has done this work already and published the results.

Unless you choose your topic carefully, there is a real danger of running out of things to say in a cause-and-effect essay. "I hung around and listened," the young

Mike Royko tells us in "Jackie's Debut" (see p. 40) "because baseball was about the most important thing in the world, and if anything was going to ruin it, I was worried." In this single sentence Royko expresses a cause-and-effect relationship. But to expand this sentence into an essay would require asking lots of other questions about what he did and why he did it.

One way to develop a cause-and-effect analysis is to use some of the other conceptual moves that are treated as separate chapters in this book: you could describe either the cause or the effect in detail, or tell stories about it, define it, give examples, prove a point, classify it, divide it, compare it, or contrast it.

Another way to develop a cause-and-effect analysis, particularly about human behavior, is to explore what philosopher Kenneth Burke identified as five essential components of human behavior: the agent (the person who does the act), the act itself (what someone does), the agency (what the person uses to commit the act), the scene (all the circumstances that surround the act), and actor's purpose (what the person expects to achieve by the act). Burke called these five elements a "pentad"—which simply means a group of five. Applied to Mike Royko's decision to hang around the tavern and listen to the men, the questions based on the pentad would work like this:

Actor. "Who was this Royko kid?" In other words, how old was he? Where did he live? What sort of family did he come from? What kind of abilities did he have? How does all of this relate to his behavior?

Act. What does he mean by "hung around and listened"? Was he an uninvited snooper? Was he a neighborhood favorite, whose company the men enjoyed? Was hanging around the tavern his way of learning how to become an adult, absorbing attitudes and behaviors from role models?

Agency. How was a twelve- or thirteen-year-old kid able to get into a tavern where men were drinking?

Scene. Just what sort of tavern are we taking about? Something like a neighborhood British pub, where children might not be out of place? Or a neighborhood beer parlor, where children and reputable women were normally not seen? Was it a highbrow establishment, or a working-class watering hole?

Purpose. What did young Royko hope to gain from eavesdropping? On one level, it was information about what the men perceived as a threat to baseball. On another, it was a way of interpreting events. Like all kids, he was looking to adults not only for information, but for clues about how to interpret events.

Studying a simple act from the perspective of Burke's pentad helps us understand how complex all human behavior is. If we were to use this system of questioning about a more serious situation (e.g., "Why did Lizzie Borden kill her parents?" or "Why did Prime Minister Neville Chamberlain sign an agreement with Adolf Hitler in Munich?"), we would likely come up with some interesting answers.

Burke's questions, like the modes and methods or conceptual moves discussed everywhere in this book, are all good tools for prying beneath the surface of data to gain a better understanding. But they are not all equally good at all times. The trick is to find out which questions help satisfy your curiosity about a given topic and which questions provide interesting and surprising answers. These are the ones that produce the substance of a good cause-and-effect essay.

One of the essays that follow in this chapter—Peter Farb's essay on the causes of success and failure (p. 160)—uses some scientific data along with analogies to explain behavioral differences. The others rely on a sort of evidence that can never be entirely conclusive—examples (in the form of likely stories) and analogies.

The Origins of Anorexia Nervosa

Joan Jacobs Brumberg

Contrary to the popular assumption that anorexia nervosa is a peculiarly modern disorder, the malady first emerged in the Victorian era—long before the pervasive cultural imperative for a thin female body. The first clinical descriptions of the disorder appeared in England and France almost simultaneously in 1873. They were written by two well-known physicians: Sir William Withey Gull and Charles Lasègue. Lasègue, more than any other nineteenth-century doctor, captured the rhythm of repeated offerings and refusals that signaled the breakdown of reciprocity between parents and their anorexic daughter. By returning to its origins, we can see anorexia nervosa for what it is: a dysfunction in the bourgeois family system. 1

Family meals assumed enormous importance in the bourgeois milieu, in the United States as well as in England and France. Middle-class parents prided themselves on providing ample food for their children. The abundance of food and the care in its preparation became expressions of social status. The ambiance of the meal symbolized the values of the family. A popular domestic manual advises, "simple, healthy food, exquisitely prepared, and served upon shining dishes and brilliant silverware . . . a gentle blessing, and cheerful conversation, embrace the sweetest communions and the happiest moments of life." Among the middle class it seems that eating correctly was emerging as a new morality, one that set its members apart from the working class. 2

At the same time, food was used to express love in the nineteenth-century bourgeois household. Offering attractive and abundant meals was the particular respon- 3 sibility and pleasure of middle-class wives and mothers. In America the feeding of middle-class children, from infancy on, had become a maternal concern no longer deemed appropriate to delegate to wet nurses, domestics, or governesses. Family meals were expected to be a time of instructive and engaging conversation. Participation was expected on both a verbal and gustatory level. In this context, refusing to eat was an unabashedly antisocial act. Anorexic behavior was antithetical to the ideal of bourgeois eating. One advice book, *Common Sense of Maid, Wife, and Mother,* stated: "Heated discussion and quarrels, fretfulness and sullen taciturnity while eating, are as unwholesome as they are unchristian."

Why would a daughter affront her parents by refusing to eat? Lasègue's 1873 description of anorexia nervosa, along with other nineteenth-century medical reports, suggests that pressure to marry may have precipitated the illness.   4

Ambitious parents surely understood that by marrying well, at an appropriate moment, a daughter, even though she did not carry the family name, could help advance a family's social status—particularly in a burgeoning middle-class society. As a result, the issue of marriage loomed large in the life of a dutiful middle-class daughter. Although marriage did not generally occur until the girl's early twenties, it was an event for which she was continually prepared, and a desirable outcome for all depended on the ability of the parents and the child to work together—that is, to state clearly what each wanted or to read each other's heart and mind. In the context of marital expectations, a daughter's refusal to eat was a provocative rejection of both the family's social aspirations and their goodwill toward her. All of the parents' plans for her future (and their own) could be stymied by her peculiar and unpleasant alimentary nihilism.   5

Beyond the specific anxieties generated by marital pressure, the Victorian family milieu in America and in Western Europe harbored a mélange of other tensions and problems that provided the emotional preconditions for the emergence of anorexia nervosa. As love replaced authority as the cement of family relations, it began to generate its own sense of emotional disorders.   6

Possessiveness, for example, became an acute problem in Victorian family life. Where love between parents and children was the prevailing ethic, there was always the risk of excess. When love became suffocating or manipulative, individuation and separation from the family could become extremely painful, if not impossible. In the context of increased intimacy, adolescent privacy was especially problematic: For parents and their sexually maturing daughters, what constituted an appropriate degree of privacy? Middle-class girls, for example, almost always had their own rooms or shared them with sisters, but they had greater difficulty establishing autonomous psychic space. The well-known penchant of adolescent girls for novel-reading was an expression of their need for imaginative freedom. Some parents, recognizing that their daughters needed channels for expressing emotions, encouraged diary-keeping. But some of the same parents who gave lovely marbled journals as gifts also monitored their content. Since emotional freedom was not an acknowledged prerogative of the Victorian adolescent girl, it seems likely that she would have expressed unhappiness in non-verbal forms of behavior. One such behavior was refusal of food.   7

When an adolescent daughter became sullen and chronically refused to eat, her 8
parents felt threatened and confused. The daughter was perceived as willfully manipulating her appetite the way a younger child might. Because parents did not want to encourage this behavior, they often refused at first to indulge the favorite tastes or caprices of their daughter. As emaciation became visible and the girl looked ill, many violated the contemporary canon of prudent child-rearing and put aside their moral objections to pampering the appetite. Eventually they would beg their daughter to eat whatever she liked—and eat she must, "as a sovereign proof of affection" for them. From the parents' perspective, a return to eating was a confirmation of filial love.

The significance of food refusal as an emotional tactic within the family de- 9
pended on food's being plentiful, pleasing, and connected to love. Where food was eaten simply to assuage hunger, where it had only minimal aesthetic and symbolic messages, or where the girls had to provide their own nourishment, refusal of food was not particularly noteworthy or defiant. In contrast, the anorexic girl was surrounded by a provident, if not indulgent, family that was bound to be distressed by her rejection of its largess.

Anorexia nervosa was an intense form of discourse that honored the emotional 10
guidelines that governed the middle-class Victorian family. Refusing to eat was not as confrontational as yelling, having a tantrum, or throwing things; refusing to eat expressed emotional hostility without being flamboyant. And refusing to eat had the advantage of being ambiguous.

In her own way, the anorexic was respectful of what historian Peter Gay called 11
"the great bourgeois compromise between the need for reserve and the capacity for emotion." The rejection of food, while an emotionally charged behavior, was also discreet, quiet, and ladylike. The unhappy adolescent who was in all other ways a dutiful daughter chose food refusal from within the symptom repertoire available to her. Precisely because she was not a lunatic, she selected a behavior that she knew would have some efficacy within her own family.

The So-What Factor. A cause-and-effect essay always involves an answer to a "how" or "why" or "what-if" question. In this case, the implied question is "Why do adolescent girls sometimes refuse to eat?" In an essay of this kind, the so-what factor is the satisfaction of solving a problem. It's an "aha!" reaction. It's "Oh, now I see what causes lightning," or "Now I understand why a falling barometer precedes bad weather," or in this case, "Now I see what motivates anorexia." What does Brumberg want us to understand, feel, or believe after reading her report? Is there a thesis statement, or is the point implied between the lines?

In paragraph 9 Brumberg argues that anorexia can exist only in an environment in which meals have meaning—and therefore refusing to eat also has meaning. Do you find this analysis persuasive? Is Brumberg's analysis of eating disorders universally valid? Would it explain eating disorders in people you know or have heard about?

What values provide the basis for Brumberg's attitude toward various anorexics, their families, and the motives to which she attributes their behavior? Or, to ask the questions Kenneth Burke might have asked, what is Brumberg's attitude toward the "agents" (their parents and the anorexics), their acts (providing or refusing food), the means available to them (money for the parents, passive aggression for the rebellious daughters), their purposes in behaving the way they do (what children hope to accomplish by refusing to eat, what parents hope to accomplish by providing lavish family meals), and the scene (the family meal, the culture in general) in which their behavior takes place? How are these various elements related to one another? Notice that in Burke's scheme of things, an "act," like refusing to eat, can also be regarded as a means or agency (in this case, means for getting at parents).

In paragraph 3 Brumberg writes that preparing meals "had become a maternal concern no longer deemed appropriate to delegate to wet nurses, domestics, or governesses." This detail has a purpose: if mothers were preparing meals themselves rather than letting servants prepare them, this would explain why mothers were all the more sensitive to their daughters' refusal to eat. And in paragraph 6, Brumberg asserts, perhaps to our surprise, that "love" caused problems in nineteenth-century families: "it began to generate its own sense of emotional disorders." This sentence is a provocative generalization, one that pulls the reader into the following paragraph to discover just how love can be a problem.

Look for other details in the essay and see if you can determine their purpose and relevance.

THE SEVEN COMMON MOVES

1. Beginning. Brumberg's opening paragraph does two things to make us curious: it announces a problem, anorexia nervosa, that most readers would find serious and puzzling; and it tells us that what we thought we knew about it—that it is a modern problem—is untrue. These two moves are intended to unsettle us enough to propel us further into the essay.

2. Ending. Just as quotations can be useful to begin an essay, they can also provide a sense of closure. In this case, Brumberg cites a famous historian, Peter Gay, to support and summarize her thesis. Notice that Gay does not seem to have been writing about anorexic behavior, but about the way feelings were expressed or suppressed by the bourgeoisie (i.e., ordinary Europeans who lived in towns and became successful at business). Brumberg is saying, in effect, that her observations about anorexia as an expression of rebellion fits right in with the larger picture that had been painted by a famous historian. The rest of the paragraph brings the essay to a close by paraphrasing and restating the thesis.

3. Detail. Even though this essay lacks footnotes and scholarly references, the details presume a great deal of research. The references to Sir William Withey Gull and Charles Lasègue in paragraph 1, the reference to "popular domestic manual" in paragraph 2, the generalizations about family meals and the quotation from *Common Sense of Maid, Wife, and Mother* in paragraph 3—in fact, the historical allusions throughout the essay are all evidence that Brumberg spent many months in libraries discovering information that would be news to her readers and interesting in the context of a puzzle—the strange behavior of anorexics—she wanted to understand. Brumberg's details are typical of those found in cause-and-effect essays not based on personal experience. They are not the sort of essays that can be written on short notice. To write an essay of this sort, you have to be prepared to spend time in research or experimentation.

4. *Organization/Plot.* Brumberg's essay could be outlined in this way:

I. Introduction: Problem and thesis (paragraph 1)
II. Family meals and their meaning in the emerging bourgeois culture of the nineteenth century (paragraphs 2 and 3)

Transition: a question and general answer (paragraph 4)

III. What an anorexic might have been rebelling against—namely, the marriage plans imposed by parents (paragraph 5) and a lack of privacy (6 and 7)
IV. Analysis of anorexia within a particular culture: it leads to pampering (paragraph 8); it worked only in families in which meals had symbolic value (paragraph 9); it was sufficiently polite as a form of rebellion (paragraph 10)
V. Conclusion: The polite rebellion of anorexics fits in with what another historian has said about nineteenth-century middle-class culture in general (paragraph 11).

This outline may be called "sui generis" (i.e., "one-of-a-kind"). Brumberg's material would not fit neatly into a standard structure, like a five-paragraph theme, so like most essayists, she created her own while she was writing, like a potter inventing a form as she molds her clay.

You can detect the plot—Brumberg's reason for arranging the parts the way she does—if you were to try to rearrange the sections in some other sequence. The beginning, of course, has to be where it is, because it states the problem and arouses our curiosity; and the ending has to be where it is because it provides closure and puts the solution in a larger context. But the other parts could not easily be rearranged without causing some confusion: each one prepares us for the information just ahead. Part II establishes the scene of the action, the family meal; after a transitional paragraph, Part III provides the motives for rebellion; and Part IV analyzes what we have observed. It just wouldn't have made much sense to put the analysis before the observation, or the action before the scene.

Brumberg's "plot," then, is to provide readers with information in the sequence in which it will make sense. It's not enough for writers to divide a topic into logical categories and label them with numerals and letters; the parts have to follow one another in a sequence that will be easy and interesting for readers to follow.

5. Style. In general, Brumberg's sentences are remarkable for what they don't do. They don't mimic the structures of ordinary conversation—as we have seen in other less formal essays, like Ernie Pyle's (p. 14), or Mike Royko's (p. 40), or Marion Winik's (p. 120). And yet they aren't terribly complex, as sentences written by scholars can sometimes be. Brumberg does not pile clause upon clause in a bewildering tangle of subordination. In fact, her sentences are short and simple. If you take away the three sentences in which she quotes more than a few words from other writers, the average length of her sentences is just a fraction above 20 words (20.42, to be precise)—not as short as Mike Royko's (12.95) or Ernie Pyle's (16.29), but still shorter than the average for magazines like *Harper's* and *Atlantic* (24.7).

Some academics seem to think that unless their prose is complex, it won't be taken seriously. Brumberg's style is a notable and successful exception. Her history of anorexia is scholarly enough to be published by Harvard University Press, and yet clear enough to be printed in the *Atlantic*, a magazine that prides itself on essays that are both clear and intelligent. Her style is arguably what every good academic writer should aspire to.

Although it is hard to find specific stylistic devices in this essay—similes, metaphors, cumulative sentences, and the like—it is still possible to discover all the subtle ways in which Brumberg's style differs from ordinary conversation. One difference is in what it lacks: it lacks fragments, digressions, and all the normal inefficiencies of conversation. Another difference is in what it has—a much broader vocabulary and tightness of structure that we don't normally encounter in ordinary social talk. You can discover these qualities by reading each sentence aloud and imagining yourself saying it spontaneously in conversation. Figure out what it is that wouldn't seem natural in speech, even though it is quite at home in print. That move, whatever it is, is part of Brumberg's style.

6. Voice/Attitude. Brumberg's essay was originally published in the same magazine that published David Foster Wallace's somewhat sassy description of clog dancing (see p. 25). And yet there is a remarkable difference in the voice and attitude projected by each writer. Wallace, you may remember, used everything from learned language to slang, and even a bit of mild profanity. Brumberg is much more polite in her diction; it would be hard to imagine words like "kickass" or a phrase like "I'd nipped in here only to get a bottle of soda pop"—the sort of phrase that makes Wallace seem relaxed and irreverent. Instead, Brumberg lets us know that she is a serious scholar right in the first paragraph when she uses a phrase that is not likely to occur in any ordinary newspaper story: "cultural imperative" (i.e., an obligation imposed by a culture)—a subtle allusion to the "categorical imperative" (i.e., an innate sense of obligation) of German philosopher, Immanuel Kant.

In fact, throughout the essay Brumberg uses words and phrases that would seem too learned for the front page of a newspaper: "a dysfunction in the bourgeois family system" (paragraph 1); "gustatory" (paragraph 3); "alimentary nihilism" (paragraph 5); "symptom repertoire" (paragraph 11). There's considerable playfulness in Wallace's voice, and considerable seriousness in Brumberg's. Her serious, professional, professorial voice is a deliberate move—an attempt to seem authoritative but not pompous. It's a move calculated to make us believe and trust. She is objective. Free of frill, foolishness, contractions, first-person pronouns. And yet her voice has the one quality that the late Canadian essayist, Hugh McLennan, considered essential to all good essays: intimacy. Brumberg still manages to write like a unique individual—even if she is quite a different sort of human being from the one implied in Wallace's essay.

7. Economy. In paragraph 2, Brumberg quotes a "popular domestic manual": "simple, healthy food, exquisitely prepared, and served upon shining dishes and brilliant silverware"? Would it have been more economical if she had just summarized that passage? Would the essay have been more effective or less effective without those details? In paragraph 10, Brumberg writes "yelling, having a tantrum, or throwing things." Wouldn't it have been more economical just to say "having a tantrum"? Would the passage be better if it had been written that way, or does Brumberg gain anything by including more detail?

Moves within Moves.   The dominant mode of this essay is a cause-and-effect analysis. But if you look closely, you will see that it includes some of the other modes and methods of development that are treated as separate chapters in this book. The body of the essay is actually a process analysis, as many cause-and-effect essays tend to be: Brumberg analyzes a process in which a set of parental values leads to a disturbing behavior in children. You will also find comparison and contrast in paragraph 1 (Brumberg's theory compared with common assumptions about anorexia) and paragraph 9 (two styles of eating habits are compared); exemplification (reference to the two doctors) in paragraph 1, paragraph 7, and in fact throughout; description in paragraph 2.

Words, Phrases, and Allusions.   The following items were taken from "The Origins of Anorexia Nervosa" in order of appearance. With the help of your classmates, locate these words in the essay and see if their context provides a clue to their meaning. If necessary, consult a dictionary, an encyclopedia, or other reference work to determine what each item means in its context. You probably know most of these words from conversation and reading, but you may not yet feel comfortable using them in your own writing.

> malady, cultural imperative, reciprocity, a dysfunction in the bourgeois family system, milieu, ambiance, domestics, Participation . . . on both a verbal and gustatory level, antithetical, taciturnity, precipitated, social aspirations, stymied, alimentary nihilism, mélange, prevailing ethic, marbled journals, prerogative, caprices, emaciation, contemporary canon of prudent child-rearing, filial love, assuage, aesthetic, provident, discreet, symptom repertoire

Notice other words and phrases in the essay that might be worth adding to your vocabulary.

Suggestion for Writing

Using Brumberg's essay as a model, write a cause-and-effect paper analyzing an example of human behavior that people find puzzling. Possible topics include any sort of human behavior that seems eccentric or at odds with the normal expectations of a culture. The journal entry suggested at the beginning of this chapter may provide you with ideas you want to develop. Although Brumberg's essay was based on research, yours might well be based on personal experience with adolescents you have known, including yourself. Within the essay, be sure to make any of the other modes and methods that might help you make your case: define, describe, compare and contrast, give examples. You might also use Kenneth Burke's pentad to help you search for clues about the causes of human behavior:

> **Actor.** Consider all the influences that make the actor what he or she is—membership in various groups (family, religious affiliation, nationality, political party, economic status, age). Do any of these factors have any bearing on the act?
>
> **Act.** What is the behavior that you find puzzling? What does it mean to the person doing it? What does it mean to persons observing it? Does it have any hidden meanings?
>
> **Agency.** What does a person need in order to behave this way? What would happen if the means were not available?
>
> **Scene.** Consider the behavior in its cultural, geographical, religious, and political contexts. Do any of these contexts help explain the behavior?
>
> **Purpose.** What do the people behaving this way hope to gain? What do other actors on the scene hope to gain from their behavior?

Don't let these questions become a burden. Try hard to answer each one, but realize that for any given behavior, you are likely to find some of these questions more productive than others.

Journal Entry.   Hardly any public policy is immune from criticism: schools, welfare, the local library, prisons, public transportation, higher education, student government, road maintenance—all these things, no matter how good they are, get blamed for not being even better. Choose a public policy that you think could be improved, but instead of just complaining, see if you can formulate a positive recommendation to eliminate the cause of failure. After you have worked on this project for a while, read the following essay in which Wilbert Rideau explains why prisons don't work. Rideau writes from experience: he had been in the Louisiana State Penitentiary thirty-one years when he published this essay in *Time*. As you read his essay, look for moves you can imitate in your own.

Why Prisons Don't Work

Wilbert Rideau

I was among 31 murderers sent to the Louisiana State Penitentiary in 1962 to be 1
executed or imprisoned for life. We weren't much different from those we found
here, or those who had preceded us. We were unskilled, impulsive and uneducated
misfits, mostly black, who had done dumb, impulsive things—failures, rejects from
the larger society. Now a generation has come of age and gone since I've been
here, and everything is much the same as I found it. The faces of the prisoners are
different, but behind them are the same impulsive, uneducated, unskilled minds that
made dumb, impulsive choices that got them into more trouble than they ever
thought existed. The vast majority of us are consigned to suffer and die here so
politicians can sell the illusion that permanently exiling people to prison will make
society safe.

Getting tough has always been a "silver bullet," a quick fix for the crime and 2
violence that society fears. Each year in Louisiana—where excess is a way of
life—lawmakers have tried to outdo each other in legislating harsher mandatory
penalties and in reducing avenues of release. The only thing to do with criminals,
they say, is get tougher. They have. In the process, the purpose of prison began to
change. The state boasts one of the highest lockup rates in the country, imposes the
most severe penalties in the nation, and vies to execute more criminals per capita
than anywhere else. This state is so tough that last year, when prison authorities
here wanted to punish an inmate in solitary confinement for an infraction, the most
they could inflict on him was to deprive him of his underwear. It was all he
had left.

If getting tough resulted in public safety, Louisiana citizens would be the safest   3
in the nation. They're not. Louisiana has the highest murder rate among states.
Prison, like the police and the courts, has a minimal impact on crime because it is a
response after the fact, a mop-up operation. It doesn't work. The idea of punishing
the few to deter the many is counterfeit because potential criminals either think
they're not going to get caught or they're so emotionally desperate or psychologically distressed that they don't care about the consequences of their actions. The
threatened punishment, regardless of its severity, is never a factor in the equation.
But society, like the incorrigible criminal it abhors, is unable to learn from its mistakes.

Prison has a role in public safety, but it is not a cure-all. Its value is limited, and   4
its use should also be limited to what it does best: isolating young criminals long
enough to give them a chance to grow up and get a grip on their impulses. It is a
traumatic experience, certainly, but it should be only a temporary one, not a way of
life. Prisoners kept too long tend to embrace the criminal culture, its distorted values and beliefs; they have little choice—prison is their life. There are some prisoners who cannot be returned to society—serial killers, serial rapists, professional hit
men and the like—but the monsters who need to die in prison are rare exceptions in
the criminal landscape.

Crime is a young man's game. Most of the nation's random violence is com-   5
mitted by young urban terrorists. But because of long, mandatory sentences, most
prisoners here are much older, having spent 15, 20, 30 or more years behind bars,
long past necessity. Rather than pay for new prisons, society would be well served
by releasing some of its older prisoners who pose no threat and using the money to
catch young street thugs. Warden John Whitley agrees that many older prisoners
here could be freed tomorrow with little or no danger to society. Release, however,
is governed by law or by politicians, not by penal professionals. Even murderers,
those most feared by society, pose little risk.

Historically, for example, the domestic staff at Louisiana's Governor's man-   6
sion has been made up of murderers, hand-picked to work among the chief-of-state
and his family. Penologists have long known that murder is almost always a once-
in-a lifetime act. The most dangerous criminal is the one who has not yet killed but
has a history of escalating offenses. He's the one to watch.

Rehabilitation can work. Everyone changes in time. The trick is to influence   7
the direction that change takes. The problem with prisons is that they don't do more
to rehabilitate those confined in them. The convict who enters prison illiterate will
probably leave the same way. Most convicts want to be better than they are, but education is not a priority. This prison houses 4,600 men and offers academic training
to 240, vocational training to a like number. Perhaps it doesn't matter. About 90%
of the men here may never leave this prison alive.

The only effective way to curb crime is for society to work to *prevent* the crim-   8
inal act in the first place, to come between the perpetrator and crime. Our youngsters must be taught to respect the humanity of others and to handle disputes with-

out violence. It is essential to educate and equip them with the skills to pursue their life ambitions in a meaningful way. As a community, we must address the adverse life circumstances that spawn criminality. These things are not quick, and they're not easy, but they're effective. Politicians think that's too hard a sell. They want to be on record for doing something now, something they can point to at re-election time. So the drumbeat goes on for more police, more prisons, more of the same failed policies.

Ever see a dog chase its tail?   9

UNDERSTANDING THE ESSAY

1. According to Wilbert Rideau, what sorts of criminals should be kept behind bars for life? What sorts ought to be rehabilitated and set free after a reasonable time? What sorts of criminals does Rideau consider most in need of watching?
2. What are the consequences, good and bad, of keeping criminals in prison after they are no longer a danger to society? What would be the consequences, good and bad, of rehabilitating them and setting them free?
3. What does Rideau mean when he says that politicians "sell the illusion that permanently exiling people to prison will make society safe"?
4. What does he mean when he says that "Crime is a young man's game"?
5. Using Kenneth Burke's pentad, analyze the various behaviors Rideau describes—the behavior of the various kinds of criminals he describes, the behavior of society in responding to these criminals.

So What and the Seven Common Moves.   Analyze this essay with the help of the questions about "So What and the Seven Common Moves" found on the back cover of this book.

Words, Phrases, and Allusions.   The following items were taken from "Why Prisons Don't Work" in order of appearance. With the help of your classmates, locate these words in the essay and see if their context provides a clue to their meaning. If necessary, consult a dictionary, an encyclopedia, or other reference work to determine what each item means in its context. You probably know most of these words from conversation and reading, but you may not yet feel comfortable using them in your own writing.

silver bullet, per capita, psychologically distressed, severity, incorrigible, abhor, penologists, escalating, rehabilitation, spawn criminality

Suggestion for Writing

Using "Why Prisons Don't Work" as a model, write an essay in which you help your readers understand why some public institution is not as successful as it might be and how you would suggest improving it. The journal entry suggested at the beginning of this selection may have given you an idea for a topic, or you may have thought of other topics as you read Rideau's essay.

In Other Words

Peter Farb

Early in this century, a horse named Hans amazed the people of Berlin by his extraordinary ability to perform rapid calculations in mathematics. After a problem was written on a blackboard placed in front of him, he promptly counted out the answer by tapping the low numbers with his right forefoot and multiples of ten with his left. Trickery was ruled out because Hans's owner, unlike owners of other performing animals, did not profit financially—and Hans even performed feats whether or not the owner was present. The psychologist O. Pfungst witnessed one of these performances and became convinced that there had to be a more logical explanation than the uncanny intelligence of a horse.

Because Hans performed only in the presence of an audience that could see the blackboard and therefore knew the correct answer, Pfungst reasoned that the secret lay in observation of the audience rather than of the horse. He finally discovered that as soon as the problem was written on the blackboard, the audience bent forward very slightly in anticipation to watch Hans's forefeet. As slight as that movement was, Hans perceived it and took it as his signal to begin tapping. As his taps approached the correct number, the audience became tense with excitement and made almost imperceptible movements of the head—which signaled Hans to stop counting. The audience, simply by expecting Hans to stop when the correct number was reached, had actually told the animal when to stop. Pfungst clearly demonstrated that Hans's intelligence was nothing but a mechanical response to his audience, which unwittingly communicated the answer by its body language.

The "Clever Hans Phenomenon," as it has come to be known, raises an interesting question. If a mere horse can detect unintentional and extraordinary subtle body signals, might they not also be detected by human beings? Professional gamblers and con men have long been known for their skill in observing the body-language cues of their victims, but only recently has it been shown scientifically that all speakers constantly detect and interpret such cues also, even though they do not realize it.

An examination of television word games several years ago revealed that contestants inadvertently gave their partners body-language signals that led to correct answers. In one such game, contestants had to elicit certain words from their partners, but they were permitted to give only brief verbal clues as to what the words might be. It turned out that sometimes the contestants also gave body signals that were much more informative than the verbal clues. In one case, a contestant was supposed to answer *sad* in response to his partner's verbal clue of *happy*—that is, the correct answer was a word opposite to the verbal clue. The partner giving the *happy* clue unconsciously used his body to indicate to his fellow contestant that an opposite word was needed. He did that by shifting his body and head very slightly to one side as he said *happy*, then to the other side in expectation of an opposite word.

Contestants on a television program are usually unsophisticated about psychology and linguistics, but trained psychological experimenters also unintentionally flash body signals which are sometimes detected by the test subjects—and which may distort the results of experiments. Hidden cameras have revealed that the sex of the experimenter, for example, can influence the responses of subjects. Even though the films showed that both male and female experimenters carried out the experiments in the same way and asked the same questions, the experimenters were very much aware of their own sex in relation to the sex of the subjects. Male experimenters spent 16 percent more time carrying out experiments with female subjects than they did with male subjects; similarly, female experimenters took 13 percent longer to go through experiments with male subjects than they did with female subjects. The cameras also revealed that chivalry is not dead in the psychological experiment; male experimenters smiled about six times as often with female subjects as they did with male subjects.

The important question, of course, is whether or not such nonverbal communication influences the results of experiments. The answer is that it often does. Psychologists who have watched films made without the knowledge of either the experimenters or the subjects could predict almost immediately which experiments would obtain results from their subjects that were in the direction of the experimenters' own biases. Those experimenters who seemed more dominant, personal, and relaxed during the first moments of conversation with their subjects usually obtained results that they secretly hoped the experiments would yield. And they somehow communicated their secret hopes in a completely visual way, regardless of what they said or their paralanguage when they spoke. That was made clear when these films were shown to two groups, one of which saw the films without hearing the sound track while the other heard only the sound track without seeing the films. The group that heard only the voices could not accurately predict the experimenters' biases—but those who saw the films without hearing the words immediately sensed whether or not the experimenters were communicating their biases.

A person who signals his expectations about a certain kind of behavior is not aware that he is doing so—and usually he is indignant when told that his experiment was biased—but the subjects themselves confirm his bias by their performances. Such bias in experiments has been shown to represent self-fulfilling prophecies. In other words, the experimenters' expectations about the results of the experiment actually result in those expectations coming true. That was demonstrated when each of twelve experimenters was given five rats bred from an identical strain of laboratory animals. Half of the experimenters were told that their rats could be expected to perform brilliantly because they had been bred especially for high intelligence and quickness in running through a maze. The others were told that their rats could be expected to perform very poorly because they had been bred for low intelligence. All the experimenters were then asked to teach their rats to run in a maze.

Almost as soon as the rats were put into the maze it became clear that those for 8 which the experimenters had high expectation would prove to be the better performers. And the rats which were expected to perform badly did in fact perform very badly, even though they were bred from the identical strain as the excellent performers. Some of these poor performers did not even budge from their starting positions in the maze. The misleading prophecy about the behavior of the two groups of rats was unfulfilled—simply because the two groups of experimenters unconsciously communicated their expectations to the animals. Those experimenters who anticipated high performance were friendlier to their animals than those who expected low performance; they handled their animals more, and they did so more gently. Clearly, the predictions of the experimenters were communicated to the rats in subtle and unintended ways—and the rats behaved accordingly.

Since animals such as laboratory rats and Clever Hans can detect body- 9 language cues, it is not surprising that human beings are just as perceptive in detecting visual signals about expectations for performance. It is a psychological truth that we are likely to speak to a person whom we expect to be unpleasant in such a way that we force him to act unpleasantly. But it has only recently become apparent that poor children—often black or Spanish-speaking—perform badly in school because that is what their teachers expect of them, and because the teachers manage to convey that expectation by both verbal and nonverbal channels. True to the teachers' prediction, the black and brown children probably will do poorly—not necessarily because children from minority groups are capable only of poor performance, but because poor performance has been expected of them. The first grade may be the place where teachers anticipate poor performances by children of certain racial, economic, and cultural backgrounds—and where the teachers actually teach these children how to fail.

Evidence of the way the "Clever Hans Phenomenon" works in many schools 10 comes from a careful series of experiments by psychologist Robert Rosenthal and his co-workers at Harvard University. They received permission from a school south of San Francisco to give a series of tests to the children in the lower grades. The teachers were blatantly lied to. They were told that the test was a newly developed tool that could predict which children would be "spurters" and achieve high performance in the coming year. Actually, the experimenters administered a new kind of IQ test that the teachers were unlikely to have seen previously. After IQ scores were obtained, the experimenters selected the names of 20 percent of the children completely at random. Some of the selected children scored very high on the IQ test and others scored low, some were from middle-class families and others from lower-class. Then the teachers were lied to again. The experimenters said that the tests singled out this 20 percent as the children who could be expected to make unusual intellectual gains in the coming year. The teachers were also cautioned not to discuss the test results with the pupils or their parents. Since the names of these children had been selected completely at random, any difference between them and the 80 percent not designated as "spurters" was completely in the minds of the teachers.

All the children were given IQ tests again during that school year and once 11 more the following year. The 20 percent who had been called to the attention of their teachers did indeed turn in the high performances expected of them—in some cases dramatic increases of 25 points in IQ. The teachers' comments about these children also were revealing. The teachers considered them more happy, curious, and interesting than the other 80 percent—and they predicted that they would be successes in life, a prophecy they had already started to fulfill. The experiment plainly showed that children who are expected to gain intellectually do gain and that their behavior improves as well.

The results of the experiment are clear—but the explanation for the results is 12 not. It might be imagined that the teachers simply devoted more time to the children singled out for high expectations, but the study showed that was not so. Instead, the influence of the teachers upon these children apparently was more subtle. What the teachers said to them, how and when it was said, the facial expressions, gestures, postures, perhaps even touch that accompanied their speech—some or all of these things must have communicated that the teachers expected improved performance from them. And when these children responded correctly, the teachers were quicker to praise them and also more lavish in their praise. Whatever the exact mechanism was, the effect upon the children who had been singled out was dramatic. They changed their ideas about themselves, their behavior, their motivation, and their learning capacities.

The lesson of the California experiment is that pupil performance does not de- 13 pend so much upon a school's audio-visual equipment or new textbooks or enriching trips to museums as it does upon teachers whose body language communicates high expectations for the pupils—even if the teacher thinks she "knows" that a black, a Puerto Rican, a Mexican-American, or any other disadvantaged child is fated to do poorly in school. Apparently, remedial instruction in our schools is misdirected. It is needed more by the middle-class teachers than by the disadvantaged children.

UNDERSTANDING THE ESSAY

1. Write a single sentence in which you say what "In Other Words" is about. Compare your sentence with your classmates' sentences.
2. What lie were teachers told as part of an experiment described in this essay? Do you think a lie of this sort is ethical for research purposes? Explain your answer.
3. The mathematical performance by Hans the horse is used as analogy for human behavior. Do you find the analogy persuasive? Give reasons.
4. What sort of inductive evidence does Farb offer to support his thesis that students perform better if teachers expect them to perform better? Is this evidence absolutely conclusive?
5. Do you agree with the last sentence in the essay? Why or why not?

So What and the Seven Common Moves.   Analyze this essay with the help of the questions about "So What and the Seven Common Moves" found on the back cover of this book.

Words, Phrases, and Allusions.   The following items were taken from "In Other Words" in order of appearance. With the help of your classmates, locate these words in the essay and see if their context provides a clue to their meaning. If necessary, consult a dictionary, an encyclopedia, or other reference work to determine what each item means in its context. You probably know most of these words from conversation and reading, but you may not yet feel comfortable using them in your own writing.

Phenomenon, elicit, linguistics, paralanguage, indignant, self-fulfilling prophecies, blatantly, lavish

Suggestion for Writing

Using "In Other Words" as a model, write an essay in which you help your readers understand the causes of failure or success. The journal entry suggested at the beginning of this selection may have given you an idea for a topic, or you may have thought of other topics as you read Farb's essay.

Journal Entry. Have you ever noticed that things can own you as much as you own them? We like to imagine that having a boat, or a car, or a cat, or a house is an act of mastery; but often, it turns out that the thing owned becomes the master, making unruly demands on our time and energy, sometimes causing even more profound changes in our personality and self-image. Think of one or several instances in which possessions become possessors. Write a cause-and-effect essay, perhaps in the form of a story, indicating how a person can be changed by ownership. After you have worked on this project for a while, read the following essay in which E. M. Forster explains how a plot of land he thought he owned actually owned him. As you read the essay, look for moves you can imitate in your own.

My Wood

E. M. Forster

A few years ago I wrote a book which dealt in part with the difficulties of the English in India. Feeling that they would have had no difficulties in India themselves, the Americans read the book freely. The more they read it the better it made them feel, and a check to the author was the result. I bought a wood with the check. It is not a large wood—it contains scarcely any trees, and it is intersected, blast it, by a public footpath. Still, it is the first property that I have owned, so it is right that other people should participate in my shame, and should ask themselves, in accents that will vary in horror, this very important question: What is the effect of property upon the character? Don't let's touch economics; the effect of private ownership upon the community as a whole is another question—a more important question, perhaps, but another one. Let's keep to psychology. If you own things, what's their effect on you? What's the effect on me of my wood?

In the first place, it makes me feel heavy. Property does have this effect. Property produces men of weight, and it was a man of weight who failed to get into the Kingdom of Heaven. He was not wicked, that unfortunate millionaire in the parable, he was only stout; he stuck out in front, not to mention behind, and as he wedged himself this way and that in the crystalline entrance and bruised his well-fed flanks, he saw beneath him a comparatively slim camel passing through the eye of a needle and being woven into the robe of God. The Gospels all through couple stoutness and slowness. They point out what is perfectly obvious, yet seldom realized; that if you have a lot of things you cannot move about a lot, that furniture requires dusting, dusters require servants, servants require insurance stamps, and the whole tangle of them makes you think twice before you accept an invitation to dinner or go for a

1

2

bath in the Jordan. Sometimes the Gospels proceed further and say with Tolstoy that property is sinful; they approach the difficult ground of asceticism here, where I cannot follow them. But as to the immediate effects of property on people, they just show straightforward logic. It produces men of weight. Men of weight cannot, by definition, move like the lightning from the East unto the West, and the ascent of a fourteen-stone bishop into a pulpit is thus the exact antithesis of the coming of the Son of Man. My wood makes me feel heavy.

In the second place, it makes me feel it ought to be larger. 3

The other day I heard a twig snap in it. I was annoyed at first, for I thought that 4 someone was blackberrying, and depreciating the value of the undergrowth. On coming nearer, I saw it was not a man who had trodden on the twig and snapped it, but a bird, and I felt pleased. My bird. The bird was not equally pleased. Ignoring the relation between us, it took fright as soon as it saw the shape of my face, and flew straight over the boundary hedge into a field, the property of Mrs. Henessy, where it sat down with a loud squawk. It had become Mrs. Henessy's bird. Something seemed grossly amiss here, something that would not have occurred had the wood been larger. I could not afford to buy Mrs. Henessy out, I dared not murder her, and limitations of this sort beset me on every side. . . .

In the third place, property makes its owner feel that he ought to do something 5 to it. Yet he isn't sure what. A restlessness comes over him, a vague sense that he has a personality to express—the same sense which, without any vagueness, leads the artist to an act of creation. Sometimes I think I will cut down such trees as remain in the wood, at other times I want to fill up the gaps between them with new trees. Both impulses are pretentious and empty. They are not honest movements toward money-making or beauty. They spring from a foolish desire to express myself and from an inability to enjoy what I have got. Creation, property, enjoyment form a sinister trinity in the human mind. Creation and enjoyment are both very, very good, yet they are often unattainable without a material basis, and at such moments property pushes itself in as a substitute, saying, "Accept me instead—I'm good enough for all three." It is not enough. It is, as Shakespeare said of lust, "The expense of spirit in a waste of shame": it is "Before, a joy proposed; behind, a dream." Yet we don't know how to shun it. It is forced on us by our economic system as the alternative to starvation. It is also forced on us by an internal defect in the soul, by the feeling that in property may lie the germs of self-development and of exquisite or heroic deeds. Our life on earth is, and ought to be, material and carnal. But we have not yet learned to manage our materialism and carnality properly; they are still entangled with the desire for ownership, where (in the words of Dante) "Possession is one with loss."

And this brings us to our fourth and final point: the blackberries. 6

Blackberries are not plentiful in this meagre grove, but they are easily seen 7 from the public footpath which traverses it, and all too easily gathered. Foxgloves, too—people will pull up the foxgloves, and ladies of an educational tendency even grub for toadstools to show them on the Monday in class. Other ladies, less educated, roll down the bracken in the arms of their gentlemen friends. There is paper, what? They are both professional teams, both located in New York. So what? Your paper will be interesting only if you find differences or similarities that strike you as odd or paradoxical, or that help you understand the subject of your essay

Here is a recipe for writing a comparison and contrast essay:

1. Choose a pair of things that you know more about than most of your readers do.
2. If the similarities between the two things are obvious, look for interesting differences; if the differences are obvious, look for interesting similarities. The key word here is interesting. If your paper points out only what is already obvious to your readers, it will lack a so-what factor.
3. Write the similarities and differences on note cards or separate slips of paper.
4. Arrange the cards or slips in the sequence that will best maintain the interest of your readers. Usually it is more effective to weave back and forth between the things you are comparing or contrasting rather than treating one first and then the other.
5. After you've selected and arranged your details, add an introduction and an ending.
6. Show a draft to fellow students in a formal or informal workshop, and see if your strategies are having the effects you want them to have. Use the checklist on the back cover to focus your discussion. Then look for errors in spelling, grammar, or punctuation that you will want to correct in your final draft.

B. Writing against the Text

Do not be intimidated by the appearance of objectivity in the essays in this chapter: Marie Winn's interpretation of modern childhood, for example, is arguably a bit skewed, colored by what she sees in a particular part of the country, and by what she *wants* to see. Even a great historian, like Bruce Catton, may be tempted to romanticize his famous pair of generals, to let us see them as he wants us to see them. Find room for disagreement in any essay in this chapter. Write a comparison/contrast essay of your own offering a different interpretation.

C. Writing from Research

Using the library and the Web, locate information about two people or things that have something important in common: for example, two battles (e.g., the attack on Pearl Harbor and the bombing of Hiroshima), two famous people (e.g., Washington and Jefferson), two cities (e.g., New York and Paris). Or consider one person or thing before and after a significant event: for example, London before and after the Great Fire, or American welfare policy before and after the Great Depression, or

Muhammad Ali before and after his debilitating illness. Look for similarities and differences that you find interesting. After you've completed your research, write a draft in your own words without consulting your sources; this will help you avoid being overwhelmed by what you read and perhaps unintentionally plagiarizing material. Then go back and add material from your research wherever you think it will make your paper more interesting or authoritative. Be sure to acknowledge the source of anything you quote or paraphrase.

there are tins. Pray, does my wood belong to me or doesn't it? And, if it does, should I not own it best by allowing no one else to walk there? There is a wood near Lyme Regis, also cursed by a public footpath, where the owner has not hesitated on this point. He had built high stone walls each side of the path, and has spanned it by bridges, so that the public circulate like termites while he gorges on the blackberries unseen. He really does own his wood, this able chap. And perhaps I shall come to this in time. I shall wall in and fence out until I really taste the sweets of property. Enormously stout, endlessly avaricious, pseudo-creative, intensely selfish, I shall weave upon my forehead the quadruple crown of possession until those nasty Bolshies come and take it off again and thrust me aside into the outer darkness.

UNDERSTANDING THE ESSAY

1. According to E. M. Forster, how does owning property affect the person who owns it?
2. Are the issues he raises of the sort that could be settled by scientific data, or are we limited to evidence based upon an intuitive sense of how people behave?
3. Forster speaks metaphorically when he says in paragraph 2 that property produces "men of weight." Is the metaphor merely decorative, an addition to what might have been said more plainly? Can this metaphor be separated from its meaning?
4. What is the point of the story about the bird in paragraph 4?
5. What parallels does Forster see between his ownership of a plot of land and England's colonization of India?

So What and the Seven Common Moves. Analyze this essay with the help of the questions about "So What and the Seven Common Moves" found on the back cover of this book.

Words, Phrases, and Allusions. The following items were taken from "My Wood" in order of appearance. With the help of your classmates, locate these words in the essay and see if their context provides a clue to their meaning. If necessary, consult a dictionary, an encyclopedia, or other reference work to determine what each item means in its context. You probably know most of these words from conversation and reading, but you may not yet feel comfortable using them in your own writing.

intersected, men of weight, crystalline entrance, Tolstoy, asceticism, ascent, fourteen-stone bishop, pulpit, antithesis, depreciating, trodden, beset, pretentious, unattainable without a material basis, meagre grove, traverses, foxgloves, grub for toadstools, bracken, spanned, gorges, Bolshies

Suggestion for Writing

Using "My Wood" as a model, write an essay about the changes ownership can make in an owner. The journal entry suggested at the beginning of this selection may have given you an idea for a topic, or you may have thought of other topics as you read Forster's essay.

RECIPES FOR WRITING ABOUT CAUSE AND EFFECT

A. Writing from Personal Experience

Writing a cause-and-effect paper about human behavior is in some ways easier than writing one about physical events. When we write about human behavior (e.g., what causes teenagers to rebel against their parents), we are essentially speculating. We are speculating even when we write about the causes of our own behavior; we do not necessarily know why we do what we choose to do, but at least we have first-hand knowledge of some evidence. When we write about physical phenomena (e.g., why diesel engines last longer than gasoline engines), readers expect us to have conducted experiments, research, or first-hand observations.

Here is a recipe for writing a cause-and-effect essay:

1. Choose a phenomenon that you already understand: it could be a physical phenomenon, or someone else's behavior, or even your own behavior.
2. Make sure your subject has causes or effects that are capable of being developed into an essay. It's not enough to say, "oceanic tides are caused by the gravitational pull of the moon." To write an essay, you have to be prepared to develop the cause or the effect by using any of the conceptual moves treated as separate chapters in this book, or, in the case of human behavior, by using Kenneth Burke's pentad as a method of analysis (see p. 146).
3. Write the causes or effects on separate slips of paper and arrange the slips in the sequence that will work best to maintain your reader's interest.
4. Develop each cause or effect by describing, narrating, exemplifying, or using any of the other conceptual moves treated as separate chapters in this book.
5. After you have written the body of the paper, add an introduction. In the case of cause-and-effect papers, often the best introduction is to describe a mystery that needs explaining (e.g., how birds find their way to destinations thousands of miles away) or an event likely to have important consequences

(e.g., how computers will affect the way students conduct writing and re-search).

6. Add an ending, perhaps a return to the beginning or a punchy last sen-tence—a zinger.

7. Show a draft to fellow students in a formal or informal workshop, and see if your strategies are having the effects you want them to have. Use the check-list on the back cover to focus your discussion. Then look for errors in spelling, grammar, or punctuation that you will want to correct in your final draft.

B. Writing against the Text

Normally, it is impossible to argue with a cause-effect analysis based on scientific data. It is, however, almost always possible to argue about the causes or effects of any sort of human behavior. You may, for example, know of people with eating dis-orders who cannot possibly be using them to escape the control of their parents. And you may know of property owners who are not at all burdened by their prop-erty the way E. M. Forster seems to have been, or you may know of criminals who, contrary to Wilbert Rideau's theory, end up committing another offense as soon as they are released from jail. Choose a cause-and-effect essay with room for disagree-ment, and rebut it in an essay of your own.

C. Writing from Research

Using the library and the Web, locate information about a subject you cannot ex-plain: fire-walking ceremonies, the migration patterns of whales, the apparent ex-plosion of genius that resulted in the Renaissance, the secret to the success of a con-troversial singer or musician. After you have completed your research, write a draft in your own words without consulting your sources; this will help you avoid being overwhelmed by what you read and perhaps unintentionally plagiarizing material. Then go back and add material from your research wherever you think it will make your paper more interesting or authoritative. Be sure to acknowledge the source of anything you quote or paraphrase.

8

Definitions with Attitude:
When Webster's Not Enough

"What's a trotline?"

Rosie Gomez wants to know. She is a federal agent in a detective novel by James Lee Burke. Of course Gomez could have looked up trotline in a dictionary, like the Merriam-Webster, where she would have found this definition: "a comparatively short setline used (as for catching catfish or crabs) near shore or along streams." But instead, she asks Dave Robicheaux, a deputy sheriff who also runs a bait shop in the swamps of Cajun country. Robicheaux knows trotlines:

> "You stretch a long piece of twine above the water and tie it to a couple of stumps or flooded trees. Then intermittently you hang twelve-inch pieces of weighted line with baited hooks into the water. Catfish feed by the moon, and when they hook themselves, they usually work the hook all the way through their head and they're still on the trotline when the fisherman picks it up in the morning." (*In the Electric Mist with Confederate Dead*, p. 124)

Like all the other modes and methods and conceptual moves discussed in this book, definition occurs universally in speech. Parents define things for children, teachers define things for students, and friends define things for friends.

In writing, definition often occurs as a phrase tucked parenthetically behind an unusual word. Definitions of this sort are common whenever the writer is more expert than the reader—legal writing, technical writing, even journalism when the reporter uses terms that ordinary readers might not understand. By putting brief definitions between commas or parentheses, writers provide help for readers who need it without insulting those who don't.

But written definitions can also be developed and extended in ways that would be impossible in conversation. They can occupy an entire paragraph, like Dave Robicheaux's definition of a "trotline"; they can even occupy entire essays, like those that serve as models in this chapter. You may have been surprised to find a process analysis—a little story with stumps, and trees, and catfish nibbling in the moonlight—as a definition. But in fact, all the modes and methods discussed as separate chapters in this book can be used to frame and develop a definition.

Sometimes the meaning of a word is controlled by the community of people who use it. Accountants, as a community, allow one another little leeway in defining terms like "debentures"; lawyers all generally agree about what "estoppel" is; for mathematicians, "surd" has a definite definition; and microbiologists do not generally argue about the difference between a "virus" and a "bacterium." Terms like these are defined by community consensus, and there is little room for individual interpretation—unless someone is prepared to start a revolution in the discipline.

Once in a while, however, a community disagrees about basic definitions, and that's when serious philosophical conflict takes place. Biologists, for example, do not all agree on the definition of life; lawyers battle in court over definitions of "contract" and "conspiracy" and "cruel and unusual" and even "person"; historians debate the definition of history itself; English professors can argue heatedly about what counts as a "novel" or a "poem," or even about what counts as "English" in the many senses of that word.

Definitions are most likely to be extended when there is no community consensus. Usually abstractions are involved—words like "freedom," "democracy," "justice," "art," "beauty," "poverty," "wealth," "happiness," "jazz," "masculinity," or "femininity"—any word whose meaning is not strictly controlled by a unified community of users. Abstractions leave room for personal definition, definition with attitude.

Attitude is at the heart of every definition essay. It's what gives the essay its energy, its so-what factor. The writer says, in effect, "I've heard all sorts of wrong definitions of *X*, and I'm here to set things straight." Writing a personal definition is a gutsy move. You happen upon a term with a contested meaning, you perceive that important things hang in the balance, so you set out to argue for the meaning you prefer. "Forget the dictionary," you say to your readers, "I'm going to tell you what this word really means." You create a definition.

For a personal definition to be effective, you have to come up with lots of details, usually in the form of examples or stories or any of the other modes or methods of development discussed as separate chapters in this book. Of course you could include a reference to a dictionary or some other authoritative source if it happens to agree with you, but the real power of a personal definition comes from original, first-hand observation. Sometimes Webster is not enough. That's when definitions become essays.

To give your own definition essay a so-what factor, choose a word about which you have strong feelings. Avoid concrete things—like apples, buttercups, calcium, and desktops; these generally lack the sort of space that you need when you create a personal definition. As you read the model essays in this chapter, be sure to notice how the writers use the other modes and methods—usually examples—to develop their definitions.

Journal Entry. Choose an abstract term, like "friendship," or "beauty," or "fairness," or "love," or "education" that you might define differently from the way most people do because you believe in it strongly. Your job is to argue for the "true" meaning of the term. Definition essays are often developed with stories or examples. But you can also develop a definition with any of the other modes or methods discussed in separate chapters of this book: description, process analysis, comparison and contrast, division and classification, and cause-and-effect analysis.

After you've worked on this project for a while, read the following essay, in which Richard Stengel offers a light-hearted definition of "personal space."

Space Invaders

Richard Stengel

At my bank the other day, I was standing in a line snaking around some tired velvet ropes when a man in a sweatsuit started inching toward me in his eagerness to deposit his Social Security check. As he did so, I minutely advanced toward the woman reading the *Wall Street Journal* in front of me, who in mild annoyance, began to sidle up to the man scribbling a check in front of her, who absent-mindedly shuffled toward the white-haired lady ahead of him, until we were all hugger-mugger against each other, the original lazy line having collapsed in on itself like a Slinky. 1

I estimate that my personal space extends eighteen inches in front of my face, one foot to each side, and about ten inches in back—though it is nearly impossible to measure exactly how far behind you someone is standing. The phrase "personal space" has a quaint, seventies ring to it ("You're invading my space, man"), but it is one of those gratifying expressions that are intuitively understood by all human beings. Like the twelve-mile limit around our national shores, personal space is our individual border beyond which no stranger can penetrate without making us uneasy. 2

Lately, I've found that my personal space is being violated more than ever before. In elevators, people are wedging themselves in just before the doors close; on the street, pedestrians are zigzagging through the human traffic, jostling others, refusing to give way; on the subway, riders are no longer taking pains to carve out little zones of space between, themselves and fellow-passengers; in lines at airports, people are pressing forward like fidgety taxis at red lights. 3

At first, I attributed this tendency to the "population explosion" and the relentless Malthusian logic that if twice as many people inhabit the planet as did twenty 4 years ago, each of us has half as much space. Recently, I've wondered if it's the season: T-shirt weather can make proximity more alluring (or much, much less). Or perhaps the proliferation of coffee bars in Manhattan—the number seems to double every three months—is infusing so much caffeine into the already jangling locals that people can no longer keep to themselves.

Personal space is mostly a public matter; we allow all kinds of invasions of per-   5
sonal space in private. (Humanity wouldn't exist without them.) The logistics of it vary according to geography. People who live in Calcutta have less personal space than folks in Colorado. "Don't tread on me" could have been coined only by some-one with a spread. I would wager that people in the Northern Hemisphere have roomier conceptions of personal space than those in the Southern. To an English-man, a handshake can seem like trespassing, whereas to a Brazilian, anything less than a hug may come across as chilliness.

Like drivers who plow into your parked and empty car and don't leave a note,   6
people no longer mutter "Excuse me" when they bump into you. The decline of manners has been widely lamented. Manners, it seems to me, are about giving peo-ple space, not stepping on toes, granting people their private domain. I've also no-ticed an increase in the ranks of what I think of as space invaders, mini-territorial expansionists who seize public space with a sense of manifest destiny. In movie theatres these days, people are staking a claim to both armrests, annexing all the elbow room, while at coffee shops and on the L.I.R.R. individuals routinely com-mandeer booths and sets of facing seats meant for foursomes.

Ultimately, personal space is psychological, not physical: it has less to do with   7
the space outside us than with our inner space. I suspect that the shrinking of per-sonal space is directly proportional to the expansion of self-absorption: people whose attention is inward do not bother to look outward. Even the focus of science these days is micro, not macro. The Human Genome Project is mapping the uni-verse of the genetic code, while neuroscientists are using souped-up M.R.I. ma-chines to chart the flight of neurons in our brains, taking snapshots of a human thought.

In the same way that the breeze from a butterfly's wings in Japan may eventu-   8
ally produce a tidal wave in California, I have decided to expand the contracting boundaries of personal space. In the line at my bank, I now refuse to move closer than three feet to the person in front of me, even if it means that the fellow behind me starts breathing down my neck.

The So-What Factor. The so-what factor in a definition essay is the sense that something important is at stake in the definition of a term. For Richard Stengel, the term "personal space" has become an issue. Although the tone of the definition is lighthearted, you might share Stengel's concern if you've ever been made uncom-fortable by the proximity of strangers. Defining "personal space" becomes a prob-lem for Stengel, and since the dictionary doesn't help, he sets out to do it for himself—and presumably for his readers as well. He tells us just exactly what he thinks personal space is, or at least what it ought to be.

What is Stengel's definition of personal space? Do you find it persuasive? What is Stengel's attitude toward space in public places?

THE SEVEN COMMON MOVES

1. Beginning. "Space Invaders" begins with a story illustrating the problem that is at the heart of the essay to follow: a scene in a bank, in which personal space seems to have disappeared. A relevant story is among the most common and effective moves for getting the attention of readers. It's a move worth imitating, perhaps in your next essay.

2. Ending. A return to the beginning: another bank scene, people standing in line. The ending that returns to the beginning is another favorite device of skilled writers. In this case, the ending also provides a plan of action: the author resolves to stand no closer than three feet behind the person ahead of him in line. This gesture, the author pretends, is likely to extend from one person to another, until everybody in the world is giving one another more personal space. This is a pleasant exaggeration, of course, but it does provide a sense of closure by suggesting a solution to the problem that was described in the opening paragraph.

3. Detail. Stengel makes use of the "writer's eye" to choose just the right details to make us imagine the scene and the actions: not just "a man," but "a man in a sweatsuit"; not just a check, but "his Social Security check"; not just "a woman," but a "woman reading the *Wall Street Journal*." These details are not random. Stengel wants to signal the variety of people who intrude on what he regards as personal space. The image of someone taking both armrests in a theater probably reminds you of an experience you've had, one in which you felt that your personal space had been invaded. The reference to the Human Genome Project—a project to map all our genes and chromosomes—is supposed to suggest that even scientists are concerned with smaller and small things within us, a variety of self-absorption that seems related to the diminution of personal space.

4. Organization/Plot. "Space Invaders" might be outlined like this:

    I. Introductory story (paragraph 1).
    II. Definition of personal space (paragraph 2).
    III. Exemplification (paragraph 3).
    IV. Analysis (paragraphs 4 through 7).
    V. Concluding resolution (paragraph 9).

Outlines reveal organization; plot, as opposed to organization, has to do with why writers choose the sequence they choose. In this case, Stengel's strategy seems to be to make us care about personal space by presenting a problem in the first paragraph and not providing a resolution until the final paragraph. He catches our attention with the beginning of a little drama in paragraph 1; he defines "personal space" in paragraph 2; and then he gives us lots of examples of how personal space is violated in paragraph 3. The "plot," then, is to make us think the problem is worth analyzing, and then to analyze it (paragraphs 4 through 7).

5. Style. Cumulative sentences—sentences in which the main clause comes first, followed by trailing clauses or phrases—are a favorite device of skilled writers:

> Manners, it seems to me, are about giving people space, not stepping on toes, granting people their private domain.

Cumulative sentences resemble freight trains: engine (i.e., main clause) first, followed by units that really could be left behind. The example above would have been grammatically complete if it had been cut off after "space" or after "toes."

Like freight trains, cumulative sentences can be extended almost indefinitely. The longest sentence in "Space Invaders" has 67 words:

> As he did so, I minutely advanced toward the woman reading the *Wall Street Journal* in front of me, who in mild annoyance, began to sidle up to the man scribbling a check in front of her, who absent-mindedly shuffled toward the white-haired lady ahead of him, until we were all hugger-mugger against each other, the original lazy line having collapsed in on itself like a Slinky.

This sentence is easy to read, despite its length, because it is cumulative: it would still be grammatically complete if it had been cut off in any of four different places—after "me," after "her," after "him," after "other."

Another way to make a long sentence easy to read is to arrange it in parallel clauses or phrases. The following sentence is readable, despite its length (62 words) because Stengel has arranged it in grammatically parallel clauses separated by semicolons:

> In elevators, people are wedging themselves in just before the doors close; on the street, pedestrians are zigzagging through the human traffic, jostling others, refusing to give way; on the subway, riders are no longer taking pains to carve out little zones of space between themselves and fellow-passengers; in lines at airports, people are pressing forward like fidgety taxis at red lights.

To learn more about parallelism and cumulative sentences, see Sentence Exercises, and p. 287.

6. Voice/Attitude. Stengel's individual voice is apparent from the first sentence: "At my bank the other day, I was standing in a line . . ." And he reveals a bit of playfulness when he writes "scribbling a check" instead of the more neutral "writing a check."

If you were looking for a famous actor to play the role of Stengel as it comes across in this essay, whom would you choose, and why? What sort of person is Stengel? And in what mood? How is his voice different from the one in paragraph 2, when someone says, "You're invading my space, man." To hear these voices and attitudes more clearly, try acting them out in class.

7. Economy. Pick any phrase in the essay and see if it serves an identifiable purpose. In paragraph 7, for example, is it worth the extra words to say what personal space is *not* after saying what it is: "Ultimately, personal space is psychological, not physical"? Does Stengel violate economy by stating virtually the same idea in the next clause: "it has less to do with the space outside us than with our inner space"? Would Stengel's essay have been improved if he had said, simply, "Personal space is psychological"—and let it go at that? Or do the extra words add something by way of density or detail that serves a purpose?

Moves within Moves.   Although "Space Invaders" is primarily an extended definition, it includes other conceptual moves that are covered as separate chapters in this book. Paragraph 1 is description (the bank scene) and narration (what people did in the bank). Paragraph 3 is exemplification (instance in which personal space has been invaded). Paragraph 4 is cause and effect analysis (what causes people to mingle more). Paragraph 5 includes comparison and contrast (Calcuttans compared with Coloradans, Englishmen compared with Brazilians). Definitions always include other moves: you can define by example, by description, by comparison and contrast. Can you identify other modes and methods within Stengel's essay?

Words, Phrases, and Allusions.   "Space Invaders" implies readers who are familiar with the following words, phrases, and allusions, which were taken from the essay in the order of appearance:

> Slinky, Malthusian logic, proximity, alluring, proliferation, logistics, "Don't tread on me," private domain, mini-territorial expansionists, manifest destiny, annexing, L.I.R.R., commandeer, self-absorption, Human Genome Project, neuroscientists, M.R.I.

With the help of your classmates (and if necessary, a dictionary, encyclopedia, or other reference work), determine what each item means in its context. Search the essay for other words and phrases that might be worth adding to your vocabulary.

Suggestion for Writing

Using "Space Invaders" as a model, write an essay on the "true" meaning of a term you think is often misdefined. Be sure to choose a topic that you feel strongly about (the journal entry suggested at the beginning of this chapter may help)—a topic about which you can tell stories, or give examples, or compare the true meaning with common misconceptions. Remember that definition requires a second step: providing examples, comparing, contrasting, giving examples, telling stories, describing, or making one of the other conceptual moves treated in separate chapters in this book.

Journal Entry. Choose a term representing a positive value that you think is often misunderstood, and write notes for a paper arguing for the "true" definition of that term. Who, for example, is a "gifted" student? Or what is the true meaning of "school spirit," or "equal rights," or "civilization?" After you have worked on this project for a while, read the following essay, in which Joan Didion explains what she means by "self-respect," distinguishing her definition from what she considers common misconceptions of that term. As you read her essay, look for moves you can imitate in your own.

On Self-Respect

Joan Didion

Once, in a dry season, I wrote in large letters across two pages of a notebook that innocence ends when one is stripped of the delusion that one likes oneself. Although now, some years later, I marvel that a mind on the outs with itself should have nonetheless made painstaking record of its every tremor, I recall with embarrassing clarity the flavor of those particular ashes. It was a matter of misplaced self-respect. 1

I had not been elected to Phi Beta Kappa. This failure could scarcely have been more predictable or less ambiguous (I simply did not have the grades), but I was unnerved by it; I had somehow thought myself a kind of academic Raskolnikov, curiously exempt from the cause-effect relationships which hampered others. Although even the humorless nineteen-year-old that I was must have recognized that the situation lacked real tragic stature, the day that I did not make Phi Beta Kappa nonetheless marked the end of something, and innocence may well be the word for it. I lost the conviction that lights would always turn green for me, the pleasant certainty that those rather passive virtues which had won me approval as a child automatically guaranteed me not only Phi Beta Kappa keys but happiness, honor, and the love of a good man; lost a certain touching faith in the totem power of good manners, clean hair, and proven competence on the Stanford-Binet scale. To such doubtful amulets had my self-respect been pinned, and I faced myself that day with the nonplused apprehension of someone who has come across a vampire and has no crucifix at hand. 2

Although to be driven back upon oneself is an uneasy affair at best, rather like trying to cross a border with borrowed credentials, it seems to me now the one condition necessary to the beginnings of real self-respect. Most of our platitudes notwithstanding, self-deception remains the most difficult deception. The tricks that work on others count for nothing in that very well-lit back alley where one keeps 3 assignations with oneself: no winning smiles will do here, no prettily drawn lists of good intentions. One shuffles flashily but in vain through one's marked cards—the kindness done for the wrong reason, the apparent triumph which involved no real effort, the seemingly heroic act into which one had been shamed. The dismal fact is that self-respect has nothing to do with the approval of others—who are, after all, deceived easily enough; has nothing to do with reputation, which, as Rhett Butler told Scarlett O'Hara, is something people with courage can do without.

To do without self-respect, on the other hand, is to be an unwilling audience of one to an interminable documentary that details one's failings, both real and imagined, with fresh footage spliced in for every screening. *There's the glass you broke in anger, there's the hurt on X's face; watch now, this next scene, the night Y came back from Houston, see how you muff this one.* To live without self-respect is to lie awake some night, beyond the reach of warm milk, phenobarbital, and the sleeping hand on the coverlet, counting up the sins of commission and omission, the trusts betrayed, the promises subtly broken, the gifts irrevocably wasted through sloth or cowardice or carelessness. However long we postpone it, we eventually lie down alone in that notoriously uncomfortable bed, the one we make ourselves. Whether or not we sleep in it depends, of course, on whether or not we respect ourselves.

To protest that some fairly improbable people, some people who *could not possibly respect themselves*, seem to sleep easily enough is to miss the point entirely, as surely as those people miss it who think that self-respect has necessarily to do with not having safety pins in one's underwear. There is a common superstition that "self-respect" is a kind of charm against snakes, something that keeps those who have it locked in some unblighted Eden, out of strange beds, ambivalent conversations, and trouble in general. It does not at all. It has nothing to do with the face of things, but concerns instead a separate peace, a private reconciliation. Although the careless, suicidal Julian English in *Appointment in Samarra* and the careless, incurably dishonest Jordan Baker in *The Great Gatsby* seem equally improbable candidates for self-respect, Jordan Baker had it, Julian English did not. With that genius for accommodation more often seen in women than in men, Jordan took her own measure, made her own peace, avoided threats to that peace: "I hate careless people," she told Nick Carraway. "It takes two to make an accident."

Like Jordan Baker, people with self-respect have the courage of their mistakes. They know the price of things. If they choose to commit adultery, they do not then go running, in an excess of bad conscience, to receive absolution from the wronged parties; nor do they complain unduly of the unfairness, the undeserved embarrassment, of being named corespondent. In brief, people with self-respect exhibit a certain toughness, a kind of moral nerve; they display what was once called *character*, a quality which, although approved in the abstract, sometimes loses ground to other, more instantly negotiable virtues. The measure of its slipping prestige is that one tends to think of it only in connection with homely children and United States senators who have been defeated, preferably in the primary, for reelection. Nonetheless, character—the willingness to accept responsibility for one's own life—is the source from which self-respect springs.

Self-respect is something that our grandparents, whether or not they had it,   7
knew all about. They had instilled in them, young, a certain discipline, the sense
that one lives by doing things one does not particularly want to do, by putting fears
and doubts to one side, by weighing immediate comforts against the possibility of
larger, even intangible, comforts. It seemed to the nineteenth century admirable, but
not remarkable that Chinese Gordon put on a clean white suit and held Khartoum
against the Mahdi; it did not seem unjust that the way to free land in California involved death and difficulty and dirt. In a diary kept during the winter of 1846, an
emigrating twelve-year-old named Narcissa Cornwall noted coolly: "Father was
busy reading and did not notice that the house was being filled with strange Indians
until Mother spoke about it." Even lacking any clue as to what Mother said, one can
scarcely fail to be impressed by the entire incident: the father reading, the Indians
filing in, the mother choosing the words that would not alarm, the child duly recording the event and noting further that those particular Indians were not, "fortunately
for us," hostile. Indians were simply part of the *donnée*.

In one guise or another, Indians always are. Again, it is a question of recogniz-   8
ing that anything worth having has its price. People who respect themselves are
willing to accept the risk that the Indians will be hostile, that the venture will go
bankrupt, that the liaison may not turn out to be one in which *every day is a holiday
because you're married to me*. They are willing to invest something of themselves;
they may not play at all, but when they do play, they know the odds.

That kind of self-respect is a discipline, a habit of mind that can never be faked   9
but can be developed, trained, coaxed forth. It was once suggested to me that, as an
antidote to crying, I put my head in a paper bag. As it happens, there is a sound
physiological reason, something to do with oxygen, for doing exactly that, but the
psychological effect alone is incalculable: it is difficult in the extreme to continue
fancying oneself Cathy in *Wuthering Heights* with one's head in a Food Fair bag.
There is a similar case for all the small disciplines, unimportant in themselves;
imagine maintaining any kind of swoon, commiserative or carnal, in a cold shower.

But those small disciplines are available only insofar as they represent larger   10
ones. To say that Waterloo was won on the playing fields of Eton is not to say that
Napoleon might have been saved by a crash program in cricket; to give formal dinners in the rain forest would be pointless did not the candlelight flickering on the
liana call forth deeper, stronger disciplines, values instilled long before. It is a kind
of ritual, helping us to remember who and what we are. In order to remember it, one
must have known it.

To have that sense of one's intrinsic worth which constitutes self-respect is po-   11
tentially to have everything; the ability to discriminate, to love and to remain indifferent. To lack it is to be locked within oneself, paradoxically incapable of either
love or indifference. If we do not respect ourselves, we are on the one hand forced
to despise those who have so few resources as to consort with us, so little perception
as to remain blind to our fatal weaknesses. On the other, we are peculiarly in thrall
to everyone we see, curiously determined to live out—since our self-image is untenable—their false notions of us. We flatter ourselves by thinking this compulsion to

please others an attractive trait: a gift for imaginative empathy, evidence of our willingness to give. Of *course* I will play Francesca to your Paolo, Helen Keller to anyone's Annie Sullivan: no expectation is too misplaced, no role too ludicrous. At the mercy of those we cannot but hold in contempt, we play roles doomed to failure before they are begun, each defeat generating fresh despair at the urgency of divining and meeting the next demand made upon us.

It is the phenomenon sometimes called "alienation from self." In its advanced   12
stages, we no longer answer the telephone, because someone might want something; that we could say *no* without drowning in self-reproach is an idea alien to this game. Every encounter demands too much, tears the nerves, drains the will, and the specter of something as small as an unanswered letter arouses such disproportionate guilt that answering it becomes out of the question. To assign unanswered letters their proper weight, to free us from the expectations of others, to give us back to ourselves—there lies the great, the singular power of self-respect. Without it, one eventually discovers the final turn of the screw: one runs away to find oneself, and finds no one at home.

UNDERSTANDING THE ESSAY

1. What does Joan Didion mean by "self-respect"?
2. What "false" definitions does she reject?
3. What modes or methods of development does Didion use to develop her definition?
4. Why is (or isn't) self-respect the sort of term she defines as one that ought to have been defined simply by consulting a dictionary?
5. What does Didion mean when she says in paragraph 4 that to do without self-respect "is to be an unwilling audience of one to an interminable documentary that details one's failings"?

So What and the Seven Common Moves.   Analyze this essay with the help of the questions about "So What and the Seven Common Moves" found on the back cover of this book.

Words, Phrases, and Allusions.   The following items were taken from "On Self-Respect" in order of appearance. With the help of your classmates, locate these words in the essay and see if their context provides a clue to their meaning. If necessary, consult a dictionary, an encyclopedia, or other reference work to determine what each item means in its context. You probably know most of these words from conversation and reading, but you may not yet feel comfortable using them in your own writing.

tremor, Raskolnikov, tragic stature, totem power, Stanford-Binet scale, amulets, non-plused apprehension, crucifix, platitudes, assignations, interminable, muff, phenobarbi-tal, instantly negotiable virtues, Khartoum, emigrating, liaison, antidote, physiological, incalculable, fancying, Cathy in *Wuthering Heights*, swoon, commiserative, carnal, Eton, cricket, liana, intrinsic, thrall, untenable, empathy, Francesca, Paolo, Hellen Keller, Annie Sullivan, ludicrous, phenomenon, alienation, self-reproach, alien, specter

Suggestion for Writing

Using "On Self-Respect" as a model, write an essay in which you define a term that has special meaning for you. The journal entry suggested at the beginning of this se-lection may have given you an idea for a topic, or you may have thought of other topics as you read Didion's essay.

Journal Entry. Definitions often put things into categories—or exclude them. Is assisted suicide murder? Is nudity obscene? Is gambling immoral? Is nicotine addictive? Definitions are at stake in each of these questions. What do you mean by "assisted suicide," or by "murder," or by any of the other key terms in these questions? Choose a disputed term that interests you and write notes for a paper indicating why that term does (or does not) belong to a particular category when both terms are properly defined. After you have worked on this project for a while, read the following essay, in which James Baldwin explains what he means by a language, and why Black English deserves to be designated as one. As you read his essay, look for moves you can imitate in your own.

If Black English Isn't a Language, Then Tell Me, What Is?

James Baldwin

The argument concerning the use, or the status, or the reality, of black English is rooted in American history and has absolutely nothing to do with the question the argument supposes itself to be posing. The argument has nothing to do with language itself but with the role of language. Language, incontestably, reveals the speaker. Language, also, far more dubiously, is meant to define the other—and, in this case, the other is refusing to be defined by a language that has never been able to recognize him. 1

People evolve a language in order to describe and thus control their circumstances or in order not to be submerged by a situation that they cannot articulate. (And if they cannot articulate it, they are submerged.) A Frenchman living in Paris speaks a subtly and crucially different language from that of the man living in Marseilles; neither sounds very much like a man living in Quebec; and they would all have great difficulty in apprehending what the man from Guadeloupe, or Martinique, is saying, to say nothing of the man from Senegal—although the "common" language of all these areas is French. But each has paid, and is paying, a different price for this "common" language, in which, as it turns out, they are not saying, and cannot be saying, the same things: They each have very different realities to articulate, or control. 2

What joins all languages, and all men, is the necessity to confront life in order, not inconceivably, to outwit death: The price for this is the acceptance, and achievement, of one's temporal identity. So that, for example, though it is not taught in the schools (and this has the potential of becoming a political issue) the south of France 3

183

still clings to its ancient and musical Provençal, which resists being described as a "dialect." And much of the tension in the Basque countries, and in Wales, is due to the Basque and Welsh determination not to allow their languages to be destroyed. This determination also feeds the flames in Ireland for among the many indignities the Irish have been forced to undergo at English hands is the English contempt for their language.

It goes without saying, then, that language is also a political instrument, means, and proof of power. It is the most vivid and crucial key to identity. It reveals the private identity, and connects one with, or divorces one from, the larger, public, or communal identity. There have been, and are, times and places, when to speak a certain language could be dangerous, even fatal. Or, one may speak the same language, but in such a way that one's antecedents are revealed, or (one hopes) hidden. This is true in France, and is absolutely true in England. The range (and reign) of accents on that damp little island make England coherent for the English and totally incomprehensible for everyone else. To open your mouth in England is (if I may use black English) to "put your business in the street." You have confessed your parents, your youth, your school, your salary, your self-esteem, and, alas, your future.   4

Now, I do not know what white Americans would sound like if there had never been any black people in the United States, but they would not sound the way they sound. *Jazz*, for example, is a very specific sexual term, as in *jazz me, baby,* but white people purified it into the Jazz Age. *Sock it to me,* which means, roughly, the same thing, has been adopted by Nathaniel Hawthorne's descendants with no qualms or hesitations at all, along with *let it all hang out* and *right on! Beat to his socks,* which was once the black's most total and despairing image of poverty, was transformed into a thing called the Beat Generation, which phenomenon was, largely, composed of *uptight*, middle-class white people, imitating poverty, trying to *get down*, to get *with it*, doing their *thing*, doing their despairing best to be *funky*, which we, the blacks, never dreamed of doing—we were funky, baby, like *funk* was going out of style.   5

Now, no one can eat his cake, and have it, too, and it is late in the day to attempt to penalize black people for having created a language that permits the nation its only glimpse of reality, a language without which the nation would be even more *whipped* than it is.   6

I say that the present skirmish is rooted in American history, and it is. Black English is the creation of the black diaspora. Blacks came to the United States chained to each other, but from different tribes. Neither could speak the other's language. If two black people, at that bitter hour of the world's history, had been able to speak to each other, the institution of chattel slavery could never have lasted as long as it did. Subsequently, the slave was given, under the eye, and the gun, of his master, Congo Square, and the Bible—or, in other words, and under those conditions, the slave began the formation of the black church, and it is within this unprecedented tabernacle that black English began to be formed. This was not, merely, as in the European example, the adoption of a foreign tongue, but an alchemy that transformed ancient elements into a new language: *A language comes*   7 *into existence by means of brutal necessity, and the rules of the language are dictated by what the language must convey.*

There was a moment, in time, and in this place, when my brother, or my mother, or my father, or my sister, had to convey to me, for example, the danger in which I was standing from the white man standing just behind me, and to convey this with a speed and in a language that the white man could not possibly understand, and that, indeed, he cannot understand, until today. He cannot afford to understand it. This understanding would reveal to him too much about himself and smash that mirror before which he has been frozen for so long. 8

Now, in this passion, this skill, this (to quote Toni Morrison) "sheer intelligence," this incredible music, the mighty achievement of having brought a people utterly unknown to, or despised by "history"—to have brought this people to their present, troubled, troubling, and unassailable and unanswerable place—if this absolutely unprecedented journey does not indicate that black English is a language, I am curious to know what definition of languages is to be trusted. 9

A people at the center of the western world, and in the midst of so hostile a population, has not endured and transcended by means of what is patronizingly called a "dialect." We, the blacks, are in trouble, certainly, but we are not inarticulate because we are not compelled to defend a morality that we know to be a lie. 10

The brutal truth is that the bulk of the white people in America never had any interest in educating black people, except as this could serve white purposes. It is not the black child's language that is despised. It is his experience. A child cannot be taught by anyone who despises him, and a child cannot afford to be fooled. A child cannot be taught by anyone whose demand, essentially, is that the child repudiate his experience, and all that gives him sustenance, and enter a limbo in which he will no longer be black, and in which he knows that he can never become white. Black people have lost too many black children that way. 11

And, after all, finally, in a country with standards so untrustworthy, a country that makes heroes of so many criminal mediocrities, a country unable to face why so many of the nonwhite are in prison, or on the needle, or standing, futureless, in the streets—it may very well be that both the child, and his elder, have concluded that they have nothing whatever to learn from the people of a country that has managed to learn so little. 12

UNDERSTANDING THE ESSAY

1. What does James Baldwin mean when he says that "Language, incontestably, reveals the speaker"?
2. What does he mean when he says that language "is meant to define the other"?

3. What does he mean when he says that the various kinds of French spoken in different parts of the world "each have very different realities to articulate, or control"?
4. Why is (or isn't) language the sort of term that ought to have been defined simply by consulting a dictionary?
5. In what way is language "a political instrument" (paragraph 4)?

So What and the Seven Common Moves. Analyze this essay with the help of the questions about "So What and the Seven Common Moves" found on the back cover of this book.

Words, Phrases, and Allusions. The following items were taken from "If Black English Isn't a Language, Then Tell Me, What Is?" in order of appearance. With the help of your classmates, locate these words in the essay and see if their context provides a clue to their meaning. If necessary, consult a dictionary, an encyclopedia, or other reference work to determine what each item means in its context. You probably know most of these words from conversation and reading, but you may not yet feel comfortable using them in your own writing.

incontestably, dubiously, Marseilles, Quebec, Guadeloupe, Martinique, Senegal, Provençal, dialect, Basque, Wales, communal identity, fatal, antecedents, qualms, diaspora, chattel slavery, Congo Square, unprecedented tabernacle, alchemy, patronizingly, inarticulate, repudiate, limbo, sustenance

Suggestion for Writing

Using "If Black English Isn't a Language, Then Tell Me, What Is?" as a model, write an essay in which you decide by definition whether a particular thing belongs to a certain category. The journal entry suggested at the beginning of this selection may have given you an idea for a topic, or you may have thought of other topics as you read Baldwin's essay.

Journal Entry. Jot down notes for a paper defining a politically loaded term, like "family values," or "patriotism," or "liberal." Don't assume that there is a single, true definition of the term, or that a dictionary can provide a definitive meaning. Use examples, anecdotes, or citations of the word used in context to establish a variety of meanings of this term, depending on who uses it and for what purposes. After you have worked on this project for a while, read the following essay, in which Gloria Naylor explains the many meanings of a common racial epithet. As you read her essay, look for moves you can imitate in your own.

The Meaning of a Word

Gloria Naylor

Language is the subject. It is the written form with which I've managed to keep the wolf away from the door and, in diaries, to keep my sanity. In spite of this, I consider the written word inferior to the spoken, and much of the frustration experienced by novelists is the awareness that whatever we manage to capture in even the most transcendent passages falls far short of the richness of life. Dialogue achieves its power in the dynamics of a fleeting moment of sight, sound, smell and touch. 1

I'm not going to enter the debate here about whether it is language that shapes reality or vice versa. That battle is doomed to be waged whenever we seek intermittent reprieve from the chicken-and-egg dispute. I will simply take the position that the spoken word, like the written word, amounts to a nonsensical arrangement of sounds or letters without a consensus that assigns "meaning." And building from the meanings of what we hear, we order reality. Words themselves are innocuous; it is the consensus that gives them true power. 2

I remember the first time I heard the word "nigger." In my third grade class, our math tests were being passed down the rows, and as I handed the papers to a little boy in back of me, I remarked that once again he had received a much lower mark than I did. He snatched his test from me and spit out that word. Had he called me a nymphomaniac or a necrophiliac, I couldn't have been more puzzled. I didn't know what a nigger was, but I knew that whatever it meant, it was something he shouldn't have called me. This was verified when I raised my hand, and in a loud voice repeated what he had said and watched the teacher scold him for using a "bad" word. I was later to go home and ask the inevitable question that every black parent must face—"Mommy, what does 'nigger' mean?" 3

And what exactly did it mean? Thinking back, I realize that this could not have been the first time the word was used in my presence. I was part of a large extended 4 family that had migrated from the rural South after World War II and formed a close-knit network that gravitated around my maternal grandparents. Their ground-floor apartment in one of the buildings they owned in Harlem was a weekend mecca for my immediate family, along with countless aunts, uncles and cousins who brought along assorted friends. It was a bustling and open house with assorted neighbors and tenants popping in and out to exchange bits of gossip, pick up an old quarrel or referee the ongoing checkers game in which my grandmother cheated shamelessly. They were all there to let down their hair and put up their feet after a week of labor in the factories, laundries and shipyards of New York.

Amid the clamor, which could reach deafening proportions—two or three con-   5
versations going on simultaneously, punctuated by the sound of a baby's crying somewhere in the back rooms or out on the street—there was still a rigid set of rules about what was said and how. Older children were sent out of the living room when it was time to get into the juicy details about "you-know-who" up on the third floor who had gone and gotten herself "p-r-e-g-n-a-n-t-!" But my parents, knowing that I could spell well beyond my years, always demanded that I follow the others out to play. Beyond sexual misconduct and death, everything else was considered harm-less for our young ears. And so among the anecdotes of the triumphs and disap-pointments in the various workings of their lives, the word "nigger" was used in my presence, but it was set within contexts and inflections that caused it to register in my mind as something else.

In the singular, the word was always applied to a man who had distinguished   6
himself in some situation that brought their approval for his strength, intelligence or drive:

"Did Johnny really do that?"   7

"I'm telling you, that nigger pulled in $6,000 of overtime last year. Said he got   8
enough for a down payment on a house."

When used with a possessive adjective by a woman—"my nigger"—it became   9
a term of endearment for husband or boyfriend. But it could be more than just a term applied to a man. In their mouths it became the pure essence of manhood—a disembodied force that channeled their past history of struggle and present survival against the odds into a victorious statement of being. "Yeah, that old foreman found out quick enough—you don't mess with a nigger."

In the plural, it became a description of some group within the community that   10
had overstepped the bounds of decency as my family defined it: Parents who ne-glected their children, a drunken couple who fought in public, people who simply refused to look for work, those with excessively dirty mouths or unkempt house-holds were all "trifling niggers." This particular circle could forgive hard times, un-employment, the occasional bout of depression—they had gone through all of that themselves, but the unforgivable sin was lack of self-respect.

A woman could never be a "nigger" in the singular, with its connotation of con-   11
firming worth. The noun "girl" was its closest equivalent in that sense, but only when used in direct address and regardless of the gender doing the addressing.

"Girl" was a token of respect for a woman. The one-syllable word was drawn out to sound like three in recognition of the extra ounce of wit, nerve or daring that the woman had shown in the situation under discussion.

"G-i-r-l, stop. You mean you said that to his face?" 12

But if the word was used in a third-person reference or shortened so that it al- 13 most snapped out of the mouth, it always involved some element of communal disapproval. And age became an important factor in these exchanges. It was only between individuals of the same generation, or from an older person to a younger (but never the other way around), that "girl" would be considered a compliment.

I don't agree with the argument that use of the word "nigger" at this social stra- 14 tum of the black community was an internalization of racism. The dynamics were the exact opposite; the people in my grandmother's living room took a word that whites used to signify worthlessness or degradation and rendered it impotent. Gathering there together, they transformed "nigger" to signify the varied and complex human beings they knew themselves to be. If the word was to disappear totally from the mouths of even the most liberal of white society, no one in that room was naive enough to believe it would disappear from white minds. Meeting the word head-on, they proved it had absolutely nothing to do with the way they were determined to live their lives.

So there must have been dozens of times that the word "nigger" was spoken in 15 front of me before I reached the third grade. But I didn't "hear" it until it was said by a small pair of lips that had already learned it could be a way to humiliate me. That was the word I went home and asked my mother about. And since she knew that I had to grow up in America, she took me in her lap and explained.

UNDERSTANDING THE ESSAY

1. Why does Gloria Naylor "consider the written word inferior to the spoken" (paragraph 1)?
2. What does she mean when she writes that "Words themselves are innocuous; it is the consensus that gives them true power" (paragraph 2)?
3. How does Naylor's use of "self-respect" (paragraph 10) compare with Didion's (p. 178)?
4. Why is (or isn't) Naylor's definition an essay? Look up "nigger" in a dictionary, and see what Naylor's definition provides that the dictionary doesn't.
5. How is it possible for the same word to be a compliment on some occasions and an insult on others? Can you think of any other words that mean different things in different contexts?

So What and the Seven Common Moves.   Analyze this essay with the help of the questions about "So What and the Seven Common Moves" found on the back cover of this book.

Words, Phrases, and Allusions.   The following items were taken from "The Meaning of a Word" in order of appearance. With the help of your classmates, locate these words in the essay and see if their context provides a clue to their meaning. If necessary, consult a dictionary, an encyclopedia, or other reference work to determine what each item means in its context. You probably know most of these words from conversation and reading, but you may not yet feel comfortable using them in your own writing.

> transcendent, dynamics of a fleeting moment, intermittent reprieve, a consensus that assigns "meaning," innocuous, nymphomaniac, necrophiliac, verified, inevitable, gravitated, maternal, mecca, simultaneously, anecdotes, inflections, term of endearment, disembodied, unkempt, connotation, communal disapproval, social stratum, internalization, degradation, impotent

Suggestion for Writing

Using "The Meaning of a Word" as a model, write an essay in which you explore the multiple meanings of a politically loaded term. The journal entry suggested at the beginning of this selection may have given you an idea for a topic, or you may have thought of other topics as you read Naylor's essay.

RECIPES FOR WRITING DEFINITION

A. Writing from Personal Experience

The key ingredient in a definition essay is attitude. You have to care about the term you define. As topics, abstractions and words that convey value judgments usually work better than concrete words because they provide more leeway for interpretation.

Here is a recipe for writing a definition essay:

1. Choose an abstraction or a value-laden word, a word that you feel strongly about.
2. Think of all the ways you can impress *your* understanding of that word on your readers: by using examples, possibly in the form of stories; by contrasting *your* meaning of the word with meanings you do not approve; by classifying various meanings of the word into categories (e.g., "There are seven

kinds of *X*") and developing each category. Any of the patterns of development treated as a separate chapter in this book can be used to define a word.

3. Write each part of the definition on a separate sheet, and then arrange your material in a sequence calculated to keep the reader's attention.
4. After you've written the body of the paper, add an introduction and an ending.
5. Show a draft to fellow students in a formal or informal workshop, and see if your strategies are having the effects you want them to have. Use the checklist on the back cover to focus your discussion. Then look for errors in spelling, grammar, or punctuation that you will want to correct in your final draft.

B. Writing Against the Text

Because definition essays are almost always loaded with the writer's personal attitude about the subject at hand, they generally provide ample room for disagreement. For example, James Baldwin's definition of "Black English" as a language would certainly encounter opposition from educational conservatives, black and white. And some people would question Joan Didion's definition of self-respect as the characteristic that enables us to forgive ourselves for our past failings. Choose a definition essay in which you find room for disagreement, and write an essay of your own in support of a definition you prefer.

C. Writing from Research

Using the library and the Web, locate information about an abstract or value-laden term that interests you. The point of your search is to cite actual occurrences of the term to show how many different meanings it can have. After you have completed your research, write a draft in your own words without consulting your sources; this will help you avoid being overwhelmed by what you read and perhaps unintentionally plagiarizing material. Then go back and add quoted and paraphrased material wherever you think it will make your paper more interesting or authoritative. Be sure to acknowledge the source of anything you quote or paraphrase.

9

Exemplification:
Paradigms and Likely Stories

"Example" is one of those words that seem simple enough, but in fact have many different meanings. An example can be a specific instance: oats, barley, wheat, and corn are examples of cereals; Trinidad, Guadeloupe, Puerto Rico, and Nassau are examples of Caribbean islands. An example can also be an illustration or a model: a dance instructor can explain a particular move by actually performing it, setting an example for her students. Examples can also be used as evidence to prove or explain a generalization. You could cite examples of what the mayor has done to deserve reelection, or explain complex business transactions or legal concepts by using specific cases. But in the realm of rhetoric—that is, in situations when we debate issues that are settled by persuasive judgments rather than by scientific proof—a particular kind of example, called a "paradigm" or "likely story" (what philosopher Kenneth Burke calls a "representative anecdote") is the primary form of evidence, sometimes the only form of evidence available.

Paradigms—"likely stories"—are to rhetoric what experimental data are to science. In science, we consider a point proven when we can support it with empirical data that are sufficient, random, and relevant. Rhetoric, however, by definition, deals with those questions for which sufficient, random, and relevant data are not available—questions of politics, ethics, esthetics, and similar topics in which there will always be dissenting points of view. You may have noticed that whenever you get into serious political or religious debates with friends or family, they (and you) almost always resort to stories—sometimes long stories, sometimes compressed stories—to bolster their (or your) point of view. That's because stories are generally the only sort of evidence available in evidence in discussions of this sort.

Preachers have been using paradigms or likely stories for centuries; in the middle ages, stories of this sort were called exempla, which is Latin for "example." Actually, the tradition of using examples in this way goes back to the Greek rhetoricians: the word normally translated as "example" in Aristotle's rhetoric is *paradeigma* in Greek, from which we get the word "paradigm" in English, meaning "pattern" or "pattern of events." Lawyers and politicians use paradigms to establish beliefs about things that cannot really be proven—like whether the United States has a vital interest in maintaining internal order in some other country, or whether executing murderers is more effective than life imprisonment as a deterrent.

Whenever we want to establish a point about human behavior, we tend to tell stories. These stories, or paradigms, will be persuasive only if people consider them typical of the way the world works or the way people behave—in other words, if the stories seem to be paradigms, patterns of events likely to be repeated in similar circumstances. They have to make people think, "If it happened once, it could happen again," or "I bet that sort of stuff happens (or could happen) all the time." We hear about teenagers who roam subway stations and fire automatic pistols into crowds of strangers. That's a likely story, we may think, and it may persuade us that society would be a bit safer if people couldn't buy guns as easily as fishing rods. Then again, we hear a story about an elderly woman who nails a would-be rapist with the .38 special she had bought the night before and concealed in her tote bag. We might think, now there's a good argument against gun control. Neither story actually proves the point; in fact, for every good example, you can usually come up with a counterexample, a different story that tends to support the opposite point.

Paradigms can be true or fictitious, as long as they are credible and analogous to the situation at hand. Even fairy tales can be persuasive. Everybody knows that the story about the boy who cried "wolf" just to create a little excitement in his village is just a fable. But it is "likely" story. It is believable. It strikes us as something that could have happened, and the result—that the villagers would not have believed that mischievous kid when a wolf really did appear—also strikes us a likely pattern of events. "The Boy Who Cried 'Wolf'" is a paradigm for what is likely to happen when people give false alarms.

Scientific examples (empirical data) result in the sort of conviction we call knowledge—a conviction universally shared by competent and impartial observers. Rhetorical paradigms result in belief. That fresh water at sea level freezes at 32 °F and that horses have from 38 to 42 teeth, depending on their age, sex, and a few other variables—these are matters of scientific knowledge based on examples that have been observed and recorded. All competent and impartial observers accept these statements as fact. But political, ethical, artistic, and religious preferences—no matter how certain they may seem to individuals who have them—are, technically, matters of belief. In these matters, rational and well-informed people can and will always disagree. Reasonable people might prefer knowledge to belief whenever they can get it; but they also know how to recognize those situations in which the comfort of scientific evidence is simply unavailable. Belief is indispensable for living—and paradigms are indispensable for establishing belief.

Paradigms may get their persuasive force from either quality or quantity—either one or two really good examples, or a large number, one after the other, an avalanche of anecdotal evidence. The point is to establish a paradigm—to make us think, "I bet this sort of stuff happens all the time."

Journal Entry. Regardless of your race or gender, you are a member of a minority: you might be left-handed, or blonde, or an athlete, or a musician, or a member of a particular religious denomination, or gifted in some way, or challenged. Whatever minority you are part of is almost certain to be stereotyped by people who do not know it well.

Choose one of the many minority groups to which you belong and explain how it feels when people treat you in a certain way because of your minority status. The examples can take the form of instances or anecdotes.

After you've worked on this project for a while, read the following essay, in which Brent Staples tells many stories—some in detail, some quickly summarized—that allow us to feel what it is like to be treated as a member of a stereotypical group rather than as an individual. As you read the essay, look for techniques that you can imitate in an essay in which you tell your own likely stories.

Just Walk on By

Brent Staples

My first victim was a woman—white, well dressed, probably in her early twenties. I came upon her late one evening on a deserted street in Hyde Park, a relatively affluent neighborhood in an otherwise mean, impoverished section of Chicago. As I swung onto the avenue behind her, there seemed to be a discreet, uninflammatory distance between us. Not so. She cast back a worried glance. To her, the youngish black man—a broad six feet two inches with a beard and billowing hair, both hands shoved into the pockets of a bulky military jacket—seemed menacingly close. After a few more quick glimpses, she picked up her pace and was soon running in earnest. Within seconds she disappeared into a cross street.

That was more than a decade ago. I was 22 years old, a graduate student newly arrived at the University of Chicago. It was in the echo of that terrified woman's footfalls that I first began to know the unwieldy inheritance I'd come into—the ability to alter public space in ugly ways. It was clear that she thought herself the quarry of a mugger, a rapist, or worse. Suffering a bout of insomnia, however, I was stalking sleep, not defenseless wayfarers. As a softy who is scarcely able to take a knife to a raw chicken—let alone hold it to a person's throat—I was surprised, embarrassed, and dismayed all at once. Her flight made me feel like an accomplice in tyranny. It also made it clear that I was indistinguishable from the muggers who occasionally seeped into the area from the surrounding ghetto. That first encounter, and those that followed, signified that a vast, unnerving, gulf lay between nighttime

1

2

pedestrians—particularly women—and me. And I soon gathered that being perceived as dangerous is a hazard in itself. I only needed to turn a corner into a dicey situation, or crowd some frightened, armed person in a foyer somewhere, or make an errant move after being pulled over by a policeman. Where fear and weapons meet—and they often do in urban America—there is always the possibility of death.

In that first year, my first away from my hometown, I was to become thoroughly familiar with the language of fear. At dark, shadowy intersections in Chicago, I could cross in front of a car stopped at a traffic light and elicit the thunk, thunk, thunk of the driver—black, white, male, or female—hammering down the door locks. On less traveled streets after dark, I grew accustomed to but never comfortable with people who crossed to the other side of the street rather than pass me. Then there were the standard unpleasantries with police, doormen, bouncers, cab drivers, and others whose business it is to screen out troublesome individuals before there is any nastiness.   3

I moved to New York nearly two years ago and I have remained an avid night walker. In central Manhattan, the near-constant crowd cover minimizes tense one-on-one street encounters. Elsewhere—visiting friends in SoHo, where sidewalks are narrow and tightly spaced buildings shut out the sky—things can get very taut indeed.   4

Black men have a firm place in New York mugging literature. Norman Podhoretz in his famed (or infamous) 1963 essay, "My Negro Problem—And Ours," recalls growing up in terror of black males; they "were tougher than we were, more ruthless," he writes—and as an adult on the Upper West Side of Manhattan, he continues, he cannot constrain his nervousness when he meets black men on certain streets. Similarly, a decade later, the essayist and novelist Edward Hoagland extols a New York where once "Negro bitterness bored down mainly on other Negroes." Where some see mere panhandlers, Hoagland sees "a mugger who is clearly screwing up his nerve to do more than just ask for money." But Hoagland has "the New Yorker's quick-hunch posture for broken-field maneuvering," and the bad guy swerves away.   5

I often witness that "hunch posture," from women after dark on the warrenlike streets of Brooklyn where I live. They seem to set their faces on neutral and, with their purse straps strung across their chests bandolier style, they forge ahead as though bracing themselves against being tackled. I understand, of course, that the danger they perceive is not a hallucination. Women are particularly vulnerable to street violence, and young black males are drastically overrepresented among the perpetrators of that violence. Yet these truths are no solace against the kind of alienation that comes of being ever the suspect, against being set apart, a fearsome entity with whom pedestrians avoid making eye contact.   6

It is not altogether clear to me how I reached the ripe old age of 22 without being conscious of the lethality nighttime pedestrians attributed to me. Perhaps it was because in Chester, Pennsylvania, the small, angry industrial town where I came of age in the 1960s, I was scarcely noticeable against a backdrop of gang warfare, street knifings, and murder. I grew up one of the good boys, had perhaps a half-dozen fist fights. In retrospect, my shyness of combat has clear sources.   7

Many things go into the making of a young thug. One of those things is the   8
consummation of the male romance with the power to intimidate. An infant discovers that random flailings send the baby bottle flying out of the crib and crashing to
the floor. Delighted, the joyful babe repeats those motions again and again, seeking
to duplicate the feat. Just so, I recall the points at which some of my boyhood
friends were finally seduced by the perception of themselves as tough guys. When a
mark cowered and surrendered his money without resistance, myth and reality
merged—and paid off. It is, after all, only manly to embrace the power to frighten
and intimidate. We, as men, are not supposed to give an inch of our lane on the
highway; we are to seize the fighter's edge in work and in play and even in love; we
are to be valiant in the face of hostile forces.

Unfortunately, poor and powerless young men seem to take all this nonsense   9
literally. As a boy, I saw countless tough guys locked away; I have since buried several, too. They were babies, really—a teenage cousin, a brother of 22, a childhood
friend in his mid-twenties—all gone down in episodes of bravado played out in the
streets. I came to doubt the virtues of intimidation early on. I chose, perhaps even
unconsciously, to remain a shadow—timid, but a survivor.

The fearsomeness mistakenly attributed to me in public places often has a per-   10
ilous flavor. The most frightening of these confusions occurred in the late 1970s and
early 1980s when I worked as a journalist in Chicago. One day, rushing into the office
of a magazine I was writing for with a deadline story in hand, I was mistaken for a burglar. The office manager called security and, with an ad hoc posse, pursued me
through the labyrinthine halls, nearly to my editor's door. I had no way of proving who
I was. I could only move briskly toward the company of someone who knew me.

Another time I was on assignment for a local paper and killing time before an   11
interview. I entered a jewelry store on the city's affluent Near North Side. The pro-
prietor excused herself and returned with an enormous red Doberman pinscher
straining at the end of a leash. She stood, the dog extended toward me, silent to my
questions, her eyes bulging nearly out of her head. I took a cursory look around,
nodded, and bade her good night. Relatively speaking, however, I never fared as
badly as another black male journalist. He went to nearby Waukegan, Illinois, a
couple of summers ago to work on a story about a murderer who was born there.
Mistaking the reporter for the killer, police hauled him from his car at gunpoint and
but for his press credentials would probably have tried to book him. Such episodes
are not uncommon. Black men trade tales like this all the time.

In "My Negro Problem—and Ours," Podhoretz writes that the hatred he feels   12
for blacks makes itself known to him through a variety of avenues—one being his
discomfort with that "special brand of paranoid touchiness" to which he says blacks
are prone. No doubt he is speaking here of black men. In time I learned to smother
the rage I felt at so often being taken for a criminal. Not to do so would surely have
led to madness—via that special "paranoid touchiness" that so annoyed Podhoretz
at the time he wrote the essay.

I begin to take precautions to make myself less threatening. I move about with   13
care, particularly late in the evening. I give a wide berth to nervous people on sub-

way platforms during the wee hours, particularly when I have exchanged business clothes for jeans. If I happen to be entering a building behind some people who appear skittish, I may walk by, letting them clear the lobby before I return, so as not to seem to be following them. I have been calm and extremely congenial on those rare occasions when I've been pulled over by the police.

And on late-evening constitutionals along streets less traveled by, I employ   14 what has proved to be an excellent tension-reducing measure: I whistle melodies from Beethoven and Vivaldi and the more popular classical composers. Even steely New Yorkers hunching toward nighttime destinations seem to relax, and occasionally they even join in the tune. Virtually everybody seems to sense that a mugger wouldn't be warbling bright, sunny selections from Vivaldi's Four Seasons. It is my equivalent of the cowbell that hikers wear when they know they are in bear country.

The So-What Factor.   What is novel, interesting, surprising, or moving about Brent Staples's examples? What does he want us to know, understand, think, or feel? In "Walk on By," the examples help white people understand what it must be like to frighten strangers unintentionally just because you happen to be a large male with a dark skin. Staples's purpose was to let people experience vicariously what they may never have experienced for themselves (or to understand the experience better if, in fact, they have had the same things happen to them). Why does Staples's experience somehow interest everybody? How do we all benefit from Staples's point of view?

THE SEVEN COMMON MOVES

*1. **Beginning.*** Brent Staples does not just presume his reader's interest. He creates it. The first sentence is a shocker, making us think, just for a moment, that we are about to read the confessions of a mugger or rapist. It turns out to be only a pose, of course, but it is a pose that gets our attention. Staples's beginning is not just a cheesy gimmick. The story illustrates the point he wants to make. Notice, too, that Staples creates a sense of unfinished business by referring to a "first victim"—implying that there were others and that the essay will not be complete until he tells us about them. Writers often use stories to get their essays started simply because good stories are hard to resist.

*2. **Ending.*** If a beginning creates momentum by presenting a problem or conflict in the form of a story, an ending can create a sense of closure by resolving the problem or ending the story. In this case, Staples brings the essay to a close with a solution for the problem that is the focus of his essay. He just whistles some classical music—music that calms strangers, who are likely to assume that people who whistle Beethoven and Vivaldi are not likely to be muggers. The solution is an implicit return to the opening paragraph; had Staples thought to whistle a few bars of the "Ode to Joy," he might not have frightened that female pedestrian in Hyde Park.

3. Detail. Notice that whenever Staples does use details, he uses "the writer's eye" and "the writer's ear"—a gift for choosing just the right sight or sound to make the scene come to life, to make his readers think, "Yes, that's it! I recognize that scene!" We recognize the "thunk, thunk, thunk of the driver . . . hammering down door locks" because we've either done that ourselves, or seen other people do it. We find it easy to imagine the defensive attitude of female pedestrians—"their faces on neutral and . . . their purse straps strung across their chests bandolier style"—because the details are specific and credible. In short, the skills you studied in the chapters on narration and description—especially the distinction between telling and showing—are important in writing persuasive examples.

4. Organization/Plot. Some essays have logical outlines—the sort that can be signaled with Roman numerals and capital letters. Others are more "organic"—an outline that grows around its subject, like a vine on a tree.

In either case, when the organization of an essay "works," it does three things:

It enables the reader to understand the significance of each bit of information as it is presented.
It keeps the reader interested—usually by saving some of the best information for last.
It avoids repeating information without good reason.

"Just Walk on By" is a good example of writing with an "organic" outline:

Introductory example (paragraph 1)
Analysis of introductory example (paragraph 2)
More examples (paragraphs 3 and 4)
References to other writers (paragraph 5)
Commentary on other writers (paragraph 6)
Cause-and-effect analysis (paragraphs 7 through 9)
More examples (paragraphs 10 and 11)
Back to one of the writers mentioned above (paragraph 12)
Conclusion: practical defenses against the problem (paragraphs 13 and 14)

It would not make a great deal of sense to add Roman numerals and capital letters to this outline, since the various parts do not have the sort of logical relationships that numerals and letters would suggest. The organization is more like a musical sonata, with an exposition (the introduction), a development section (paragraphs 2 through 11), and what might be called a recapitulation, a return to the beginning. Like a musical composition, the various parts of Staples's essay could conceivably have been arranged in many other ways; there is nothing inherently and unalterably logical about this outline. And yet it "works"—which is all anyone can ask of an outline.

5. *Style.* In paragraph 11, Staples writes a cumulative sentence—a sentence in which the main clause (in this case, "She stood") comes first, followed by a series of trailing phrases.

> She stood, the dog extended toward me, silent to my questions, her eyes bulging nearly out of her head.

Cumulative sentences are worth noticing and imitating; they are considered characteristic of modern American prose, particularly in narrative and descriptive writing, which of course can occur within any of the other modes.

Staples also makes a number of other stylistic moves, many of them with traditional names. You may not want to bother with learning the Greek names for these moves; still, it is worth learning the moves themselves, perhaps by writing sentences of your own in imitation of Staples's sentences.

There is an example of onomatopoeia (words that imitate sounds, e.g., bow wow, meow, tick tock, choo choo, etc.) in paragraph 3:

> "the thunk, thunk, thunk of the driver . . . hammering down the door locks."

Staples's phrase, "streets less traveled by" (paragraph 14) is a subtle allusion to a famous poem by Robert Frost ("The Road Less Traveled"). And in paragraph 8, three classical moves are packed into a single sentence: anaphora (a series of phrases beginning with the same word), asyndeton (the omission of a conjunction between the last two items of a series), and isocolon (a series of phrases of roughly equal length):

> We, as men, are not supposed to give an inch of our lane on the highway; we are to seize the fighter's edge in work and in play and even in love; we are to be valiant in the face of hostile forces.

6. *Voice/Attitude.* In many ways, Staples's attitude resembles a newspaper reporter's. He doesn't seem angry, or upset, or judgmental. In fact, his emotional coolness probably makes it easier to believe what he tells us. He doesn't seem to have a chip on his shoulder.

But unlike a traditional reporter, Staples use the first person (*I, my, me*) throughout, giving himself a personal voice in the essay, and the voice he assumes is educated, comfortable with references to famous authors and composers and with words like "errant," and "warrenlike," "ad hoc," "solace," "perilous," "labyrinthine," and "constitutionals." Staples's voice shows us, without showing off, that he is anything but the dangerous thug that he is often taken to be.

Staples also uses a bit of street language (when he describes a mugger's victim as a "mark" in paragraph 8) to show that not all of his education took place in the classroom. He also uses contractions ("I'd," "I've"), colloquialisms ("the bad guy," "thug"), and a sentence fragment ("Not so") to make his voice intimate and unpretentious. The result of these moves is a voice that is intelligent, unpretentious, and wordly-wise, along with an attitude that seems cool, objective, and credible.

7. Economy. In exemplification essays, details can take the form of stories, and stories can be summarized in a phrase or two or expanded to cover several paragraphs. In paragraph 2, Staples packs three likely stories into a single sentence:

> I only needed to turn a corner into a dicey situation, or crowd some frightened, armed person in a foyer somewhere, or make an errant move after being pulled over by a policeman.

In a sense, it is more "economical" to summarize stories this way, rather than to expand them. But the trick is to know when summarizing is a false economy, and when it serves a purpose. First, imagine what sort of stories could have been spun out of the sentence above. And then discuss with your classmates whether Staples's essay would have been strengthened by expanding those stories. What factors might a writer consider in determining when to expand and when to condense?

Moves within Moves.   An exemplification essay is often developed with the other modes and methods. In paragraph 6, for example, Staples provides a cause-and-effect analysis of why women are frightened of him on the street, and in paragraphs 8 and 9 he provides a cause-and-effect analysis to explain why many young men grow up to be violent. And of course, examples blossom into narration in paragraphs 1 (the story of his first victim), 10 (the story about being mistaken for a burglar), and 11 (the stories about the Doberman in the jewelry store and about the reporter being mistaken for a murderer)—often with lots of descriptive detail.

Words, Phrases, and Allusions.   "Just Walk on By" presumes readers who are familiar with the following words, phrases, and allusions, which were taken from the essay in the order of appearance:

> discreet, uninflammatory, menacingly, unwieldy, foyer, errant, elicit, taut, Norman Podhoretz, constrain, Edward Hoagland, panhandlers, warrenlike, bandolier, perpetrators, solace, alienation, entity, lethality, mark, cowered, bravado, ad hoc, labyrinthine, affluent, paranoid, wide berth, congenial, constitutionals, streets less traveled by, Vivaldi's Four Seasons, cowbell that hikers wear

With the help of your classmates (and if necessary, a dictionary, encyclopedia, or other reference work), determine what each item means in its context. Pay particular attention to words and phrases that might be worth adding to your vocabulary.

Suggestion for Writing

Using "Just Walk on By" as a model, tell what it feels like to be in situations in which people react to you as a member of a group rather than as an individual.

Reread the model for specific techniques you might imitate in your own essay. You might find things to write about in the journal entry suggested at the beginning of this chapter. Another possibility would be to find a spot in "Just Walk on By" where you think there might be room for other examples, or for telling the same examples from another point of view. Use this as the starting point for an exemplification essay of your own.

Virus Zero

Val Schaffner

In precomputer days the editor at my newspaper would blame typos on "the printer's devil." Today, when popular dread has assumed a medical rather than a theological form, we call it something else: a bug, or a virus. 1

The most notorious of viruses was perversely named after an artist, albeit one of diabolical genius: Michelangelo. The hackers who concoct them proceed from deviltry, an urge to cause havoc, destruction, and grief in artistically ingenious ways. 2

Where old-fashioned vandals burned libraries and looted material wealth, these techies target the magnetic repositories of information which constitute virtual wealth. So far their attacks have been random. But suppose they join forces with terrorists. They have already caused such pain, these cyberspace outlaws whose mischief is innocent of politics; imagine what will happen when radical revolutionaries go on line. 3

Imagine, for instance, some ferociously utopian hacker who, on the theory that money is the root of all evil, puts his or her programming genius to work getting rid of it. Money. All of it, everywhere. 4

Before computers, this was impossible. Money used to be something you could touch and carry around and hide. The only revolutionary who seriously tried to abolish money was Cambodia's Pol Pot. Despite his extreme tactics many Cambodians managed to bury their savings, in the form of gold—to be retrieved, if they survived, after the reign of terror had passed. 5

In the postindustrial West, however, money has become more and more abstract. Gold (or silver or cowrie shells) was the ancient first stage of abstraction, a portable substitute for the actual goods to be bartered. Then came bank notes, less 6 trouble to carry around than ingots or coins and still representing the existence of actual gold or silver that was kept in some bank vault to back their value.

Those were replaced in this century by bank notes that no longer had any tangible backing—only their own reputations backed by that of the government. Everyone went on agreeing to accept these numbered pieces of paper in exchange for goods, in the belief that everyone else would do so, and most were ready to hand them over to banks in the belief that the bankers would keep accurate accounts of who owned what and would hand back equivalent pieces of paper on demand. 7

This system enabled the invention of checks, with which people wrote their own personal money, which was accepted in the belief that it was backed by actual government money in the check writer's bank account. Checks further speeded up the economy, as they could be mailed as well as carried from place to place. 8

Today we have arrived at an even higher level of abstractions: electrons. The bank notes that substituted for the gold that substituted for the goods are in turn substituted for by computerized bank records, by the magnetic strips on credit cards and ATM cards, and by the electric currents that convey information about transactions from shop to credit card company or from bank to bank with lightning speed along telephone wires. 9

Never has money moved so fast, nor so hypothetically. Only the poor, or those with illicit gains to hide, rely exclusively on cash. The more money people have, the less likely they are actually to see it or touch it. Wealth inheres in a little black stripe on a piece of plastic and in the magnetic patterns that represent numbers in the computer memories of the banking system. 10

This has given rise to a new class of criminal, who steals by tampering with the electrons. Rather than the old physical work of walking into a bank with a gun and carrying off bundles of bank notes, a thief with the right programming skills need only gain access to the right computer: a more humane and devious form of bank robbery in which no one gets shot and, often, no one gets caught. 11

In one subtle heist, a larcenous cyberpunk invaded a bank's computer and altered the program that credited account holders with the interest on their deposits. Normally the computer would round fractions of a cent up or down to the nearest whole cent. The hacker instructed it to round every payment down to the lower cent, and to deposit the leftover fractions of cents in his own account. He figured that no one would ever notice this, and, in the years before he was somehow caught, the fractions of cents he siphoned off daily from the bank's many thousands of accounts added up to a lot of money. 12

By the same electronic token, government can do the tampering. I myself was a victim, several years ago, in the course of a dispute with the Internal Revenue Service. One day my bank's cash machine failed to respond to the usual ritual of dipping the ATM card and typing the access code. According to the machine, my balance was now zero. The IRS had done this, electronically seizing my account as a hostage to its claim. 13

At least one dystopian novelist has recognized the possibilities here. In Margaret Atwood's *The Handmaid's Tale*, religious fundamentalists carry out a putsch against the U.S. government and, as a first step in their male-chauvinist program, cause the banking system's computers to abolish all accounts whose owners are female. 14

Which brings me back to my hypothetical Pol Pot virus. There is at work even today, let's imagine, a brilliant hacker motivated by an ideology of extreme radical egalitarianism. He is able to gain access to a computer in a bank somewhere, into which he introduces an insidious software program that, over time, in the course of electronic transfers from bank to bank, infects every computer in the capitalist world's monetary system. 15

On a certain date—May Day, let's say—the virus causes the entire system to crash. Every bank balance, every credit card balance, every electronically recorded account balance of any kind whatever, suddenly changes to zero. All the money in the developed world disappears, except for whatever negligible amount of cash people happen to be carrying in their wallets that day. 16

The Dow Jones average is zero. The federal budget is zero, but so is the deficit. The rich are aghast. They demand that all bank accounts and brokerage accounts and so on be reconstructed from the paper trail of checks and deposit slips and so forth. But there are trillions of these pieces of paper; the job would take years. 17

Meanwhile the middle class, finding its debts changed to zero, and the poor, lacking bank accounts in the first place, are not at all unhappy with the new state of affairs. They don't see why the government should go to all the trouble of sifting through those trillions of documents. Much simpler just to start over and divide the wealth equally. The government doesn't see it that way, of course, but because the virus has temporarily made it impossible for special interests to make campaign contributions, the incumbents are all voted out. The economy begins anew with everyone at the same starting line. 18

Can it happen? I don't see why not. Watch your ATM machine and see. 19

UNDERSTANDING THE ESSAY

1. What does the title have to do with Schaffner's subject matter?
2. Why does Schaffner tell us about his troubles with the IRS?
3. What does Schaffner mean by describing gold, silver, and cowrie shells as "the ancient first stage of abstraction"?
4. What were the later stages?

5. Although several of Val Schaffner's stories are obviously fictional, do they strike you as possible or even likely? Do you think it is possible that the sort of computer terrorism he describes really could occur?

So What and the Seven Common Moves.   Analyze this essay with the help of the questions about "So What and the Seven Common Moves" found on the back cover of this book. Jot down answers to the questions. As you do, keep your own writing in mind; the point of examining the work of other writers is to discover moves you can make in an essay of your own.

Words, Phrases, and Allusions.   The following items were taken from "Virus Zero" in the order of appearance. With the help of your classmates, locate these words in the essay and see if their context provides a clue to their meaning. If necessary, consult a dictionary, an encyclopedia, or other reference work to determine what each item means in its context. Pay particular attention to words and phrases that might be useful in your own writing.

albeit, diabolical, havoc, vandals, virtual wealth, cyberspace, innocent of politics, utopian, Cambodia's Pol Pot, postindustrial West, cowrie shells, ingots, tangible, hypothetically, illicit, inheres, devious, heist, larcenous, cyberpunk, siphoned, electronic token, dystopian, Margaret Atwood's *The Handmaid's Tale*, religious fundamentalists, ideology, radical egalitarianism, insidious, negligible, aghast, brokerage accounts, incumbents

Suggestion for Writing

Using "Virus Zero" as a model, try writing a "what-if" essay, using lots of imaginary but credible examples to show your readers what would happen if, say, aliens invaded, or if the stock market crashed, or if universities were to give generous scholarships to all qualified students. The journal entry suggested at the beginning of this selection may have given you an idea for a topic, or you may have thought of other topics as you read Schaffner's essay. You can choose a serious topic or a frivolous one, as long as you demonstrate your ability to find or invent persuasive examples.

Journal Entry. Something unusual happens where you live, and it happens often. Something unusual happens where everyone lives. What is it in your case? What sort of behavior or event makes you think, "Only here—only in this residence—does this sort of thing happen with such frequency"?

Jot down as many instances as you can to exemplify the way things are at your house. After you have worked on this project for a while, read Marion Winik's essay about the way things disappear at her house. Look for moves you could imitate in an essay of your own.

Things Don't Just Disappear

Marion Winik

Today we are looking for my car keys, a pair of sunglasses, the baby's yellow swim trunks. In addition to today's specials, we are, as always, keeping an eye out for my driver's license and video club card, miscellaneous kitchen utensils, earrings, and small wooden toys, the one pacifier preferred above all others, the personal statement I wrote when I applied to law school five or ten years ago. Whatever made me think to look for that old thing and, finding it gone, spend the rest of the summer searching and mourning? As if I had lost the young, earnest part of me that wrote it. 1

We are tearing apart the house, going through drawers and file cabinets and toy chests. Checking the dumpster, the laundry hamper, the refrigerator. One time we found a missing pair of scissors in the egg compartment. A string of pearls in the recycling bin. We will not rest; we cannot think of anything else. Why are we always looking for things, asks Tony wearily. He sounds as if he's about to cry. 2

As a person who naturally maintains a warm, solicitous relationship with the material objects in his life, he cannot fathom the stubborn streak of carelessness to which the afflicted state of my possessions bears witness. If they are not lost altogether, my things are stained or scratched or broken, in sad and urgent need of cleaning and mending. *His* things are well taken care of, polished, folded, neatly stored. They don't go flying out of his pocket, slipping into the garbage, jumping into somebody else's car. They stick to him like glue. 3

The only thing that sticks with me is a kind of fitful, half-baked antimaterialism, an impatience with the tyranny of objects. Because of it, I just don't notice what kind of car other people drive, or the puddle I'm about to step into, or where I set down my bag when I got home. And this leaves the door wide open to the cold wind of chaos, which sweeps through my life at unpredictable intervals to exact its 4

207

toll. There wasn't a bone in my body that wanted to lose my heirloom engagement ring two weeks after it was given to me. I only wore it to a party on the outside of a glove because I wanted to be able to look at it all night long. And then it was days before my husband-to-be could drag me out of the hedges and pry the rented metal detector from my frozen hands.

If objects I actually cherish are not exempt from the curse, the outlook is grim-   5
mer still for things for which I feel no love. In early adolescence, for example, I lost seven or eight pairs of eyeglasses in one year. I dropped them in the street while hurrying to the bus stop and found them run over on the way home, a million sparkly blue plastic pieces on the pavement. I accidentally put them in my lunch bag with the remainder of a baloney sandwich and flicked the whole thing into the trash. My mother telephoned the school in a panic; a janitor was dispatched to go through the incinerator. One pair after the next, those glasses flew off my face and out of my life, propelled by some strange centrifugal force.

Back then, my looking was all for show. I'll search the bedroom, Ma, I'd call,   6
and take one quick peek in the closet. Then I'd flop on the bed with a magazine till she came to check on me. I looked everywhere, I'd tell her. They're gone. I pictured something in the way of a distant galaxy, where tennis balls, orthodontic retainers, geography books, combs, and puppies rotated slowly in the luminous violet air. Whoosh, my glasses were sucked in by a powerful vacuum. Zip, the entrance to the place seamed up like a tent.

My mother took a wholly different attitude. The fact that anything could be lost   7
at all was an affront to her worldview. She put something away, it stayed there. If it didn't, she tracked it to the ends of the earth. She determined when it was last seen, where, and by whom. She lined up the usual suspects: me, my sister, the dog. Who took the good pen out of my purse? She pulled the refrigerator away from the wall; she carefully sorted through old newspapers. It's got to be somewhere, she muttered. Things don't just disappear.

When my family went to see the circus at Madison Square Garden, my mother   8
lost a contact lens in the crowded cement passageway that led to our seats. Hold it! shouted my father, flat-palmed like a traffic cop, and a circular space cleared around us. Men, women, and children were down on their knees, nose to tail like elephants, seeking the tiny transparent circle on the dusty floor. My mother stood motionless in the center, scouting with her one working eye as my father patted down her woolen suit. I'm not related to them, I told anyone who would listen.

In my mother's opinion, to lose something due to carelessness was a sin that re-   9
quired penance. To atone for one's failure to keep track of one's little flock of objects, one had to devote oneself completely to the pursuit of the lost lamb, be it a ballpoint pen or a ten-dollar bill. Whatever it was, in becoming lost it achieved a significance far greater than any it had ever known.

Now I spend half my life blithely leaving restaurants without my purse or my   10
jacket and the other half maniacally searching my house for the cat-food coupon I put away so carefully. For God's sake, Marion, says Tony three days into the drama, is it still that damn coupon? Of course not, I lie.

But sometimes the obsession pays off. Like the time Hayes had his little friend 11
Emily Rose over and they scattered every piece of every toy he owns from one end
of the house to the other. When the dust settled, an octagonal green puzzle piece
had completely disappeared. I called up Emily Rose's mother, Carole. Look in your
diaper bag, I ordered.

But it wasn't in the diaper bag, or in our garbage disposal, or on the bookshelf, 12
or in any of the thousand other places I looked in the weeks that followed. I called
up the toy store the puzzle came from and inquired about ordering a replacement
part. They laughed at me.

Then one day I was in the bathroom, thinking about nothing, looking at the 13
hole in the wall that was made when the toilet paper holder fell off and took a big
hunk of Sheetrock with it. Suddenly I had an inspiration. Reaching into the hole and
down toward the floor, I brushed something with my fingertips. Could it be? I
crammed in my arm up to the shoulder. Exultant, I called Tony at work. The green
thing! I shouted.

That's great, he said. But what about the cat-food coupon? 14

And let us not forget the famous incident of Sandye's glove in Chinatown. Ever 15
since we were in fifth grade, every time I borrowed something from Sandye I would
lose it or break it or wreck it. After fifteen years of this she said, Enough. You better
not borrow anything from me anymore.

Then Tony and I came up from Texas to visit her in New York and it was a 16
very cold day and I had no gloves and we hadn't seen each other in a while, so despite everything, she lent me a pair and sent us off for the afternoon. Imagine my
horror a few hours later when one of my coat pockets was suddenly empty. We
looked, we looked, we retraced our steps, we went back to Hong Fat, where we'd
had lunch. By then, it had begun to grow dark.

It took forever to get out of Chinatown, rush-hour traffic two weeks before 17
Christmas, streets and sidewalks filled with people scurrying home. I was despon-
dent in the backseat, staring out the window as if somehow the glove might appear.
And against all probability, it did. One wool-lined leather glove, returned from the
ethers only slightly trampled, lying in the middle of Mott Street. Tony, I cried out.
Stop the car.

I keep at least a dozen pens in my purse at all times and force myself not to 18
count them to make sure they're all there. I do not favor one over the others, for I
know that will make it disappear. I never purposely hide a thing from myself, or put
it in a safe and secret place. If I do, I will never see it again.

When my mother comes to visit, I lose something big, just to give us something 19
to do. A credit card, my watch, the recipe for vinaigrette. Then we are overtaken by
the rhythm of looking, like aging actors staffing in a revival of their first hit show.
Our lines come back as if it were yesterday. It'll turn up, don't worry. Oh, I know,
I'm sure it will. Did you have it when you went to the supermarket? Have you already looked in the car?

At my father's funeral, my mother, my sister, and I were given small badges 20
made from a piece of black grosgrain ribbon to wear during the period of mourning.

The ribbon had a cut in it to symbolize the rending of garments traditionally performed by members of the bereaved Jewish family. I remember pinning the strange decoration on my dress with a kind of bitter pride.

Later that day or the next, in a noisy house filled with plates of food and vats of coffee and half-empty highball glasses, I looked down and saw the ribbon was gone. My hand flew up to my heart. It's okay, honey, said my mother, you can have mine. I don't want yours, I half-screamed at her, and went crazy, tearing up the house, crawling under the couch, yanking out drawers that hadn't been opened in years. Finally I threw myself on my childhood bed in despair. 21

Then Tony and Sandye burst into my room, all flushed with their little conspiracy, shouting, Look, Mar, it was in the car! It was in the car! Tony brandished a torn black ribbon, but I knew it wasn't mine. At first I wasn't going to take it. Then, as I looked at their eager, helpful faces, something gave in me. I wiped my eyes, pinned the false ribbon on my shift, and did not search anymore. I took it home with me to Texas and placed it in my lingerie drawer, where it is at this very moment. I never look at it. 22

My first ribbon, the original ribbon, is somewhere in my mother's house. It will turn up. Unlike people, things don't just disappear. 23

UNDERSTANDING THE ESSAY

1. What does the title have to do with Winik's subject matter?
2. Why does Winik tell us about finding a missing pair of scissors in the egg compartment? What does this reveal about her household?
3. Why does she tell us about losing the heirloom engagement ring?
4. What are Marion Winik's examples, examples of? What does she want you to think they are typical of?
5. What does she want you to know or understand or feel or believe as a result of reading her essay? Is it, in fact, an essay? Has Winik succeeded in making the topic interesting to you? Does she interpret a subject, or merely report it?

So What and the Seven Common Moves.   Analyze this essay with the help of the questions about "So What and the Seven Common Moves" found on the back cover of this book.

Words, Phrases, and Allusions.   The following items were taken from "Things Don't Just Disappear" in the order of appearance. With the help of your classmates, locate these words in the essay and see if their context provides a clue to their meaning. If necessary, consult a dictionary, an encyclopedia, or other reference work to determine what each item means in its context. Pay particular attention to words and phrases that might be useful in your own writing.

> miscellaneous, solicitous, fathom, antimaterialism, tyranny of objects, cold wind of chaos, intervals, exact its toll, heirloom, incinerator, luminous, affront, Madison Square Garden, blithely, maniacally, obsession, exultant, despondent, ethers, vinaigrette, grosgrain ribbon, rending of garment, bereaved, lingerie

Suggestion for Writing

Using "Things Don't Disappear" as a model, write an essay about something strange that happens with some frequency where you live, giving lots of examples. The journal entry suggested at the beginning of this selection may have given you an idea for a topic, or you may have thought of other topics as you read Winik's essay.

On Boxing and Pain

Joyce Carol Oates

Years ago in the early 1950s when my father first took me to a Golden Gloves boxing tournament in Buffalo, New York, I asked him why the boys wanted to fight one another, why they were willing to get hurt. As if it were an explanation my father said, "Boxers don't feel pain quite the way we do." 1

Pain, in the proper context, is something other than pain. 2

Consider: Gene Tunney's single defeat in a thirteen-year career of great distinction was to a notorious fighter named Harry Greb who seems to have been, judging from boxing lore, the dirtiest fighter in history. Greb was infamous for his fouls—low blows, butting, "holding and hitting," rubbing his laces against an opponent's eyes, routine thumbing—as well as for a frenzied boxing style in which blows were thrown from all directions. (Hence, "The Human Windmill.") Greb, who died young, was a world middleweight champion for three years but a flamboyant presence in boxing circles for a long time. After the first of his several fights with Greb the twenty-two-year-old Tunney was so badly hurt he had to spend a week in bed; he'd lost an astonishing two quarts of blood during the fifteen-round fight. Yet, as Tunney said some years later: 3

> Greb gave me a terrible whipping. He broke my nose, maybe with a butt. He cut my eyes and ears, perhaps with his laces . . . My jaw was swollen from the right temple down the cheek, along under the chin and partway up the other side. The referee, the ring itself, was full of blood . . . But it was in that first fight, in which I lost my American light-heavyweight title, that I knew I had found a way to beat Harry eventually. I was fortunate, really. If boxing in those days had been afflicted with the Commission doctors we have today–who are always poking their noses into the ring and examining

superficial wounds–the first fight with Greb would have been stopped before I learned how to beat him. It's possible, even probable, that if this had happened I would never have been heard of again.

Tunney's career, in other words, was built upon pain. Without it he would never have moved up into Dempsey's class.

Tommy Loughran, light-heavyweight champion in the years 1927–29, was a 4 master boxer greatly admired by other boxers. He approached boxing literally as a science—as Tunney did—studying his opponents' styles and mapping out ring strategy for each fight, as boxers and their trainers commonly do today. Loughran rigged up mirrors in his basement so that he could watch himself as he worked out, for, as he said, no boxer ever sees himself quite as he appears to his opponent. He sees the opponent but not himself as an opponent. The secret of Loughran's career was that his right hand broke easily so that he was forced to use it only once each fight: for the knockout punch or nothing. "I'd get one shot, then the agony of the thing would hurt me if the guy got up," Loughran said. "Anybody I ever hit with a left hook I knocked flat on his face, but I would never take a chance for fear if my [left hand] goes, I'm done for."

Both Tunney and Loughran, it is instructive to note, retired from boxing well be- 5 fore they were forced to retire. Tunney became a highly successful businessman, and Loughran a highly successful sugar broker on the Wall Street commodities market. (Just to suggest that boxers are not invariably stupid, illiterate, or punch-drunk.)

Then there was Carmen Basilio!—much loved for his audacious ring style, his 6 hit-and-be-hit approach. Basilio was world middle and welterweight champion 1953–57, stoic, determined, a slugger willing to get hit in order to deal powerful counter-punches of his own. Onlookers marveled at the punishment Basilio seemed to absorb though Basilio insisted that he didn't get hit the way people believed. And when he was hit, and hit hard—

> People don't realize how you're affected by a knockout punch when you're hit on the chin. It's nerves is all it is. There's no real concussion as far as the brain is concerned. I got hit on the point of the chin [in a match with Tony DeMarco in 1955]. It was a left hook that hit the right point of my chin. What happens is it pulls your jawbone out of your socket from the right side and jams it into the left side and the nerve there para- lyzed the whole left side of my body, especially my legs. My left knee buckled and I al- most went down, but when I got back to my corner the bottom of my foot felt like it had needles about six inches high and I just kept stamping my foot on the floor, trying to bring it back. And by the time the bell rang it was all right.

Basilio belongs to the rough-and-tumble era of LaMotta, Graziano, Zale, Pep, Sad- dler; Gene Fullmer, Dick Tiger, Kid Gavilan. An era when, if two boxers wanted to fight dirty, the referee was likely to give them license, or at least not to interfere.

Of Muhammad Ali in his prime Norman Mailer observed, "He worked appar-   7
ently on the premise that there was something obscene about being hit." But in
fights in his later career, as with George Foreman in Zaire, even Muhammad Ali
was willing to be hit, and to be hurt, in order to wear down an opponent. Brawling
fighters—those with "heart" like Jake LaMotta, Rocky Graziano, Ray Man-
cini—have little choice but to absorb terrible punishment in exchange for some advantage (which does not in any case always come). And surely it is true that some
boxers (see Jake LaMotta's autobiographical *Raging Bull*) invite injury as a means
of assuaging guilt, in a Dostoyevskian exchange of physical well-being for peace of
mind. Boxing is about being hit rather more than it is about hitting, just as it is about
feeling pain, if not devastating psychological paralysis, more than it is about winning. One sees clearly from the "tragic" careers of any number of boxers that the
boxer prefers physical pain in the ring to the absence of pain that is ideally the condition of ordinary life. If one cannot hit, one can yet be hit, and know that one is still
alive.

It might be said that boxing is primarily about maintaining a body capable of   8
entering combat against other well-conditioned bodies. Not the public spectacle, the
fight itself, but the rigorous training period leading up to it demands the most discipline, and is believed to be the chief cause of the boxer's physical and mental infirmities. (As a boxer ages his sparring partners get younger, the game itself gets more
desperate.)

The artist senses some kinship, however oblique and one-sided, with the pro-   9
fessional boxer in this matter of training. This fanatic subordination of the self in
terms of a wished-for destiny. One might compare the time-bound public spectacle
of the boxing match (which could be as brief as an ignominious forty-five seconds—the record for a title fight!) with the publication of a writer's book. That
which is "public" is but the final stage in a protracted, arduous, grueling, and frequently despairing period of preparation. Indeed, one of the reasons for the habitual
attraction of serious writers to boxing (from Swift, Pope, Johnson to Hazlitt, Lord
Byron, Hemingway, and our own Norman Mailer, George Plimpton, Ted Hoagland,
Wilfrid Sheed, Daniel Halpern, et al.) is the sport's systematic cultivation of pain in
the interests of a project, a life-goal: the willed transposing of the sensation we
know as pain (physical, psychological, emotional) into its polar opposite. If this is
masochism—and I doubt that it is, or that it is simply—it is also intelligence, cun-
ning, strategy. It is an act of consummate self-determination—the constant reestab-
lishment of the parameters of one's being. To not only accept but to actively invite
what most sane creatures avoid—pain, humiliation, loss, chaos—is to experience
the present moment as already, in a sense, past. *Here* and *now* are but part of the design of *there* and *then*: pain now but control, and therefore triumph, later. And pain
itself is miraculously transposed by dint of its context. Indeed, it might be said that
"context" is all.

The novelist George Garrett, an amateur boxer of some decades ago, remi-   10
nisces about his training period:

I learned something . . . about the brotherhood of boxers. People went into this brutal and often self-destructive activity for a rich variety of motivations, most of them bitterly antisocial and verging on the psychotic. Most of the fighters I knew of were wounded people who felt a deep, powerful urge to wound others at real risk to themselves. In the beginning. What happened was that in almost every case, there was so much self-discipline required and craft involved, so much else besides one's original motivations to concentrate on, that these motivations became at least cloudy and vague and were often forgotten, lost completely. Many good and experienced fighters (as has often been noted) become gentle and kind people . . . They have the habit of leaving all their fight in the ring. And even there, in the ring, it is dangerous to invoke too much anger. It can be a stimulant, but is very expensive of energy. It is impractical to get mad most of the time.

Of all boxers it seems to have been Rocky Marciano (still our only undefeated heavyweight champion) who trained with the most monastic devotion; his training methods have become legendary. In contrast to reckless fighters like Harry "The Human Windmill" Greb, who kept in condition by boxing all the time, Marciano was willing to seclude himself from the world, including his wife and family, for as long as three months before a fight. Apart from the grueling physical ordeal of this period and the obsessive preoccupation with diet and weight and muscle tone, Marciano concentrated on one thing: the upcoming fight. Every minute of his life was defined in terms of the opening second of the fight. In his training camp the opponent's name was never mentioned in Marciano's hearing, nor was boxing as a subject discussed. In the final month Marciano would not write a letter since a letter related to the outside world. During the last ten days before a fight he would see no mail, take no telephone calls, meet no new acquaintances. During the week before the fight he would not shake hands. Or go for a ride in a car, however brief. No new foods! No dreaming of the morning after the fight! For all that was not *the fight* had to be excluded from consciousness. When Marciano worked out with a punching bag he saw his opponent before him, when he jogged he saw his opponent close beside him, no doubt when he slept he "saw" his opponent constantly—as the cloistered monk or nun chooses by an act of fanatical will to "see" only God.

Madness?—or merely discipline?—this absolute subordination of the self. In   11 any case, for Marciano, it worked.

UNDERSTANDING THE ESSAY

1. Why, according to Oates, do boxers prefer pain to its absence (see paragraph 7)? What evidence does she give? Do you believe her?
2. What does Oates think boxers have in common with writers?
3. Who was Gene Tunney? Jack Dempsey? Rocky Marciano? What do these boxers have in common? In what ways is each unique? See if you can find

information about the various boxers Oates mentions in your library or on the Web.

4. Do you think everybody would share Oates's attitude about boxing?

5. In several places, Oates quotes other people, sometimes at length. Find each quoted passage and see if you can determine why Oates chooses to quote rather than to paraphrase. Develop advice for writers about when to quote and when to paraphrase—advice that you might follow in your own research papers.

So What and the Seven Common Moves. Analyze this essay with the help of the questions about "So What and the Seven Common Moves" found on the back cover of this book.

Words, Phrases, and Allusions. The following items were taken from "On Boxing and Pain" in the order of appearance. With the help of your classmates, locate these words in the essay and see if their context provides a clue to their meaning. If necessary, consult a dictionary, an encyclopedia, or other reference work to determine what each item means in its context. Pay particular attention to words and phrases that might be useful in your own writing.

Golden Gloves, notorious, flamboyant, afflicted, Wall Street commodities market, audacious, welterweight, stoic, era, Norman Mailer, assuaging, Dostoyevskian, rigorous, infirmities, sparring partners, oblique, ignominious, protracted, arduous, grueling, masochism, consummate self-determination, parameters of one's being, reminisces, antisocial, verging on the psychotic, monastic devotion, seclude, cloistered

Suggestion for Writing

Using "On Boxing and Pain" as a model, write an essay using lots of examples to show that your favorite spectator activity is, in fact, worth watching. Address the concerns of people who, for one reason or another, do not enjoy watching this same activity. The journal entry suggested at the beginning of this selection may have given you an idea for a topic, or you may have thought of other topics as you read Oates's essay.

RECIPES FOR WRITING EXEMPLIFICATION

A. Writing from Personal Experience

Exemplification is the use of stories or analogies to prove a point. It is often used in politics. People arguing for or against any proposed law or policy are bound to give examples or precedents to indicate how the rule makes sense (or fails to make sense) because of the way it affects individuals or groups whose cases are represented by the examples. We can argue *against* trimming the federal education budget, for example, by telling specific stories about how budget cuts will affect the lives of students; or we can argue *for* cuts in the education budget by citing examples of students who have abused aid programs by refusing to repay loans or by using the money to take luxurious spring vacations. An exemplification paper almost always includes narrative passages (the examples are likely to be anecdotal).

Here is a recipe for writing an exemplification essay:

1. Pick an issue of current political interest about which you have a firm opinion based on personal experience.
2. Tell one extended story or several brief stories illustrating why you feel the way you do about the issue at hand.
3. Do not hesitate to add fictional stories, but make sure not to present these stories as if they were true.
4. Arrange your stories in the sequence that will best maintain the interest of your reader.
5. After you've written the body of the paper, add an introduction and an ending.
6. Show a draft to fellow students in a formal or informal workshop, and see if your strategies are having the effects you want them to have. Use the checklist on the back cover to focus your discussion. Then look for errors in spelling, grammar, or punctuation that you will want to correct in your final draft.

B. Writing against the Text

All examples imply counterexamples—other likely stories that may modify or in some cases disprove whatever point the original examples had made. What stories would Brent Staples's "victims" have experienced or heard to make them react instinctively with fear? (Staples is careful to acknowledge these stories in a general way in paragraph 6.) What stories about boxing could be told to argue that it is, in fact, a brutal and inhumane sport? Choose any exemplification essay in this chapter and write a response to it using examples of your own.

C. Writing from Research

Examples are often used to support or oppose proposed legislation or policy. Choose a side in any issue currently debated in Congress. Use the Web and the library to find as many examples as you can to use as precedents or analogs to support your side of the debate. As you conduct your research, also notice examples cited by people who support the other side of the issue; you might mention these examples and then explain why they are not entirely persuasive. After you've completed your research, write a draft without consulting your sources; this will help you avoid being overwhelmed by what you read and perhaps unintentionally plagiarizing material. Then go back and add material from your research wherever you think it will make your paper more interesting or authoritative. Be sure to acknowledge the source of anything you quote or paraphrase.

10

Argument, Persuasion, and Conflict Resolution:
Making Belief and Making Up

Persuasive essays are never absolutely persuasive; someone, somewhere, is always unpersuaded. This is because persuasive essays deal with issues that cannot be settled by the sort of evidence we use in logic and science. We *can* get conclusive evidence to determine whether there is fuel in the tank, or whether there are holes in the ozone layer, or whether the angles of a trapezoid add up to 360°—evidence that reasonable and well-informed people are likely to accept. But the questions persuasion deals with are much more elusive than these. They include questions with "should" or "ought" in them, questions about values, and questions about events that depend upon human behavior. These questions reside in the realm of rhetoric, the realm of belief—belief about the way things are, or ought to be, or are likely to be, particularly in human affairs.

In fact, rhetoric can be defined as the study of belief and of the way we arrive at it. It is the art of dealing with questions for which the answers are always merely plausible, not conclusive. Everything else in rhetoric—modes, moves, style, organization—is secondary.

To understand rhetoric as a study of belief, it helps to contrast it with other ways of knowing. The most certain kind of knowledge is mathematical. Geometry often uses a form of reasoning called the "syllogism," drawing conclusions from a pair of premises that no one can argue with. Here is an example:

> If A is greater than B
> And B is greater than C
> Then A is greater than C

There is no room for arguing with this kind of thinking. In geometry, logic actually proves things. But that's because everybody who understands geometry understands the premises and the rules of reasoning in precisely the same way. And geometry deals only in abstractions—abstract As and Bs, ideal lines and triangles—avoiding the murky imprecision of real Apples and Bananas and imperfect lines and triangles.

Laboratory science is a second kind of knowledge. It falls between the absolute precision and certitude of geometry and the endlessly debatable conclusions of rhetoric. Science uses the same sort of reasoning that geometry uses; but it never reaches quite the same level of precision because it has to work with real, physical things—real frogs and chromosomes and comets and neutrons—which are never as cooperative as the ideal circles and triangles and abstractions of geometry. Scientists always have to admit that their observations are precise only up to a certain point, and that some hitherto unknown datum will turn up, some wrinkle in the structure of the universe, contrary to what they thought were laws of nature, making them modify or even abandon what they thought they knew for sure.

Rhetoric is a third kind of knowledge, less certain than the other two, but much broader in its scope. Rhetoric takes on questions that are beyond the reach of mathematics and science, questions like, "Should government subsidize the arts?" "Should youthful offenders be tried as adults?" "Should states use lotteries to support education?" "What will happen if the United States were to ban capital punishment, or normalize relations with Cuba?" Mathematical reasoning and scientific proofs may be helpful in answering questions like these, but they never actually settle them. There will always be room for reasonable and well-informed debate.

If this were not true, all the tough debates in the world would be settled by logic or science. There would be as much basic agreement among politicians—and for that matter, among religious leaders, art critics, and economists—as there is among geometricians or physicists. All reasonable and well-informed people would belong to the same political party, support the same foreign and domestic policies, and share the same religious beliefs. They would all like the same music and art, the same sports, the same style of architecture. But of course, they don't. And life would be boring if they did. It wouldn't even be life.

Rhetoric has a special kind of reasoning of its own—reasoning based upon **assumptions** about the way the world works (beliefs) or ought to work (values). These assumptions can never be conclusively proved or refuted; and yet they are the foundation of all rhetorical reasoning. Everybody has assumptions: scientists, atheists, saints, Republicans, Democrats, professors, hairdressers, taxi drivers, cheerleaders, gymnasts, and astronauts. There is an absolute democracy in the universe of belief.

In rhetoric, assumptions become part of a peculiar form of reasoning called the **enthymeme**. Enthymemes are to rhetoric what syllogisms are to logic. They often occur as compressed syllogisms, in which premises may be implied rather than stated; and they are always based on assumptions.

Here is an enthymeme:

> Americans will buy more foreign cars this year because the dollar is strong.

If we were to put this enthymeme in the form of a syllogism, it would look like this:

> Whenever the dollar is strong, Americans buy more foreign cars.
> This year the dollar is strong.
> Therefore, this year Americans will buy more foreign cars.

In this case, the premise that Americans buy more foreign cars when the dollar is strong is an assumption. It may be true, normally, but not always. For this reason, the conclusion is not exactly airtight. Any number of things could happen to discourage or even prevent Americans from buying foreign automobiles, no matter how strong the dollar might be.

Enthymemes are a kind of reasoning, different from syllogisms in that they have no set forms and in that they derive debatable conclusions from premises that are not at all certain. They can, in addition, be extremely complex while seeming quite simple: whole chains of implied syllogisms may be buried within a single enthymeme. This complexity can make them very efficient (which is why they are often used in public discourse) but also impossible to untangle. Although the name of this particular kind of reasoning may seem odd (it's Greek, actually, for "in the mind"), everybody uses enthymemes in every formal or informal debate. We learn to use them almost as soon as we learn language itself.

In science, evidence usually occurs in the form of observed data. In rhetoric, however, evidence usually occurs in the form of **paradigms**. Paradigms are examples, analogous situations, or likely stories, the sort of stories we use to make generalizations about how people behave or to make educated guesses about the consequences of a particular policy or course of action. Paradigms can be either historical or fictitious. The American experience in Viet Nam is often used as an historical paradigm to argue against sending troops to other foreign wars. The fable about "The Boy Who Cried 'Wolf!'" is often used to persuade children that false alarms can be dangerous. Paradigms appeal to the belief that human behavior is likely to repeat itself in similar circumstances.

Paradigms never *prove* a point—but we often find them persuasive anyway. The conclusions we draw from paradigms are always "hasty," strictly speaking. They always leave room for debate—for counterexamples or for a different interpretation of events. Someone is sure to interpret every paradigm differently ("Well, we *could* have won in Viet Nam, if only we had . . .") or cite a competing paradigm

("Sure, Viet Nam was a mistake, but this situation is more like Granada, or Kuwait, or Nazi Germany). If someone uses "The Boy Who Cried 'Wolf!'" as evidence against giving false alarms, someone else might propose ordinary fire drills as evidence in support of them—deliberate false alarms calculated to save lives in the event of a real emergency.

Rhetoric is "relativistic." It recognizes few absolutes, if any. But it does have **consequences**. Sooner or later, someone will turn out to be right, or at least partially right, and someone else wrong, or at least partially wrong. When a fire breaks out, the preparatory drills will either keep people calm and save their lives, or they will cause lives to be lost because people will have become accustomed to not taking the alarms seriously. When we send troops abroad, the result will be either triumph or defeat or an endless entanglement—just as somebody had predicted. Rhetorical reasoning may lack the precision of geometry and the solidity of science, but much depends upon our ability to do it well.

Rhetoric, as the anatomy of belief, has two major uses. One is to unravel the assumptions, enthymemes, paradigms, and consequences at the heart of every argument so we can identify the basis of disagreement. Once we do this, we can construct strategies to convert people who disagree with us, by appealing to assumptions, enthymemes, paradigms, and consequences that they will find even more persuasive than the ones that support their position. We might call this "Rhetoric A"—the rhetoric of persuasion. A second use of rhetoric is to examine beliefs, not so much to convert people, but to discover the ideologies that prevent people or groups of people from getting along with each other, and perhaps to discover some common ground for the peaceful resolution of conflict. We might call this "Rhetoric B"—the rhetoric of understanding.

We all have ideologies—beliefs we consider sacred and unquestionable. We generally do not think of them as beliefs, however; we think of them as "common sense," or "conscience," or "self-evident truths," or "divine revelation"—even when we encounter intelligent people of good will whose beliefs contradict our own. Ideologies are both positive and negative in their effects: they are the interpretive lenses that enable us to make sense of our lives; they are the "glue" that bonds social units and enables them to achieve things that no single individual could achieve; but they also make us resistant to change, even when change would be for the better.

Identifying our own ideologies is generally difficult: we tend to believe what we believe because, for some reason, we *have* to believe it. It is usually easier to identify ideologies in other people, especially ideologies we happen not to share. We have no difficulty recognizing that political positions we disagree with are, ultimately, ideological; but we generally have difficulty seeing the ideological basis of our own political convictions. In some discussions, "ideology" is considered a bad word, an intellectual disease that makes people close-minded. But everybody has ideologies. We need them. They are the basis of every political or religious or philosophical position. Even scientists and geometricians have ideologies—beliefs that they choose to leave unexamined.

Groups that share the same ideologies can be called "communions."

Communions are essential to human cooperation and achievement. Without them, we could have no science, no civilization, no group identity, or school spirit, or teamwork, or civic or ethnic pride, or political alliances, or corporate achievements, or religious denominations. But communions have a negative side, too. By establishing a sense of "us," they necessarily establish an implicit sense of "them," a sense of "the other"—other clubs, other countries, other ethnic groups, other religions, other kinds of science, even other kinds of geometry. The very thing that makes cooperation possible also sets up the possibility of conflict.

From a rhetorical perspective, communions can be either an aid or a hindrance to persuasion. Sometimes writers can establish a sense of communion with their readers. "*People like us,*" they might say or imply—meaning "members of *our* particular religious group, or neighborhood, or region, or social class, or economic level, or professional organization"—"People like us consider the beliefs and values implicit in my argument to be sacred." The appeal to membership in a communion is often difficult to resist. To abandon the beliefs of a communion, to abandon an ideology, can feel like disloyalty or heresy.

But it can also feel like a conversion—a new way of seeing things, a way that makes more sense or has more desirable consequences. If you've read the story about "Jackie's Debut" (p. 40), you may recognize that the young Mike Royko was undergoing a conversion. The communion of the neighborhood included a belief about segregation. It must have been difficult for Royko, as a boy, to reject that belief, in effect rejecting the communion of people for whom he quite properly felt love and respect. Conversions can be painful, but they are a normal part of growing up and a necessary ingredient in a civil society.

Weedee Peepo

José Antonio Burciaga

> We the people of the United States, in order to form a more perfect union, establish justice, insure domestic tranquillity, provide for the common defense, promote the general welfare, and secure the blessings of liberty to ourselves and our posterity, do ordain and establish this Constitution for the United States of America.
>
> Preamble to the Constitution

Twenty-five years ago, when my parents were studying for their naturalization tests, they would ask each other in Spanish, "Have you learned *el Weedee Peepo*?" 1

It took me a while to figure out what they were talking about. Weedee Peepo 2 was the way my parents pronounced the first words of the preamble to our Constitution. They had to memorize it.

It was a happy and proud day when they went to the courthouse to be sworn in 3 as United States citizens. My father got a haircut, shined his shoes and wore his best suit. A snappy dresser all his life, he cherished this special occasion, especially since he changed clothes from a maintenance janitor at a synagogue in El Paso.

He also bought an autograph book and had all his friends sign it with little con- 4 gratulatory messages, from the rabbi and the cantor to the judge who swore them in.

My mother was more subdued. She had been a very patriotic Mexican school- 5 teacher who had lived and taught Mexico's revolutionary history. For her, becoming a U.S. citizen was more of a convenience after having lived in this country for

224

many years. For fifteen years she had to carry a passport that would allow her to cross the international bridge five times a week to buy produce or visit her mother and sisters. Besides, her six children were all U.S.A.-born. Five years later, I would march off to the wild blue yonder with the Air Force.

But that day at the courthouse was the beginning of their lives as United States 6
citizens. They took their voting rights seriously. At that time, voters in Texas had to pay a poll tax that came to about $1.75. In a family with six children that was a substantial amount twenty-five years ago. Nonetheless, my father insisted on doing his duty as a good citizen.

Before voting in each election, he would ask my older sister Lupita and me for 7
our views on the candidates and the issues. Though he spoke English, it was harder for him to read politically technical literature comfortably. In Spanish, Lupita and I would summarize the propaganda and tell him what we thought was the best choice. But he was not to be conned into our choice. He always made his own decision even if it was based on intuition, which most of the time was right on target.

At seventy-six he still voted, but with the help of bilingual voting ballots. I 8
didn't have to translate for him. Besides, living in California, I know zilch about recent Texas politics.

There are people who would condemn my father and other such people for sup- 9
posedly failing to make an effort to read and write English. He did learn, despite the fact that he usually worked ten to twelve hours a day, six days a week. But he was more comfortable and confident in his native tongue.

His home, El Paso, is a town whose population is officially sixty-two percent 10
Mexican-American (unofficial estimates go as high as seventy percent). Seventy percent of the population speak Spanish, and retail sales in Spanish account for at least fifty percent of the business. This does not include the enormous business the city conducts with Mexico. The communications media are fifty percent Spanish-speaking.

Recently El Paso celebrated its four-hundredth anniversary. Spanish has been 11
spoken there much longer than English. The Spanish arrived in El Paso in 1581; two hundred and twenty-five years later, in 1806, Zebulon Pike became one of the first English speakers to enter El Paso. The Southwest has not been completely conquered.

And so, despite their limited English my parents became United States citizens. 12
They knew what Weedee Peepo meant. It meant *Nosotros el pueblo,* We the People.

Whatever language we speak, we have the same goals stated in our Constitu- 13
tion. If people need a translator when their children are no longer at their side and the government does not consider the job its responsibility, God help this nation.

The So-What Factor.   What is novel, interesting, surprising, or moving about José Burciaga's essay? Does it make you think about an issue in a way you may not have thought about it before?

In "Weedee Peepo" the issue is whether the government should provide language assistance for American citizens whose primary language is other than English; or more specifically, whether the government should provide bilingual ballots for voters who speak a language other than English (see paragraph 7). This is properly a rhetorical issue—one for which facts and logic may provide some assistance, but not an answer. It is an issue based on values and belief. Burciaga's point is that speakers of languages other than English can be loyal and productive American citizens if the government will assist them by providing official documents in their native languages. The contrary position is implied rather than stated: it is the notion that English should be declared the official language of the United States.

Assumptions. To be effective, a persuasive essay has to be built on assumptions that the audience shares. There has to be "common ground." In this essay, Burciaga attempts to establish common ground by the reference to God in the last line and to the Constitution in the title—"Weedee Peepo." The reference to God is intended to invoke a religious solidarity with his readers, establishing an "us" relationship that transcends the "us/them" relationship (immigrants/people born in this country). The reference to the Constitution is intended to invoke a shared ideology, a belief that all Americans are presumed to share: that all people are created equal.

Burciaga also attempts to transcend an us/them relationship by mentioning that his father (presumably a Roman Catholic) worked in a Jewish synagogue, where the rabbi and the cantor were among his closest friends. The point is that America has a long tradition of absorbing cultural and ethical communions into something much larger.

There are other assumptions implicit in Burciaga's story, assumptions about what it means to be an American and a responsible citizen. There is also an implicit sympathy for ordinary people, even if they happen to be different from the majority. And there are assumptions about the responsibilities of government ("ought" assumptions). Do you share these assumptions? Do you bring other, competing assumptions to bear on this issue? Could you be persuaded to change them? If not, can you analyze the causes of your resistance?

Enthymemes. If you asked a dozen experts to untangle the reasoning buried in a persuasive essay, they would probably come up with a dozen different answers. This is what makes persuasion interesting, at least for people who can live with a certain amount of indeterminacy (i.e., the lack of certitude and simple solutions). One way of outlining the underlying reasoning of "Weedee Peepo" would be this:

> Wherever a large portion of the population speaks a language other than English, the government has a responsibility to provide ballots in the language they speak.
> In El Paso, Texas, Spanish is the primary language of a large portion of the population.

In El Paso, Texas, the government has a responsibility to provide ballots in Spanish.

You know this is an enthymeme—a rhetorical syllogism rather than a mathematical one—because you can imagine reasonable people disagreeing with it, sputtering, "But where do you draw the limits?" or "But how many languages should the government be expected to accommodate?" or "But wouldn't it be simpler if everyone learned English?" These objections, of course, would be supported by enthymemes and assumptions of their own.

You will find enthymemes persuasive only if you share assumptions in the premises and if you accept the facts or examples that go along with them.

Here are some other enthymemes buried or implied in "Weedee Peepo":

Good citizens are people who show pride in their country, work hard to support themselves, take part in the political process, live peaceably with their neighbors, and serve their country.
The Burciagas are people who show pride in their country, work hard to support themselves, take part in the political process, live peaceably with their neighbors, and serve their country.
The Burciagas are good citizens.

Good citizens deserve the assistance of the government.
People like the Burciagas are good citizens.
People like the Burciagas deserve the assistance of the government.

It is in the best interest of America to provide voters with ballots in a language they can understand.
In Spanish-speaking communities, ballots can be understood by voters only if they include a Spanish version.
It is in the best interest of America to provide voters in Spanish-speaking communities with ballots that include a Spanish version.

What other enthymemes can you discover? Which do you find plausible? Which implausible? Why?

Paradigms.   The story of Burciaga's parents is a paradigm—a story intended to be perceived as typical of a certain category of events. To be persuasive, a paradigm has to strike you as a likely story—in this case, a story that typifies the experience of immigrants or at least of a significant number of them.

In rhetorical reasoning, stories often do battle with other stories. What sorts of stories and examples would be told by people who oppose Burciaga's point of view? Which set of stories do you find more persuasive? Why is it that you will prefer one set of stories while some of your classmates will prefer the competing stories?

Consequences.   What good consequences does Burciaga imagine resulting from his position? What bad consequences from the opposing position? Burciaga seems to think that linguistic diversity within the United States is not such a bad thing—perhaps even a very American thing. What good consequences can you imagine if Burciaga's side ends up winning the "English only" debate? What bad consequences can you imagine if his side loses? (You can ask the same questions about the opposing point of view as well.)

THE SEVEN COMMON MOVES

1. Beginning. The first paragraph makes us curious by repeating the strange phrase we have already encountered in the title: "Weedee Peepo." Because Burciaga has provided us with a bit of the Constitution, we may already guess what the phrase means, but we're still curious about who pronounced it that way, and why. This is the sort of curiosity that makes for a good beginning. And of course, it is not just some random mystery: this particular phrase and this particular pronunciation of it are central to Burciaga's thesis.

2. Ending. The last two paragraphs may be considered the ending. "And so," Burciaga writes, clearly signaling a "conclusion" in more senses than one. Like many writers, Burciaga achieves a sense of closure by circling back to the beginning, in this case, by echoing and translating the key phrase, "Weedee Peepo." The final sentence is a clincher, repeating the thesis and ending in a strong phrase that at once appeals to what is presumably a shared belief (in this case, a religious belief), and is at the same time a powerful expletive.

3. Detail. Because details in persuasive writing often take the form of likely stories, the skills you learned in the chapters on description and narration can be very useful. The heart of description is "things that mean"; the heart of narration is "action that means" and dialogue that reveals the character of the speakers. What is revealed by the Burciagas' asking each other, "Have you learned el Weedee Peepo?" What is revealed by the fact that Mr. Burciaga "got a haircut, shined his shoes and wore his best suit" for the naturalization ceremony? What other details can you recall from the essay even without looking back at it? Return to those details, and ask yourself what makes them memorable and what they mean in relation to the point of the essay.

4. Organization/ Plot. The structure of "Weedee Peepo" has two main parts: The first part is the story of how Burciaga's parents became United States citizens and exercised their responsibilities (paragraphs 1 through 8); the second part (paragraphs 9 through 13) deals indirectly with a movement to make English the official language of the United States, a movement that would make it difficult for people like the Burciagas to participate fully in the economic and political life of the United States.

In persuasive writing, the word "plot" takes on new meaning. In addition to being a pattern of concealing and revealing information to maintain the readers' interest, plot in persuasive papers is a strategy, a plan of assault, an attempt to rout out old beliefs and replace them with new ones. To succeed, the writer may have to infiltrate the readers' defenses, gaining their good will. This is why Burciaga waits until paragraph 9 to announce the central issue of the essay. First he lets us get to know his parents, perhaps even to like and admire them. Once he has done this, we may feel the shock he wants us to feel when he says, "There are people who would condemn my father and other such people for supposedly failing to make an effort to learn to read and write English." Had he announced his thesis at the outset, readers who are inclined to disagree with him would have mounted all sorts of defenses against the implications of his story. When you expect readers to resist your conclusions, it is smart to postpone your thesis until they have had a chance to consider your best evidence with an open mind.

5. Style. There is considerable craft in Burciaga's sentences, even though they seem like ordinary speech. Notice, for example, how they range in length, from five words to thirty-one (paragraph 5, "For fifteen years . . ."). The short sentences, in context, are real zingers: "They had to memorize it"; "My mother was more subdued." The variety of sentence length creates a pleasing rhythm, but it also serves to emphasize what Burciaga wants to emphasize.

Burciaga pays attention to sentence endings, saving the best part for last. For example, he could have written this:

> My parents would ask each other in Spanish, "Have you learned *el Weedee Peepo?*" when they were studying for their naturalization tests twenty-five years ago.

But instead, he wrote this:

> Twenty-five years ago, when my parents were studying for their naturalization tests, they would ask each other in Spanish, "Have you learned *el Weedee Peepo?*"

The second version focuses on the final phrase, "Weedee Peepo," which is important to the thesis of this essay. Experiment with other sentences in Burciaga's essay and see how their effect would have been altered if he had arranged to end other than the way they do. Pay particular attention to the final sentence.

6. Voice/Attitude. Burciaga sounds like a particular human being, an individual speaking, instead of a newspaper reporter neutrally and objectively reporting the facts. He uses the first-person pronoun ("I"). He reveals his values and opinions.

Notice, too, his occasional use of slang, or informal diction: "march off to the wild blue yonder"; "he was not to be conned into our choice"; "I know zilch about recent Texas politics." These phrases are designed to help Burciaga seem friendly, informal, unpretentious, nonthreatening.

7. Economy. An essay is economical if every detail serves a point. What is the point of the story about the way Burciaga's father dressed for the ceremony? What is the point of the story about Burciaga's mother's attachment to her native culture? What is the point of the story about the Burciaga children helping their parents interpret political propaganda? Find other stories in the essay and explain what point they are intended to make. Are there any stories or parts of stories that are unrelated to Burciaga's main point? Are there any words that could have been omitted, or phrases that could have been condensed without any discernible loss?

Moves within Moves.   Overall, "Weedee Peepo" is a persuasive essay. But within that framework it's easy to find instances of modes and methods treated as separate chapters in this book. Most of the essay is an example, which is developed by techniques discussed in the chapters on narration and description. There is also a bit of comparison and contrast between the father and the mother (the point of which may be to show that not everyone is absolutely wild about giving up their own heritage to become U.S. citizens—nor need they be). There is a quick contrast between the clothes Mr. Burciaga wore to the ceremony and those he wore to work. Paragraph 7 is a process analysis—explaining how Mr. Burciaga used to vote when he still had children at home to interpret things for him.

Words, Phrases, and Allusions.   "Weedee Peepo" implies readers who are familiar with the following words, phrases, and allusions, which were taken from the essay in the order of appearance:

> domestic tranquillity, posterity, naturalization tests, cantor, subdued, wild blue yonder, poll tax, propaganda, conned, bilingual, Zebulon Pike, Nosotros el pueblo

With the help of your classmates (and if necessary, a dictionary, encyclopedia, or other reference work), determine what each item means in its context. Pay particular attention to words and phrases that might be useful in your own writing.

Suggestion for Writing

Using "Weedee Peepo" as a model, write an essay defending your position on the issue you chose to discuss in the journal entry suggested in the introduction to the essay. Use examples as evidence—either one extended example or several shorter ones. Use the life stories of people you know, perhaps people in your own family. Tell the story in the context of assumptions and values you think your classmates will share—assumptions about the way the world works or ought to work. Decide whether it would be more effective to put your thesis up front, or to delay it until you have presented some of your best evidence in the form of examples, or perhaps simply to imply it—to have it whispered between the lines. After you have written a draft, try it out on fellow students in a formal or informal workshop, and see if your strategies are having the effects you want them to have.

Journal Entry. Whenever a few people begin to question established customs, they are likely to be considered a radical fringe—even though these radical fringes occasionally turn out to be right. The notion that voting rights should be extended to women and minorities and to people who do not own real estate was considered radical at one time. So was the notion that people in the thirteen colonies need not remain subject to the laws of England. Of course, not all radical ideas turn out to be good ones. Think of a "sacred cow"—some custom or practice in American life that some people have started to call into question, even though that custom or practice may be supported by law or by religious groups. Identify the assumptions and paradigms that might support tradition in this matter—as well as assumptions and paradigms that might indicate a need for change. Then read Barbara Ehrenreich's essay about widespread attitudes toward divorce. Look for moves you might imitate in an essay of your own.

In Defense of Splitting Up

Barbara Ehrenreich

No one seems much concerned about children when the subject is welfare or Medicaid cuts, but mention divorce, and tears flow for their tender psyches. Legislators in half a dozen states are planning to restrict divorce on the grounds that it may cause teen suicide, an inability to "form lasting attachments" and possibly also the piercing of nipples and noses.

But if divorce itself hasn't reduced America's youth to emotional cripples, then the efforts to restrict it undoubtedly will. First, there's the effect all this antidivorce rhetoric is bound to have on the children of people already divorced—and we're not talking about some offbeat minority. At least 37% of American children live with divorced parents, and these children already face enough tricky interpersonal situations without having to cope with the public perception that they're damaged goods.

Fortunately for the future of the republic, the alleged psyche-scarring effects of divorce have been grossly exaggerated. The most frequently cited study, by California therapist Judith Wallerstein, found that 41% of the children of divorced couples are "doing poorly, worried, under-achieving, deprecating and often angry" years after their parents' divorce. But this study has been faulted for including only 60 couples, two-thirds of whom were deemed to lack "adequate psychological functioning" even before they split, and all of whom were self-selected seekers of family therapy. Furthermore, there was no control group, say, miserable couples who stayed together.

As for some of the wilder claims, such as "teen suicide has tripled as divorces   4
have tripled": well, roller-blading has probably tripled in the same time period too,
and that's hardly a reason to ban in-line skates.

In fact, the current antidivorce rhetoric slanders millions of perfectly wonder-   5
ful, high-functioning young people, my own children and most of their friends included. Studies that attempt to distinguish between the effects of divorce and those
of the income decline so often experienced by divorced mothers have found no lasting psychological damage attributable to divorce per se. Check out a typical college
dorm, and you'll find people enthusiastically achieving and forming attachments
until late into the night. Ask about family, and you'll hear about Mom and Dad . . .
and Stepmom and Stepdad.

The real problems for kids will begin when the antidivorce movement starts   6
getting its way. For one thing, the more militant among its members want to "re-
stigmatize" divorce with the cultural equivalent of a scarlet *D*. Sadly though, divorce is already stigmatized in ways that are harmful to children. Studies show that
teachers consistently interpret children's behavior more negatively when they are
told that the children are from "broken" homes—and, as we know, teachers' expectations have an effect on children's performance. If the idea is to help the children
of divorce, then the goal should be to *de*-stigmatize divorce among all who interact
with them—teachers, neighbors, playmates.

Then there are the likely effects on children of the proposed restrictions them-   7
selves. Antidivorce legislators want to repeal no-fault divorce laws and return to the
system in which one parent has to prove the other guilty of adultery, addiction or
worse. True, the divorce rate rose after the introduction of no-fault divorce in the
late '60s and '70s. But the divorce rate was already rising at a healthy clip *before*
that, so there's no guarantee that the repeal of no-fault laws will reduce the divorce
rate now. In fact, one certain effect will be to generate more divorces of the rancorous, potentially child-harming variety. If you think "Mommy and Daddy aren't
getting along" sounds a little too blithe, would you rather "Daddy (or Mommy) has
been sleeping around"?

Not that divorce is an enviable experience for any of the parties involved. But   8
just as there are bad marriages, there are, as sociologist Constance Ahrons argues,
"good divorces" in which both parents maintain their financial and emotional responsibility for the kids. Maybe the reformers should concentrate on improving the
quality of divorces—by, for example, requiring prenuptial agreements specifying
how the children will be cared for in the event of a split.

The antidivorce movement's interest in the emotional status of children would be   9
more convincing if it were linked to some concern for their physical survival. The
most destructive feature of divorce, many experts argue, is the poverty that typically
ensues when the children are left with a low-earning mother, and the way out of this
would be to toughen child-support collection and strengthen the safety net of support-
ive services for low-income families—including childcare, Medicaid and welfare.

Too difficult? Too costly? Too ideologically distasteful compared with de-   10
nouncing divorce and, by implication, the divorced and their children? Perhaps. But

sometimes grownups have to do difficult and costly things, whether they feel like doing them or not. For the sake of the children, that is.

UNDERSTANDING THE ESSAY

1. What does Ehrenreich mean when she says that children of divorced parents have "to cope with the public perception that they're damaged goods"?
2. What flaws does Ehrenreich point out in the research report she mentions in paragraph 3?
3. What is the main issue in this essay? Is this an issue that can be settled by logic or science, or is it properly a rhetorical issue (an issue of values and belief)?
4. Everyone has some personal knowledge of divorce and its consequences. What stories could you tell to add evidence to Ehrenreich's position on divorce? What stories could you tell to argue against her position?
5. If a person seeking a divorce were required to prove that the other had been guilty of "adultery, addiction, or worse," would the consequences be beneficial to children (by making divorce more difficult to obtain) or would they be cruel to children (by pitting parents against each other in a bitter lawsuit)?

(See Additional Questions for Persuasive Essays, p. 242)

So What and the Seven Common Moves.   Analyze this essay with the help of the questions about "So What and the Seven Common Moves" found on the back cover of this book.

Words, Phrases, and Allusions.   The following items were taken from "In Defense of Splitting Up" in order of appearance. With the help of your classmates, locate these words in the essay and see if their context provides a clue to their meaning. If necessary, consult a dictionary, an encyclopedia, or other reference work to determine what each item means in its context. You probably know most of these words from conversation and reading, but you may not yet feel comfortable using them in your own writing.

pyches, cope, psyche-scarring effects, deprecating, control group, slanders, a scarlet *D*, stigmatized, rancorous, blithe, enviable, prenuptial agreements, ensues, ideologically distasteful, denouncing, implication

Suggestion for Writing

Using "In Defense of Splitting Up" as a model, write an essay examining a custom or practice that is currently being called into question. You could argue one side or the other, or perhaps find enthymemes and examples that favor each side, so that your essay merely indicates how complex the issue is. The journal entry suggested at the beginning of this selection may have given you an idea for a topic, or you may have thought of other topics as you read Ehrenreich's essay.

Journal Entry.   Most people resent being treated as quaint objects or curios. In many countries, for example, people object to tourists who ask them to pose for snapshots (presumably to show the folks back home how strange these natives look). Think of a situation in which a person or a group of persons is reduced to an icon or stereotype—like Uncle Ben on the rice box, or the Italian mama in spaghetti ads. Write notes for an essay distinguishing between stereotypes that people properly find offensive and those that are really harmless, even flattering. After you have worked on this project for a while, read Michael Dorris's essay about a practice that continues today, despite objections from native Americans. Look for moves that you can imitate in your own essay.

Crazy Horse Malt Liquor

Michael Dorris

People of proclaimed good will have the oddest ways of honoring American Indi- 1
ans. Sometimes they dress themselves up in turkey feathers and paint to boogie on fifty-yard lines. Sometimes otherwise impeccably credentialed liberals get so swept up into honoring that they beat fake tom-toms or fashion their forearms and hands into facsimiles of the axes European traders used for barter and attempt, unsuccessfully, to chop their way to victory. Presumably they hope that this exuberant if ethnographically questionable display will do their team more good against opponents than those rituals they imitate and mock did for nineteenth-century Cheyenne or Nez Percé (men and women who tried, with desperation and ultimate futility, to defend their homelands from invasion.)

Everywhere you look such respects are paid: the street names in woodsy, af- 2
fluent subdivisions, mumbo jumbo in ersatz male-bonding weekends and Boy Scout jamborees, geometric fashion statements, weepy anti-littering public service announcements. In the ever popular noble/savage spectrum, red is the hot, safe color.

For five hundred years flesh and blood Indians have been assigned the role of a 3
popular culture metaphor. Today, they evoke fuzzy images of Nature, The Past, Plight, or Summer Camp. War-bonneted apparitions pasted to football helmets or baseball caps act as opaque, impermeable curtains, solid walls of white noise that for many citizens block or distort all vision of the nearly two million contemporary Native Americans. And why not? Such honoring relegates Indians to the long ago

and thus makes them magically disappear from public consciousness and conscience. What do the three hundred federally recognized tribes—with their various complicated treaties governing land rights and protections, their crippling unemployment, infant mortality, and teenage suicide rates, their often chronic poverty, their manifold health problems—have in common with jolly (or menacing) cartoon caricatures, wistful braves, or raven-tressed Mazola girls?

Perhaps we should ask the Hornell Brewing Company of Baltimore, manufac-   4
turers of The Original Crazy Horse Malt Liquor, a product currently distributed in New York with packaging inspired by, according to the text on the back, "the Black Hills of Dakota, *steeped* [my italics] in the History of the American West, home of Proud Indian Nations, a land where imagination conjures up images of blue-clad Pony Soldiers and magnificent Native American Warriors."

Whose imagination? Were these the same blue-clad lads who perpetrated the   5
1890 massacre of two hundred captured, freezing Lakota at Wounded Knee? Are Pine Ridge and Rosebud, the two reservations closest to the Black Hills and, coincidentally, the two counties in the United States with the lowest per capita incomes, the Proud Nations? Is the "steeping" a bald allusion to the fact that alcohol has long constituted the number one health hazard to Indians? Virtually every other social ill plaguing Native Americans—from disproportionately frequent traffic fatalities to arrest statistics—is related in some tragic respect to ethanol, and many tribes, from Alaska to New Mexico, record the highest percentage in the world of babies born disabled by fetal alcohol syndrome and fetal alcohol effect. One need look no further than the warning label to pregnant women printed in capital letters on every Crazy Horse label to make the connection.

The facts of history are not hard to ascertain: the Black Hills, the *paha sapa*,   6
the traditional holy place of the Lakota, were illegally seized by the U.S government, systematically stripped of their mineral wealth—and have still not been returned to their rightful owners. Crazy Horse, in addition to being a patriot to his people, was a mystic and a religious leader murdered after he voluntarily gave himself up in 1887 to Pony Soldiers at Fort Robinson, Nebraska. What, then, is the pairing of his name with forty ounces of malt liquor supposed to signify?

The Hornell brewers helpfully supply a clue. The detail of the logo is focused   7
on the headdress and not the face; it's pomp without circumstance, form without content. Wear the hat, the illustration seems to offer, and in the process fantasize yourself more interesting (or potent or tough or noble) than you are. Play at being a "warrior" from the "land that truly speaks of the spirit that is America."

And if some humorless Indians object, just set them straight. Remind them   8
what an honor it is to be used.

UNDERSTANDING THE ESSAY

1. What does Dorris mean when he says that "Such honoring relegates Indians to the long ago and thus makes them magically disappear from public consciousness and conscience"?
2. What are the double meanings of "steeped" in paragraph 4?
3. What is the main issue in this essay? Is this an issue that can be settled by logic or science, or is it properly a rhetorical issue (an issue of value or belief)?
4. Is it always an insult to a group of people if their name or their culture is used to identify a product or a team? How do you distinguish insult from honor in this practice?
5. In what way could creating an image of native Americans as "noble savages" help or hinder them politically or economically?

(See Additional Questions for Persuasive Essays, p. 242)

So What and the Seven Common Moves.   Analyze this essay with the help of the questions about "So What and the Seven Common Moves" found on the back cover of this book.

Words, Phrases, and Allusions.   The following items were taken from "Crazy Horse Malt Liquor" in order of appearance. With the help of your classmates, locate these words in the essay and see if their context provides a clue to their meaning. If necessary, consult a dictionary, an encyclopedia, or other reference work to determine what each item means in its context. You probably know most of these words from conversation and reading, but you may not yet feel comfortable using them in your own writing.

impeccably credentialed liberals, facsimiles, exuberant, ethnographically questionable, Cheyenne, Nez Percé, futility, affluent, ersatz, popular culture, metaphor, apparitions, opaque, impermeable, white noise, contemporary, relegates, caricatures, raven-tressed Mazola girls, steeped, blue-clad Pony Soldier, Lakota at Wounded Knee, ethanol, fetal alcohol syndrome, ascertain, mystic, pomp without circumstance

Suggestion for Writing

Using "Crazy Horse Malt Liquor" as a model, write an essay exploring the public use of stereotypes. You could argue one side or the other, or perhaps find enthymemes and examples that favor each side, so that your essay merely indicates how complex the issue is. The journal entry suggested at the beginning of this selection may have given you an idea for a topic, or you may have thought of other topics as you read Dorris's essay.

Journal Entry. If you are like most people, you've probably inherited your attitude toward animals from your family, your community, and even (believe it or not) your religion (the world's religions, after all, are vastly different in their beliefs about the role animals play in the spirit world). Think about your most memorable encounter with an animal. It could have been a pet, a farm animal, a laboratory animal, or wild animal. In your journal, discuss whether you think this animal had any sort of consciousness of its own, and whether it has any "rights." Then read Alice Walker's story about a horse she once knew to see if she makes any moves that you might imitate in an essay of your own.

Am I Blue?

Alice Walker

"Ain't these tears in these eyes tellin' you?"

For about three years my companion and I rented a small house in the country that stood on the edge of a large meadow that appeared to run from the end of our deck straight into the mountains. The mountains, however, were quite far away, and between us and them there was, in fact, a town. It was one of the many pleasant aspects of the house that you never really were aware of this.

It was a house with many windows, low, wide, nearly floor to ceiling in the living room, which faces the meadow, and it was from one of these that I first saw our closest neighbor, a large white horse, cropping grass, flipping its mane, and ambling about—not over the entire meadow, which stretched well out of sight of the house, but over the five or so fenced-in acres that were next to the twenty-odd that we had rented. I soon learned that the horse, whose name was Blue, belonged to a man who lived in another town, but was boarded by our neighbors next door. Occasionally, one of the children, usually a stocky teen-ager, but sometimes a much younger girl or boy, could be seen riding Blue. They would appear in the meadow, climb up on his back, ride furiously for ten or fifteen minutes, then get off, slap Blue on the flanks, and not be seen again for a month or more.

There were many apple trees in our yard, and one by the fence that Blue could almost reach. We were soon in the habit of feeding him apples, which he relished, especially because by the middle of summer the meadow grasses—so green and succulent since January—had dried out from lack of rain, and Blue stumbled about munching the dried stalks half-heartedly. Sometimes he would stand very still just

1

2

3

by the apple tree, and when one of us came out he would whinny, snort loudly, or stamp the ground. This meant, of course: I want an apple.

It was quite wonderful to pick a few apples, or collect those that had fallen to the ground overnight, and patiently hold them, one by one, up to his large, toothy mouth. I remained as thrilled as a child by his flexible dark lips, huge, cubelike teeth that crunched the apples, core and all, with such finality, and his high broad-breasted enormity; beside which, I felt small indeed. When I was a child, I used to ride horses, and was especially friendly with one named Nan until the day I was riding and my brother deliberately spooked her and I was thrown, head first, against the trunk of a tree. When I came to, I was in bed and my mother was bending worriedly over me; we silently agreed that perhaps horseback riding was not the safest sport for me. Since then I have walked, and prefer walking to horseback riding—but I had forgotten the depth of feeling one could see in horses' eyes.

I was therefore unprepared for the expression in Blue's. Blue was lonely. Blue was horribly lonely and bored. I was not shocked that this should be the case; five acres to tramp by yourself, endlessly, even in the most beautiful of meadows—and his was—cannot provide many interesting events, and once rainy season turned to dry that was about it. No, I was shocked that I had forgotten that human animals and nonhuman animals can communicate quite well; if we are brought up around animals as children we take this for granted. By the time we are adults we no longer remember. However, the animals have not changed. They are in fact completed creations (at least they seem to be, so much more than we) who are not likely to change; it is their nature to express themselves. What else are they going to express? And they do. And generally speaking, they are ignored.

After giving Blue the apples, I would wander back to the house, aware that he was observing me. Were more apples not forthcoming then? Was that to be his sole entertainment for the day? My partner's small son had decided he wanted to learn how to piece a quilt; we worked in silence on our respective squares as I thought . . .

Well, about slavery: about white children, who were raised by black people, who knew their first all-accepting love from black women, and then, when they were twelve or so, were told they must "forget" the deep levels of communication between themselves and "mammy" that they knew. Later they would be able to relate quite calmly, "My old mammy was sold to another good family." "My old mammy was———" Many years later a white woman would say: "I can't understand these Negroes, these blacks. What do they want? They're so different from us."

And about the Indians, considered to be "like animals" by the "settlers" (a very benign euphemism for what they actually were), who did not understand their description as a compliment.

And about the thousands of American men who marry Japanese, Korean, Filipina, and other non-English-speaking women and of how happy they report they are, "blissfully," until their brides learn to speak English, at which point the marriages tend to fall apart. What then did the men see, when they looked into the eyes of the women they married, before they could speak English? Apparently only their own reflections.

I thought of society's impatience with the young. "Why are they playing the 10 music so loud?" Perhaps the children have listened to much of the music of oppressed people their parents danced to before they were born, with its passionate but soft cries for acceptance and love, and they have wondered why their parents failed to hear.

I do not know how long Blue had inhabited his five beautiful, boring acres be- 11 fore we moved into our house; a year after we had arrived—and had also traveled to other valleys, other cities, other worlds—he was still there.

But then, in our second year at the house, something happened in Blue's life. 12 One morning, looking out the window at the fog that lay like a ribbon over the meadow, I saw another horse, a brown one, at the other end of Blue's field. Blue appeared to be afraid of it, and for several days made no attempt to go near. We went away for a week. When we returned, Blue had decided to make friends and the two horses ambled or galloped along together, and Blue did not come nearly as often to the fence underneath the apple tree.

When he did, bringing his new friend with him, there was a different look in his 13 eyes. A look of independence, of self-possession, of inalienable horseness. His friend eventually became pregnant. For months and months there was, it seemed to me, a mutual feeling between me and the horses of justice, of peace. I fed apples to them both. The look in Blue's eyes was one of unabashed, "this is itness."

It did not, however, last forever. One day, after a visit to the city, I went out to 14 give Blue some apples. He stood waiting, or so I thought, though not beneath the tree. When I shook the tree and jumped back from the shower of apples, he made no move. I carried some over to him. He managed to half-crunch one. The rest he let fall to the ground. I dreaded looking into his eyes—because I had of course noticed that Brown, his partner, had gone—but I did look. If I had been born into slavery, and my partner had been sold or killed, my eyes would have looked like that. The children next door explained that Blue's partner had been "put with him" (the same expression that old people used, I had noticed, when speaking of an ancestor during slavery who had been impregnated by her owner) so that they could mate and she conceive. Since that was accomplished, she had been taken back by her owner, who lived somewhere else.

Will she be back? I asked. 15

They didn't know. 16

Blue was like a crazed person. Blue was, to me, a crazed person. He galloped 17 furiously, as if he were being ridden, around and around his five beautiful acres. He whinnied until he couldn't. He tore at the ground with his hooves. He butted himself against his single shade tree. He looked always and always toward the road down which his partner had gone. And then, occasionally, when he came up for apples, or I took apples to him, he looked at me. It was a look so piercing, so full of grief, a look so human, I almost laughed (I felt too sad to cry) to think there are people who do not know that animals suffer. People like me who have forgotten, and daily forget, all that animals try to tell us. "Everything you do to us will happen to you; we are your teachers, as you are ours. We are one lesson" is essentially it, I think. There are those who never once have even considered animals' rights: those who have been taught that animals actually want to be used and abused by us, as small children "love" to be frightened, or women "love" to be mutilated and raped. . . . They are the great-grand children of those who honestly thought, because someone taught them this: "Women can't think," and "niggers can't faint." But most disturbing of all, in Blue's large brown eyes was a new look, more painful than the look of despair: the look of disgust with human beings, with life, the look of hatred. And it was odd what the look of hatred did. It gave him, for the first time, the look of a beast. And what that meant was that he had put up a barrier within to protect himself from further violence; all the apples in the world wouldn't change that fact.

And so Blue remained, a beautiful part of our landscape, very peaceful to look   18
at from the window, white against the grass. Once a friend came to visit and said, looking out on the soothing view: "And it would have to be a white horse; the very image of freedom." And I thought, yes, the animals are forced to become for us merely "images" of what they once so beautifully expressed. And we are used to drinking milk from containers showing "contented" cows, whose real lives we want to hear nothing about, eating eggs and drumsticks from "happy" hens, and munching hamburgers advertised by bulls of integrity who seem to command their fate.

As we talked of freedom and justice one day for all, we sat down to steaks. I   19
am eating misery, I thought, as I took the first bite. And spit it out.

UNDERSTANDING THE ESSAY

1. What double meaning does the title have?
2. What does the epigraph ("Ain't these tears in these eyes tellin' you?") have to do with the title of the essay, and with the essay itself?
3. What does Walker mean when she says that calling pioneers "settlers" is a "very benign euphemism" (paragraph 8)?
4. What is the main issue in this essay? Is this an issue that can be settled by logic or science, or is it properly a rhetorical issue (an issue of values or belief)?
5. The references to slaves and Indians and mixed marriages and young people (paragraphs 7 through 10) are paradigms—examples used as analogies. Do they help explain Walker's insight about Blue? Do they also work the other way around—the experience of Blue somehow throwing light on relationships between powerful and powerless people?

(See Additional Questions for Persuasive Essays, p. 242)

So What and the Seven Common Moves.   Analyze this essay with the help of the questions about "So What and the Seven Common Moves" found on the back cover of this book.

Words, Phrases, and Allusions.   The following items were taken from "Am I Blue?" in order of appearance. With the help of your classmates, locate these words in the essay and see if their context provides a clue to their meaning. If necessary, consult a dictionary, an encyclopedia, or other reference work to determine what each item means in its context. You probably know most of these words from conversation and reading, but you may not yet feel comfortable using them in your own writing.

> ambling, relished, succulent, enormity, completed creations, respective, benign euphemism, inalienable, unabashed, impregnated, mutilated

Suggestion for Writing

Using "Am I Blue?" as a model, write an essay exploring the issue of animal rights. You could argue one side or the other, or perhaps find enthymemes and examples that favor each side, so that your essay merely indicates how complex the issue is. The journal entry suggested at the beginning of this selection may have given you an idea for a topic, or you may have thought of other topics as you read Walker's essay.

ADDITIONAL QUESTIONS FOR PERSUASIVE ESSAYS

Assumptions.   What beliefs and values does the author expect us to share, so that we react to the examples with the same pattern of approval and disapproval? What assumptions is the author arguing against in this essay? Why would some people find it difficult to abandon these assumptions? Do any these assumptions form the basis of communions of "us" (vs. "them")?

Enthymemes.   What enthymemes can you discover in the essay? If you had to express the implicit reasoning as a pair of premises and a conclusion, what would they be? (You can expect members of your class to come up with a number of different good answers to this question).

Paradigms.   What examples or "likely stories" does the author tell? Do they strike you as relevant and typical? Do they strike you as credible evidence to be used in a debate about the issue in this essay? Why or why not?

Consequences. What consequences, bad and good, can you imagine if the writer's view were to public policy? What consequences, bad and good, can you imagine if the opposite position prevails?

RECIPES FOR WRITING PERSUASION

A. Writing from Personal Experience

Persuasion A. "Persuasion A" is the kind of persuasion that we need when a situation will not allow us to tolerate two opposing points of view: for example,when we have to decide whether a defendant is guilty or innocent, or when we have to decide between candidates, or policies, or incompatible options of any kind.

1. Browse through the editorial pages of several newspapers until you discover an issue about which we must choose between two irreconcilable options.
2. After you have made your own choice, draft a letter to a real or imaginary person who has made the opposite choice.
3. In the first part of the letter, demonstrate how thoroughly you understand the other person's point of view by expressing it as forcefully as you can in language that the other person would appreciate, with reasons (perhaps in the form of examples) that the other person is likely to find persuasive. Identify the assumptions that color the way the other person interprets whatever evidence there might be, and describe those assumptions as sympathetically as you can. In other words, demonstrate your ability to get inside the other person's mind, to see the world as that person sees it.
4. In the second part of the letter, use examples to explain why you prefer the option you prefer. If possible, identify assumptions or values that the other person might actually share—a point of view from which the other person would see a different conclusion in the available evidence.
5. If in the process of writing this letter, you find yourself agreeing with the position you had set out to attack, feel free to change your mind and write your letter from the opposite point of view.
6. After you have completed the letter, change it to an editorial essay by providing a suitable beginning and ending and by changing all second-person references ("you") to third-person references.
7. Show a draft to fellow students in a formal or informal workshop, and see if your strategies are having the effects you want them to have. Use the checklist on the back cover to focus your discussion. Then look for errors in spelling, grammar, or punctuation that you will want to correct in your final draft.

Persuasion B. "Persuasion B" is the kind of persuasion that we need when a situation *will* allow two opposing points of view to exist simultaneously, even though the people who hold those points of view have been unable to settle their differences peaceably. The world is full of Persuasion B situations—where warring tribes or political parties or ethnic groups or religious denominations are convinced that their own interests or even their own existence is jeopardized by the other. There are often "ideological" conflicts at the basis of these conflicts—differences based on beliefs that neither side is willing to examine, beliefs (or assumptions) of a sort that can never be proved or disproved. These beliefs may be rooted in mythology, or tradition, or religion, or political doctrine, or simply "taste"; they are nonetheless very real, and must be taken into consideration if negotiations are to succeed.

Either side may allege facts to support its own position or to demonstrate the injustice of the other side's position. As an impartial mediator, your job is to decide whether these factual allegations are the sort that can be adjudicated (as in Persuasion A), or whether they represent interpretations of events that are either undecidable or beyond remedy.

In situations like these, the group with the upper hand typically thinks of the other as inferior, while the second group typically thinks of the first as oppressors. If the oppressed group ever gets the upper hand, it tends to regard itself as revolutionary or politically correct, and to regard the other group as old fashioned, selfish, and reactionary. Assuming that people involved in such conflicts are unlikely to change their beliefs, write a balanced essay for the few people on either side who may, in fact, be willing to consider another point of view. Assume that logic and facts will have little effect on the attitudes of either side. You should correct any gross logical or factual errors you encounter, but this will only clear the ground for persuasive tactics in the form of examples (stories like those José Antonio Burciaga tells about his family) or appeals to shared cultural or ethical values (like the appeals to patriotic and religious traditions that Dr. Martin Luther King, Jr., makes in his famous "I Have a Dream" speech, p. 277 in this book).

It would be preposterous to suppose that something as simple as a recipe could resolve deep-seated hostilities that opposing factions may have been nursing for centuries. The process outlined below is intended simply to help identify the causes of conflict and possibly discover shared beliefs or values that might eventually be the basis of a peaceful resolution.

1. Browse through the editorial pages of several newspapers until you discover a conflict between individuals or groups who are forced to live in proximity to each other.
2. Study the arguments advanced by both sides, identifying the assumptions and the examples that support them.
3. Identify factual allegations that might be settled by investigation or adjudication (e.g., allegations of war crimes or illegal appropriation of property). Hold these issues in reserve.

4. Identify the ideological conflicts that separate the contending parties—differences in culture, attitude, style, religion, or assumptions about how the world works or ought to work.

5. In the first part of your paper, demonstrate how thoroughly you understand each side's point of view by expressing it as forcefully as you can, with reasons (perhaps in the form of examples) that that side is likely to find persuasive (even though the other side will not). Then identify the assumptions that cause people on each side to interpret the examples differently.

6. If, after viewing all the information, you still think there is room for the opposing factions to cooperate in a pluralistic society, explain how tolerance and respect can be achieved. Use examples in the form of stories to help the party with the upper hand see people on the other side in a more sympathetic light (the essays in chapter 10 use many examples of this sort). Directly or implicitly invoke common sense or values shared by both sides as a basis for a peaceable resolution of conflict. These values may be expressed in sacred texts common to both sides, or they may be embodied in a hero, real or mythical, a political figure or even an entertainment celebrity.

7. If, after viewing all the information, you discover that the factions are divided by ideological differences that are truly irreconcilable, offer a resolution that reasonable and impartial observers would find acceptable.

8. Add a suitable beginning and ending.

9. Discuss your draft with classmates, using the "So-What and the Seven Common Moves" checklist to help you identify what you've done well and where you could use some improvement.

B. Writing against the Text

For every argument in the realm of rhetoric, there is a counterargument, one that could be made by providing different examples or by applying a different set of values and assumptions. If you found yourself thinking "Yes, but . . ." as you read any of the essays in this chapter, you have already thought of counterarguments. You may have found yourself thinking, "But where do you draw the line?" Or more specifically, "How many hundreds of languages should the government be expected to accommodate?" or "Shouldn't we all become total vegetarians and stop wearing leather shoes if we're serious about animal rights?" Choose an essay in which you found room for reasonable disagreement and write an essay of your own in support of a different interpretation of the subject.

C. Writing from Research

Using the library and the Web, locate information about issues that have been decided by the United States Supreme Court, but with strong dissenting opinions.

Study the majority and the dissenting opinions and either analyze them from a rhetorical perspective (identifying paradigms, enthymemes, assumptions, and consequences in the arguments on each side) or write an essay of your own, defending one side of the issue but acknowledging the arguments from the other side.

After you have completed your research, write a draft in your own words without consulting your sources; this will help you avoid being overwhelmed by what you read and perhaps unintentionally plagiarizing material. Then go back and add quoted material wherever you think it will make your paper more interesting or authoritative. Be sure to acknowledge the source of anything you quote or paraphrase.

11

Reflections on the Essay:
Five Classic Examples

All essays have one thing in common: the author assumes a voice, a personality, a presence. This makes essays different from, say, legislative writing, courthouse records, writing on billboards, accident reports, lab reports, and certain kinds of newspaper writing, particularly front page reporting.

As you will have noticed from the examples in this book, a great variety of personal voices is possible: Mike Royko does not sound like Annie Dillard, who does not sound like Joan Didion, who does not sound like David Foster Wallace, who does not sound like Brent Staples, who does not sound like Marion Winik. One of the interesting things about essays as a genre is that they allow writers to be unique individuals on paper, to be themselves, or at least to create selves that they would like to be—or in some cases (as in the essay by Jonathan Swift in this chapter) to create a self that they might *not* like to be.

No one would argue that personal voice is appropriate in every sort of writing; but we find it in unexpected places, and find it pleasing. Even scholarly writing can be personal, and when it is, it reaches a much larger audience. Joan Brumberg's essay on anorexia nervosa (p. 148) and Bruce Catton's essay on Grant and Lee (p. 111) have been read by many people who are not sociologists or historians precisely because the voices in these essays seem personal. Scholarly essays of this sort raise an interesting question: Why can't all scholars write this way? Does the pose of "objectivity" in scholarly journals really serve a useful purpose? Or is it a tradition that needs to be examined?

A second quality of all essays is that they do not merely convey information; they *interpret* it. In fact, the point of an essay is always the interpretation of the subject, not the subject itself. It is Ernie Pyle's interpretation of the debris on the Normandy beachhead (p. 14), and Donna Tartt's interpretation of cheerleading in junior high (p. 29), and José Antonio Burciaga's interpretation of his parents experience (p. 224), and Joan Jacobs Brumberg's interpretation of anorexia nervosa (p. 148) that make these essays worth reading. In a good essay, there is an element of surprise in the writer's interpretation: not just a surprise ending or a surprising twist in a plot, but a surprising "take" on the subject, an understanding that we might not have discovered on our own, a point of view different from what ordinary, intelligent people ordinarily think, or in the case of scholarly essays, an interpretation that adds to or argues with previous interpretations of the same subject. This is what gives essays the so-what factor that makes them worth reading.

Interpretation and voice are always closely related. To interpret is to reveal your sense of good and bad, interesting and dull, tasteful and tacky. Personality is normally suppressed in the "objective" pose of scholarly, technical, and legal writing, just as it is (or is supposed to be) in newspaper reporting. In essays, however, personality—the writer's values and assumptions—are always detectable.

The third essential quality of an essay is the element of style. Essayists are never content merely to interpret information. They want their language to be polished, tight, efficient, and if the situation allows, pleasing, even playful. They are never content with sentences that merely communicate. They want each sentence, each phrase, to have a certain energy about it that would be lacking in a transcript of ordinary conversation. To achieve this, they make writerly moves, moves that require a bit of effort—words, phrases, and allusions carefully chosen, sentences more economical, more formal, more decorative, and in general more cultivated than would be possible in ordinary speech.

The fourth essential quality of essays is that they are intended for readers who have no practical reason or obligation to read them (which makes essays different from, say, laws and legal opinions and textbooks and airline schedules and cookbooks). This is why essays are particularly challenging to write. The author cannot presume interest, and therefore has to earn it, right from the outset, with a beginning that grabs the reader's attention, a sequence of information that maintains the reader's curiosity, and above all, an interpretation of the subject matter that is unusual and credible enough to deserve the reader's attention.

A fifth essential quality of essays is that they are intended for a large group of readers (which makes essays different from, say, letters, contracts, diaries, and grocery lists). It is easy to write notes to ourselves, perhaps a bit more difficult to write to an individual or a small group of people. But essays are designed for a large group of readers, most of them unknown to the author.

As a form of writing, essays are just over four hundred years old. Before the invention of the printing press (roughly 1450), it was hard to imagine a large and anonymous group of readers because duplicating texts was difficult and expensive. When the only means of "publication" was to make individual copies by hand, the only things worth publishing were things that seemed destined to last forever, or at least for a reasonably long time—like the Bible and serious works of science, philosophy, theology, literature, and sacred texts. It was not practical to produce writing that was relatively casual, like conversations with friends and family.

Even after printing was invented, the duplication of texts was quite expensive: paper had to be made by hand, and a barrel of ink was a major investment. The disposable texts that we take for granted today—newspapers, magazines, paperbacks—were a long way in the future. It was not until the Renaissance, with its revolutionary sense of the value of the individual, that anyone might have dared to publish the personal musings of an individual writer; and even then, it took a remarkable person to invent the essay as a form of writing, and to invent it in a way that would appeal to sufficient readers to make printing profitable.

That someone was a Frenchman by the name of Michel Eyquem de Montaigne, who inherited an estate from his father, and along with it, lots of leisure in which he worried that his mind was going to waste, like a field growing nothing but weeds.

To make his mind ashamed of itself, Montaigne says, he began writing down his thought. In 1580 he published a book called *Essaís*, in which he both invented a particular kind of writing and gave it a name that has lasted ever since. The word "essay" has two forms with numerous meanings in English, "essay" and "assay," each of which can be used as a noun or as a verb. To "essay" can mean to try something, perhaps to try it tentatively; it can also mean to put something to a test. To "assay" means to examine closely—for example, to perform a chemical analysis on a sample of ore to discover what it contains. Montaigne's essays are tentative analyses of topics that interested him, trial writings—not pretending to be great literature or scholarship. As it turns out, however, Montaigne's essays were so delightful that they are still read today, and they established a genre that is still very much alive.

In this chapter, you will examine six classic essays—essays that have earned themselves a permanent place in history because they continue to be interesting. All of them are, in varying degrees, a bit antique in style, so you may have to work a bit to make sense of them. The first was written by Montaigne himself: the first essay in the first volume of his work—arguably the world's first essay—in which Montaigne speculates about the best way to win mercy from people we have offended. There you will discover all the essential moves that launched the essay as a genre that is still alive and well four hundred years later.

The second essay, "A Modest Proposal" (1729), is in the voice of a fictional character—an economist who would like to reduce the number of poor people in Ireland more or less the way we might reduce a surplus of livestock. The author, Jonathan Swift, does not tell us at the outset that he is not writing in his own voice; he lets us discover this on our own, as his modest proposal becomes more and more outrageous.

The third essay, by Virginia Woolf (published posthumously in 1942), returns to the tradition of an author writing in her own voice. The subject seems, at first, trivial: a moth dying on a windowsill. But Woolf's interpretation transforms this event into an emblem of a great contest between vastly unequal forces in which we ourselves are doomed to lose.

The fourth essay is by E. B. White, whose books (*Charlotte's Web, Stuart Little, The Trumpeter Swan*) you may have encountered as a child. White is generally considered one of the best essayists of this century, and his reflections on taking his son to the same lake he had visited in his own childhood are like Virginia Woolf's, in that the event itself seems ordinary, but the writer's interpretation of the event makes it memorable and moving.

The fifth essay was originally a speech, delivered by the Reverend Dr. Martin Luther King, Jr., on August 28, 1963, from the steps of the Lincoln Memorial in Washington, D.C. The subject and the occasion were momentous, and King used many of the rhetorical devices common to classical rhetoric and good down-home preaching to make his pleas for peaceful change both forceful and memorable.

But first, the earliest essay of them all: Montaigne's reflections on a human paradox—that when one method of getting what we want from other people fails to work, the exact opposite of that method will sometimes work.

By Diverse Means We Arrive at the Same End

Michel Eyquem de Montaigne

The commonest way of softening the hearts of those we have offended, when, vengeance in hand, they hold us at their mercy, is by submission to move them to commiseration and pity. However, audacity and steadfastness (entirely contrary means) have sometimes served to produce the same effect.

Edward, prince of Wales, the one who governed our Guienne so long (a person whose traits and fortune have in them many notable elements of greatness), having suffered much harm from the Limousins, and taking their city by force, could not be halted by the cries of the people and of the women and children abandoned to the butchery, who implored his mercy and threw themselves at his feet until, going farther and farther into the city, he saw three French gentlemen who with incredible boldness were holding out alone against the assault of his victorious army. Consideration and respect for such remarkable valor first took the edge off his anger; and he began with these three men to show mercy to all the inhabitants of the city.

As Scanderbeg, prince of Epirus, was pursuing one of his soldiers in order to kill him, this soldier, after trying by every sort of humility and supplication to appease him, resolved in the last extremity to await him sword in hand. This resoluteness of his put a sudden stop to the fury of his master, who, having seen him take such an honorable stand, received him into his favor. This example may suffer another interpretation from those who have not read about the prodigious strength and valor of that prince.

Emperor Conrad III, having besieged Guelph, duke of Bavaria, would not come down to milder terms, no matter what vile and cowardly satisfactions were offered him, than merely to allow the gentlewomen who were besieged with the duke to go out, their honor safe, on foot, with what they could carry away on them. They, great-heartedly, decided to load their husbands, their children, and the duke himself on their shoulders. The Emperor took such great pleasure in the nobility of their courage that he wept with delight and wholly subdued the bitter and deadly hatred which he had borne against this duke, and from that time forward treated him and his humanely. 4

Either one of these two ways would easily win me, for I am wonderfully lax in the direction of mercy and gentleness. As a matter of fact, I believe I should be likely to surrender more naturally to compassion than to esteem. Yet to the Stoics pity is a vicious passion; they want us to succor the afflicted, but not to unbend and sympathize with them. 5

Now these examples seem to me more to the point, inasmuch as we see these souls, assailed and tested by these two means, hold up unshaken against one and bow beneath the other. It may be said that to subdue your heart to commiseration is the act of easygoing indulgence and softness, which is why the weaker natures, such as those of women, children, and the common herd, are the most subject to it; but that, having disdained tears and prayers, to surrender simply to reverence for the sacred image of valor is the act of a strong and inflexible soul which holds in affection and honor a masculine and obstinate vigor. 6

However, in less lofty souls, astonishment and admiration can engender a like effect. Witness the people of Thebes: having put their generals on trial for their lives for continuing in their posts beyond the time prescribed and foreordained for them, they just barely absolved Pelopidas, who bowed under the weight of such accusations and used only pleas and supplications to protect himself; whereas with Epaminondas, who came out and related proudly the things done by him and reproached the people with them in a haughty and arrogant manner, they did not have the heart even to take the ballots into their hands, and the assembly broke up, greatly praising the loftiness of this man's courage. 7

Dionysius the Elder, having taken the city of Rhegium after extreme delays and difficulties, and in it the captain Phyto, a first-rate man, who had defended it most obstinately, decided to make him a tragic example of vengeance. First he told him how the day before he had had his son and all his relatives drowned. To which Phyto replied only that they were thereby happier than he by one day. After that he had him stripped and seized by executioners, who dragged him through the town, whipping him very ignominiously and cruelly and, in addition, heaping on him slanderous and insulting words. But Phyto kept his courage steadfast, not letting himself go, and with a firm countenance persisted in recalling loudly the honorable and glorious cause of his death (that he had refused to surrender his country into the 8 hands of a tyrant) and in threatening that tyrant with prompt punishment by the gods. Instead of growing angry at this defiance of a conquered enemy, the rank and file of Dionysius' army showed in their countenance that, disregarding their leader and his triumph, they were softened by astonishment at such rare valor; so that, seeing them on the point of mutiny and about to snatch Phyto from the hands of his sergeants, Dionysius had his martyrdom stopped and secretly, sent him to be drowned in the sea.

Truly man is a marvelously vain, diverse, and undulating object. It is hard to   9
found any constant and uniform judgment on him. Here is Pompeius pardoning the whole city of the Mamertines, against which he was greatly incensed, in consideration of the valor and magnanimity of the citizen Stheno, who took the fault of the people upon himself alone and asked no other favor but to bear the punishment alone. Yet Sulla's host, who displayed similar valor in the city of Praeneste, got nothing out of it, either for himself or for the others.

And directly contrary to my first examples, the bravest of men and one very   10
gracious to the vanquished, Alexander, forcing the city of Gaza after many great difficulties, came upon Betis (who was in command there and of whose valor he had experienced marvelous proofs during this siege), now alone, abandoned by his men, his armor cut to pieces, all covered with blood and wounds, still fighting on in the midst of many Macedonians who were attacking him from all sides. Stung by such a dearly won victory (for among other damage Alexander had received two fresh wounds on his person), he said to him: "You shall not die as you wanted, Betis; prepare yourself to suffer every kind of torment that can be invented against a captive." The other, with a look not only confident but insolent and haughty stood without saying a word to these threats. Then Alexander, seeing his proud and obstinate silence: "Has he bent a knee? Has any suppliant cry escaped him? I'll conquer your muteness yet; and if I cannot wring a word from it, at least I'll wring a groan." And turning his anger into rage, be ordered Betis' heels to be pierced through and had him thus dragged alive, torn, and dismembered, behind a cart.

Could it be that hardihood was so common to Alexander that, not marveling at   11
it, he respected it the less? Or did he consider it so peculiarly his own that he could not bear to see it at this height in another without passionately envious spite? Or was the natural impetuosity of his anger incapable of brooking opposition? In truth, if it could have been bridled, it is probable that it would have been in the capture and desolation of the city of Thebes, at the sight of so many valiant men, lost and without any further means of common defense, cruelly put to the sword. For fully six thousand of them were killed, of whom not one was seen fleeing or asking for mercy, but who were on the contrary seeking, some here, some there, through the streets, to confront the victorious enemy and to provoke an honorable death at his hands. Not one was seen so beaten down with wounds as not to try even in his last gasp to avenge himself, and with the weapons of despair to assuage his death in the death of some enemy. Yet the distress of their valor found no pity, and the length of a day was not enough to satiate Alexander's revenge. This slaughter went on to the

last drop of blood that could be shed, and stopped only at the unarmed people, old men, women, and children, so that thirty thousand of them might be taken as slaves.

The So-What Factor.   The so-what factor is whatever is novel or interesting or surprising about the writer's thesis—whether it is stated explicitly or implied between the lines. In this case, the surprise is that sometimes we can win mercy by demonstrating bravery, even defiance, instead of humility or contrition. But by the end of the essay, Montaigne offers the examples of Pompey and Alexander to show that this technique may backfire. And so he arrives at yet another observation worth thinking about: that people are fundamentally unpredictable—which is what Montaigne means when he says, "It is difficult to found a judgment on him which is steady and uniform."

THE SEVEN COMMON MOVES

*1. **Beginning.*** The traditional thesis sentence can be a good move for capturing a reader's attention, particularly if the thesis is contrary to common opinion. Montaigne opens with a generalization that is not particularly surprising: that the most common way to get mercy is to be submissive. But he immediately switches to a contrary thesis—that people can win mercy by refusing to be submissive. This is a surprising statement, one that should make readers curious to know if Montaigne has any evidence to prove his point.

*2. **Ending.*** Montaigne's ending does not wrap things up with a neat moral. In fact, the latter part of his essay provides examples that seem to work against his thesis—examples in which showing bravery and defiance resulted in even worse punishment. The last example is more horrendous than all the rest. And the last paragraph, by providing a commentary on this climactic example, creates the sense of an ending. There is a compelling honesty about this conclusion, as if Montaigne were not so wedded to his original thesis that he would ignore evidence against it. In fact, Montaigne seemed in general to believe that the behavior of human beings is rarely predictable—which makes it a particularly apt subject for a tentative, exploratory form of writing like the essay.

*3. **Detail.*** The detail in this essay consists of a long series of instances and likely stories, the sort of stories that are discussed in chapter 9. In the Middle Ages and the Renaissance, stories of this sort were called *exempla* (i.e., "examples," or "likely stories," or "paradigms," or "representative anecdotes" as discussed in chapters 9 and 10). A typical education for upper-class boys during the Renaissance, like the one Montaigne received, would have included exercises in using historical and mythological stories from classical sources to prove a point in just this way.

4. Organization/Plot. Montaigne announces his thesis in the first paragraph and then provides a series of examples to prove his point, each example in some way more remarkable than the one before it. An outline of his essay might look like this:

Introduction and thesis (paragraph 1)

Three examples in which mercy was shown by people who were not particularly inclined to vengeance—the Prince of Wales (paragraph 2), the Prince of Epirus (paragraph 3), and the Emperor Conrad III (paragraph 4)

Two brief paragraphs of commentary (5 and 6).

One example in which mercy was shown by people who had, until that point, shown no mercy at all—the citizens of Thebes (paragraph 7).

An example in which the victim's bravery did not win mercy, but did win sympathy from everyone who witnessed his behavior (paragraph 8).

At this point, Montaigne switches to examples that run counter to his thesis, in effect proving a larger point: that we just cannot predict what human beings are likely to do.

In paragraph 9 Montaigne tells the stories about how demonstrating bravery won mercy on one occasion but had no effect on another.

In paragraph 10 he tells how the Greek general Alexander, who was known for his generosity, refused to show mercy to one of his bravest opponents.

In the final paragraph, Montaigne reflects on the meaning of his last and most compelling example.

There is an overall plot in this outline: Montaigne begins with a surprising thesis; proves it with examples; and then deals with the surprising exceptions to the thesis, leading to an insight about the unpredictability of human behavior. He maintains the interest of his readers by replacing one surprising observation with another.

5. Style. It may be impossible to sense Montaigne's style accurately since we are reading it in translation, and since what seems a bit old fashioned to modern readers would have seemed quite normal to Montaigne's contemporaries. In other essays, Montaigne tells us he writes just as he speaks: "I speak to the paper just as I speak to the first person I happen to run into" (III, 1). He also admires people who can speak ordinary language with ordinary people: "I envy those who can come down to the level of the meanest on their staff and make conversation with their own servants" (III, 3). And since Montaigne dictated his essays (III, 3, 806B), and thought of his readers as family and friends ("*parens & amis,*" preface to the first edition), we would hardly expect him to write in the style of formal oratory or serious scholarship.

But like all good writers, Montaigne constructs sentences that are not likely to occur in ordinary conversation. Not even Montaigne is likely to have said, spontaneously,

Edward, prince of Wales, the one who governed our Guienne so long (a person whose traits and fortunes have in them many notable elements of greatness), having suffered much harm from the Limousins, and taking their city by force, could not be halted by the cries of the people and of the women and children abandoned to the butchery, who implored his mercy and threw themselves at his feet until, going farther and farther into the city, he saw three French gentlemen who with incredible boldness were holding out alone against the assault of his victorious army.

We can, however, imagine Montaigne *dictating* such a sentence—pacing about, thinking aloud, having his scribe read back what he had written so Montaigne could add or delete or move a phrase, change a few words here and there, until he produced the sentence you have just read. The result is a style that is not quite the same as speech written down; it would not be credible as dialogue. But it is friendly and intimate, like a personal letter, free of the sort of artificial ornament and learned diction that were common in oratory and scholarship in Montaigne's day. Although Montaigne seems to have intended from the outset to publish his essays, he wrote them *as if* his readers were friends and family. He invented a new kind of audience, an audience of "intimate strangers." And he invented a style appropriate for that audience. It is a style we take for granted today because we see so much of it in newspapers and magazines. It is as different from the anonymous style of legal and technical writing today as it was when Montaigne invented it.

6. Voice/Attitude. "I am myself the subject of my book," Montaigne tells his readers in a note at the beginning of the first edition. He knew that his essays would reveal himself, even when they seemed to be about some other subject. And then he adds, "there is no reason for you to use your free time on such a frivolous and vain subject." Obviously Montaigne did not consider his work unworthy of the attention of strangers, or else he would not have gone to the trouble of having them printed. And so his pose of humility is just that—a pose, a necessary gesture that helps construct the person he wants us to imagine, someone who takes his thoughts seriously, but not too seriously.

The fact that Montaigne wrote in French is also revealing. Latin was the language used by writers who hoped to be taken seriously by educated readers throughout Europe. To write in French was a daring move—a risk, perhaps a presumption, that his essays would not be read outside of France. This choice of ordinary language instead of the learned language reveals something about the person. Montaigne wanted to be understood by those who were less well educated than himself.

The *Essais* as a whole provide us with the self-portrait of Montaigne as he reflects on great matters and small—on life, and death, and social customs, and human behavior—the same sort of topics that essayists still find interesting to write about. In this particular essay, we meet a person who enjoys studying human motivation, who values mercy over harshness, and who respects classical authorities and knows them well.

7. Economy. One of the more obvious differences between Montaigne's style and the style of modern essayists is in the length of his sentences. Long sentences are not necessarily uneconomical; in fact, they can be every bit as economical as short sentences, as long as every word serves a purpose. But does every word, in fact, serve a purpose in Montaigne's writing? For example, his first sentence could be reduced from this:

> The commonest way of softening the hearts of those we have offended, when, vengeance in hand, they hold us at their mercy, is by submission to move them to commiseration and pity.

to this:

> Usually we try to get mercy from people we've offended by acting submissively.

The second version is obviously shorter than the first, but is it really any better? Does the second version lose any essential details? Does it lose a bit of the original tone and flavor? Is it, in fact, more economical, or simply shorter? After discussing these questions with your classmates, try your hand at shortening some of Montaigne's sentences to see if it can be done without any significant losses.

Moves within Moves. As a whole, the essay is an exercise in exemplification, which would have been among the techniques for writing that Montaigne had learned in school. He establishes a thesis, and then supports it with lots of stories from classical sources. But the essay includes other moves: it starts out with a contrast (the most common means of getting mercy, followed by its opposite); and the examples themselves are miniature narratives, each with moments of description within it. The modes and methods of development that were identified centuries later by rhetoricians have existed in essays right from the beginning.

Words, Phrases, and Allusions. The following words, phrases, and allusions, which were taken from "By Diverse Means We Arrive at the Same End" in the order of appearance. With the help of your classmates (and if necessary, a dictionary, encyclopedia, or other reference work), determine what each item means. Often you can figure out what an unusual word means from its context. Pay particular attention to words and phrases that might be worth adding to your vocabulary. Notice, however, that some of these words are old fashioned, chosen by the translator to give an antique flavor to the style.

> commiseration, Edward, Prince of Wales, Guienne, Limousins, valor, supplication, extremity, prodigious, besieged, Stoics, succor, obstinate, Thebes, countenance, martyrdom, diverse, Pompeius, Alexander, impetuosity, valiant, avenge

Suggestion for Writing

Using "By Diverse Means We Arrive at the Same End " as a model, write an essay in which you explain how we sometimes have to choose between opposite tactics to get other people to do things we would like them to do. The journal entry suggested at the beginning of this chapter might provide you with a good topic. Another possibility would be to stick closely to the topic Montaigne wrote about—how to get mercy when we need it—substituting examples from ordinary, modern life at home, at school, or on the job. A third possibility would be to write an essay of your own on what becomes Montaigne's secondary thesis—that human beings are fundamentally unpredictable.

A Modest Proposal

Jonathan Swift

For Preventing the Children of Poor People in Ireland
from Being a Burden to Their Parents or Country,
and for Making Them Beneficial to the Public

It is a melancholy object to those who walk through this great town or travel in the country, when they see the streets, the roads, and cabin doors, crowded with beggars of the female sex, followed by three, four, or six children, all in rags and importuning every passenger for an alms. These mothers, instead of being able to work for their honest livelihood, are forced to employ all their time in strolling to beg sustenance for their helpless infants, who, as they grow up, either turn thieves for want of work, or leave their dear native country to fight for the Pretender in Spain, or sell themselves to the Barbadoes. 1

I think it is agreed by all parties that this prodigious number of children in the arms, or on the backs, or at the heels of their mothers, and frequently of their fathers, is in the present deplorable state of the kingdom a very great additional grievance; and, therefore, whoever could find out a fair, cheap, and easy method of making these children sound, useful members of the commonwealth would deserve so well of the public as to have his statue set up for a preserver of the nation. 2

But my intention is very far from being confined to provide only for the children of professed beggars; it is of a much greater extent, and shall take in the whole number of infants at a certain age who are born of parents in effect as little able to support them as those who demand our charity in the streets. 3

259

As to my own part, having turned my thoughts for many years upon this impor- 4 tant subject, and maturely weighed the several schemes of other projectors, I have always found them grossly mistaken in their computation. It is true, a child just dropped from its dam may be supported by her milk for a solar year, with little other nourishment; at most not above the value of two shillings, which the mother may certainly get, or the value in scraps, by her lawful occupation of begging; and it is exactly at one year that I propose to provide for them in such a manner as instead of being a charge upon their parents or the parish, or wanting food and raiment for the rest of their lives, they shall on the contrary contribute to the feeding, and partly to the clothing, of many thousands.

There is likewise another great advantage in my scheme, that it will prevent 5 those voluntary abortions, and that horrid practice of women murdering their bastard children, alas! too frequent among us! sacrificing the poor innocent babes, I doubt, more to avoid the expense than the shame, which would move tears and pity in the most savage and inhuman breast.

The number of souls in this kingdom being usually reckoned one million and a 6 half, of these I calculate there may be about two hundred thousand couples whose wives are breeders; from which number I subtract thirty thousand couples who are able to maintain their own children (although I apprehend there cannot be so many under the present distress of the kingdom); but this being granted, there will remain an hundred and seventy thousand breeders. I again subtract fifty thousand for those women who miscarry, or whose children die by accident or disease within the year. There only remain an hundred and twenty thousand children of poor parents annually born. The question therefore is, how this number shall be reared and provided for, which, as I have already said, under the present situation of affairs, is utterly impossible by all the methods hitherto proposed. For we can neither employ them in handicraft or agriculture; we neither build houses (I mean in the country) nor cultivate land; they can very seldom pick up a livelihood stealing till they arrive at six years old, except where they are of towardly parts; although I confess they learn the rudiments much earlier, during which time they can, however, be looked upon only as probationers, as I have been informed by a principal gentleman in the country of Cavan, who protested to me that he never knew above one or two instances under the age of six, even in a part of the kingdom so renowned for the quickest proficiency in that art.

I am assured by our merchants that a boy or a girl before twelve years old is no 7 saleable commodity; and even when they come to this age they will not yield above three pounds, or three pounds and half a crown at most on the Exchange; which cannot turn to account either to the parents or the kingdom, the charge of nutriment and rags having been at least four times that value.

I shall now therefore humbly propose my own thoughts, which I hope will not 8 be liable to the least objection.

I have been assured by a very knowing American of my acquaintance in Lon- 9 don, that a young healthy child well nursed is at a year old a most delicious, nourishing, and wholesome food, whether stewed, roasted, baked, or boiled; and I make no doubt that it will equally serve in a fricassee or a ragout.

I do therefore humbly offer it to public consideration that of hundred and   10
twenty thousand children, already computed, twenty thousand may be reserved for
breed, whereof only one-fourth part to be males, which is more than we allow to
sheep, black cattle, or swine; and my reason is that these children are seldom the
fruits of marriage, a circumstance not much regarded by our savages; therefore one
male will be sufficient to serve four females. That the remaining hundred thousand
may, at a year old, be offered in sale to the persons of quality and fortune through
the kingdom, always advising the mother to let them suck plentifully in the last
month, so as to render them plump and fat for a good table. A child will make two
dishes at an entertainment for friends; and when the family dines alone, the fore or
hindquarter will make a reasonable dish, and seasoned with a little pepper or salt
will be very good boiled on the fourth day, especially in winter.

I have reckoned upon a medium that a child just born will weigh twelve   11
pounds, and in a solar year, if tolerably nursed, increaseth to twenty-eight pounds.

I grant this food will be somewhat dear, and therefore very proper for land-   12
lords, who, as they have already devoured most of the parents, seem to have the best
title to the children.

Infant's flesh will be in season throughout the year, but more plentiful in   13
March, and a little before and after: for we are told by a grave author, an eminent
French physician, that fish being a prolific diet, there are more children born in
Roman Catholic countries about nine months after Lent than at any other season;
therefore, reckoning a year after Lent, the markets will be more glutted than usual,
because the number of popish infants is at least three to one in this kingdom; and
therefore it will have one other collateral advantage, by lessening the number of Papists among us.

I have already computed the charge of nursing a beggar's child (in which list I   14
reckon all cottagers, laborers, and four-fifths of the farmers) to be about two
shillings per annum, rags included; and I believe no Gentleman would repine to
give ten shillings for the carcass of a good fat child, which, as I have said, will make
four dishes of excellent nutritive meat, when he hath only some particular friend or
his own family to dine with him. Thus the squire will learn to be a good landlord,
and grow people among the tenants; the mother will have eight shillings net profit,
and be fit for work till she produces another child.

Those who are more thrifty (as I must confess the times require) may flay the   15
carcass; the skin of which artificially dressed will make admirable gloves for ladies,
and summer boots for fine gentlemen.

As to our city of Dublin, shambles may be appointed for this purpose in the   16
most convenient parts of it, and butchers we may be assured will not be wanting; although I rather recommend buying the children alive, and dressing them hot from
the knife as we do roasting pigs.

A very worthy person, a true lover of his country, and whose virtues I highly   17
esteem, was lately pleased in discoursing on this matter to offer a refinement upon
my scheme. He said that many gentlemen of his kingdom, having of late destroyed
their deer, he conceived that the want of venison might be well supplied by the bod-

ies of young lads and maidens, not exceeding fourteen years of age nor under twelve, so great a number of both sexes in every county being now ready to starve for want of work and service; and these to be disposed of by their parents, if alive, or otherwise by their nearest relations. But with due deference to so excellent a friend and so deserving a patriot I cannot be altogether in his sentiments; for as to the males, my American acquaintance assured me from frequent experience that their flesh was generally tough and lean, like that of our schoolboys, by continual exercise, and their taste disagreeable; and to fatten them would not answer the charge. Then as to the females, it would, I think with humble submission, be a loss to the public, because they soon would become breeders themselves; and besides, it is not improbable that some scrupulous people might be apt to censure such a practice (although in deed very unjustly) as a little bordering upon cruelty; which, I confess, hath always been with me the strongest objection against any project, how well soever intended.

But in order to justify my friend, he confessed that this expedient was put into 18 his head by the famous Psalmanazar, a native of the island Formosa, who came from thence to London above twenty years ago, and in conversation told my friend that in his country when any young person happened to be put to death, the executioner sold the carcass to persons of quality as a prime dainty; and that in his time the body of a plump girl of fifteen, who was crucified for an attempt to poison the emperor, was sold to his Imperial Majesty's prime minister of state, and other great mandarins of the court, in joints from the gibbet, at four hundred crowns. Neither indeed can I deny that if the same use were made of several plump young girls in this town, who without one single groat to their fortunes cannot stir abroad without a chair, and appear at the playhouse and assemblies in foreign fineries which they never will pay for, the kingdom would not be the worse.

Some persons of a desponding spirit are in great concern about that vast num- 19 ber of poor people who are aged, diseased, or maimed, and I have been desired to employ my thoughts what course may be taken to ease the nation of so grievous an encumbrance. But I am not in the least pain upon that matter, because it is very well known that they are every day dying and rotting by cold and famine, and filth and vermin as fast as can be reasonably expected. And as to the younger laborers, they are now in almost as hopeful a condition. They cannot get work and consequently pine away for want of nourishment to a degree that at any time they are accidentally hired to common labor, they have not strength to perform it; and thus the country and themselves are happily delivered from the evils to come.

I have too long digressed, and therefore shall return to my subject. I think the 20 advantages by the proposal which I have made are obvious and many, as well as of the highest importance.

For first, as I have already observed, it would greatly lessen the number of 21 Papists, with whom we are yearly overrun, being the principal breeders of the nation as well as our most dangerous enemies; and who stay at home on purpose to deliver the kingdom to the Pretender, hoping to take their advantage by the absence of so many good Protestants, who have chosen rather to leave their country than to stay at home and pay tithes against their conscience to an Episcopal curate.

Secondly, the poorer tenants will have something valuable of their own, which by law may be made liable to distress, and help to pay their landlord's rent, their corn and cattle being already seized, and money a thing unknown.

Thirdly, whereas the maintenance of an hundred thousand children, from two years old and upwards, cannot be computed at less than ten shillings apiece per annum, the nation's stock will be thereby increased fifty thousand pounds per annum, besides the profit of a new dish introduced to the tables of all gentlemen of fortune in the kingdom who have any refinement in taste. And the money will circulate among ourselves, the goods being entirely of our own growth and manufacture.

Fourthly, the constant breeders, besides the gain of eight shillings sterling per annum by the sale of their children, will be rid of the charge of maintaining them after the first year.

Fifthly, this food would likewise bring great custom to taverns, where the vintners will certainly be so prudent as to procure the best receipts for dressing it to perfection, and consequently have their houses frequented by all the fine gentlemen, who justly value themselves upon their knowledge in good eating; and a skillful cook, who understands how to oblige his guests, will contrive to make it as expensive as they please.

Sixthly, this would be a great inducement to marriage, which all wise nations have either encouraged by rewards or enforced by laws and penalties. It would increase the care and tenderness of mothers toward their children, when they were sure of a settlement for life to the poor babes, provided in some sort by the public, to their annual profit instead of expense. We should see an honest emulation among the married women, which of them could bring the fattest child to the market. Men would become as fond of their wives during the time of their pregnancy as they are now of their mares in foal, their cows in calf, or sows when they are ready to farrow; nor offer to beat or kick them (as is too frequent a practice) for fear of a miscarriage.

Many other advantages might be enumerated. For instance, the addition of some thousand carcasses in our exportation of barreled beef, the propagation of swine's flesh, and improvements in the art of making good bacon, so much wanted among us by the great destruction of pigs, too frequent at our tables, which are no way comparable in taste or magnificence to a well-grown, fat, yearling child, which roasted whole will make a considerable figure at a lord mayor's feast or any other public entertainment. But this and many others I omit, being studious of brevity.

Supposing that one thousand families in this city would be constant customers for infants' flesh, besides others who might have it at merry meetings, particularly weddings and christenings, I compute that Dublin would take off annually about twenty thousand carcasses, and the rest of the kingdom (where probably they will be sold somewhat cheaper) the remaining eighty thousand.

I can think of no one objection that will possibly be raised against this proposal, unless it should be urged that the number of people will be thereby much lessened in the kingdom. This I freely own, and it was indeed one principal design in offering it to the world. I desire the reader will observe, that I calculate my remedy for this one individual kingdom of Ireland and for no other that ever was, is, or I think ever can be upon earth. Therefore let no man talk to me of other expedients: of taxing our absentees at five shillings a pound: of using neither clothes nor household furniture except what is of our own growth and manufacture: of utterly rejecting the materials and instruments that promote foreign luxury: of curing the expensiveness of pride, vanity idleness, and gaming in our women: of introducing a vein of parsimony, prudence, and temperance: of learning to love our country, in the want of which we differ even from Laplanders and the inhabitants of Topinamboo: of quitting our animosities and factions, nor acting any longer like the Jews, who were murdering one another at the very moment their city was taken: of being a little cautious not to sell our country and conscience for nothing: of teaching landlords to have at least one degree of mercy toward their tenants: lastly, of putting a spirit of honesty, industry, and skill into our shopkeepers; who, if a resolution could now be taken to buy only our native goods, would immediately unite to cheat and exact upon us in the price, the measure, and the goodness, nor could ever yet be brought to make one fair proposal of just dealing, though often and earnestly invited to it.

Therefore, I repeat, let no man talk to me of these and the like expedients, till 30 he hath at least some glimpse of hope that there will ever be some hearty and sincere attempt to put them in practice.

But as to myself, having been wearied out for many years with offering vain, 31 idle, visionary thoughts, and at length utterly despairing of success, I fortunately fell upon this proposal; which, as it is wholly new, so it hath something solid and real, of no expense and little trouble, full in our own power, and whereby we can incur no danger in disobliging England. For this kind of commodity will not bear exportation, the flesh being of too tender a consistence to admit a long continuance in salt, although perhaps I could name a country which would be glad to eat up our whole nation without it.

After all, I am not so violently bent upon my own opinion as to reject any offer 32 proposed by wise men, which shall be found equally innocent, cheap, easy, and effectual. But before something of that kind shall be advanced in contradiction to my scheme, and offering a better, I desire the author or authors will be pleased maturely to consider two points. First, as things now stand, how they will be able to find food and raiment for an hundred thousand useless mouths and backs. And secondly, there being a round million of creatures in human figure throughout this kingdom, whose sole subsistence put into a common stock would leave them in debt two millions of pounds sterling, adding those who are beggars by profession to the bulk of farmers, cottagers, and laborers with their wives and children who are beggars in effect; I desire those politicians who dislike my overture, and may perhaps be so bold to attempt an answer, that they will first ask the parents of these mortals whether they would not at this day think it a great happiness to have been sold for food at a year old in this manner I prescribe, and thereby have avoided such a perpetual scene of misfortunes as they have since gone through by the oppression of landlords, the

impossibility of paying rent without money or trade, the want of common sustenance with neither house nor clothes to cover them from the inclemencies of the
weather, and the most inevitable prospect of entailing the like or greater miseries
upon their breed forever.

I profess, in the sincerity of my heart, that I have not the least personal interest in   33
endeavoring to promote this necessary work, having no other motive than the public
good of my country, by advancing our trade, providing for infants, relieving the poor,
and giving some pleasure to the rich. I have no children by which I can propose to get
a single penny; the youngest being nine years old, and my wife past childbearing.

UNDERSTANDING THE ESSAY

1. Who is the speaker in this essay? Is it Jonathan Swift, speaking in his own
   voice and expressing his own values, or is it someone else, expressing a set
   of values that Swift would not approve? What evidence can you give to support your answer?
2. If the speaker is someone Swift disagrees with, how does the essay manage
   to be an argument in favor of values that Swift approves? How does Swift
   make it possible for us to hear *his* voice, even when he seems to be speaking
   in the voice of an invented character?
3. What is the main issue in this essay? Is this an issue that can be settled by logic
   or science, or is it properly a rhetorical issue (an issue of values or belief)?
4. What does the title have to do with the subject matter? Is the proposal really
   modest?
5. Whom does the speaker cite as an authority on the use of children as food
   (paragraph 9), and what British bias would this citation have appealed to
   when the essay was written (1729)?
6. What religious biases does the speaker presume his readers will share (paragraphs 13 and 21)?
7. What is the double meaning of "devoured" in paragraph 12?
8. The speaker rejects a series of alternate proposals in paragraph 29. What are
   they? Do you think Swift intends for his readers to reject them as well, or do
   you think he intends them as responsible solutions to the problem of poverty
   in Ireland?
9. What clue does paragraph 30 give you about Swift's attitude?
10. The key to this essay is the way in which the speaker lures the reader in by
    expressing assumptions and value judgments they probably share, and then
    switching to other assumptions, generally unstated, that they do not share.
    You probably agree, for example, that it is "melancholy" (sad) to see "roads,
    and cabin doors, crowded with beggars" (paragraph 1). But do you agree

with the assumptions implicit in a statement like "A child will make two dishes at an entertainment for friends" (paragraph 10)?

11. Can you find passages in which human beings are described in terms ordinarily used for farm animals? How do descriptions of this sort affect your attitude toward the speaker?

12. Choose any passage in this essay and examine its assumptions, implicit or expressed. Which assumptions do you think Jonathan Swift personally approves, and which do you think he wants his readers to recognize as grotesque?

13. Notice the assumptions that are presumed to be shared, dividing people into an "us" (English Protestants) against a "them" (Irish Catholics). Can you find evidence in the text to show that Swift approved or disapproved this sort of divisiveness?

(See Additional Questions for Persuasive Essays, p. 242)

So What and the Seven Common Moves   Analyze this essay with the help of the questions about "So What and the Seven Common Moves" found on the back cover of this book.

Words, Phrases, and Allusions.   The following items were taken from "A Modest Proposal" in the order of appearance. With the help of your classmates, locate these words in the essay and see if their context provides a clue to their meaning. If necessary, consult a dictionary, an encyclopedia, or other reference work to determine what each item means in its context. Which of these words are no longer part of ordinary English? Which are still part of the English language but with slightly different meanings?

importuning, sustenance, the Pretender in Spain, Barbadoes, prodigious, deplorable, grievance, dropped from its dam, raiment, the Exchange, nutriment, fricassee, ragout, reserved for breed, prolific, popish, collateral advantage, per annum, repine, carcass, nutritive, squire, flay the carcass, censure, mandarins, gibbet, desponding, vermin, vintners, receipts, emulation, disobliging, consistence

Suggestion for Writing

Using "A Modest Proposal" as a model, write an essay from the point of view of someone you disagree with. Take the assumptions implicit in that point of view to their logical—and presumably unacceptable—conclusions. An essay of this sort can be grim, like Swift's, or it can be lighthearted, poking fun at a position that is insensitive or politically pious. The journal entry suggested at the beginning of this selection may have given you an idea for a topic, or you may have thought of other topics as you read Swift's essay.

Journal Entry. Walt Whitman once said that the entire universe is contained in a blade of grass. Essayists often discover important philosophical meaning in seemingly tiny places and trivial events—like a battle between ants or the death of a bug. Choose an event that may seem unimportant in itself, but can in fact be seen as an emblem of something much larger. After you have worked on this project for a while, read the following essay and look for moves you might use in your own.

The Death of the Moth

Virginia Woolf

Moths that fly by day are not properly to be called moths; they do not excite that 1
pleasant sense of dark autumn nights and ivy-blossom which the commonest yellow
underwing asleep in the shadow of the curtain never fails to rouse in us. They are
hybrid creatures, neither gay like butterflies nor sombre like their own species. Nevertheless the present specimen, with his narrow hay-coloured wings, fringed with a
tassel of the same colour, seemed to be content with life. It was a pleasant morning,
mid-September, mild, benignant, yet with a keener breath than that of the summer
months. The plough was already scoring the field opposite the window, and where
the share had been, the earth was pressed flat and gleamed with moisture. Such
vigour came rolling in from the fields and the down beyond that it was difficult to
keep the eyes strictly turned upon the book. The rooks too were keeping one of their
annual festivities; soaring round the tree-tops until it looked as if a vast net with
thousands of black knots in it has been cast up into the air; which, after a few moments sank slowly down upon the trees until every twig seemed to have a knot at
the end of it. Then, suddenly, the net would be thrown into the air again in a wider
circle this time, with the utmost clamour and vociferation, as though to be thrown
into the air and settle slowly down upon the tree-tops were a tremendously exciting
experience.

The same energy which inspired the rooks, the ploughmen, the horses, and 2
even, it seemed, the lean bare-backed downs, sent the moth fluttering from side to
side of his square of the window-pane. One could not help watching him. One was,
indeed, conscious of a queer feeling of pity for him. The possibilities of pleasure
seemed that morning so enormous and so various that to have only a moth's part in
life, and a day moth's at that, appeared a hard fate, and his zest in enjoying his meagre opportunities to the full, pathetic. He flew vigorously to one corner of his compartment, and, after waiting there a second, flew across to the other. What remained

for him but to fly to a third corner and then to a fourth? That was all he could do, in spite of the size of the downs, the width of the sky, the far-off smoke of houses, and the romantic voice, now and then, of a steamer out at sea. What he could do he did. Watching him, it seemed as if a fibre, very thin but pure, of the enormous energy of the world had been thrust into his frail and diminutive body. As often as he crossed the pane, I could fancy that a thread of vital light became visible. He was little or nothing but life.

Yet because he was so small, and so simple a form of the energy that was 3 rolling in at the open window and driving its way through so many narrow and intricate corridors in my own brain and in those of other human beings, there was something marvelous as well as pathetic about him. It was as if someone had taken a tiny bead of pure life and decking it as lightly as possible with down and feathers, had set it dancing and zig-zagging to show us the true nature of life. Thus displayed one could not get over the strangeness of it. One is apt to forget all about life, seeing it humped and bossed and garnished and cumbered so that it has to move with the greatest circumspection and dignity. Again, the thought of all that life might have been had he been born in any other shape caused one to view his simple activities with a kind of pity.

After a time, tired by his dancing apparently, he settled on the window ledge in 4 the sun, and the queer spectacle being at an end, I forgot about him. Then, looking up, my eye was caught by him. He was trying to resume his dancing, but seemed either so stiff or so awkward that he could only flutter to the bottom of the windowpane; and when he tried to fly across it he failed. Being intent on other matters I watched these futile attempts for a time without thinking, unconsciously waiting for him to resume his flight, as one waits for a machine, that has stopped momentarily, to start again without considering the reason for its failure. After perhaps a seventh attempt he slipped from the wooden ledge and fell, fluttering his wings, on to his back on the window-sill. The helplessness of his attitude roused me. It flashed upon me that he was in difficulties; he could no longer raise himself; his legs struggled vainly. But, as I stretched out a pencil, meaning to help him to right himself, it came over me that the failure and awkwardness were the approach of death. I laid the pencil down again.

The legs agitated themselves once more. I looked as if for the enemy against 5 which he struggled. I looked out of doors. What had happened there? Presumably it was midday, and work in fields had stopped. Stillness and quiet had replaced the previous animation. The birds had taken themselves off to feed in the brooks. The horses stood still. Yet the power was there all the same, massed outside, indifferent, impersonal, not attending to anything in particular. Somehow it was opposed to the little hay-coloured moth. It was useless to try to do anything. One could only watch the extraordinary efforts made by those tiny legs against an oncoming doom which could, had it chosen, have submerged an entire city, not merely a city, but masses of human beings; nothing, I knew, had any chance against death. Nevertheless after a pause of exhaustion the legs fluttered again. It was superb, this last protest, and so frantic that he succeeded at last in righting himself. One's sympathies, of course, were all on the side of life. Also, when there was nobody to care or to know this gigantic effort on the part of an insignificant little moth, against a power of such magnitude, to retain what no one else valued or desired to keep, moved one strangely. Again, somehow, one saw life, a pure bead. I lifted the pencil again, useless though I knew it to be. But even as I did so, the unmistakable tokens of death showed themselves. The body relaxed, and instantly grew stiff. The struggle was over. The insignificant little creature now knew death. As I looked at the dead moth, this minute wayside triumph of so great a force over so mean an antagonist filled me with wonder. Just as life had been strange a few minutes before, so death was now as strange. The moth having righted himself now lay most decently and uncomplainingly composed. O yes, he seemed to say, death is stronger than I am.

UNDERSTANDING THE ESSAY

1. What is novel, interesting, or surprising about Woolf's interpretation of the event she describes?

2. What connection does Woolf find between the moth and the huge forces of nature outside her window? Between the moth and herself? Between the moth and you, her reader? Does this connection seem credible?

3. Why does Woolf describe the activity beyond her window in such great detail? Why does she also describe the absence of activity (paragraph 5) at the moment of the moth's death?

4. What opposing forces are at work in nature as Woolf describes it? In what sense are these opposing forces actually the same force? What is the "power" mentioned in paragraph 5, and in what sense is it "opposed to the little hay-colored moth"? Is it also opposed to the rooks and the horses described elsewhere, or is it a friendly force to them?

5. What is Woolf's attitude toward the events she narrates? Do you think everybody would have the same attitude about these events?

So What and the Seven Common Moves.   Analyze this essay with the help of the questions about "So What and the Seven Common Moves" found on the back cover of this book.

Words, Phrases, and Allusions.   The following items were taken from "The Death of the Moth" in the order of appearance. With the help of your classmates, locate these words in the essay and see if their context provides a clue to their meaning. If necessary, consult a dictionary, an encyclopedia, or other reference work to determine what each item means in its context. Are any of these words no longer part of ordinary English? Do any strike you as British English as opposed to American English?

> hybrid, scoring, share, vigor, rooks, vociferation, lean bare-backed downs, bossed, garnished, circumspection, cumbered

Suggestion for Writing

Using "The Death of the Moth" as a model, write an essay about a small event that has large implications. The journal entry suggested at the beginning of this selection may have given you an idea for a topic, or you may have thought of other topics as you read Woolf's essay.

Journal Entry.   Perhaps the most clichéd essay topic of all is "My Summer Vacation." But any topic—even a summer vacation—can be the basis of an unforgettable essay. It's not just what happened during the vacation that matters; it's what those events mean. Do you remember a sequence of events on a vacation or on a trip that taught you something about life itself? Jot down notes for turning that experience into an essay in which you can surprise your readers with your interpretation of events that might otherwise seem ordinary. Then read E. B. White's classic essay in which he returns with his son to the same lake that he used to with his own father—only to discover something eerie about the way time seems to bend back on itself in a spiral instead of a straight line.

Once More to the Lake

E. B. White

One summer along about 1904, my father rented a camp on a lake in Maine and took us all there for the month of August. We all got ringworm from some kittens and had to rub Pond's Extract on our arms and legs night and morning, and my father rolled over in a canoe with all his clothes on; but outside of that the vacation was a success and from then on none of us ever thought there was any place in the world like that lake in Maine. We returned summer after summer—always on August 1st for one month. I have since become a salt-water man, but sometimes in summer there are days when the restlessness of the tides and the fearful cold of the sea water and the incessant wind that blows across the afternoon and into the evening make me wish for the placidity of a lake in the woods. A few weeks ago this feeling got so strong I bought myself a couple of bass hooks and a spinner and returned to the lake where we used to go, for a week's fishing and to revisit old haunts. 1

I took along my son, who had never had any fresh water up his nose and who had seen lily pads only from train windows. On the journey over to the lake I began to wonder what it would be like. I wondered how time would have marred this unique, this holy spot—the coves and streams, the hills that the sun set behind, the camps, and the paths behind the camps. I was sure that the tarred road would have found it out, and I wondered in what other ways it would be desolated. It is strange how much you can remember about places like that once you allow your mind to return into the grooves that lead back. You remember one thing, and that suddenly reminds you of another thing. I guess I remembered clearest of all the early mornings, when the lake was cool and motionless, remembered how the bedroom smelled of 2 the lumber it was made of and of the wet woods whose scent entered through the screen. The partitions in the camp were thin and did not extend clear to the top of the rooms, and as I was always the first up I would dress softly so as not to wake the others, and sneak out into the sweet outdoors and start out in the canoe, keeping close along the shore in the long shadows of the pines. I remembered being very careful never to rub my paddle against the gunwale for fear of disturbing the stillness of the cathedral.

The lake had never been what you would call a wild lake. There were cottages   3 sprinkled around the shores, and it was in farming country, although the shores of the lake were heavily wooded. Some of the cottages were owned by nearby farmers, and you would live at the shore and eat your meals at the farmhouse. That's what our family did. But although it wasn't wild, it was a fairly large and undisturbed lake and there were places in it which, to a child at least, seemed infinitely remote and primeval.

I was right about the tar: it led to within half a mile of the shore. But when I got   4 back there, with my boy, and we settled into a camp near a farmhouse and into the kind of summertime I had known, I could tell that it was going to be pretty much the same as it had been before—I knew it, lying in bed the first morning, smelling the bedroom, and hearing the boy sneak quietly out and go off along the shore in a boat. I began to sustain the illusion that he was I, and therefore, by simple transposition, that I was my father. This sensation persisted, kept cropping up all the time we were there. It was not an entirely new feeling, but in this setting it grew much stronger. I seemed to be living a dual existence. I would be in the middle of some simple act, I would be picking up a bait box or laying down a table fork, or I would be saying something, and suddenly it would be not I but my father who was saying the words or making the gesture. It gave me a creepy sensation.

We went fishing the first morning. I felt the same damp moss covering the   5 worms in the bait can, and saw the dragonfly alight on the tip of my rod as it hovered a few inches from the surface of the water. It was the arrival of this fly that convinced me beyond any doubt that everything was as it always had been, that the years were a mirage and there had been no years. The small waves were the same, chucking the rowboat under the chin as we fished at anchor, and the boat was the same boat, the same color green and the ribs broken in the same places, and under the floor-boards the same fresh-water leavings and debris—the dead helgramite, the wisps of moss, the rusty discarded fishhook, the dried blood from yesterday's catch. We stared silently at the tips of our rods, at the dragonflies that came and went. I lowered the tip of mine into the water, tentatively, pensively dislodging the fly, which darted two feet away, poised, darted two feet back, and came to rest again little farther up the rod. There had been no years between the ducking of this dragonfly and the other one—the one that was a part of memory. I looked at the boy, who was silently watching his fly, and it was my hands that held his rod, my eyes watching. I felt dizzy and didn't know which rod I was at the end of.

We caught two bass, hauling them in briskly as though they were mackerel,   6 pulling them over the side of the boat in a businesslike manner without any landing net, and stunning them with a blow on the back of the head. When we got back for a swim before lunch, the lake was exactly where we had left it, the same number of inches from the dock, and there was only the merest suggestion of a breeze. This seemed an utterly enchanted sea, this lake you could leave to its own devices for few hours and come back to, and find that it had not stirred, this constant and trustworthy body of water. In the shallows the dark, water-soaked sticks and twigs, smooth and old, were undulating in clusters on the bottom against the clean ribbed sand, and the track of the mussel was plain. A school of minnows swam by, each minnow with its small individual shadow, doubling the attendance, so clear and sharp in the sunlight. Some of the other campers were in swimming, along the shore, one of them with a cake of soap, and the water felt thin and clear and unsubstantial. Over the years there had been this person with the cake of soap, this cultist, and here he was. There had been no years.

Up to the farmhouse to dinner through the teeming, dusty field, the road under our sneakers was only a two-track road. The middle track was missing, the one with the marks of the hooves and splotches of dried, flaky manure. There had always been three tracks to choose from in choosing which track to walk in; now the choice was narrowed down to two. For a moment I missed terribly the middle alternative. But the way led past the tennis court, and something about the way it lay there in the sun reassured me; the tape had loosened along the backline, the alleys were green with plantains and other weeds, and the net (installed in June and removed in September) sagged in the dry noon, and the whole place steamed with midday heat and hunger and emptiness. There was a choice of pie for dessert, and one was blueberry and one was apple, and the waitresses were the same country girls, there having been no passage of time, only the illusion of it as in a dropped curtain—the waitresses were still fifteen; their hair had been washed, that was the only difference—they had been to the movies and seen the pretty girls with the clean hair. 7

Summertime, oh summertime, pattern of life indelible, the fadeproof lake, the woods unshatterable, the pasture with the sweetfern and the juniper forever and ever, summer without end; this was the background, and the life along the shore was the design, the cottages with their innocent and tranquil design, their tiny docks with the flagpole and the American flag floating against the white clouds in the blue sky, the little paths over the roots of the trees leading from camp to camp and the paths leading back to the outhouses and the can of lime for sprinkling, and at the souvenir counters at the store the miniature birch-bark canoes and the post cards that showed things looking a little better than they looked. This was the American family at play, escaping the city heat, wondering whether the newcomers in the camp at the head of the cove were "common" or "nice," wondering whether it was true that the people who drove up for Sunday dinner at the farmhouse were turned away because there wasn't enough chicken. 8

It seemed to me, as I kept remembering all this, that those times and those summers had been infinitely precious and worth saving. There had been jollity and peace and goodness. The arriving (at the beginning of August) had been so big a business in itself, at the railway station the farm wagon drawn up, the first smell of 9 pine-laden air, the first glimpse of the smiling farmer, and the great importance of the trunks and your father's enormous authority in such matters, and the feel of the wagon under you for the long ten-mile haul, and at the top of the last long hill catching the first view of the lake after eleven months of not seeing this cherished body of water. The shouts and cries of the other campers when they saw you, and the trunks to be unpacked, to give up their rich burden. (Arriving was less exciting nowadays, when you sneaked up in your car and parked it under a tree near the camp and took out the bags and in five minutes it was all over, no fuss, no loud wonderful fuss about trunks.)

Peace and goodness and jollity. The only thing that was wrong now, really, was   10
the sound of the place, an unfamiliar nervous sound of the outboard motors. This was the note that jarred, the one thing that would sometimes break the illusion and set the years moving. In those other summertimes all motors were inboard; and when they were at a little distance, the noise they made was a sedative, an ingredient of summer sleep. They were one-cylinder and two-cylinder engines, and some were make-and-break and some were jump-spark, but they made a sleepy sound across the lake. The one-lungers throbbed and fluttered, and the twin-cylinder ones purred and purred and that was a quiet sound too. But now the campers all had outboards. In the daytime, in the hot mornings, these motors made a petulant, irritable sound; at night, in the still evening when the afterglow lit the water, they whined about one's ear like mosquitoes. My boy loved our rented outboard, and his great desire was to achieve singlehanded mastery over it, and authority, and he soon learned the trick of choking it a little (but not too much), and the adjustment of the needle valve. Watching him I would remember the things you could do with the old one-cylinder engine with the heavy flywheel, how you could have it eating out of your hand if you got really close to it spiritually. Motor boats in those days didn't have clutches, and you would make a landing by shutting off the motor at the proper time and coasting in with a dead rudder. But there was a way of reversing them, if you learned the trick, by cutting the switch and putting it on again exactly on the final dying revolution of the flywheel, so that it would kick back against compression and begin reversing. Approaching a dock in a strong following breeze, it was difficult to slow up sufficiently by the ordinary coasting method, and if a boy felt he had complete mastery over his motor, he was tempted to keep it running beyond its time and then reverse it a few feet from the dock. It took a cool nerve, because if you threw the switch a twentieth of a second too soon you would catch the flywheel when it still has speed enough to go up past center, and the boat would leap ahead, charging bull-fashion at the dock.

We had a good week at the camp. The bass were biting well and the sun shone   11
endlessly, day after day. We would be tired at night and lie down in the accumulated heat of the little bedrooms after the long hot day and the breeze would stir almost imperceptibly outside and the smell of the swamp drift in through the rusty screens. Sleep would come easily and in the morning the red squirrel would be on the roof, tapping out his gay routine. I kept remembering everything, lying in bed in

the mornings—the small steamboat that had a long rounded stern like the lip of a Ubangi, and how quietly she ran on the moonlight sails, when the older boys played their mandolins and the girls sang and we ate doughnuts dipped in sugar, and how sweet the music was on the water in the shining night, and what it had felt like to think about girls then. After breakfast we would go up to the store and the things were in the same place—the minnows in a bottle, the plugs and spinners dis-arranged and pawed over by the youngsters from the boys' camp, the fig newtons and the Beeman's gum. Outside, the road was tarred and cars stood in front of the store. Inside, all was just as it had always been, except that there was more Coca Cola and not so much Moxie and root beer and birch beer and sarsaparilla. We would walk out with a bottle of pop apiece and sometimes the pop would backfire up our noses and hurt. We explored the streams, quietly, where the turtles slid off the sunny logs and dug their way into the soft bottom; and we lay on the town wharf and fed worms to the tame bass. Everywhere we went I had trouble making out which was I, the one walking at my side, the one walking in my pants.

One afternoon while we were there at that lake a thunderstorm came up. It was   12 like the revival of an old melodrama that I had seen long ago with childish awe. The second-act climax of the drama of the electrical disturbance over a lake in America had not changed in any important respect. This was the big scene, still the big scene. The whole thing was so familiar: the first feeling of oppression and heat and a gen-eral air around camp of not wanting to go very far away. In midafternoon (it was all the same) a curious darkening of the sky, and a lull in everything that had made life tick; and then the way the boats suddenly swung the other way at their moorings with the coming of a breeze out of the new quarter, and the premonitory rumble. Then the kettle drum, then the snare, then the bass drum and cymbals, then crack-ling light against the dark, and the gods grinning and licking their chops in the hills. Afterward the calm, the rain steadily rustling in the calm lake, the return of light and hope and spirits, and the campers running out in joy and relief to go swimming in the rain, their bright cries perpetuating the deathless joke about how they were getting simply drenched, and the children screaming with delight at the new sensa-tion of bathing in the rain, and the joke about getting drenched linking the genera-tions in a strong indestructible chain. And the comedian who waded in carrying an umbrella.

When the others went swimming my son said he was going in too. He pulled   13 his dripping trunks from the line where they had hung all through the shower, and wrung them out languidly, and with no thought of going in, I watched him—his hard little body, skinny and bare, saw him wince slightly as he pulled up around his vitals the small, soggy, icy garment. As he buckled the swollen belt, suddenly my groin felt the chill of death.

UNDERSTANDING THE ESSAY

1. What meaning does E. B. White find in an event that is, after all, merely a trip to an ordinary lake?
2. What connection does White discover between himself and his son as they visit the lake? Between himself and his father? Why would these connections be of interest to people who are not members of E. B. White's family?
3. Why does White describe the activity on and near the lake in such great detail?
4. What are the opposing forces at work in this essay? In what sense are these opposing forces actually the same force?
5. What does the last line mean, and how is it connected to the rest of the essay?

So What and the Seven Common Moves.   Analyze this essay with the help of the questions about "So What and the Seven Common Moves" found on the back cover of this book.

Words, Phrases, and Allusions.   The following items were taken from "Once More to the Lake" in the order of appearance. With the help of your classmates, locate these words in the essay and see if their context provides a clue to their meaning. If necessary, consult a dictionary, an encyclopedia, or other reference work to determine what each item means in its context.

gunwale, primeval, helgramite, undulating, mussel, cultist, indelible, tranquil, sedative, flywheel, sarsaparilla, premonitory

Suggestion for Writing

Using "Once More to the Lake" as a model, write an essay about an ordinary experience that has large implications. The journal entry suggested at the beginning of this selection may have given you an idea for a topic, or you may have thought of other topics as you read White's essay.

Journal Entry. Various essays throughout this text have dealt with some version of an us-versus-them problem: men versus women, ethnic majorities versus ethnic minorities, humans versus animals, our kind of childhood versus another kind of childhood, even cheerleaders like us versus cheerleaders like them. Society generally makes room for both groups; but every once in a while, the difference leads to conflicts that have to be resolved.

Think of an us-versus-them situation that you have encountered, one in which people are at odds with one another because of different values, different beliefs, different ways of reading the world. Shared ideological differences generally create what we called communions in chapter 10. Can you think of a larger communion to which both groups belong, a communion that may provide the basis for a resolution?

Jot down notes for an essay in which you invoke this larger communion as a way of making peace. Then read the classic speech by Dr. Martin Luther King, Jr., in which he uses numerous patriotic and religious allusions to remind black and white people that they belong to two or three communions larger than the obvious ones that were pitting them against one another at that time.

I Have a Dream

Martin Luther King, Jr.

I am happy to join with you today in what will go down in history as the greatest demonstration for freedom in the history of our nation. 1

Fivescore years ago, a great American, in whose symbolic shadow we stand today, signed the Emancipation Proclamation. This momentous decree came as a great beacon light of hope to millions of Negro slaves who had been seared in the flames of withering injustice. It came as a joyous daybreak to end the long night of their captivity. 2

But one hundred years later, the Negro still is not free; one hundred years later, the life of the Negro is still sadly crippled by the manacles of segregation and the chains of discrimination; one hundred years later, the Negro lives on a lonely island of poverty in the midst of a vast ocean of material prosperity; one hundred years later, the Negro is still languishing in the corners of American society and finds himself in exile in his own land. 3

So we've come here today to dramatize a shameful condition. In a sense we've come to our nation's capital to cash a check. When the architects of our republic wrote the magnificent words of the Constitution and the Declaration of Indepen- 4 dence, they were signing a promissory note to which every American was to fall heir. This note was the promise that all men, yes, black men as well as white men, would be guaranteed the unalienable rights of life, liberty, and the pursuit of happiness.

It is obvious today that America has defaulted on this promissory note in so far as her citizens of color are concerned. Instead of honoring this sacred obligation, America has given the Negro people a bad check; a check which has come back marked "insufficient funds." We refuse to believe that there are insufficient funds in the great vaults of opportunity of this nation. And so we've come to cash this check, a check that will give us upon demand the riches of freedom and the security of justice. 5

We have also come to this hallowed spot to remind America of the fierce urgency of now. This is no time to engage in the luxury of cooling off or to take the tranquilizing drug of gradualism. Now is the time to make real the promises of democracy; now is the time to rise from the dark and desolate valley of segregation to the sunlit path of racial justice; now is the time to lift our nation from the quicksands of racial injustice to the solid rock of brotherhood; now is the time to make justice a reality for all God's children. It would be fatal for the nation to overlook the urgency of the moment. This sweltering summer of the Negro's legitimate discontent will not pass until there is an invigorating autumn of freedom and equality. 6

Nineteen sixty-three is not an end, but a beginning. And those who hope that the Negro needed to blow off steam and will now be content, will have a rude awakening if the nation returns to business as usual. 7

There will be neither rest nor tranquility in America until the Negro is granted his citizenship rights. The whirlwinds of revolt will continue to shake the foundations of our nation until the bright day of justice emerges. 8

But there is something that I must say to my people who stand on the warm threshold which leads into the palace of justice. In the process of gaining our rightful place we must not be guilty of wrongful deeds. 9

Let us not seek to satisfy our thirst for freedom by drinking from the cup of bitterness and hatred. We must forever conduct our struggle on the high plane of dignity and discipline. We must not allow our creative protest to degenerate into physical violence. Again and again we must rise to the majestic heights of meeting physical force with soul force. 10

The marvelous new militancy which has engulfed the Negro community must not lead us to a distrust of all white people, for many of our white brothers, as evidenced by their presence here today, have come to realize that their destiny is tied up with our destiny and they have come to realize that their freedom is inextricably bound to our freedom. This offense we share mounted to storm the battlements of injustice must be carried forth by a biracial army. We cannot walk alone. 11

And as we walk, we must make the pledge that we shall always march ahead. We cannot turn back. There are those who are asking the devotees of civil rights, "When will you be satisfied?" We can never be satisfied as long as the Negro is the victim of the unspeakable horrors of police brutality. 12

Additional Sentences for Analysis and Imitation

Each of the following sentences includes one or more of the moves exemplified in the exercises above. Read them aloud and identify what would make them seem unusual in dialogue, even though they seem perfectly natural in print. These are the moves that generally require a little more time and more than is ordinarily possible in speech. Practice your ability to analyze sentence structure by naming as many moves as you can find in each example. More importantly, write sentences of your own, imitating the moves you like best.

The family is never asked whether they want an open-casket ceremony; in the absence of their instruction to the contrary, this is taken for granted.

—Jessica Mitford

They drank beer, made out with boys in the hallways, and had horrible black hickeys all over their necks.

—Donna Tartt

That kind of self-respect is a discipline, a habit of mind that can never be faked but can be developed, trained, coaxed forth.

—Joan Didion

Ever since we were in fifth grade, every time I borrowed something from Sandye I would lose it or break it or wreck it.

—Marion Winik

The hackers who concoct them proceed from deviltry, an urge to cause havoc, destruction, and grief in artistically ingenious ways.

—Val Schaffner

With that genius for accommodation more often seen in women than in men, Jordan took her own measure, made her own peace, avoided threats to peace. . . .

—Joan Didion

They would appear in the meadow, climb up on his back, ride furiously for ten or fifteen minutes, then get off, slap Blue on the flanks, and not be seen again for a month or more.

—Alice Walker

Greb was infamous for his fouls—low blows, butting, "holding and hitting," rubbing his laces against an opponent's eyes, routine thumbing—as well as for a frenzied boxing style in which blows were thrown from all directions.

—Joyce Carol Oates

What do the three hundred federally recognized tribes—with their various complicated treaties governing land rights and protections, their crippling unemployment, infant mortality, and teenage suicide rates, their often chronic poverty, their manifold health problems—have in common with jolly (or menacing) cartoon caricatures, wistful braves, or raven-tressed Mazola girls?

—Michael Dorris

How surprised he would be to see how his counterpart of today is whisked off to a funeral parlor and is in short order sprayed, sliced, pierced, pickled, trussed, trimmed, creamed, waxed, painted, rouged and neatly dressed—transformed from a common corpse into a Beautiful Memory Picture.

—Jessica Mitford

You went out for a pass, fooling everyone.

—Annie Dillard

We were standing up to our boot tops in snow on a front yard on trafficked Reynolds Street, waiting for cars.

—Annie Dillard

Meeting the word head-on, they proved it had absolutely nothing to do with the way they were determined to live their lives.

—Gloria Naylor

Feeling that they would have had no difficulties in India themselves, the Americans read the book freely.

—E. M. Forster

And it was perhaps the first time she had heard me give a lengthy speech, using the kind of English I have never used with her.

—Amy Tan

Our audience requires us to be sympathetic and patient teachers, ever willing to simplify and clarify—whereas we would rather soar high above the crowd, singing like nightingales.

—Kurt Vonnegut

Untouched by human hand, the coffin and the earth are now united.

—Jessica Mitford

One pair after the next, those glasses flew off my face and out of my life, propelled by some strange centrifugal force.

—Marion Winik

Other ladies, less educated, roll down the bracken in the arms of their gentlemen friends.

—E. M. Forster

He rarely does own his wood, this able chap.

—E. M. Forster

[T]hey were targets all but wrapped in red ribbons, cream puffs.

—Annie Dillard

Some trees bordered the little flat backyard, some messy winter trees.

—Annie Dillard

The older two Fahey boys were there—Mikey and Peter—polite blond boys who lived near me on Lloyd Street. . . .

—Annie Dillard

They have already caused such panic, these cyberspace outlaws whose mischief is innocent of politics. . . .

—Val Schaffner

I came upon her late one evening on a deserted street in Hyde Park, a relatively affluent neighborhood in an otherwise mean, impoverished section of Chicago.

—Brent Staples

It was in the echo of that terrified woman's footfalls that I first began to know the unwieldy inheritance I'd come into—the ability to alter public space in ugly ways.

—Brent Staples

A restlessness comes over him, a vague sense that he has a personality to express— the same sense which, without any vagueness, leads the artist to an act of creation.

—E. M. Forster

Wordless, we split up.

—Annie Dillard

Embalming is indeed a most extraordinary procedure, and one must wonder at the docility of Americans who each year pay hundreds of millions of dollars for its perpetuation, blissfully ignorant of what it is all about, what is done, how it is done.

—Jessica Mitford

It took forever to get out of Chinatown, rush-hour traffic two weeks before Christmas, streets and sidewalks filled with people scurrying home.

—Marion Winik

Then Tony and Sandye burst into my room, all flushed with their little conspiracy, shouting. . . .

—Marion Winik

Men, women, and children were down on their knees, nose to tail like elephants, seeking the tiny transparent circle on the dusty floor.

—Marion Winik

Before me extends a low hill trembling in yellow brome, and behind the hill, filling the sky, rises an enormous mountain ridge, forested, alive and awesome with brilliant blown lights.

—Annie Dillard

I began to wonder what God thought about Westley, who certainly hadn't seen Jesus either, but who was now sitting proudly on the platform, swinging his knickerbockered legs and grinning down at me, surrounded by deacons and old women on their knees praying.

—Langston Hughes

Ignoring the relation between us, it took fright as soon as it saw the shape of my face, and flew straight over the boundary hedge into a field, the property of Mrs. Henessy, where it sat down with a loud squawk.

—E. M. Forster

We were always freezing in our skimpy plaid skirts, our legs all goose pimples as we clapped and stamped on the yellowed wooden floor.

—Donna Tartt

Moodily, they stared out the windows, dreaming of backseats, and letter jackets, and smooching with their repulsive boyfriends.

—Donna Tartt

Buddies, for example, are the workhorses of the friendship world, the people out there on the front lines, defending you from loneliness and boredom.

—Marion Winik

All that returns to me now is the way the breeze blew up there, stirring the leaves, not at all like the breeze on the ground.

—Jaime O'Neill

Basilio was world middle- and welterweight champion 1953–57, stoic, determined, a slugger willing to get hit in order to deal powerful counter-punches of his own.

—Joyce Carol Oates

We kept running, block after block; we kept improvising, backyard after backyard, running a frantic course and choosing it simultaneously, failing always to find small places or hard places to slow him down, and discovering always, exhilarated, dismayed, that only bare speed could save us—for he would never give up, this man—and we were losing speed.

—Annie Dillard

It was a house of many windows, low, wide, nearly floor to ceiling in the living room, which faced the meadow, and it was from one of these that I first saw our closest neighbor, a large white horse, cropping grass, flipping its mane, and ambling about . . . over the entire five or so fenced-in acres that were next to the twenty-odd that we had rented.

—Alice Walker

13

Additional Ideas for Writing

1. Experimenting with Point of View. Choose any essay written in the first person (e.g., "Jackie's Debut," "Salvation," "Falling into Place"). How would the essay be different if it were told from a different point of view? How would "Jackie's Debut" be different if it were told from Jackie Robinson's, or from the point of view of the man who bought the baseball, or from the point of view of the Cub players or of the wise men at the tavern who seemed to be so worried? How would "Salvation" be different if it were told from the point of view of the preacher, or of the narrator's Auntie Reed? Choose one of the people mentioned in any essay in this book and rewrite the essay from that person's point of view.

2. Essays about Essays.

Option A: Choose any two essays in the book and write a critique comparing and contrasting the moves the writers make. You might use the checklist "So What and the Seven Common Moves" to help you discover categories of comparison. Don't feel obliged to use the entire checklist; just use those items that lead to the most interesting observations.

Option B: Define the term "essay," using examples to distinguish essays from other kinds of writing.

3. Revealing the Writer. Choose an essay and identify the words, phrases, and other rhetorical devices that reveal the personality of the writer. Once you've collected your observations, draw a conclusion from them. It could be a generalization about the essay itself, or about the topic, or about the author. Let this generalization serve as the thesis of an essay of your own.

Suggestion: if you cannot think of anything to say about the personality of any one writer, take a look at two essays and see if you can find interesting similarities or differences between the writers revealed in each.

4. Writing against the Text.

Option A: One of the defining characteristics of an essay is interpretation—the writer's personal "take" on the subject at hand. But because interpretation is so personal, chances are you will find yourself disagreeing with an essay from time to time. Pick an essay that you disagree with and write an essay of your own in support of a different and more persuasive interpretation of the same subject.

Option B: Choose an essay that you think is poorly written and write a review indicating why you think the essay is bad and how you think it could be improved. Use examples to prove your point.

Option C: The introduction to each chapter offers several generalizations about the kind of writing covered in that chapter. Write an essay in which you argue, citing examples from the essays themselves, that the generalizations in the introduction are or are not valid.

5. Research Papers.

Option A: Using the library and the Web, locate information about the subject of any essay you have already written. After you have read as much as you can, write a new essay incorporating what you have learned. Write the new essay in two stages: First, write it from beginning to end in your own words without looking at your research—leaving blanks that you intend to fill later with quotations or paraphrases taken from your sources. Then write it a second time, adding quotations or/and paraphrases wherever they will help you make a point. Be careful not to paste material into your paper without properly introducing it. Usually an introductory phrase will provide a smooth connection between your own voice and the voice of anyone you want to quote (e.g., "As Mary Brown says in *Coping with Poverty*, 'third world countries would benefit from . . .' "). Be sure to acknowledge the source of anything you quote or paraphrase. Refer to any standard handbook for the proper forms of footnotes and bibliographic entries.

Option B: You can find interesting topics for research not only in the subjects covered by the essays in this book, but also in many of the references and allusions that are mentioned in passing within each essay. Use the library and the Web to locate information about a topic that interests you. Then write an essay of your own, following the two-stage process outlined above in Option A.

About the Authors

JAMES BALDWIN

James Baldwin (1924–1987) was born in Harlem to an impoverished family, and for a time in his teens he served as a preacher in a local church. Without the financial resources to pursue a college education, Baldwin turned to writing to make his name, and by the time he was twenty-four, his articles and reviews were being published in such journals as *The Nation* and *Partisan Review*. To escape the racial prejudice of the United States, Baldwin moved to Paris in 1948; there he wrote his first two novels, *Go Tell It on the Mountain* (1953) and *Giovanni's Room* (1956), and continued to write essays, collected in *Notes of a Native Son* (1955). He returned to the United States in 1957 and began a close involvement with the civil rights movement. Much of his later work, including the essay collections *Nobody Knows My Name* (1961), *The Fire Next Time* (1963), and *No Name in the Street* (1972), reflects his frustration with and anger over the state of race relations in his home country. After the early 1970s, Baldwin spent much of his time in Europe. The essay on p. 183 was written in 1979 for the *New York Times*'s Op-Ed page.

JOAN JACOBS BRUMBERG

Joan Jacobs Brumberg was born in Mount Vernon, New York, in 1943. A graduate of the University of Virginia with a doctorate in American history, she is currently on the faculty at Cornell University, where she teaches a unique combination of history, human development, and women's studies. Her books include *Mission for Life: The Story of Adoniram Judson* (1980), a biography; *Fasting Girls: The Emergence of Anorexia Nervosa* (1988), an examination of the historical origins of that condition, beginning in Victorian times; and, most recently, *The Body Project: An Intimate History of American Girls* (1997), which traces the changing attitudes of young women toward their bodies from the 1920s to the present. Her work has been recognized by the Guggenheim Foundation and the National Endowment for the Humanities, among others. The essay on p. 148 was adapted from *Fasting Girls* for *Harper's* magazine.

JOSÉ ANTONIO BURCIAGA

Born in El Chuco, Texas, in 1940, José Antonio Burciaga served in the U.S. Air Force before graduating from the University of Texas at El Paso and attending art school in Washington, D.C., and San Francisco. He worked for a number of years as a technical illustrator and published his first collection of essays, poems, and drawings, *Drink Cultura Refrescente,* in 1976. In 1985 he became a resident fellow at Stanford University and in 1988 published the collection *Weedee Peepo*, which included the essay on p. 224. He also wrote editorials for the *Los Angeles Times* and contributed pieces to magazines such as *Texas Monthly* as well as a variety of Spanish-language publications. He was a founder of both a Spanish-language publishing house and of a comedy troupe, Culture Clash. His later books include *Undocumented Love: Amor Indocumentado* (1992) and *Spilling the Beans: Loteria Chicana* (1994), an autobiography. A winner of the National Book Award, Burciaga died in 1996.

BRUCE CATTON

Noted historian Bruce Catton (1899–1978) grew up in small-town Michigan and later attended Oberlin College. After serving in Europe during World War I, he settled in Cleveland, Ohio, working there as a journalist for the *Cleveland Plain Dealer* and later for the War Production Board during World War II. Never trained in historical study, Catton pursued these interests—particularly his interest in Civil War history—on his own. After publishing his first book, *The War Lords of Washington,* at the age of forty-nine, Catton went on to write some eighteen more, including *Mr. Lincoln's Army* (1951); *A Stillness at Appomattox* (1953), for which he was awarded the Pulitzer Prize; *The Hallowed Ground* (1956); and *The Centennial History of the Civil War* (1961–65). Beginning in 1954, he also edited the historical magazine *American Heritage* until his death at the age of seventy-nine. "Grant and Lee" (p. 111), about the two Civil War generals, was originally composed for radio, one of a series of addresses by eminent historians, and later revised for the collection *The American Story.*

JERRY DENNIS

Nature writer Jerry Dennis has traveled extensively to pursue his interest in outdoor subjects. He has contributed articles to the *New York Times, Audubon, Smithsonian, Sports Afield,* and *Outdoor Life.* He also writes the monthly "Natural Enquirer" column for *Wildlife Conservation.* A native of northern Michigan, Dennis has also published a number of guidebooks for canoe and bicycle touring, as well as two volumes explaining natural phenomena for popular audiences: *It's Raining Frogs and Fishes: Four Seasons of Natural Phenomena and Oddities in the Sky* (1992) and *The Bird in the Waterfall: A Natural History of Oceans, Rivers, and Lakes* (1996). The essay on p. 127 is a chapter from *It's Raining Frogs and Fishes.*

JOAN DIDION

Born in Sacramento, California, in 1934, Joan Didion has been hailed as one of America's foremost prose stylists. After graduating from the University of California at Berkeley in 1956, Didion moved to New York, where she worked as a staff writer at *Vogue* magazine until 1963. She then returned to California with her husband, writer John Gregory Dunne, and began contributing a series of essays to *The Saturday Evening Post.* Some of these were collected in *Slouching Towards Bethlehem* (1968), the book that established her coolly ironic literary voice. Her other essay collections are *The White Album* (1979) and *After Henry* (1992). Didion has also written four novels, including the best-selling *Play It As It Lays* (1971) and two book-length works of nonfiction reportage, *Salvador* (1983) and *Miami* (1987), in addition to collaborating with Dunne on a number of film screenplays. "On Self-Respect" (p. 178) was written in 1961, when Didion was twenty-eight, and collected in *Slouching Towards Bethlehem.*

ANNIE DILLARD

Essayist, novelist, and nature writer Annie Dillard came to immediate literary prominence with the publication of her first book, *Pilgrim at Tinker's Creek,* in 1974. Its lyrical observations of the natural world won her a Pulitzer Prize for nonfiction. Subsequent books include *Holy the Firm* (1977), a deeply felt meditation on human spirituality; *Teaching a Stone to Talk* (1982), a second collection of essays focusing on the natural world; *An American Childhood* (1987), a memoir; *A Writer's Life* (1989), in which she ponders the mysteries of the creative process; and *The Living* (1992), a historical novel. In "Catch It If You Can" (p. 22), from *Pilgrim at Tinker's Creek,* Dillard vividly describes what she encounters during a chance stop at a remote gas station in rural Virginia."The Chase" (p. 55) appears as a section in her autobiographical *An American Childhood* (1987), which focuses on her early years in Pittsburgh.

MICHAEL DORRIS

Known for his sensitivity to Native American concerns, Michael Dorris was born in Louisville, Kentucky, in 1945 to a family of distant native lineage. He received his

Ph.D. from Yale University in 1970 and in 1972 founded the Native American Studies program at Dartmouth. In addition to a short story collection, *Working Men* (1993), and a novel, *A Yellow Raft in Blue Water* (1987), Dorris published a number of works of nonfiction. These include *A Guide to Research on North American Indians* (1988); *The Broken Cord* (1989), about the death of his adopted Native American son, who suffered from fetal alcohol syndrome; and *Rooms in the House of Stone* (1993), about his visits to Mozambican refugee camps as a board member of the Save the Children Foundation. He also coauthored books with his wife, novelist Louise Erdrich, from whom he was later estranged. Dorris committed suicide in 1997. The essay on p. 235 originally appeared on the *New York Times* Op-Ed page in April, 1992, and was later collected in his *Paper Trails: Essays* (1994).

BARBARA EHRENREICH

Born in 1941 in Butte, Montana, Barbara Ehrenreich grew up in a fiercely independent, free-thinking family, greatly suspicious of the power establishment of wealth and organized religion. As a contemporary social critic and feminist, she has often trained her sights on these same targets. A graduate of Reed College and a Columbia University Ph.D., Ehrenreich taught at the university level for several years before beginning her career as a full-time writer. She has contributed essays and investigative articles to a wide variety of mostly liberal publications, and her recent books include *The Worst Years of Our Lives* (1990), about the period of Ronald Reagan's presidency; *The Snarling Citizen* (1995), a critique of the level of public debate initiated by commentators such as Rush Limbaugh; and *Blood Rites: Origins and History of the Passions of War* (1997). Ehrenreich is also a regular contributor to *Time* magazine's "Essay" page, where the essay on p. 231 originally appeared in 1996.

PETER FARB

A naturalist, linguist, and anthropologist, Peter Farb (1929–1980) was able to reach a wide popular audience by writing about the natural and human sciences. Born in New York City, Farb attended Vanderbilt University and Columbia. He began writing in his twenties and published his first best-selling work, *Living Earth,* in 1959. Later books include *The Insects* (1962, 1977), *The Land and Wildlife of North America* (1964, 1978), *Humankind* (1978), and *Consuming Passions: The Anthropology of Eating* (1980). For many years, Farb served as a consultant to the Smithsonian Institution in Washington, and he was a curator of American Indian cultures at the Riverside Museum in New York. The essay on p. 160, a chapter from his *Word Play: What Happens When People Talk* (1974), is characteristic of the lively, readable style that made Farb's work so popular.

E. M. FORSTER

Edward Morgan Forster (1879–1970), one of Britain's most highly regarded novelists, graduated from Cambridge University and then lived for a time in Italy and

Greece. He published his first novel, *Where Angels Fear to Tread,* in 1905, and later works include *A Room with a View* (1908), *Howard's End* (1910), and *A Passage to India* (1924), his final novel. (*Maurice* was completed in 1914 but not published until 1971, after Forster's death, because of the open homosexuality of its main character.) In later years Forster turned primarily to essays and other nonfiction prose, including *Aspects of the Novel* (1927), an influential critical work, and the essay collections *Abinger Harvest* (1936) and *Two Cheers for Democracy* (1951). Forster became a fellow at King's College, Cambridge, in 1946 and continued to live there until his death. His soulful comedies of manners have received renewed attention in recent years through a series of award-winning film adaptations, successful with critics and audiences alike. "My Wood" (p. 165) was written in 1926 and published in the *New Leader,* a literary journal.

JUDITH HERBST

Judith Herbst was born in Queens, New York, in 1947. A former junior high school teacher, Herbst is now a full-time freelance writer who specializes in explaining unusual scientific concepts and phenomena for young adult audiences. Her books include *Sky Above and Worlds Below* (1983); *Bio Amazing: A Casebook of Unsolved Human Mysteries* (1985) and its sequel, *Animal Amazing* (1991); and *The Mystery of UFOs* (1997). Her research has supported an adventurous spirit, allowing her to tramp through the Amazon, snorkle with sea lions, and camp her way across America. Her essay on p. 73 is a chapter from *Animal Amazing,* a book that in its publisher's words "probes the mysteries of the animal kingdom with a scientific eye and amazing flair."

LANGSTON HUGHES

A primary figure of the Harlem Renaissance, a flowering of black artistic expression centered in New York City in the 1920s, Langston Hughes published his first collection of poetry, *The Weary Blues* (1926), when he was twenty-four. Its success allowed him to attend Lincoln University in Pennsylvania, where he received his degree in 1929. Later works include the poetry collections *Shakespeare in Harlem* (1942), *One-Way Ticket* (1949), *Montage of a Dream Deferred* (1951), and *Ask Your Mama* (1961); the play *Mulatto* (1935); the children's book *The First Book of Negroes* (1952); a collection of dialect pieces, *The Best of Simple* (1961); and two volumes of autobiography, *The Big Sea* (1940) and *I Wonder as I Wander* (1956). All of his work is marked by the spirit and traditions of African-American life. Hughes died in 1967. "Salvation" (p. 48), a chapter from *The Big Sea,* recounts a painful experience from the poet's youth.

MARTIN LUTHER KING, JR.

One of the towering figures of the twentieth century, civil rights leader Martin Luther King, Jr., was born in Atlanta, Georgia, in 1929. His father was a Baptist minister, and King himself entered the ministry at the age of eighteen. In 1955, after receiving his doctoral degree in theology from Boston University, King threw himself wholeheartedly into the struggle for desegregation and equal opportunity for American blacks. His first major act was to lead a year-long boycott of the segregated municipal transit system in Montgomery, Alabama, where he was then a minister; the buses were ultimately integrated. Leading subsequent protests in cities across the South, King was arrested on numerous occasions. While more militant blacks challenged his philosophy, King never abandoned the methods of nonviolent resistance he had adapted from the teachings of Mahatma Ghandi. He was awarded the Nobel Peace Prize in 1964, fours years before his tragic assassination at the age of thirty-nine. In August of 1963, King organized a massive march on Washington, D.C.; more than 200,000 people of all races gathered to commemorate Lincoln's Emancipation Proclamation and show their support for civil rights legislation then being considered by Congress. There, King stirringly delivered the speech on p. 277, now a classic among American documents.

Merrill Markoe

A graduate of the University of California at Berkeley, Merrill Markoe taught art in southern California for several years before turning to stand-up comedy, honing her act at the Los Angeles Comedy Store and other clubs. In 1978, she met David Letterman and later became head writer for both his first major television effort, *The David Letterman Show,* and the hugely popular *Late Night with David Letterman,* for which she conceived such features as Stupid Pet Tricks and the roving camera remotes. After winning several Emmys, Markoe left the show in 1987 to become a contributor to *Not Necessarily the News* and to return to stand-up comedy. Since then she has also written columns for *New York Woman* and other national magazines and published three books of irreverent humor: *What the Dogs Have Taught Me and Other Amazing Things I've Learned* (1992), *How to Be Hap- Hap- Happy Like Me* (1994), and *Merrill Markoe's Guide to Love* (1997). The essay on p. 63 originally appeared in *New York Woman.*

Jessica Mitford

As an investigative journalist and social critic, Jessica Mitford (1917–1996) wrote with a scathing wit and attention to human foible that led her to be tagged the "Queen of the Muckrakers." Mitford was born into an eccentric aristocratic family in Batsford Mansion, England, but early on embraced radical ideology, eventually joining the Communist party. After immigrating to the United States and renouncing communism in the 1950s, she remained outspoken in her support of liberal causes. Her groundbreaking exposés include *The American Way of Death* (1963), an eye-opening account of the funeral industry that was attacked by funeral directors but led to many reforms; *Unusual Punishment: The Prison Business* (1973), a critique of the American penal system; and *The American Way of Birth* (1992), an examination of the technology of obstetrics. Mitford also wrote numerous articles for periodicals and two volumes of memoirs. The essay on p. 78 is one of the most famous—and gruesome—chapters from *The American Way of Death.*

MICHEL EYQUEM DE MONTAIGNE

One of the acknowledged masters of the literary essay, Michel Eyquem de Montaigne (1533–1592) in many senses invented the form. Born to a wealthy family in Perigord, France, Montaigne—at his father's insistence—heard and spoke only Latin until he was six years old. Trained in the law, he served as a magistrate for much of his career, and later was mayor of Bordeaux. After his retirement in 1571, Montaigne began work on his *Essaís,* literally "trials" or "attempts," to explore a variety of philosophical, political, and social subjects. The first two volumes were published in 1580, a third along with extensive revisions of the previous volumes in 1588, and final revised versions in 1595. Throughout these works, Montaigne's motto is "Que sais-je?" ("What do I know?"), and by exploring the limits of his own knowledge he leads readers to a deeper understanding of human nature. Informal in style, often witty and digressive, the *Essaís* of Montaigne have been influential worldwide in establishing the essay form.

GLORIA NAYLOR

Gloria Naylor was born in New York City in 1950 to parents who had recently arrived from Mississippi. She attended Brooklyn College and later earned a master's degree in Afro-American studies from Yale. While completing her studies at Yale, she had a story accepted by *Essence* magazine, her first published work, in 1977. Her first novel, *The Women of Brewster Place,* appeared in 1982; it received an American Book Award and was later dramatized for a highly successful television production. Later novels include *Linden Hills* (1985), *Mama Day* (1988), and *Bailey's Cafe* (1992). "Technically," Naylor has written, "I'm a New Yorker who grew up in a southern home. That meant I heard stories all my life about the South. And being a quiet kid, I was the one who sat still long enough to listen to them." The recollection of her childhood (p. 187) originally appeared in the *New York Times* in 1986.

JAIME O'NEILL

Born in 1944 in Freeport, Illinois, Jaime O'Neill grew up in then rural Safety Harbor, Florida, and later received his master's degree from California State University—Hayward. Currently a professor of English composition and literature at Butte College in Oroville, California, O'Neill is also a freelance writer. His books include *What Do You Know?: The Ultimate Test of Common (and Not So Common) Sense* (volume 1, 1990; volume 2, 1993), *The Ultimate Test of TV Trivia* (1994), and *We're History: The 20th Century Survivor's Final Exam* (1998); and his work has been published in periodicals such as *The Threepenny Review* and *Newsweek.* The essay on p. 51 appeared in 1993 in the *New York Times Magazine*'s "About Men" column, a former biweekly feature in which male writers reflected on issues of gender and identity. O'Neill sometimes uses it in his own composition classes as an example of personal narrative.

JOYCE CAROL OATES

As a novelist, short story writer, playwright, literary critic, social observer, and (pseudonymous) mystery author, Joyce Carol Oates has established herself as one of the most prolific and wide-ranging voices in American letters. Born in 1938 in rural upstate New York, she attended Syracuse University and began writing early, winning a *Mademoiselle* award before her graduation. Her first collection of stories was published when she was twenty-five, and just over thirty she won the National Book Award for her third novel, *them* (1969). The settings of her over forty novels and short story collections have ranged from violent inner cities to well-heeled suburbs, from a darkly imagined nineteenth-century Gothic past to the richly detailed circumstances of her own girlhood home, from blue-collar tract housing to the campuses of the Ivy League. In choosing her subject matter, the highly literate Oates has always exhibited the power to surprise, and the essay on p. 212 is no exception. It appeared in her 1987 work of nonfiction, *On Boxing*.

ERNIE PYLE

Ernest Taylor Pyle (1900–1945) grew up in an Indiana farming community and later attended Indiana University, where he edited the school newspaper. He left university before graduating to write for the *La Porte Herald,* then worked as a reporter and columnist for the *Washington Daily News,* the *New York Evening World,* and the *New York Evening Post.* He is best remembered today for his reporting as a war correspondent during the Second World War, when he traveled to England, Ireland, North Africa, Italy, France, and the South Pacific. Describing the day-to-day life of the average soldier, Pyle tempered realism with an innate sense of optimism that appealed to a broad popular audience. His columns on the war were collected in the books *Here Is Your War* (1943), *Brave Men* (1944), and *Last Chapter* (1946), and his reporting won him a Pulitzer Prize in 1944. Pyle was killed by sniper fire while covering the landing of the U.S. troops on an island near Okinawa, but his work remains a model of journalistic reporting and writing more than fifty years after his death.

WILBERT RIDEAU

Convicted of murder in his late teens, Wilbert Rideau has been incarcerated at the Louisiana State Penitentiary at Angola since 1962. During his first eleven years on death row, he taught himself to write, and after his sentence was commuted to life imprisonment, he began contributing articles to *The Angolite,* the prison's uncensored news publication. Since 1975 he has served as editor-in-chief, and the magazine has won a number of awards and reached a wide audience both within and outside prison walls. With another prisoner, Ron Wikberg, Rideau edited the book *Life Sentences: Rage and Survival behind Bars* (1992), a collection of pieces from *The Angolite* that is "dedicated to fostering a better public understanding of criminal justice." A long-time spokesman for prison reform, Rideau has been especially critical of media depictions of crime and prison life. The essay on p. 156 appeared in *Time* magazine in March 1994 at a time when many "get-tough-on-crime" arguments were being advanced by state and federal legislators.

MIKE ROYKO

Mike Royko (1923–1997) was born in Chicago in 1923, the son of parents who ran a saloon. After attending junior college and serving in the U.S. Air Force, he began a career in journalism, first as a reporter and editor for the *Chicago Daily News* and later as a columnist for the *Chicago Sun Times* and the *Chicago Tribune*. Writing in a down-to-earth voice that appealed strongly to working class readers, Royko was for many years one of Chicago's most prominent journalists. He was also well known nationally through syndication, and he won a Pulitzer Prize for commentary in 1972. His columns have been collected in the books *Up Against It* (1967), *I May Be Wrong but I Doubt It* (1968), *Sez Who? Sez Me* (1982), and *Like I Was Sayin'* (1984), among others; he also wrote *Boss: Richard J. Daly of Chicago* (1971), a sharp attack on the controversial long-time mayor. Royko died in 1997.

MYRA SADKER AND DAVID SADKER

As a research team, Myra Sadker (1943–1995) and her husband David (b. 1942) produced numerous studies on gender bias in education, asserting that girls suffer because teachers generally give boys more attention, encouragement, and support. Both professors of education at The American University in Washington, D.C., they jointly directed more than a dozen federal equity grants and were involved in training programs to combat sexism and sexual harassment across the country and overseas. Their work provided the basis for the 1993 report by the American Association of University Women, "How Schools Shortchange Girls," and has been reported widely in major newspapers and magazines. Their books include *Beyond Pictures and Pronouns: Sexism in Teacher Education Texts* (1980), *Sex Equity Handbook for Teachers* (2nd edition, 1990), and *Teachers, Schools, and Society* (3rd edition, 1993). The essay on p. 98 is from their final book together, *Failing at Fairness: How America's Schools Cheat Girls* (1994), the Sadkers look at what young students themselves have to say about the comparative merits of being a boy or a girl.

SCOTT RUSSELL SANDERS

Currently a professor of English at Indiana University, Scott Russell Sanders is also a prolific writer who has published a number of collections of personal essays, several novels, works for young adult readers including science fiction stories, children's books, and journalistic reportage. Sanders was born in 1945 to a Tennessee cotton-farming family and spent much of his boyhood in Ohio. A scholarship student at Brown University studying English and physics, he graduated first in his class in 1967. His writing often focuses on science and the arts, and he has said that in all his work he is "concerned with the ways in which human beings come to terms with the practical problems of living on a small planet, in nature and in communities . . . with the life people make together in marriages and families and towns. . . ." The essay on p. 131—which appeared in Sanders' award-winning first collection, *The Paradise of Bombs* (1987)—focuses on memories of his working-class childhood and his later experiences at Brown.

VAL SCHAFFNER

Val Schaffner (b. 1951) grew up in New York City, the son of a writer and a literary agent and grandson of the poet Hilda Doolittle (H.D.). A newspaper reporter and editor since his early twenties, he currently writes a regular column for the *East Hampton* (N.Y.) *Star,* for which he has won several journalism awards. His first book was *Algonquin Cat* (1980), a fantasy novella that has been translated into Japanese, German, and Russian. In 1993 he published *Lost in Cyberspace,* a collection of essays mostly adapted from his columns, which take a humorous, slightly skeptical look at the advantages of modern technology. "Virus Zero" (p. 203) appeared in that collection. Schaffner advises that writers "have to pull readers along fast, in as few words as possible"; for him, "a piece of writing is like a racing bicycle; the leaner and lighter it is, the faster it goes."

BRENT STAPLES

Brent Staples was born to a working class family in Chester, Pennsylvania, in 1951. A scholarship student at Widener University, he later received a Ph.D. in psychology from the University of Chicago. After teaching for several years, he turned to a career in journalism, writing for the *Chicago Sun-Times* among other local publications. In 1985 he moved to the *New York Times*, where he writes a regular column on cultural and political issues, and in 1990 he was the first African American to be appointed to the paper's editorial board. In addition to contributing articles to periodicals such as *Ms.* and *Harper's,* Staples has published *Parallel Time: A Memoir* (1994), in which he describes his childhood, his education, and the very different life choices made by his brother, a petty criminal killed in a dispute over drugs. "Just Walk on By" (p. 195) originally appeared in *Ms.* in 1986.

RICHARD STENGEL

Born in New York City in 1955, Richard Stengel graduated from Princeton University and in 1981 joined the staff at *Time* magazine, where he continues to be a regular contributor. He has also written for such diverse publications as the *New York*

Times, Vanity Fair, Rolling Stone, and *The Smithsonian.* He has published one book, *January Sun: One Day, Three Lives, a South African Town* (1990), which focuses on the lives of three ordinary citizens living under the system of apartheid. The essay on p. 173 originally appeared in *The New Yorker* in 1995.

JONATHAN SWIFT

Probably best remembered today for his fantastical *Gulliver's Travels* (1726), Jonathan Swift (1667–1745) wrote during what might be considered a golden age of satire, a literary form of which he was a master. Born to English parents who had settled in Ireland, Swift was rebellious by nature and barely managed to graduate from Trinity College in Dublin. After his ordination as an Anglican priest, the thoroughly secular Swift was never able to obtain more than a modest living. A friend of many of the literary lights of England, where he lived off and on, Swift began his writing career in the late 1690s. His *A Tale of a Tub,* satirizing religious excess, was published in 1704, and the equally ironic *Argument against Abolishing Christianity,* the first of a series of pamphlets concerning contemporary religious controversies, in 1708. Throughout his career, Swift dealt with many of the most contentious issues of his day. "A Modest Proposal" (p. 259) was written in response to the inhumanely unjust taxes levied by the English government on a desperately impoverished Irish population. Its biting satire can shock even today.

AMY TAN

A former corporate communications specialist, Amy Tan began writing stories in 1984 as a kind of self-therapy to distract her from the rigors of her job. The result was *The Joy Luck Club* (1987), a novel made up of interconnected stories, which was published when she was thirty-eight. It met with immediate critical and popular acclaim and established her as one of the most important voices of her generation. The daughter of Chinese immigrants, Tan grew up in Oakland, California, and studied linguistics at San Francisco State University. Much of her work—including the subsequent novels *The Kitchen God's Wife* (1991) and *The Hundred Secret Senses* (1995)—focuses on generational differences between Chinese immigrant parents and their children and on the melding of old-world ways with new-world sensibilities. *The Joy Luck Club,* for example, interweaves the memories of four Chinese immigrant mothers with those of their four very different American-born daughters. In the essay on p. 105, originally published in the literary journal *Threepenny Review,* Tan looks at her relationship with her own mother as it has played out through the "Englishes" they speak.

DEBORAH TANNEN

Linguistics researcher Deborah Tannen (b. 1945) has written a number of highly regarded scholarly texts in the field of communication. She is best known, however, for bringing the results of her research on communicating across difference to a wide popular audience through talk-show appearances, magazine articles, and books such as *That's Not What I Meant!: How Conversational Style Makes or Breaks Relationships* (1986), *You Just Don't Understand: Men and Women in Conversation* (1990), and *Talking 9 to 5: How Men's and Women's Conversational Styles Affect Who Gets Ahead, Who Gets Credit, and What Gets Done at Work* (1994). In her latest book, *The Argument Culture: Moving from Debate to Dialogue* (1998), she looks at the lack of civility and substance in much current political debate and offers suggestions for change. A graduate of the State University of New York and the University of California at Berkeley, Tannen is currently a professor at Georgetown University. The essay on p. 136 is taken from *Talking 9 to 5,* which originally appeared in *Redbook* magazine.

DONNA TARTT

Born in 1964 in Greenwood, Mississippi, Donna Tartt spent a year at the University of Mississippi by later transferred to Bennington College in Vermont because she felt stifled by the South of her childhood. After graduation she worked some eight years on her first novel, a story of a murder among an elitist clique of intellectual students at a small private college much like Bennington. Championed by best-selling novelist (and former classmate) Brett Easton Ellis, *The Secret History* (1992) sparked a publishing bidding war and considerable publicity for Tartt and went on to become a best-seller. Since its publication, Tartt has been working on a second novel and has contributed short stories and essays to magazines such as *The New Yorker* and *Harper's.* Her reminiscence of high school cheerleading in the 1970s (p. 29) originally appeared in *The Oxford American,* a literary journal; this slightly shortened version was adapted for *Harper's.*

KURT VONNEGUT

One of the United States' premier novelists, Kurt Vonnegut was born in Indianapolis in 1922. Educated at Cornell University and the University of Chicago, Vonnegut worked for a time as a newspaper reporter and a teacher before publishing his first novel, *Piano Player,* in 1952. He was virtually ignored by critics at the beginning of his career, but by the early 1960s he had been discovered by a group of younger writers who shared his countercultural vision and interest in stylistic experimentation. Among his popular later novels—many of which mix deeply humane social commentary with darkly comic surrealism—are *Cat's Cradle* (1963); *Slaughterhouse Five* (1969), based on his harrowing experiences in Germany as a member of the Army infantry during World War II; *Jailbird* (1979); *Hocus Pocus* (1990); and *Timequake* (1997), which Vonnegut claims will be his last. He wrote the essay on p. 69 at the request of the International Paper Company to be presented as part of a series of advertisements focused on the art of writing.

ALICE WALKER

Perhaps most well known for her best-selling—and Pulitzer Prize–winning—novel *The Color Purple* (1982), Alice Walker is among the most distinguished of American writers. Born in 1944 to a sharecropping family in rural Georgia, Walker received scholarships to Spelman College in Atlanta and Sarah Lawrence in New York. After publishing several poetry collections in the late 1960s, she found immediate critical acclaim with her first novel, *The Third Life of George Copeland* (1970), followed by the equally successful *Meridian* (1976), based on Walker's experiences in the civil rights movement. Her influential essay collection *In Search of Our Mother's Gardens: Womanist Prose* (1983), which looks at ways in which black women translate the African-American experience into art, added to her reputation, as did two collections of short stories. Subsequent works include the novels *The Temple of My Familiar* (1989) and *Possessing the Secret of Joy* (1992), which revisit some of the characters in *The Color Purple,* and a memoir about the making of the film version of that novel. The essay on p. 238 originally appeared in *Ms.* magazine in 1986 and was collected in *Living by the Word* (1988).

DAVID FOSTER WALLACE

David Foster Wallace grew up in the Midwest, a mathematics whiz and a highly ranked junior tennis player. After schooling at Amherst and the University of Arizona, he began his writing career, publishing his first novel, *The Broom of the System* (1987), when he was twenty-five. A collection of short stories, *Girl with Short Hair,* appeared in 1989 and a second novel, *Infinite Jest,* in 1996. Wallace has also written nonfiction for a number of popular periodicals. Noted for "his sardonic humor and complicated style," as one critic put it, he has been called "Generation X's first literary hero," and Frank Bruni of the *New York Times* wrote that Wallace "is to literature what Robin Williams or perhaps Jim Carrey is to live comedy." The essay on p. 25 originally appeared in *Harper's* magazine as a section of a larger piece about the Illinois State Fair; it is also collected in his most recent book, *A Supposedly Funny Thing I'll Never Do Again: Essays and Arguments* (1997).

E. B. WHITE

Arguably the finest American essayist of the twentieth century, Elwyn Brooks White (1899–1986) published his first piece of writing when he was ten years old in *The Ladies' Home Journal.* Born in Mount Vernon, New York, and a graduate of Cornell University, White in 1927 began an eleven-year stint writing for *The New Yorker,* shaping that sophisticated magazine's style as much as the magazine did his. Interested in relocating his family from New York City to the rural coast of Maine, he gave up his job at *The New Yorker* in 1938 and began contributing monthly essays to *Harper's* in the column "One Man's Meat"; many of these were collected in a book of the same title in 1942. Two successful children's books—*Stuart Little* (1945) and *Charlotte's Web* (1952)—followed, along with a popular book-length essay about New York City and a second essay collection, *The Second Tree from the Corner* (1952). White's revision of *The Elements of Style* (1959), a writer's handbook first put together by a former teacher, William Strunk, Jr., remains a classic, advising the kind of directness, grace, and precision that was a hallmark of all White's work. The essay on p. 271 appeared in *Harper's* in 1941 and was included in *One Man's Meat.*

MARION WINIK

Marion Winik has been called "a voice both cosmic and karmic, a communal voice for our own off-the-edge times." Born in 1958, she grew up in suburban New Jersey. Her writing first came to prominence when National Public Radio's *All Things Considered* began broadcasting her reading a series of her essays focusing on personal quirks and foibles. Her work also appeared in *Redbook, Texas Monthly, The Utne Reader,* and *The Austin* (Texas) *Chronicle.* In 1996 she published *First Comes Love,* a highly praised memoir about her charismatic husband's battle with HIV, its effect on their two sons, and his eventual assisted suicide. Her earlier collection of essays, *Telling: Confessions, Concessions, and Other Flashes of Light* (1994), brings together several pieces that premiered on *All Things Considered,* including the essays on p. 120 and 207.

MARIE WINN

Born in Czechoslovakia in 1936, Marie Winn immigrated to the United States with her family when she was three. After attending Radcliffe College and Columbia University, Winn began a career as a freelance writer, publishing articles in a variety of periodicals including the *New York Times* and the *Village Voice.* The author of a number of books for children, Winn has also written about childhood issues of concern to parents, most notably the effects of the media on contemporary children's development. Her books on this topic include *The Plug-In Drug: Television, Children, and the Family* (1977), *Children without Childhood* (1983), and *Unplugging the Plug-In-Drug* (1987). In recent years she has turned her attention to urban wildlife in her native New York City, the subject of *The Secret Life of Central Park* (1997) and *Red-Tails in Love: A Wildlife Drama in Central Park* (1998). The essay on p. 89 appeared in *Children without Childhood.*

VIRGINIA WOOLF

Born into a prominent London literary family in 1882, Virginia Stephen Woolf had no formal schooling but read extensively in her father's private library. She turned to writing in her early twenties, contributing book reviews and commentaries to English and American journals. In 1912 she married Leonard Woolf, whom she had met through a collection of artists and intellectuals known as the Bloomsbury group, and in 1915 she published *The Voyage Out,* the first of her eight influential novels. Her first collection of critical essays, *The Common Reader,* appeared in 1925, the same year as *Mrs. Dalloway,* one of Woolf's most widely read novels; a second collection with the same title was published in 1932. Considered one of the most meticulous and luminous of English prose stylists, Woolf saw the essay as a unique literary form, at its best able "to sting us awake and fix us in a trance which is not sleep but rather an intensification of life—a basking with every faculty alert in the sun of pleasure." Having suffered bouts of depression and mental illness since childhood, Woolf took her life in 1941. The essay on p. 267 was collected posthumously by her husband in *The Death of the Moth and Other Essays* in 1942.

Index of Titles

Index of Authors